Enid was born in Golcar in 1933, later the family moved to Quarmby Fold where they stayed until she was 17. They then moved to Bradley and it was while living there that she got married.

Educated at Oakes Junior School and later Royds Hall Grammar School she left at 16 and went to work as a bindery assistant at Wheatley Dysons printers in New Street, Huddersfield. While there she met an apprentice compositor called William and love blossomed.

They married in 1954 and set up home in Lewisham Road, Slaithwaite. It was here that Heather and Howard were born. As the family increased with the arrivals of Melanie and Louise they moved to Stuart Grove and later to Manchester Road just below the Bath Hotel (no longer there now). In 1970 shortly after the arrival of Amanda they moved into a large Victorian semi by Slaithwaite Police Station. As the children got older, married and had families of their own, William and Enid moved to Marsh in 1982.

Enid had various jobs before getting married but following the birth of Heather became a full-time mother and continued to be one until youngest daughter Amanda attended Colne Valley High School.

Enid then started work as a part-time librarian in Slaithwaite and remained there until she retired aged 60.

In these pages she puts herself down somewhat, in dress sense, appearance, cooking and bowling. She was in fact very attractive, an excellent cook and quite a useful bowler as you will gather when you read her stories and see the photographs.

ISBN No. 1-905546-02-5

Published by Write Books CPR Ltd
Units 9/10 Ferrybridge Workspace
Pontefract Road, Ferrybridge
West Yorkshire, WF11 8PL

It took me about three months to type and print out twelve prototype copies of this book on my PC. Following an article in the Huddersfield Examiner about the book I was inundated by requests for a copy. After talking it over with my children we decided to go ahead and have it printed professionally.

I would like to thank the Huddersfield Daily Examiner for allowing me the use of their library to copy all of Enid's writings and to Write Books CPR Ltd of Ferrybridge and Swiftprint of Huddersfield for the production of this book.

William, Enid's husband of 49 years

The Thoughts of a Colne Valley Mother

by

Enid Blackburn

In 1973 Enid Blackburn wrote her first article for the Colne Valley Guardian, a weekly newspaper which was published in the village of Slaithwaite where she lived.

She was always keen on writing as a hobby, thanks she said, to an excellent English teacher at Royds Hall Grammar School.

Whilst bringing up a family of five children she had little opportunity to pursue her interest, but kept jotting down little notes and happenings and special events in case they may be useful later on. She was also an avid reader, often reading as many as five novels a week, mainly thrillers. Enid was a regular user of Slaithwaite Public Library and eventually got a post there as a part-time librarian, a position she held for about 15 years.

When the Huddersfield Examiner purchased the Colne Valley Guardian it was printed at the Examiner but retained its own identity until it was amalgamated into the Huddersfield and District Weekly Examiner. Enid was then asked if she would like to contribute a weekly column.

Working in the library she came into contact with hundreds of borrowers and often picked up little bits of gossip, as she did on her weekly trip to the hairdressers. In her effort to remain 'incognito' she decided to write under a pen name, and after a family summit meeting Kay Bennett was born.

Enid continued to write her weekly column until 1981 when she was knocked down when crossing the road on her way home from work at the library. It was touch and go for a while as she lay in a coma at Huddersfield Royal Infirmary having suffered amongst other things a fractured skull. Eventually she was allowed home but subsequent tests showed she had lost her sense of smell and taste, a bit upsetting when your other main hobbies are baking and cooking!

After some months she attempted to return to her writing but her powers of concentration and wicked sense of humour had deserted her and she decided to call it a day.

However, she regained her strength and for the next 20 years or so she spent most of her time helping to bring up twelve grandchildren, (which also restored her sense of humour) with each one holding a special place in her heart.

Enid sadly passed away on April 27th, 2004, and this book is printed as a tribute to a wonderful wife, mother, grandma and friend to many.

Overleaf is Enid's first ever published article, which was titled 'A kind of loving - sometimes called Bowling the Jack'

IN Spring a young man's fancy turns to thoughts of love. But what about the middle aged man? What are his thoughts turning to?

What's all this muttering and mumbling on the street corners and in the fish and chip shops? About 'thumb pegs' and 'funny marks.' You've guessed it, the bowling bag brigade are coming out of hibernation once more.

Bad backs, which have kept sufferers confined to armchairs all winter, are cured like magic! The sprained wrist too weak to lift the coal bucket is now 'in need of exercise, love.'

Husbands are fondly emptying the newly spring-cleaned cupboards in search of their 'woods.' The ones discarded last year as rubbish! Grown men are cooing like doves as they polish their oil-covered bowls with the wife's best duster.

Weak, frail-bodied males, with hardly the strength to lift a pint to their lips are now preparing for battle with their opponents and the elements on the bowling greens of Yorkshire.

The long, the short and the corpulent are to be seen prancing prettily across the greens as they accompany their bowls into the gutter.

Faithful wives whose normal conversation with hubby is 'wipe your feet!' are now shouting kindly with tears in their eyes, 'gerrum up lad!'

Tight-lipped women sit framing the greens, knitting needles clicking and the picnic bag bulging. If it rains each one, quick as a conjuror, transforms her mate into an Icelandic fisherman, with waterproof cap, leggings and jacket.

To the inexperienced viewer it may look a simple game of rolling bowls up and down the grass. But it takes years of practice.

First there is the delivery. One foot on the tiny mat, which is quite invisible to the more developed figure, knees bent, back foot raised, then hold this position so the other chap can't follow 'the road.' It's not easy.

Then the special walk across the green, one leg dragging or twisted behind the other. Some lean back as far as possible after delivering the wood in the hope it will slow its progress down, some perform something similar to a tango stamping the feet in the hope the wood will run further.

What an excellent team spirit there is amongst the lads! Eager volunteers are helping the greenkeeper whiten the boards and cutting and rolling the green while wives are wading through the back lawn searching for their washing!

It's remarkable how they stick together on 'away' matches. 'I couldn't come home any sooner pet, we had to stop and support George, he was the last man on, you know.'

But at sunset when cricketers have downed their cocoa and said their prayers, dedicated bowlers can still be seen, supporting each other gallantly as they stagger under the floodlights of the more affluent clubs. Revealing such intimate confessions as 'I like mine' or 'You've a good length, Joe.'

Did Sir Francis Drake realise what he had started when he kept the Spanish fleet waiting? I wonder.

Breezy, bracing Blackpool

ALTHOUGH it's not considered fashionable in these affluent times when working men's clubs spend their annual trips at exotic places like Magaluf, for a good feed, a good laugh and a liberal helping of childhood nostalgia, you can't beat a day at Blackpool.

It's smelly, noisy, but oh boy, it's matey and it's fun.

Last week I persuaded the man about the house to let his remaining hair down and indulge us in a coach trip to this popular resort. The last time I travelled there by bus my dad offered a silver threepenny bit to the first one to see the Tower.

During the exhausting three-hour drive this was the only thing that kept my sister and I sociable.

What a difference today! The same journey takes just over an hour via the Motorway. Some friends often 'pop over' just for the night.

Departure time was 8.30am. When we arrived five minutes early the bus was brimming with smiling day-trippers.

I could see why they were smiling when we were allocated our seating arrangements. Our three girls were eventually accommodated at the rear, dad in the front seat and me behind him. The emotion displayed by our daughters at this temporary parting would have been quite touching if I hadn't remembered the packet of mints was in my handbag.

My seating companion was a middle-aged boy clutching a black and white dog to his chest. It was only when I stroked it and the black came off on my hand that I realised it was actually white. His devoted parents across the aisle kept in touch with little hand signals and occasionally pulled a few funny faces for the dog's benefit.

The only other diversion was when another bus overtook us and we were treated to a glorious side view of the passionate back seat Romeo.

Blackpool Tower came and went unnoticed by everyone – except me.

Half-an-hour before we arrived, our driver pulled into a café car park and awarded us a thirty-minute break.

But eventually we arrived. Then follow the crowds past the fancy hats and the annual 'closing down' sales now being challenged by the 'opening' sales- and it's all there. The same old promenade with its clanging trams and haunting smells. Hot sugar, fried onions with just a hint of the briny stimulating the nearly forgotten memories – sixpenny Fairyland rides – twopenny cornets from Pablos – the good old days when people could still spare a copper for the Salvation Army box.

Yes the Army band is still playing at the top of the beach steps, but the sound of dropping copper is coming from the insatiable 'Pleasureland' slot machines.

But the sight of all the enormous quantities of candy floss, ice cream and other goodies being continually masticated proved too much for my taste buds. I vulnerably succumb to my favourite – fresh mussels. Threepence a small plate, but who cares at Blackpool. The children watch in horrified disgust as they queue for a lolly.

But unfortunately the modern urge for ugly architecture is ripe here, too.

The Victorian aura is gradually being obliterated. No need to dash between the horses and the trams to reach the tower, there's a disfiguring pedestrian bridge to carry you across.

'The Golden Mile' has forfeited some of its old glitter, but the happy teenagers in their uniforms of slogan T- shirts and denim jeans are too much in tone to notice. It's either couples or gangs of predatory males or females all searching for the magic ingredient – love.

Makes you feel a bit conspicuous, but it's difficult trying to hold your hero's hand when he's carrying a bulging picnic bag and doing his best to control three capricious daughters.

Although there is no lack of amusement here, one could spend an interesting hour just observing the crowds. Here is Hilda Baker-land at its funniest. There is an air of notoriety, people do things here they wouldn't dare attempt at home. Grandads roll up their Sunday trousers for an icy paddle, while grannies sport a daring inch of pink interlock as they relax in the deck chair. Lads and lasses hardly out of their spots are locked together in full view. Snatches of their romantic conversations linger on their tobacco smoke. 'Mind me new earrings, you dope,' he says.

We ignored the tempting offers of any delight you could mention-with chips. My dad had booked our meal at the friendly boarding house were he was staying, just a small homely board residence, but the best value in Blackpool. We enjoyed a tasty three-course meal, then off to the Pleasure Beach to round off the day, with half-mile queues to subdue hubby and my pleasure. The day ended before we had time to visit one of the piers and they are packed with talent, as usual.

Yes, a happy day enjoyed by all. The change did us good, but there wasn't much left at the end of the day.

Where is this sex discrimination farce going to end? It has now been decided that children's books, which advocate mother being dependent on father, are out. John and Mary can still go to the dairy but Mary has to carry the can as well.

If this continues I can see our old traditional stories coming under censorship. Cinderella will have two ugly brothers, ladies in drag naturally.

What will happen to our history books? Should we let our children see Sir Walter throwing down his cloak for his Queen? Because of a moment's courtesy will he now be branded Walter the Weak. The whole idea is too ludicrous! What is wrong with the idea that mother bears and breast-feeds the children, while father protects and provides. Let's face it, there is a difference whichever way you look at it.

Waiting for the big freeze-up

'WHAT size is your freezer?' she asked matily as we stood holding our PTA coffee.

I had been expecting this question all through the exciting adventures of her latest 'freezing' epic. We had just spent a yawning ten minutes discussing her excellent prowess at freezing joints. But any conversation will do when you are alone in a PTA crowd. Better a frost report than a cold shoulder.

'Er, well, we don't have one actually,' I confessed, trying not to look too primitive. 'But they have one next door,' I added, hoping this information would exonerate me, at least until I'd eaten my biscuit ration.

She could not have looked more surprised if I'd said I was Elizabeth Taylor in disguise.

'I cannot imagine life without my freezer,' she shuddered, clasping her frost-bitten fingers around the scalding hot plastic cup with apparently no side effect. Nodding sympathetically I transferred my coffee to my other thickly gloved hand. I understand this sort of relationship, having the same attachment to my husband.

Hoping to prove I was not too much out of touch, I did a quick boast about the wonders of my electric mixer, but she had already lost interest and was scanning the crimplene mixtures for a bright and freezy friend.

These frozen food addicts are everywhere. I seem to be the only surviving member of a dying breed. We are becoming almost as extinct as the Welsh frogs.

Not that I am completely anti-freeze, I have been known to lick a lolly, perhaps de-frost a bird and enjoyed liberal helpings of champion John Curry 'on ice.' But although some of my best friends are firm freezers I have no icy ambitions myself.

One couple have so much frozen food stacked away it always feels a sin to keep them talking with all that meat waiting to be eaten. Another conscientious projector spends hours filling her home with delicious tempting aromas then proceeds to stuff the freshly baked delights into the hungry freezer. Whenever I baked double quantity I always seem to choose the day when everyone's had a rotten dinner and they come home with double appetites.

It would be full-time occupation keeping them and a freezer fully stocked.

Like most modern indulgences there are bound to be side effects, but is anyone brave enough to point them out.

Is it an economical proposition or as one courageous owner points out-convenience?

Considering the initial outlay plus additional cost of insurance, electric, servicing and remembering that price paid per pound for meat in bulk usually includes fat and bone – does it pay to freeze.

As my husband is fond of saying on certain occasions, how much will this money saving cost me? The answer to this question, act as an overwhelming deterrent in our case. Apart from anything else does anything taste as good as fresh food? Is anything else as nourishing?

We used to be fortunate enough to grow our own vegetables. Half an hour before a meal they would be soaking up the sunshine in the garden. Their tender succulent taste is beyond comparison and far above any of the frozen varieties, in my opinion. Would my voracious family be content to eat left-overs on toast for supper while succulent steaks lie a-frosting? I have always been thankful that we suffer our worst hunger pangs after 9pm when most of the shops are closed. But the strongest argument against – is my treacherous memory.

Would I remember to plan dinner ahead or should we all be draped around the table on the verge of starvation waiting for our meal to thaw out?

My absent-mindedness has often been my downfall. Would I be able to cope with this, the family and the added responsibility of a deep freezer – I wonder!

Take yesterday morning for instance. It started out as a typical day, cold, miserable with a hint of rain. Gazing through the window in my usual stupor and marvelling how the little birds found the strength to fly before dinner, I turned on the tap to wash up. The water gushed down forcefully on to an upturned cup and hit me full in the face! Then I expertly chopped an onion a la Fanny Craddock, after carefully putting the skins in the frying pan I threw the onions in the fire. I waved goodbye to my neighbour as I boarded a bus to town, then quarter of an hour later I waved again as I panted up the garden path to retrieve my purse from the kitchen table.

My husband finds it necessary to consider these little idiosyncrasies before making investments.

But I am sometimes a right pleader, and there is a wistful note creeping into our bedroom conversation of late.

'Do you think we ought to have one?'

'No.'

'But I haven't said what –.'

'Whatever it is we can't afford it and take those blasted icicles off my back!

Well – perhaps when the better weather comes.

Yes, I realise it's all in the mind

IT is sad but true that we are inclined to remember people for the wrong reasons.

Have you heard conversations something like: 'Wasn't that whatsisname?'

'Who?'

'You know, he used to (hand over mouth whisper, whisper) in the corner of the mill yard.'

'Oh yes, I remember.'

Years have passed, but whatsisname will always be remembered for this reason.

I recognised an old school teacher of mine the other day as soon as she smiled. The only other time I have seen her do this was when a few of us sneaked an eyeful through the staff room keyhole. She was on the headmaster's knee laughing her head off. So this was what they did while we shivered outside in the playground!

The image sprang to mind immediately I saw her again. But when I submitted my maiden name to jog her memory, her smile disappeared probably engulfed by some endearing memory of me, I hoped.

14

It's the same with our beloved dog. His reputation goes before him. Because of his amorous nature, he will sit outside a gate for hours for one glimpse of his lady-love. Anyway, as I keep telling irate bitch owners, there is a nasty bad dog wandering about who looks exactly like ours (but its not!).

*

SEEING all the tantalising exhibits of the Ideal Homes show reminds me of the one we visited at Queen's Hall, Leeds. We wandered around enthusiastically soaking up the atmosphere, dying to make a purchase. Everything was very expensive, but we did eventually find something within our price range – a plastic egg whisk!

But if the furniture prices are too breathtaking, why not ignore the home for once and treat yourself to a new hairstyle? Try a style completely different, which is what I did last week. I decided to go short and curly and toddled off to the hairdressers.

The girl in a pink overall arrived just in time. I had seen the price list and was on my way out. After I granted permission to remove my split ends, and my dead hair lay defacing the lino, I was given a magazine full of exotic damsels, all with long, straight hair trailing over their built-up shoulders.

As my hair disappeared and my face grew fatter, I could see it had been a ghastly mistake. But my head was quickly pushed under the tap, probably a well-known cure for hysterics, I thought, and before I had time to brood, my berollered head was pushed into a plastic cap. When this had been pulled over my forehead and tied at the back I saw my reflection for the first time.

What bliss! This is my favourite part. A few blasts of hot air and I become delirious. I could see my spouse filled with passion at the sight of my new hair-do, floating slowly towards me through the buttercups, arms extended – and me bouncing from the other direction, my beautiful curls dangling provocatively as our hands touched.

'She wants neutralising!' The hood is lifted and I am back to the tearful eye-stinging process. This is the worst part. Stinging solution drips down your neck into your eyes leaving its blotchy trail all over your face, but this is the last lap.

When it has been combed out and you are expected to look in the mirror and give your verdict, for once in my life, I must admit, I am lost for words.

'That's beautiful,' sounds conceited. 'Not so bad,' a bit ungrateful. I decided on a compromise, 'looks thicker.' We both smiled our relief.

Half an hour later I poked my shrunken head around the dining room door.

Silence - then all together, 'Oh no! and 'What the . . . .?'

Actually, after a week adjusting a curl here, and pushing a grey hair under there, I believe it's starting to grow on me!

But however glamorous my new hairstyle, I suspect my hairdresser will always remember me as a red-nosed, berollered drip, ripening under the drier!

The hidden pleasure of Easter

I THINK Easter holidays are about as exciting as an attack of the flu. Cold, shivery and considering the exorbitant pricing of today's fancy packaging, could leave me in a poor condition.

Easter egg buying looks like being a costly business. If only this product could be affected by bad weather or perhaps the Easter chicks could become egg-bound. Unfortunately, however great the demand, prices remain diabolically high.

It was the rising prices of this chocolate luxury that gave us the idea years ago to introduce 'Easter Bunny' into our household. As our family increased, the size of their Easter eggs decreased accordingly. Hoping to make this less noticeable we decided 'Easter Bunny' would hide them secretly the night before. Perhaps in the excitement of the hunt they would forget for once their legends concerning the gigantic and numerous eggs that tantalisingly adorned their pals' sideboards.

We hoped it would also help to preserve them, perhaps for once we could enjoy our boiled eggs without the pervading smell of vanilla.

During my burst of enthusiasm I hadn't realised how difficult the task of burying five Easter eggs, three at dwarf level, was going to be. After desperate scrutineering, the job was eventually completed. As the clock on the mantelpiece ticked us into Sunday morning, I awakened our bored egg marketer to tell him it was time for bed and the moment our eyelids closed the rampage started, or so it seemed.

Doors slammed, drawers and contents scattered then five minutes later – blissful silence, broken only by the sickening sound of five busy jaws indulging in their favourite occupation of chocolate eating. Unfortunately the participants enjoyed their expedition so much it has now become our Easter ritual, with the added burden of clues, in rhyme of course.

But I confess it works, everyone becomes so involved, the size of the prize is forgotten! If you can find a sneaky hiding place they also last twice as long.

*

ONLY a few more days to go and the youngsters will be filling the kitchen table with their artistic creations, and we shall all be biting back our curiosity and trying not to say 'What is it?'

When one of our children started school she was greatly honoured to have one of her drawings pinned on the classroom wall, 'Come and see,' she pleaded.

True enough, there it was. I recognised it straight away, a lifelike portrait of me. White haunted face, trimmed abundantly with black scribbly hair, a gigantic pair of bright red hands with matching nose completed the picture. As last seen at the breakfast table no doubt! In case there was any doubt teacher had kindly printed underneath in bold letters 'Here is Heather's Mummy.'

*

I NOTICE that crash helmets are now being advocated for car riders, I still haven't mastered the seat belts. We recently had the displeasure of a trip to Reading via the motorway.

After spending five feverish hours strapped in the front seat like someone about to be electrocuted, while our three out-of-reach 'monsters' went berserk on the back seat, and trying to retrieve the fallen road map with my feet as our driver frantically enquires if this is our turn off, I think I could find the addition of a crash helmet a trifle inhibiting. But my enthusiasm for family motorway trips is definitely on the wain. Travelling with a family can be really hazardous – one has to be prepared for anything.

During one hot return journey from the coast, we were speeding happily up the motorway, the children fighting merrily in the back, me doing my elastic neck act in the front – you know the feeling the moment your eyes close an elasticated reflex drags you dislocatingly back. Suddenly there was a terrifying explosion from the rear.

Speaking in an unknown language, which roughly translated meant 'What the hell?' our driver braked sharply throwing us in all directions.

After a deathly silence we discovered a thin piece of rubber tied with string, the remains of a dog-shaped balloon presented to our youngest the preceding evening. For the rest of the journey we were all suitably subdued!

So whatever your plans this Easter be prepared – and drive carefully.

Out on the town

NOT all our colourful birds fly south for the winter. Some have been busily accumulating a secret 'nest egg' in joyful anticipation of that favourite Northern winter sport, the annual 'club dinner.'

These loyal team-mates have been faithfully robbing the 'housekeeping' all summer, to celebrate their bowling victories in the atmosphere of Yorkshire's famous Batley Variety Club.

Unfortunately, due to circumstances beyond our control and my erratic bowling, we hadn't a victory to celebrate. Naturally, this didn't deter us. Like a plague of feverish moths we emerge from our 'woolly-boy' bowling image and normally flutter towards the bright lights of Batley. We take our 'hair-dropping' event very seriously and last year's was enough to straighten anyone's.

Noting the idyllic expressions which seemed to light up the faces of our male club members after their annual outing, we decided to follow their wavering footsteps and book our evening out at the same place, an athletic establishment 'over the tops.'

Of course their 'trip' takes a different form to ours. It takes them twenty-four hours to unwind, preferably during the stifling heat of summer, so they can find themselves a cool oasis to freshen up immediately they arrive at their destination. They have to start exceptionally early, as soon as they are out of earshot it's time for breakfast and the first lubrication. With such a long day ahead, parched throats are a particular hazard and the dreaded fear of 'seizing up' haunts most active trippers. Regular dosage is generously applied. But their needs are simple, casual clothes plus two week's spending money and the nearest coastal resort will do.

After two or three hours refreshment they all trip merrily down to the sands, flushed and contented, where, extremely out of character, they all play football. This sounded so unusual, I once asked my husband where they obtained the football, but he ignored me. When pain stops play they carry each other to tea, and friendly waitresses who dress and look 'just like your mother, love' wean them on to solids.

Next follows the race back to the outskirts of home. Here, according to husbands, they all lean against the back wall of some sophisticated haunt and soberly watch everyone else have a good time.

Last year's time sounded so good we ladies promptly booked into the same establishment. We ate a pleasant meal in a quite refrigerated dining-room, shivered into the cloakroom to whiten our blue noses and hopefully knocked on the two wrestlers who guarded the entrance to the 'cabaret.'

When our mascara cleared and we became accustomed to the haze, we wondered if we could have possibly have walked on to a 'Wild West' film set by mistake.

Lifting our long skirts and avoiding the broken glass we waded to our reserved table an inch from the stage, expecting John Wayne to ride in any minute.

An orange-haired girl who was rapidly growing out of her dress finished her song and, accompanied by noisy conversations from everyone, told the microphone how happy she was to be there. Then everyone had a good cough while she promised 'Tomorrow I'm off to sunny Spain.' Our table was so near the stage we had an excellent worm's eye view of every nostril that came on. We could diagnose sinus trouble in a performer before they sang a note.

The highlight of my evening was when someone asked if I had ever appeared on television. It dimmed slightly when he said 'You are a comedienne aren't you!' Another Hylda Baker fan. The acoustics were so acute we could here the arguments at the back of the room clearer than the singer, until two heftys placed amplifying equipment next to my chair. This worked so successfully I still have a faint echo lurking near my left eardrum.

When they had recovered from our vivid disappointment, our horrified males all agreed we had chosen the wrong night. But this year Batley restored our equilibrium, even though we had to have our handbags disconcertingly searched before we could enter. It could have been worse, they might have had to grope through a collection of antique cough sweets, bus tickets, chewing gum wrappers, a family album and a large white pebble with a hole in it, but I left my handbag at home. Inside the theatre we were enveloped in the fashionable semi-darkness, flattering to the over forties, but slightly disappointing when you are covered in new clothes that no one can see.

The vast auditorium, like a massive, shadowy underground cave of twitching animals was soon frighteningly full. I felt a moment's panic, was that a bomb throbbing under our table? But I adjusted my bunions and the resident band soon blasted away our inhibitions.

The scampi and chips in a basket were oddly garnished with free shampoos – so we thought – until we discovered it was tartar sauce in a plastic packet. That multi-talented Yorkshire group 'The Grumbleweeds' were well worth the long wait. Their humorous gimmicks and impersonations had us all in ruptures.

This droll climax and the other exhilaration's of the evening, including the presentation of a plaque from my team-mates 'a nail to hang your bowls on during the winter' – the tonic of being one of the three who refrained from a cloakroom visit, thereby gaining a dancing partner, who fortunately seemed to be the elected driver of his jovial group – helped to make it a bumper fun-packed annual!

But next time I go 'Out on the Town' it would be comforting to feel that the rest of the family noticed my absence and are not all sleeping comfortably behind locked and bolted doors when I creep happily homeward without key!

'Theatre science'

SINCE I had almost recovered from the harrowing brain tumour operation I saw on television a few years ago, I was granted permission to watch last week's TV programme, showing a housewife's terrifying experience on the operating table.

But after witnessing the distressing scene where the surgeon probed her exposed brain until she almost reached breaking point and hearing her fully conscious pleas for him to 'Please don't do that again,' I confess I suffered a relapse.

Oh, the wonders of science. By the simple flick of a switch we can be transported to all portions of the human body. One moment we can be coping reasonably with our simmering ailments then after a detailed and colourful visit to a 'theatre' we are immediately re-analysing our symptoms. Before the miracle of television, operations were something aunts whispered about, with painful upward glances, and lots of head shaking. Today the cameras sweep up to the bedside and we are almost hand in glove with the surgeon. Auntie can discuss in lucid detail the wonders of heart a transplant or the various techniques of hysterectomy without setting foot in a hospital.

Erudite descriptions concerning scalpels and sutures are on almost everyone's lips, a visit to a practitioner must be nearly as awe-inspiring for him. At one time we complained, 'It's my back, doctor,' now it's 'Spasmodic pressure in the pelvic region.'

But can we cope with all this medical insight being doled out between the adverts, is it really healthy?

A little knowledge can be dangerous, but a lot can be downright fatal.

A friend often tells me how well she feels after visiting anyone sick in hospital. It has the reverse effect on me. Half-an-hour at a bedside and I seem to develop everyone's symptoms and by the time I leave I have aged ten years. It doesn't help me to see other people suffer.

Mind you, I am a practising coward with phobic tendencies, but I suspect there are others who share my affliction. After a cancer operation was televised recently, everyone at our house seemed to spend twice as long in the bathroom. I can't speak for all members, but I know some of us were surreptitiously searching. The heart operations leave us breathlessly confined to armchairs for longer stretches than usual.

I wonder if these programmes have any effect on the surgery ratings?

Do they line the walls with anxiously pale hypochondriacs like myself? I long to peep, but these places are so well guarded I suppress my curiosity.

It takes enough courage to face the appointments system when you are sick. One always feels so vulnerable when facing the white-smoked receptionists, wondering if they know all one's shameful history. Perhaps they are a necessary deterrent for our overworked doctors.

We have progressed a long way from the days when a chap in bicycle clips called for the weekly payment towards the doctor's bill, the days when it was considered 'nobler in the mind to suffer the slings and arrowroots' of friendly neighbours rather than add to this expense. The sound of scraping mudguards reminds me of our collector. This was the signal for my mother to hide the cigarette packet and suppress her bronchitis, either of these would evoke his favourite topic of conversation – the evils of tobacco. Having previously been a heavy smoker, he was an abstained of the worst kind. He could tell fearsome morbid epics about dying smokers that made my mother so nervous she smoked twice as much the rest of the day!

I often reflect on our old and beloved family doctor. His surgery was always overflowing – sometimes standing room only. He liked to hand out a humorous anecdote along with the prescription – all part of the treatment. I remember with gratitude his three visits during one week when our eldest was ill, his bass baritone rendering of 'Onward Christian Soldiers' heralding his arrival and departure, whatever the hour.

Yes, we have come a long way since then. Perhaps this heartening message I saw scrawled on a cricket club door in bold whitewash may cheer some 'When you die, you go to Leeds.'

All is not lost.

Inconsistencies – and understanding

DO YOU really understand your child?

Or are there mysterious quirks in his otherwise lovable nature, which obviously come from your partner's family strain, but are nevertheless baffling?

Shakespeare wasn't just play-acting when he said 'It's a wise father who knows his own child.' Today he would probably have gone a step further and added 'But his teacher knows him better.'

Yes, if you want to know Junior, study his school report. Somewhere among the prescription-like handwriting hides a vital clue to his amorphous personality, and you could pick up a few hints on teachers' too.

My unique gifts were discovered immediately I entered grammar school and duly entered on my first report. Memories of that exciting Friday teatime come rushing back, me running homeward through the green fields, the precious manila envelope in my brown blazer pocket, stopping only to rifle the contents, digest the insults and creep tearfully home.

But having a dad fighting for his country from a deckchair in West Africa had its compensations. My work-weary mother had enough to concern her without having to read my agony. So to relieve some of it I translated for her, while she listened to Vera Lynn begging us for the umpteenth to wish her luck as we waved her goodbye.

The theme was always the same. 'Has ability but is not consistent in her efforts.' Naturally I only felt it necessary to burden her with the first two words. As time passed I became quite adept at this.

But this enlightening revelation, repeated at monthly intervals, made a profound impression on my innocent mind, and it eventually dawned on my mother, unfortunately.

I realised even at this tender age it was useless to fight. Others would gain the honours my painful inconsistencies denied me. What a handicap!

Of course I never give up striving. Well actually I do after a while, but it's something I have to live with (sniff).

Only last week I decided to try to be a perfect mother. (No, honestly, I swear it had nothing to do with March 28.)

We were all drying our eyes after the latest fairy story from 'The Waltons.' Our son had been late for work two consecutive mornings. Poor neglected lad, I thought, as I tucked his dwindling wage packet in my pocket. Getting up on his own and snatching a lonely breakfast as the rest of us slumber on, what he needs is the loving care of a mother – or a sledgehammer. Settling back in my favourite armchair, my toes as near the flames as possible without melting my tights, I had a cosy vision of myself the following morning.

There I was rising cheerfully at the crack of dawn, putting on my gingham apron and lighting the fire, a merry song on my lips while the eggs and bacon sizzle invitingly in the pan. Then when the delicious aroma of percolated Blue Mountain blend is almost too much to bear, I creep gently upstairs tenderly to awake our sleeping engineer.

When breakfast is over, I wave him on to the bus with my best Momma Walton smile.

Unhappily, it didn't exactly happen like that. The alarm rang and after wrestling with my inconsistent abilities for half-an-hour I felt my way to his bedroom without opening my eyes, shook him until his rattling teeth dislodged his eyelids, then I am ashamed to say, contrary to all promises, I crept back to my warm patch.

I was formally accused and stood trial at the tea table. Surrounded by expressions of disgust I tried to defend myself, but in the end had to plead guilty. But what can I do? I blame it all on the manila envelope.

In my defence, perhaps I ought to mention my son's similar affliction. One of his teachers once inscribed the immortal phrase, 'Does not like to exert himself.' How dare she we thought, gazing fondly at our son as he dozed peacefully beside the dog.

'Does this mean he is lazy?' we demanded, on parents' evening.

'Yes,' she replied. So parents be warned, do read the small print, even if it takes a telescope. The key to the future may be disguised in the scribble.
*

WAS it something I'd said, I wondered, as I noticed our seven-year-old curled up like a watch-spring in the corner with her head poking out from the mess at a ghoulish angle? Then I noticed the yoga book. How does she do it? After months of practice I still can't face the cross-legged position without a pain -killer.

Less of this horse nonsense!

I HAVE never been a horse fancier, and I wouldn't dream of donning puffy breeches and attempting to climb one of these formidables, even if my legs did reach the other side.

I usually leave this form of excitement to the double-barrel sports that get a kick out of a regular bounce in the saddle.

The only way I can watch the aptly-named horse trials with any pleasure is to imagine the scene in reverse. That is the riders performing acrobatics over the sticks with the horses saddled to their backs.

Yes, it requires a lot of imagination, especially when there is a fall. Who can visualise a horseless rider carrying on or being shot because of a broken limb?

I think the horse trials would be a lot more interesting without the overworked horses. Look how much fun it would be watching the ladies toss their manes as they dive head first over the sticks.

Imagine the mounting tension as they scramble through the mud trying to get a foothold on the slimy bank as someone lends a few posterial whip-lashes for encouragement. Then I would really feel like applauding the winner.

Surely the sad death during the Badminton horse trials raises a few questions?

Isn't it time we treated this noble breed with a little more respect? Is it necessary to inflict such merciless and undignified endurance tests?

Once, at a Honley Show, I tried to be brave and watch a few rounds of the pony jumping. I sat there cringing, not just because I was painfully placed between two jerky seats, but the nauseating sound of snorting, perspiring horseflesh cracking continuously against the unrelenting fences brought tears to my eyes. But my patience was rewarded when one intelligent animal threw its owner and went on to perform its only clear jump of the round. 'Well done,' I cried, with no help from my friends, who seemed more concerned with the prostrate rider.

Cruelty crusaders whine enough about the terrors of fox-hunting, but no-one seems to care about the poor old horses who are forced to spend their weekends clattering over precarious country walls, or wading through icy ditches, whether they fancy it or not.

Let's be more down to earth about it. Why not come down off the tall horse and hunt on foot? This should make everyone happy and give an equal sporting chance. I'd like to drop a hint imperial and ask one to consider the advantages of a jaunt on one's shank's pony. One and one's friend might find gambolling together giving merry chase quite topping fun. What! Pip Pip, Tallyho! Might even curb the predatory instincts.

Actually it was a horse that came between me and the Girl Guides. I know I promised to do my duty to God and the Queen, but that before someone had put a horse in the field I had to walk through to the meetings.

My one and only horseback thrill took place on Blackpool sands. I was too young to realise that big does not always mean beautiful and demanded a ride on 'the tall donkey,' which was really a wild horse in disguise, probably a great relative of Red Rum.

My dad was just showing me which strap to hold when the beastly Pegasus suddenly had an overwhelming desire to reach the pier - and back – before the Woolworth's clock moved its minute hand. I was nearly turned inside out in the rush, and never found the correct rein, his tatty mane was all that stood between me and a broken neck. Naturally it's been terra firma for me ever since.

Last year I was playing beach cricket with 'our gang' in my usual position of silly mid off, when I inadvertently got mixed up with a muddle of donkeys. I had no choice but to run with the pack. I try not to upset anything bigger than myself – except my husband. Thank goodness we don't play bowls on horseback. I can cope with the cats that show their claws occasionally, but horses – never.

A question of values

DID YOU ever hear the Goon Show episode where someone bursts noisily into a room and an outraged George Saunders-type voice protests 'How dare you burst in here, this is the living-room?'

The implication that someone has had the nerve to explode all over the carpet is certainly amusing, but judging by the photographs in some magazines, living-rooms are definitely places to be found dead in.
Their fictional build-ups of elegant lifeless dining-rooms, spotted with ubiquitous and wire-less, yet magically lit reading lamps, the gleaming polished halo complete with candles and cut-glass surrounded with symmetrically placed dining chairs – leave me gasping in wonder.

It is like trying to solve a 'find the missing article' puzzle in a children's quiz book.

Where are the pump bags? Are there really sideboards without an ornamented display of this week's homework and last week's flowers? No switches, no newspapers – in fact no life! Are all those coffee tables really necessary? And what happens to the jardiniere when dad walks in reading his newspaper?

I suppose it is really a question of values. Do you prefer a house or a home?

Unfortunately I can never work up enough enthusiasm to dedicate myself fully to unresponsive objects like houses and furniture. It has always been a lukewarm relationship. I find the human element more satisfying.

Pretending to spring clean, I find the newspaper linings I the drawers more interesting than the job in hand. Having spent most of my working life under pressure, I can easily make three school skirts the day before a new term starts, or clean the house from top to bottom the morning our guests are expected for tea. But I find it very difficult to clean the front step because it's Friday or to wash the clothes because it's Monday.

I envy the pedantics who care enough about paint scratches to be stood by, ever ready with paint and touching up brush, who cannot bear to be parted from the ironing board, however urgently the sun and the children call. They will always be dearly remembered for their domestic prowess: 'She never sits down you know. You could eat your dinner from her kitchen floor.' At least At least this will never be my epitaph! I should regard it as complimentary as 'She would have been a good singer, if it hadn't been for her voice.'

My family will not retain many memories of my hygienic feats, but I hope they will remember the happy days we spent fishing for tadpoles, visiting museums or just picnics on the canal bank.

Another missing article is the family pet, not even a budgie! Mind you animals can be allowed too much freedom. Accepting a lift once, three daughters and me had to share the back seat with a giant dog, that didn't look too happy about the idea. While I was struggling desperately not to sit on its knee, our driver was nearly breaking his neck watching that out toddler did not rest her new sandals on the car seat.

I often wonder what it would be like to sink my ten stone into the pale upholstery of the enormous settees depicted in the 'glossies' – instead of making a mad dash to reach the left cushion which balances on a dodgy spring and lets you down almost to the floor – before the guest. Actually it becomes quite comfy, after a while you almost forget you are a few inches lower than her. That is why I probably didn't notice the broken bus seat I sat on recently. It was only when I waived at my friend and she didn't recognise me that I realised my seat was so low down all she could see was a pair of brown eyes peering over the window ledge and a hand waving frantically.

Putting the family first does have its drawbacks. One summer during a halcyon existence of picnics and leisurely rambles my son turned round and accused me of leading a workless life. He imagined the flexible and relaxed routine that I adopted especially for his benefit during school holidays was an indication of my regular lifestyle! An attitude he maintains to this day.

Naturally it helps to have two handy men. They can design and build a guinea pig home with two bedrooms, dining area leading to sun lounge, in one afternoon. Of course inside jobs, like replacing faulty door handles and painting the rest of the bedroom door requires years of careful planning.

I have resolutely trained myself to believe that the state of the house is secondary to the welcome shown, and hope this disguises its shortcomings. But the old homestead doesn't look too bad when everything is in its place.

The dog covering the worn patch on the hearth rug, my slippers hiding the gap between carpet and fireplace, and what stately residence does not benefit from a few seasonal touches like the faded Christmas bauble still hanging from the front-room ceiling or the various cards our youngest can't stop creating, which she replaces faster than I can destroy.

Long ago when I still believed that problems were the thing 'Auntie Audrey' solved on the back page, we spent long evenings worshipping the monthly journals and planning our perfect retreat. But four girls and a boy, two tame mice, one wild dog, a guinea-pig and a continual stream of mates has helped me overcome our materialistic ambitions.

I was brought up with the idea that an open house is a happy house. Anyone who stayed at ours longer than two minutes was entitled to a cup of tea, my mother's cure for all ills.

Consequently it was always full – and the kettle whistled eternally. The day war broke out my aunt arrived with two cousins and a large suitcase to stay until it ended. After three weeks of hilarious fun with our cousins, she got tired of waiting and we all had to wave a tearful goodbye.

No, don't come to our house if you are expecting a magazine layout. Otherwise come in, move the books, take a seat and I'll just pop the kettle on.

Liberation? I'll give you a few hints

MARGARET THATCHER revealed an endearingly feminine trait in her make-up the other day. She confessed she is not pleased with the way she looks on TV, especially her hair. In fact she has decided to change her image and go in for the unkempt look.

By a strange coincidence I am just emerging from this and may be able to offer a few hints. Actually I am aiming for the liberated look, but unfortunately I finished up with a weary, bedraggled appearance that could definitely be described as unkempt.

I tend to fluctuate from one image to another, depending on what book I am reading, the serial I am currently viewing or which daughter goes shopping with me.

But I achieved my unkempt look by discarding all visible means of support. As our teenage daughter, still under the influence of her Margaret Morrison diploma, is fond of saying, muscles were made before Lycra.

Accustomed as I am to my vacillating personality I didn't burn my bra, just left it in the airing cupboard for a day, but I couldn't quite shake off the feeling that I ought to get dressed.

There are certain rules necessary during this liberation movement, I discovered. You have to breathe in more often than you breathe out, don't laugh too heartily and never run. Most important, if there is an East wind about, do keep you arms folded.

The success of this 'loose' living depends on how much you have been holding back and for how long. In my case I think the liberated layers had been imprisoned for too long, freedom was just one big let down! When I gave myself a truthful scrutiny in the bathroom mirror I could see I had left it too late to be a 'drop out.' Teenagers have the right idea though, they don't hamper their figures with unnatural girdles, they use muscle elasticity instead.

Old habits die hard. My mother still believes it is immoral not to wear a vest. When I scan the brief undies, which nearly cover my children I can see we've come a long way from the brown interlock hold-alls which used to cover my suspenders. They also had another use at our house for when my sister and I used to play at 'Ladies' we wore them draped on our heads with a hat on top. They were a boon when you were dying for long curls like Rita Hayworth instead of the short back and sides we were forced to endure.

Now I am all set for a touch of elegance blatantly displaying my grey streaks and cunningly disguising my unredeeming features. Unfortunately the private vision we have of ourselves does not always coincide with the public picture we present.

Margaret Thatcher worries about cartoonist impressions of herself, but my family's opinion of my appearance leaves a lot to be desired. It varies according to how long they have known me. Graduating from 'nice and fat' to indecipherable mutterings which sound suspiciously like 'useless' and 'pathetic.'

I do not agree with the yearnings of poet Robbie Burns to see ourselves as others see us, I prefer to keep my illusions. The sight of one of our daughter's first boy friend shattered one or two.

Judging from her exciting description Robert Redford had better watch out. The elaborate preparations that preceded their meetings, the hair-washing and trouser pressing had us all on tenterhooks to meet him, but she was reluctant to bring him home. I managed to get a glimpse of him, by peeping around Silvio's corner once as she went to meet him. Surely this Airforce greatcoat resting cosily on the off-grey plimsolls, a cigarette poking carelessly through the dense brown curtains was not Robert Redford's rival. What a shock! Only the super rich can really afford to be scruffy. Look at the Beatles, fame and wealth transformed them from four smart lads into four bearded pump wearers.

Jean Marsh, the upstairs maid of TV fame, left all her inhibitions and part of her underwear at home when she went to America and discovered she is not such an old-fashioned girl underneath after all.

But my life seems to be a continuous metamorphosis. I am like a chameleon and change my image to suit the surroundings. At school interviews I am covered in my parental concern image, at parties I'm nonchalantly carefree, pretending the gas bill is paid and forgetting the telephone row.

When I'm alone I concentrate on my night-club image. I practise my cabaret act. Yes one day I intend to take the world by storm (even if I haven't been asked to swell the chapel choir). I gaze lecherously at the vac, my wet lips pouting sulkily and break into the sexiest song I know all the words to. Usually its Marlene Dietrich's 'Lili Marlene.' Then I do my sultry hip roll down the hall (just missing the dog), my big toe poking seductively through the hole in my slipper, trying to fight my way through the writhing mass of admirers who are dying of unrequited passion by the kitchen door.

Or sometimes I serenade the dog with my heartbreaking and tragic rendition of 'Oh my beloved father.' This is so realistic, I am nearly in tears myself and even the dog started to tremble.

I have learned from experience to keep away from windows during these 'rehearsals.' Once I had been practising my provocative Shirley Bassey expression in front of the mirror by the kitchen window when I noticed our new neighbour's face peering through the ivy that covers our adjoining fence. Seeing as she had previously witnessed my vigorous version of the 'Dying Swan' starring my Margot Fonteyn-image through the front room window, I felt I ought to give her a rest for a while.
*

SOMEONE chided me recently about my unkind references to my beloved's sad parting of his waves. Perhaps I ought to amend this somehow. Well I would like to say although he has outgrown his hair, his head is still the same size and it is a lovely colour. How's that.
*

ARE you playing your part in water conservation? I have cut our washing up down to twice a day. Since I saw the painful scene of one diligent housewife washing her front steps in the rain with an umbrella held over her hairnet, I have cut this chore out altogether!

At last it's looking forward week

IT HAS finally arrived, my favourite week of the year! The one week I drift around in blissful euphoria, smiling at the children, answering my husband, walking around the dog's tail. Why?

Because in exactly three weeks we are off on holiday and this is the exciting part, the looking forward week. Next week I shall be up to my headache in buttonless shirts and fallen hems, probably asking myself 'Is it worth it?'

The week after, piles of clothes and cases are a clutter, and I find myself constantly surveying tongues and tonsils, on the look-out for that fearful holiday-spoiling epidemic.

But at the moment I am walking on air. As I whistle my rousing brass band repertoire – no crisis can defeat me! Even the blood-curdling cry from our third daughter, 'Mum, my hair's started going greasy,' when we have just steered her sister through a bad bout of adolescence, has little effect. Her brother's consoling reply 'had your head in the chip pan again' fails to penetrate my congeniality.

All I can think of is the bright yellow sand stretching out forever under the coffee-stained sky (I must stop reading this brochure at breakfast). This charming resort has been built just for us.

The shops are eagerly awaiting our custom, restaurants are living only for that magical day when we dine at their overstocked tables and children are especially adored and catered for - it says here.

I keep trying to inject the others with a dose of my enthusiasm, but everyone seems suddenly preoccupied with money-boxes and the falling rate of spending money. Our youngest is hard at work on her latest profitable enterprise, loosening her front teeth. The dog is the only one that looks excited, but unfortunately (whisper, whisper), he won't be coming.

One year after countless expensive experiments we reluctantly decided to join the self-catering ranks. We enjoyed it so much it has now become our regular habit. The joys of full board were proving too much for dad.

At breakfast he had to eat through a nest of unwanted eggs passed on surreptitiously by our faddy brood. Lunch saw his plate piled high with cast offs. By afternoon he was so full of 'board' we had to wait ages for him to sleep it off!

A week spent under canvas drove us all wild with pleasure, until a thousand wasps became addicted to our culinary delights.

Over the years we have become a trifle wary of the glowing descriptions which disguise the small print. We answered one advert for a 'modern bungalow – one owner has caravan in garden.'

We arrived to discover it was actually on the back doorstep and they had forgotten to mention the communal toilet and 'grandad.' He had a gammy leg and could only walk with the aid of an upturned broom tucked under his arm. Because of his weak bladder 'Long John Silver' was a frequent visitor for the next seven days. The brochure ought to have read 'lonely owner not happy in caravan on doorstep.'

Self-catering cottages are ideally relaxing for all the family. Chores are shared and there are all sorts of missed treats to threaten them with. I spend as little time as possible in the kitchen depending heavily on dehydrateds.

Anything accompanied with a bottle of Riesling goes.

When our brood were very young, I used to pop a casserole in the oven while we were babysitting. No need to dress for dinner and we never dressed for breakfast. We enjoyed an enormous three-course breakfast, packed a picnic for lunch then cooked an evening meal when we returned.

One year when we were deliriously situated a pebble's throw from the beach I left a chicken cooking slowly, while we sunned it up on the sands. Then we took chips back to accompany chicken and what was left of it went with a salad into the beach bag for tea. Remember picnicking cuts washing-up down to the minimum.

Part of our holiday entertainment is reading the exclusive menus pinned outside the delicious smelly entrances to restaurants. This appetising activity leads up to the highlight of the week – our Friday treat. Providing there is enough money left in the 'kitty' we 'eat out.' Children embarrass us all week, scanning the menus and shouting up the crowded pavements, 'Come and look at this – and it's cheap.'

Friday is also the day when we indulge in the strawberry cream flans we have been making eyes at all week.

If you want something hot, but don't feel like cooking, lots of bakers sell freshly made Cornish pasties, eaten from a deck-chair, liberally sprinkled with sand, followed by an ice-cream cornet, it's the height of self-catering luxury.

If you find you have inadvertently chosen the monsoon season, it is no problem. Out come the dominoes or Scrabble for adults, crayons and books for the tots. Liquid refreshments in varying strengths all round and the terrors of rain swiftly evaporate.

Unfortunately our holiday does contain a sad note this year. I share this moment of grief, if I may. It will cause relief in certain areas of my family when I confess two articles of clothing will be missing from my pile this year. Until we buy a new camera I refuse to pack my swimsuit and shorts. It seems to have developed an aggravating effect that makes me look wider and everyone else narrower.

It is surprising though what vast energy the thought of a holiday can generate. I find myself cleaning out cupboards, brushing out corners and who will see the results, I ask myself? It's as if the only way to enjoy a holiday is by wearing yourself out first!

To cut down on expenses I usually bake two 'sticky loaves.' These are easy to pack and delicious eaten with or without butter. Like most of my recipes they need little effort to prepare and are cheap and economical.

Just boil together in a pan for five minutes two cups of sugar, two cups of water, 8oz margarine, and about 1lb of dried fruit. When cool mix with four cups of self-raising flour, bake for about one and a half hours in a square tin or two loaf tins and enjoy.

Yes I can't wait to don my holiday gear once more. Anyone can be anything they desire on holiday providing the kids don't give you away!

Everyone needs a break in my opinion, a time off from the daily grind, to relax and enjoy whatever activity brings the most pleasure, or perhaps just to sit and 'consider the lilies.' When our children grow up and leave us (sob), hubby and me plan to indulge ourselves in one of the five star hotels we try and not to notice at the moment.

We intend to enjoy our freedom for a while anyway – until grandchildren arrive on the scene – that is!

Saying what you mean

OK' I ventured and stood back, waiting and watching for the give-away 'body language.'

Signs that according to writer, zoologist and monkey watcher Desmond Morris, would tell me exactly what my spouse thought about my paint daubing activities on the three cupboard doors he had grudgingly allowed me to undercoat. A promising step up from my regular position as sand-paper pusher, I might add.

His face was a picture of non-expressiveness (so he's been reading it too!) as I looked for the tell-tale indications of his inner feelings. But no –

he did not scratch is nose, tap his feet or flutter his paint-spattered eyelids. I observed his fingers neatly stuck to the paintbrush handle – no, his grip did not tighten, thereby signifying a suppressed longing for his mother. All he did was bravely force his mouth into an upward curve and nod slowly. So how did I know that his inner thoughts were unprintable?

It's all in the eyes, and I didn't need a sneak preview of Desmond Morris's new book 'Manwatching' to tell me this.

Recently he bewitched Michael Parkinson on TV (Desmond Morris, not my husband!) by hinting that our hand-clasping and finger-sucking habits imply a deep and insecure yearning for 'Mum.' When we are toddlers mother's hand is the last thing we want to hold but as we mature it seems to be the support we most need.

So the eminent professor has turned his binoculars towards human behaviour. Something I suspect most of us have been doing less lucratively for years and we can probably translate what we see without his specialised help, thank you!

For instance we don't need to be told that foot-tapping and shifty eyes are the outward signs of a liar.

His statement that intimacy increases the length of time that couples gaze at each other should certainly revolutionise the Christmas party season. He labels 'long-looking' as a sign of loving. It seems we can only stare into each other's eyes at length when we are, or want to be, on intimate terms with each other. 'The man who finds a beautiful colleague unusually arousing' he writes 'may not show his feelings in other ways, but when their eyes meet, holds her fractionally longer than usual.' Oh really? We'll see about that.

I foresee a festive season scene of foot-tapping wives, with one eye on the clock and the other on him and hands clasped rigidly together – and it's all his mother's fault! Wondering if I practised this 'long look' often enough I tried it out with my partner the other day during conversation.. He was indulging in his basic insecurity of pulling hairs from his nostrils at the time, which did prove a little distracting, but he returned my gaze for at least half a second the inquired in intimate terms 'What's up!'

Instead of reading the paper during his breakfast time quiz, I tried looking into the deep red eyes of our son. He pursed his lips, fluttered his eyelashes, rolled his eyeballs until they disappeared then accused me of pinching his pen. 'I can tell it's you by your eyes,' he said.

When I tried it on our youngest she did an exaggerated squint back and in best schoolyard style branded me a 'stare-cat.'

But we can all easily recognise our nearest's warning signals. My husband can convey disapproval, resignation or distaste, simply by breathing out through his teeth. No other complicated body or eye twitching is necessary.

Clothes have a language all their own. At a local school meeting the interesting guest speaker amused us all with a few anecdotes concerning an old Slaithwaite family who dated back to 1700. The mood of one member could always be determined by the tilt of his bowler hat. When worn straight all was well, the more his temper deteriorated the further back it was pushed. If it reached the back of his head, everybody ducked!

I must confess anyone who translates the message my clothes convey must be severely astute. I dress according to mood; on average this consists of baggy trousers, red knee socks (no one else will wear them) and whichever comfortable sweater my groping early morning fingers find first. Unfortunately as visitors never call when I am in my 'little housewife' mood adorned in frilly pinny and nylons, I do most of my entertaining in baggy pants.

When couples meet, eyes are supposed to centre upon three points: eyes, hair and mouth. This has not always been my experience.

We once had an insurance agent whom I swear could never pick my face out in a crowd, but would recognise my 'C' cup anywhere. I didn't need a Desmond Morris to analyse his thoughts, perhaps he just couldn't bear the sight of my face!

An unexpected visit from the clergy had me in animated conversation one afternoon. I was particularly thankful for his visit, it detained my planned and much-detested cellar overhaul. His three focal points were the five empty beer cans I would keep absently resting my foot on, the two crates of empty whisky and wine bottles just resurrected from the cellar, and although he did his best to ignore it, a gaping void in my under arm area.

But here up North it's not so much the facial expression and arm-waving that reveals feelings. Yorkshire people don't go in much for that sort of language anyway. We believe in speaking our minds.

I remember one toothless old 'pot and rag' man who used to ride into our village regularly on his horse-drawn cart. On one occasion we instantly recognised his appearance had changed somewhat. Overnight, by courtesy of National Health, he had acquired a brilliant smile, which we couldn't help noticing, threatened to become permanently fixed. His new teeth were so large his tight lips couldn't hope to conquer them, and with forthright Yorkshire veracity one customer gleefully informed him – 'He lad, tha looks just like thi 'orse,'

Needless to say there is a lot of this 'body language' about these days. Our weekly Yoga class tells a painful story, which translated spells 'Aaargh' 'help' and 'ooer' and it's all coming from my direction.

Yes, Mr Morris, good luck with your 'Manwatching,' we don't waste time with intricate sign language up here lad, we say exactly what we think.

Time for packing up!

I SEE husbands at a Birmingham engineering firm are demanding extra time off work to help with baby. They have the full support of their union, who say they should have two weeks' paid leave to help mother back on her feet again. I'll vote for that.

And what about another extra week before the holiday to help with the preparation, and to stop mother collapsing on the sands in an exhausted heap the moment they get there?

Due to bad planning on someone's part our pre-holiday week happens to fall during a school holiday week. Instead of the quiet time I blissfully envisaged, with me calmly packing the cases, and coping perfectly with all the usual last-minute catastrophies, I find an excited committee of 'advisers' surround me. I have developed a desperate need for Dad!

A doctor once confided that the week preceding the six week's school holidays always brings a rush of mums crying 'Help.' Pardon my bad mood, but if we ever do manage to pack all this lot into all that little, then come Saturday morning we are off.

I read in my morning paper that a swarm of stinging fish have already arrived and are hidden in the sand happily awaiting our arrival.

It has rained steadily ever since I replaced the woollies with cotton dresses. Proving that at least some of us have our prayers answered. Perhaps my heatwave is next on the list.

I think our dog has finally realised he is not included in our holiday plans. He is either stood in front of the television giving his soleful impression of Clement Freud, or spreading his black frame across the kitchen doorway, just as I emerge with an armful of ironing.

Our washing up rota which took longer to agree to than a wage claim has disappeared. There's a strong odour of sabotage lingering among the greasy dishes and a mighty war rages around the kitchen sink as we all look back in anger three times a day,

As my entertaining vocal arrangements have been banned, there is no light relief, Jimmy Young rules and it's not OK. I am sincerely sorry he was not awarded more for the car injuries he sustained recently. He deserves an early retirement,

Naturally now the children do not have to rise early for school, they are awake and in my bed before dad reaches his shaving tackle. Searching questions, straight from the heart, start early. Ranging from 'Can I count your wrinkles' or 'Why did you get married?' to the inevitable 'When are you getting up?'

Like a KGB grilling this painful question is repeated until the right answer is received. 'In half an hour is tortuously reduced to 'In five minutes.' Then the countdown starts – one second – two seconds – until – I soar through breaking point and shriek 'SHURRUP!'

An item on the jolly holiday fun one can enjoy, with two scarves catches my bleary eyes at breakfast. When your hair is a wet and hopeless mess, tie one scarf around your head, twist the other into a rope and tie this on top, it works wonders – it says here. After trying it I don't know which would cause the most amusement – my impression of Lawrence of Arabia or wet, hopeless hair.

But here's another helpful suggestion, tie one scarf around the bosom – yes – and another around the hips, like a sarong – yes. Well, I suppose I could walk about like this but would I get locked up.

Actually my sense of humour has deserted me this week. I refuse to be amused by the regular wisecracks that accompany my meals. When I bravely ask if my home-made bread is a little on the heavy side I can do without our diners falling to the ground unable to lift their stomachs.

I can also do without the weatherman and his depressing 'Further Outlooks.' I could even manage without the ever-loving telephone.

The other day while I was in the attic, three dragging flights up watering hubby's hopeful boost to our economy – four frail tomato plants – you've guessed – the phone rang.

Accompanied by the dog and a milkbottle full of water, I fell down the first flight and managed to limp down the second arriving at the telephone just in time for the frustrating purring tone. Naturally as soon I had regained the topmost step it rang again and I ignored it, 'But who was it I ask myself continuously.'

*

THERE seems to be a distinct shortage of knicker elastic at the moment, most of ours is doing a stretch between two chairs. It's the latest side effect of the 'common market' called 'French skipping.' Unfortunately for

36

everyone I, also unwisely, chose this week to 'run-in my new corselette, to the uncontrolled disgust of my daughters. But who cares, it's quicker than dieting. In one uplifting experience my midriff concertina has been straightened out considerably. But I admit I haven't felt quite as choked since I got the hang of the adjustable straps.
*

CAREER concern is rearing its worrying head at our house just now. Our seven-year-old can't make up her mind whether to be a 'café lady' or a doctor. We have a budding psychotherapist and a zoologist. Now all we need is a career for our eldest who finishes her teacher's training course next year.

Our son always wanted to be a fireman until he discovered they put fires out and do not light them as he had always fondly believed.

But please let dads have this extra week's holiday before the holiday. This is the last week's holiday for me. In future I'm planning a month at least.

Tentatively tottering through the tango!

WHAT marvellous machines we humans are! It takes at least three days of concentrated sea-air and sunshine to erode the ugly scars of daily routine. But as soon as one returns home, a simple click of the back door Yale and Voila!

The salubrious holiday buoyancy, that kept you floating through all mundane adversity for those gloriously happy fun-filled days, is swiftly and truly punctured.

A few moments' careful reflection of the previous week's mail and you realise that the bank balance is a shade deflated too.

But isn't it great to spend money like there is no tomorrow for once in your dull little life Indulging in life's occasional luxuries, fish and chips for supper at 45p? That's nine shillings in old currency, and all last week I couldn't stop myself reverting to the old prices.

One blistering afternoon we guiltily enjoyed five ice-cream sodas at 15p each (three bob). We had actually intended to indulge in my favourite holiday luxury – a knickerboker glory, but at £2.50 for five, that was one glory we could do without.

Life on the beach is the usual round of whining and dining, sometimes the drama can be quite hair-raising! Tiny-tots tossing precariously from wave to wave in pathetic plastic dinghies, while dad dons his sunglasses for a spot of bikini watching.

I wish these death-traps could be confined to the safety of the inland paddling pools, although the bikinis present a serious threat to some of us.

One of the most popular beach games is 'find the children.' After an hour's anguish for one mother, her prodigal eventually returned clutching a precious bucket of sea water. They tearfully embraced as little sister happily poured the priceless liquid into the hole he had just excavated, smiling to herself as she watched it disappear.

Another irate woman stormed and raved across our picnic at a little boy in front of us as he sat peacefully watching the yachts glide across the horizon.

'Where the curse, curse, have you been? The police are searching everywhere and your mother is breaking her heart,' as she greeted him, with a stunning belt to his right ear. What a blessed relief to all of us when he eventually started to cry and she could proceed to kiss him better.

During our holiday, we discovered a strange new world. We followed the trail of sequins and diamante and entered the 'Saunter' and 'Gavotte' land of the dedicated old-time dance competitors.

What a magnificent sight! A beautiful oak-lined ballroom hung with delicately coloured lanterns. Nostalgic strains of 'Goodnight Vienna' setting our corns on fire with desire, tantalising flowery odours titillating our sunburned nostrils as the highly lacquered coiffures fluttered past (and some of the ladies smelled rather nice too.)

I don't know which was the most appetising the savoury smell drifting in from the adjoining restaurant or the frothy creations worn by the competitors. There must have been miles of tulle gathered into each misty cloud of candy floss all in delicious mouth-watering shades, peppermint greens, sugary pinks and ice-cool lemons. When I realised it was not Danny la Rue, I paid court to one glittering blonde with a chandelier dangling from each ear. She confessed these magnificent dresses do often get in the way. During the passion of a tango they tend to bunch up between you and your partner and spoil the togetherness somewhat, probably evoking the dreaded 'this is bigger than both of us' feeling.

Before the competition there is a big cover-up operation. Ladies wear floaty nylon sleeveless over dresses and the men have little silk hankies draped over their stiff collars, only unveiling their vast splendour at the last minute. Once the numbers are pinned to their backs the men swirl their ladies into position on the polished parquet and they are off!

The excitement begins. 'What number?' a voice incites over the microphone and most of us shout back in frenzy. A few nights later and the rest of the family cynics succumb to this 'plebeian' pastime. Judging by the rigid upper backs extra points must be gained by maintaining a correct aristo- cratic position throughout. This must become a little wearing after a while. What starts out as a spontaneous smile often ends in a frightening leer.

No reflection on my dancing partner, but I never realised before what graceful movers men can be. I thought they looked so captivating as they waltzed by, a white-gloved hand resting elegantly on the hip, whatever my husband said. And I loved their expressive faces, especially the pencil moustache who had obviously trapped a part of his anatomy quite recently and still suffered inwardly.

Hoping to join in at least one dance during the evening I persuaded (well threatened) my spouse to attend an afternoon learners' session.
I don't know whether it was the dehydrating choice of music – selections from 'The Desert Song' or the throat constricting jerks of the tango, but after two or three attempts my reluctant partner was soon pointing his pretty little calluses in the direction of the 'hops' at the other side of the bar. Mind you, this is a pleasure that has to be taken seriously and requires the utmost dedication.

One sweet couple won the 'Over Fifties' cup, and danced into the final six of the open four-dance competition all on the same night! They also joined in the general dancing in between. Couples twice my age can't get on the dance floor quick enough. Instead of clearing the floor for the competitions, they are all gaily applauding for more, their stamina is exhausting to behold. Judging from their carefree expressions, they enjoy every fatiguing minute!

They certainly kept us entertained. I shall be whistling and waltzing through the next few weeks anyway, without a partner naturally.
*
BEING the coward I am I spent the latter part of my holiday worrying about my imminent dental appointment, but it didn't hurt me at all to have my tooth filled. The pain came later when I received a bill for £3.

It increased considerably when my waiting-room companion, who confessed that unlike me she was not a regular attender, told me she had had eight fillings for £3.50. Does it pay to have regular dental check-ups then?

Every time I open my mouth
I put my foot in it!

I RESOLUTELY believe we all have a unique talent for something. Sometimes these gifts lay deeply hidden and are only revealed in unusual circumstances.

For instance it took the boxer, Richard Dunn a trip to Munich and a heavy bashing to realise what a great talent he had for scaffolding.

The former Miss World, Marjorie Wallace, is currently doing wonders for Jimmy Connors' tennis.

Noele Gordon, who stands stoically at the 'Crossroads' four times week, doesn't know it but has turned our garden into a showpiece. It takes only one sentence of her windy consonants 'Whhhere is Hhhugh and Whhhy?' and our reluctant gardener is enthusiastically weeding out the bones from under the rhododendrons.

I seem to have a highly developed dexterity for doing and saying the 'wrong thing.' Well, it's more of a gift really. It isn't something I consciously work at but seems to occur naturally. Without any premeditation, clumsy clangers fall like misjudged cricket balls from my innocent lips. One minute I'm chatting gaily to a receptive friend, next minute she is preparing to leave.

Like the time a pregnant woman and I were awaiting our weekly prod at the maternity hospital. We were soon deeply engrossed in intellectual baby talk. 'We don't seem to be able to decide on a girl's name this time,' I confided, leaving out the fact that this was our fifth time round and suitable names were becoming a bit scarce.

She helpfully suggested a few which included the name of a relative's slobbery-mouthed dog. 'I wouldn't even insult our dog with that name,' I laughed, appreciating her sense of humour. My smile soon disintegrated, how-ever when she called her small daughter over using the same name.

Sometimes I commit these endearing faux pas with faces. I once greeted an acquaintance in a cloakroom at a dance and playfully patted her mother's rear as she bent down to adjust her evening shoes. Image my surprise when she straightened up into an unknown teenager, with a red unfriendly face.

My mumbled apology, 'Oops, sorry love, I thought you were her mother,' had little effect on her hostile expression. But let's be honest, we all make similar mistakes, don't we.'

When we read the newspaper write-up of our wedding I discovered my blunderous ability was obviously shared.

There was our photograph, immediately recognisable. We had just survived an aggressive confetti battle. My head-dress was poised at an unusual angle and my husband was the only bridegroom on the page without eyes, his hair covered two-thirds of his face. Looking back I wonder if this image was purposefully contrived as living proof to our generation that, contrary to the sparse display of today, at least father did enjoy the luxury of pre-marital hair. Underneath all the Swiss lace and roses there it was for all to see – and remember for a long time to come – 'The bride went away on her honeymoon in a petrel-blue coat with . . . the organist.' He was most displeased and wrote in and complained to the newspaper. I preferred the 'tan accessories' which were supposed to accompany my petrel-blue coat.

The following morning as we started our life together in scintillating Slaithwaite, our friends and relatives popped in and out, probably curious to see if we were still together. It was then I dropped my first wifely clanger. I told my father-in-law I had hardly slept a wink all night.

Everyone sniggered and spelled out the old cliches so vigorously no-oneheard the rest of my sentence referring to the resounding church bells at the end of our street and their quarterly chimes.

Most of us has carried on a personal conversation with what we believed was our beloved, only to discover, in an intimate confession later, that a stranger stands beside us with baited breath waiting for the final details, while husband is looking in the next door shop window.

Once I took the arm of a complete stranger and pressed him hard against a jeweller's window, 'That's the one I want,' I demanded, pointing to a diamond engagement ring. When I eventually saw the poor chap's frightened expression, I realised my prospective fiance had done his usual bunk at the sight of the black velvet pads.

Unless I am sporting my spectacles, I have stopped using my favourite surprise greeting 'OK lady I am a store detective, you are under arrest,' I said to the back view of a friend, who unfortunately turned out to be a complete stranger.

But it happens to the best of us. The other day Margaret Thatcher arrived at Liverpool FC's clubhouse wearing Everton colours, and ignoring advice, lifted the heavy cup they had just won and damaged the base. I am learning though, she had the sense to cover her colour error with a red scarf tied neatly round her neck. That's the secret folks, it's not the mistakes you make, but the way you cover them up that counts.

41

AFTER visiting a safari park on one of last week's hot and dusty days, I wonder if all this dragging animals from their natural environment wasn't a sad misjudgement. The Tarzan sound effects in the background didn't do much for any of us. I have seen more life in a sheepskin rug than we saw in some of the predatory animals and wonder if they had read the legend displayed outside their cages. 'These animals are dangerous.' As we surveyed a chimp hanging at a jaunty angle, I couldn't quite make up my mind who was watching who

Seeing some of them in the flesh destroys the majestic illusion the excellent TV series 'World About Us' creates. There seems to be no justifiable reason to place an animal whose prime instinct is to hunt for food, in a wired prison. The lions were well fed but did not show any interest in the chunk of raw meat chucked in the corner.

I suppose it's the same with most of us. Take away a chap's daily job, and what is left? Most of us do not want life handed to us on a plate, we prefer to go out and work for it. Most of us, even the late Paul Getty admitted he was happiest when he was working.

Everything in the garden

WELL we've done it, another dry and feverish month of clout-casting survived. Spring is not the sap-rising season poets would have us believe. The suicide rate is high and according to chronobiologists, stomach ulcers are on the throb. A young man's fancy may turn to thoughts of love, but he'd better see the doctor first, but enough of that, let's burst triumphantly into the month of June.

Our garden is a thriving mass of activity at this time of year. Pretty dandelion cushions blooming profusely on the front lawn, chickweed fighting a rising arm of willowherb for supremacy in the flower beds and me fighting the war of the roses with a nasty platoon of greenfly.

Brooding sparrows happily blocking our fallpipes are splattering their messages all over my clean washing, in fact, Flaming June is a pest.

During a recent spell of gardening weather I was contemplating the weeds from the safety of my deck chair, when I observed two birds having a slight disagreement. It looked as if one of them wanted a 'piggy back,' but the other was less enthusiastic. After a moment's rumination I realised what was going on. Judging from the female's obstructive display and ruffling of feathers, Daddy bird was about to be denied his favourite spring sport. I am not an ornithologist, but I recognised her call immediately as

42

the unmatey cry of the reluctant 'moodybird,' 'I have a headache, I have a headache.'

Our rambling rose transmits quite the opposite message, more like 'Come and get it!' Last year I dosed the invasion of aphids with a suggested detergent solution. My son had an unusual fit of energy while I was out and repeated the process. It worked though, next day the pests were dried up black specks, and so were the roses.

As I continued my serious meditation, this time on the pleasures of concrete lawns, a large bee landed on one of the remaining rose leaves beside me, buzzed around a bit then flew off with half the leaf! I could hardly believe my eyes. But sure enough there was a large chunk missing, just as if someone had taken a bite.

There seems to be some sort of conspiracy. I hopped on a bus the other day and was just adopting a timorous expression to accompany my pound note, when there was an almighty crack near the back of my head. I screamed and ducked like a cretin, chanting wild curses concerning galloping turban rot. The apologetic conductor helped me to my seat and pointed to the two wriggling halves of a dying wasp on the floor. What a relief! It had nothing to do with him being short of change. I wasn't being attacked after all!

The following morning I walked into our local Post Office quite oblivious of the large black spider dangling from my left ear. When I eventually investigated the pleasant tickling sensation I saw the enormous tickler run across my hand, I shrieked and threw it straight at the postmaster. 'It won't hurt you,' he said, picking it up with two thick brown envelopes and an ashtray, his heartbeat showing through his shirt.

But I have been covered in imaginary crawly creatures ever since. During earnest conversations I find myself sneaking a hand down the back of my neck, making a quick grab, a sharp retreat and then sprinkling the air with invisible horrors. Or sometimes I can feel six hairy feet creeping tentatively up my leg, I bear this James Bond torture bravely until they reach my knee-cap then a cartilage shattering blow and I'm sprinkling the air once more. It's proving to be a conversational handicap though, even for me.

Although our son used to be a spider-keeper, I have never learned to love them. One year we had a massive garden spider in each corner of the porch and a snake occupied a wooden box on the floor. Although we had a recurring safari of stray school-boys the postman and I spent a nervous summer that year – our animal escape record is higher than 'Colditz!'

43

One morning I discovered our letter-bearer gingerly lifting the lid of an empty shoe-box on the window sill. The poor man probably thought it contained some macabre addition to our menagerie.

Thank goodness our youngest is still at the bluebell collecting stage. I truly believed our Sunday school teacher when she told us flowers were a gift from God. Our house was filled with a glamorous selection from most of the herbaceous borders en-route to school.

My sister and I once livened up a dull Saturday afternoon by sharing out all the flowers in Lindley church graveyard. We were only satisfied when all the jam jars were full and each grave had its quota of blooms. Our deed would not go unrecognised we felt sure and hoped that God would see fit to reward us, before we went to Heaven, if possible.

When we reached home the benevolent mood lingered on and I decided to put a stop to mother's nagging at my dad to keep up with the experts next door. Nipping over the fence I performed a flora transplant, half and half, equal shares. I sat on our front step waiting for my reward. I could almost feel the halo revolving around my short back and sides.

My reward followed shortly in painful duplicate and I fell out with God for ages. Right until the evacuee, who played Tarzan to my mate's Jane, finally succumbed to my advances, and I stood in our 'cave,' a wick infested rhodo-dendron clipped to my fringe, waiting for him to return from the jungle to his mouth-watering appendix-bursting meal of chopped rhubarb and crab apples. Yes, everything in the garden was really lovely then and I can only surmise that whoever said that gardening is emotionally therapeutic must have had an excellent gardener.

Let's have some more bare chests!

WITH heat and tempers soaring into the nineties making England hotter than Spain, I think the effects of the sizzling heat-wave could be quite long-lasting.

Judging from the shopping battles I saw last week some of the whiney tots will be nursing their 'tanning' scars for some time to come. Tears and sweat were flowing all over the town centre. The 'Can I have' becoming 'I want' and the 'No you can't,' becoming a belt to the nearest ear.

But although the sunshine brings out the worst in some of us, it certainly has a gorgeous ripening effect on others. I spent a wonderful lunch hour on the Piazza gaping at all the bare torsos and hairy legs of our splendid

Yorkshire males. The invigorating sight of all the young and beautiful bodies certainly put new life into my brown bread and lettuce.

In my youth brawn and biceps were only allowed a quick boil in suntan lotion once a year on the sands, so perhaps that's why I can't stop gawping (either that or the fact that I am forty-three on Saturday). I heard someone recently complain about the copious nude females who habitually adorn certain newspapers. Yes, I agree, it is shocking. All these undressed women on display. When are we going to see some manly chests, for a change?

But this weather takes some dressing down for. One minute the children emerge from their ransacked wardrobes in shorts and vests, next it's long sleeves and long faces because they are burning. In between postman and insurance callers, I have managed to give my spare tyre an airing. Unfortunately as soon as I sprawl out in plump abandon, every fly in the neighbourhood decides it is time for the family to leave the rotting vegetation and go walkies on me.

Instead of half-an-hours relaxation, I am banging my bulges together or swiping myself viciously in the vain hope of mutilating at least one offender.

Incidentally, whoever said wasps don't sting if you keep still is a liar. If you don't move they think you like it and sting again. Actually, I consider wasp killing one of the pleasures of summer. It's nearly as aggression-relieving as blue-bottle swatting. I love to hear the crunch as their crackly bodies squelch against the window and find it most amusing to watch one wasp become two wiggling halves. But they probably found it just as much fun the year they stung us out of the bilberry patch and then set their ant mates on us when we sat down.

But if the long hot days are difficult to struggle through, the nights present one or two sticky problems. What to wear? Man-made fibres are useless and only keep the heat in. The double-layered nylon nighties have a built-in hazard - if hubby falls asleep on a corner of the top layer you could be imprisoned all night. One friend told me she once nearly hung herself trying to turn around and hadn't realised she was trapped until she heard the rip of nylon and discovered she had lost a layer.

Chanel No 5 may be cosy for film stars, but it can be a clammy experience. Bodies can become so riveted together that parting is not only 'sweet sorrow' it's seethingly painful. No, it's either comfortable cotton or the garden wall for me.

I can remember long, humid twilights during the war when neighbours' late night gossip swapping used to enliven many a restless night for my sister and I as we listened at our bedroom window.

We soaked up all the exciting adventures they had endured in Ward 2 and wondered how Mrs So-and-So dare venture out on windy days when she had had 'everything taken away.' We imagined her as light as a feather with nothing inside her. But some of the juicier bits were told in whispers and we never did find out why the glamorous Mrs B managed to get bananas without a green ration book!

Psychiatrists get crazier. One article I read recently advocated making love as a body cooler. My advice to you Doc is change your girlfriend. Perhaps Paul Getty Jnr had read the same article – he was fined £10 for keeping cool in this way in a London Park. Our paper shop sells the cheapest icy shivers in a polythene strip for 1p with a friendly chat thrown in.

The summer fete season is in full swing again. What joy. You spend all week being cajoled into designing a fancy dress. The fete-ful day arrives. Everyone dressed up and ready to go. Then 'I don't want to dress up' says our temperamental Victorian lady throwing her lovingly designed and extremely pinned and delicate headgear at the dog. 'Alright then don't,' says patient and ever-loving mum proceeding to undo pins.

'No don't, I do,' she says in her own special language. After this performance has been repeated several times, we then move on to the 'What if I don't win,' parable, with glib lies about the taking part. 'You are just entering for the fun of it love,' I say as I stick another pin into the uncomfortable straw hat and wrap the prickly net shawl around her neck, resisting the temptation to pull it tight! At least our fete organiser presents all competitors with a bar of chocolate, which quells the disappointment of some of the children.

Yes, take advantage of the sunshine, it's salubrious, it's heart-warming and there is no bill at the end of it. No fireplaces to clean and in my case no coal to haul in! Great.

Who says it's a holiday?

TEACHERS are smiling once more and mums are wearing their white, haunted, end-of-term expression again.

A nervous tick is developing around Dad's left eye. Deliriously happy juniors will be swinging home tomorrow with all their term's toil squashed into a carrier bag.

The older scholars will be dragging home under the weight of their efforts an ominous sealed envelope cunningly concealed. Yes, we may as well face it this is no nightmare, the stark reality of what is aptly called the summer 'break' has almost begun.

When junior lovingly empties all her own work over the tea table, it always brings a lump to my throat. What a pity we cannot return the compliment and send one back, filled with all our unwanted 'masterpieces.'

But what cannot be cured must be endured, we only have to 'suffer the little children' for six weeks. Things could be worse; you could be struck with galloping malaria in the middle of the Market Hall on a hot day. I hope all these platitudes help you more than they help me.

Actually, it's just a matter of keeping them occupied and quelling the 'What can I do?' before it takes root.

My mutinous crew's insatiable lust for spending money has proved to be a valuable asset during our six weeks' incarceration. They are interested in doing anything if it is lucrative and not too uncomfortable.

Our son was a willing helper during his holidays and never reused to do any job, if the price was right and it didn't mean moving from his buffet. Mind you, with the help of his sisters, who trusted him implicitly, until they learned to count, it is surprising the amount of jobs he did accomplish with his sitting position.

If you decide to introduce this 'daily worker' system there is no need to sit in anxious trepidation wondering what you can sell when they present their gigantic bill for daily services. This problem is painlessly reduced by the introduction of 'taxes.' All their aggravating habits are taxable.

You may notice a rapid personality change at this stage and might even start taking them to auntie's again. Don't worry too much, this angel phase does not last.

Planning a special day's outing each week is a good idea. As long as it is a flexible arrangement which can be cancelled at a moment's tantrum. It is wiser not to mention it, though, unless you are definitely prepared to go through with it, because once they know, nothing, but nothing, will put them off. If you develop rattling pneumonia you would have to go to the intensive care unit via the pre-arranged outing.

One of my golden rules is never promise anything you cannot fulfil or better still never promise anything. 'We'll see how you behave,' is a safer bet.

Finding an outing to suit all tastes is a mammoth task. Forget you enjoyment – that is bottom of their list. Remember these happy outings are for their benefit.

This is where Dad's help is vital. On these occasions he must be ready and waiting with a suitable anaesthetic the minute Mum is dragged in. What she needs now is an instant babysitter and an immediate childless evening off. Never make the mistake of expecting gratitude from young children. After an expensive day trip you could find on return their friends have enjoyed a blissful day fishing in the canal across the road, and the pity you expect them to feel for their stay-at-home mates will probably sound like 'Why couldn't we . . . ? Next to money, children love water, preferably dirty with treacherous tight-tearing access. In fact outings need not be expensive. We have three well-equipped parks and Ravenknowle Museum is well worth a visit. Pretty streams and woodland are within easy reach for most of us.

Children love picnics. No need for elaborate cuisine. I can still remember the exquisite pleasure my sister and I enjoyed as we shared a bottle of water and a bundle of jam sandwiches in my father's hen-run. It's just the fun of eating outside in the soft grass, with only the sound of birds and rustling leaves.

I once took my Sunday school class of vigorous nine-year-olds on a picnic to Longwood Edge, a childhood haunt of mine. Mums gave me some quizzical glances as we set off. First we climbed the rocks, then the pork-pie tower. We surveyed our bird's eye kingdom then took it in turns to make a speech from the pulpit-shaped stone in a grass valley.

Our fish paste sandwiches was voraciously eaten to the accompaniment of a hidden cricket. It was inconceivable that these lads who made my Sunday mornings so wretched could transform a Saturday afternoon so pleasantly.

For the very young a table-over tent in the backyard takes a lot of beating. Or perhaps a short expedition 'lucky' stone collecting. Another excellent pastime for the artistically inclined is to bring back as many holiday shells and pebbles as Dad can carry. Using Polycel cement they can clutter up a vase, plant pot, or anything else you never liked anyway.

When you go out take a sketch pad, they will probably end up playing noughts and crosses but if it's occupational, it's fun. Buy them a scrapbook, they can spend many happy hours sticking in useless pictures. It's all messy, but less frustrating than fuss.

If you have a short-sighted gardener let them loose on the front lawn, a home-made game of Jokari or clockwork golf will keep them happy for a while.

We went through a hiking phase once. It lasted until we got out of the car at Edale village, turned the corner and everyone saw the ice-cream van.

On one optimistically planned ramble, feeling tired, I told everyone about a white lie about hidden Neolithic treasure near by. I was about to uncover my corns when our excited archaeologists returned with what looked like a load of old iron to me. It turned out to be an ancient working tool.

Don't forget you local library, not just for the children, but also as a relaxation for Mum. Let them browse on their own while you do the same. Our friendly librarians have provided me with countless passports to tranquillity.

It pays to plant the idea that everyone needs a quiet time, even Mum, from a very early age.

I often spent sewing time in the children's playpen. They always seemed happier gazing in at me from the outside. But whatever you have planned for the next hectic weeks – the best of luck!

Smile please, I want a photo of your knees

JUST talking about your ephemeral holiday adventures is not enough, these days you need a picture to prove it.

That's the way most of us spend part of our holiday, clicking the shutter. The exposing season is in full swing. Miles of celluloid is on its way to enlightening development.

It could be an inspiring close-up of your left ear snapped by a hidden professional while you were looking the other way or just a scintillating view of hubby's tonsils as he eventually got the joke. Whichever way you look at it, most of us find these exposures irresistible, no holiday would be complete without one.

You may consider your holiday expensive, but the plastic-coated memory could be even dearer than you anticipated. These 'masterpieces' are not executed in oils but they are almost as extravagant. Nevertheless, it is a vital part of the holiday fun. Sharp clicks here, a blinding flash there and another technicolour memory is preserved for the family album.

Living proof that dad lifted his head out of the deck chair, took off his jumper and said 'cheese' last Friday.

Or just evidence for work-mates that flesh and blood does exist beneath the overall. It's on eternal record that toddler actually parted his pout and bared his front teeth one sunny afternoon by the sea.

Casual epics so carefully contrived – big sister just happened to be posing in her bikini, one leg seductively bent and stomach muscles rigidly controlled while boy friend is calmly relaxing on the beach towel with fists rigorously clenching his bulging muscles to bursting point.

Photograph albums are splendid conversation pieces, something to laugh and browse through during the sombre winter evenings. My 'snaps' are very aptly named. They have a disjointed, slightly sinister appearance. Here we see three smiling legless bodies, accompanied by half a Father. This is a scintillating Father before his swim, although he hasn't a face the legs are unmistakable. Now this stranger emerging from the pool looks divine, but who is it? Oh yes, it's really a picture of youngest daughter Amanda, that is the top of her bathing cap in the bottom left corner.

Unfortunately some will always remain a mystery. What special significance do the three telephone wires have, and is there a family lurking behind the enormous rock? I ask myself. Perhaps this 'gift' is inherited from my father whose photographic genius has been a continuous surprise for over sixty years. He always spent holidays with a camera strapped to his chest.

Incidentally, he never had a cough until he sold it and bought a movie camera. But his avid enthusiasm was not infectious. We have a large box at home filled with black and white versions of my mother's differing negative expressions.

One year she persuaded us all, except Dad, into a studio for what she described as 'a real photo'- a still-life version of our holiday. None of us were prepared for the eye-boggling explosion of the flash bulb. The result looked like the all-winners of an Eddie Cantor lookalike competition.

This situation has altered now of course. My Father has now become a 'Movie Mogul.' But the transition from midget Brownie to the wide screen is not easy. We first had to sit through the life history of his garden, featuring the third rose from the left, followed by the exciting adventures of an aeroplane, followed by negative comments from Mother and snores from the dog.

These cameras take some mastering. I used a whole film capturing the antics of our troupe on a seaside skating rink, without learning the technique I felt like Ken Russell as I zoomed the lens from one exhibitionist to another without taking my finger off the button.

The result made slightly billious viewing with skaters and sky spinning furiously past. When I turned up the lights and wheeled in the supper, I noticed a pale green tinge on our guests' bewildered faces and the snacks went much further than I expected.

But we love them really and spend many felicitous evenings enjoying them all over again. We have built up quite a collection over the years and my Dad has become most proficient. As he often threatens, he has enough film to run for a week!

But it must be most satisfying to posses the photogenic features of the magazine model. Exquisite bone structure and deeply set eyes are a definite asset. I long to emulate the mysterious, sulky expression they seem so fond of portraying, but annoyingly, if I don't show my teeth I look as if someone's just told me I have only a month to live.

And how do they achieve the cool windswept romantic aura, with a gentle breeze caressing their sun-bleached silken strands? All a gentle breeze does for me is whip my frizz into a frenzy.

But an unsightly clumsiness seems to be creeping into some of the fashion features lately. The tall angulars are poised in ugly hip-thrusting positions. Our teenage daughter pointed out an advert the other day. The photograph showed the back view of a young girl in red cotton shorts and a black halter neck sweater. She was gracelessly perched on a wooden form with her thighs spread inelegantly, hands on hips. I used to sit like this when I was eight months pregnant, for an obvious reason! But my daughter had not noticed the ugliness, she was just interested in the red shorts.

So it ain't the way you wear it after all – it's what you wear, OK. Happy postulating.

It's all in the Games!

I COULD see the shop assistant was exhausted when she had to carry the wafer biscuits for my ice cream, one at a time, using both hands.

'It's these Olympics,' she explained uncovering her bloodshot eyeballs for a moment. 'These Olympics' and their late night antics seem to be setting quite a few optic nerves on edge. At our house it is not just the Olympic games that leave me breathless, but all the accompanying channel switching. We sound like a group of frustrated 'Mediums' constantly demanding 'Is there anything on the other side?' Life seems to be a continual switchback.

Of course during the school holidays, some of us, those with the wrong priorities, as my husband lovingly puts it, can stay in bed for an extra blissful hour. Sounds wonderful . . . so, why isn't it? Somehow sleeping late is not half as much fun when it is allowed. On normal early-rising days, the celestial luxury of sneaking an illicit five minutes in the warm hollow your sleeping partner has just vacated is unsurpassable delight. With a little precision you can prolong the euphoria for another glorious five minutes. I can submerge in my cosy cocoon until the third bathroom sink-plug deluge and still have breakfast prepared before my lot have found their shoes. My eyelids take a while longer to rise. During the night they

51

gain extra weight and I haven't the necessary strength to lift them until my third cup of coffee.

But now we can stay in bed longer they have changed miraculously. As soon as my mate leaves, they shoot back like roller blinds. By the time he has walked into the wardrobe to collect his glasses I am wide awake! However hard I try I can never recapture the snug and sleepy school morning raptures. It is diabolically unfair.

The other evening on retiring, my snoring partner and I had a melodious surprise. Our heads were just creaking into the pillows, when a bird opened its throat and proceeded to serenade us full blast! 'How lovely,' I smiled drowsily, 'How tuneful,' he sighed dreamily. Half an hour's continuous lullaby later, 'How blinking aggravating' we both screamed!

But I confess the entertaining part of the Games ends for me when the Queen sits down. I spend the rest of the time hoping to get another glimpse of her, and think she's a real record-breaker. Standing there so regally and showing no sign of strain as the nations file past, makes me feel so ashamed. I can't wait five minutes for a bus before giving in and sitting on the wall.

When I'm not looking for the Queen I am held in suspense by the fashions and the hairstyles and, whisper, whisper, those gorgeous hunks of manhood leaping about all over the place.

I often contemplate when the victors accept their medals and applause, how they will cope with their success. As my son sardonically remarks after he has achieved another victory in our family sport, bowling, 'You'll never know that feeling, will you mum!'

Just because I haven't won a game yet this season – actually I could possibly be included in the Guinness Book one day if my record continues.

On holiday once in Colwyn Bay my expert tennis-playing husband booked a court for an hour. During that time I never stopped running, the racket never left my hand, I hardly hit a ball, and a smile never passed my husband's lips. It's true!

I may not know much about success, but I am an accomplished loser, I know all the tricks. Other members of my team chew spearmint to concentrate but it serves two purposes for me. It gives me a firm jawline and stops the dreaded chin wobble when defeat is imminent – a boon for born losers. I find it useful to wear something around my neck, something to keep the fingers busy and take my mind off strangling my opponent.

Some wag once remarked that bowling is the best game for cutting a person down to size. If it reduces me any more I could eventually disappear.

NOW the children have recovered from their first good mood flush of the school holidays, breakfast conversation has resumed the usual quizzical turn.

'Mum,' our toastmaster inquired the other morning, 'Is this toast burned enough yet?'

Then after a sidelong glance at my unique breakfast hairstyle, 'Dad did you wear glasses before you were married?'

Half an hour later our insect lover walked in with a matchbox full of ladybirds. 'Look what I found on your roses,' I hadn't the heart to tell her Dad had carefully placed them there the night before. Our roses were the only part of England the swarm of ladybirds had not invaded. He had lovingly carried them half a mile.

I can see where I'm going now!

SO Kenneth Kendall has finally succumbed to spectacles, what a trans-formation! No more gentle reports from the silver-haired newscaster, the heavy dark frames have added a ruthless dimension to his benign personality.

Does he realise, I wonder, what a gigantic step he has taken? Once we have seen him 'framed' shall we ever again be able to stand the sight of him without them?

Glasses give wearers a new 'lens of life' and I have never seen a permanent wearer yet who didn't look ill and strained without them. They disguise the parts that contact lenses never reach, although the latter can be an attractive replacement for the marble-thick glasses. I still concede that some people look prettier in 'specs.'

Our maths teacher used to nearly frighten us into working when he donned his ugly, thick tortoise-shells, but he was not too loveable when he took them off, either. I can see him now, chewing on the frames, making mouth-watering sounds, which drove me enviously to bite another chunk off my ink-rubber.

He was a versatile lens wearer and performed all sorts of fascinating tricks. When he got tired of sucking he would part his hair and dig at his dandruff for a while. He could hitch them up or down his nose without using his hands. In fact he could do anything, except teach me algebra.

But my chance to join the esoterics came with the introduction of National Health frames. Like many others I realised my 'need.' It was easy, a cursory test plus an eye-watering confession concerning headaches.

Lots of head-holding from me and a little short-sightedness from the optician and I was soon chewing on the pink plastic.

I spent hours in front of the mirror enraptured by the intelligence that shone out of the new glasses. They added rare sincerity to my well-rehearsed wage-increase 'soliloquy,' that I was sure no boss could resist. Once I had mastered the art of keeping them on my non-adhesive, almost non-existent nose, my future was secure.

During the early years of marriage I had a strange encounter which made me think twice about wearing them. I was playing my usual part 'The Constant Wife,' clicking my needles and watching the clock, when I heard someone tap on the door with what sounded like a wooden leg. Not a salubrious sound at that late hour. Unable to control my feline curiosity I opened the door half an inch. All I could see was darkness until a hand gripped my ankle, and I saw a man stretched out at my feet, holding a walking stick. Realising it was not my husband I helped him to his feet. It seemed he had fallen and could not rise without the aid of his other stick, which was out of reach.

As he turned to thank me he begged me to throw my glasses away! Well I never saw myself as another Grace Kelly, but . . . he explained he had not worn his for twenty years and his eyesight was perfect. It never occurred to me to ask how he had fallen, and I obediently followed his advice.

Recently, I decided it was time to face facts. The other side of the road was not fading into the distance, people were not walking about without features – I needed glasses!

This time it was not as easy as the opticians was twice as big, with double staff, who all talked in whispers and tiptoed everywhere. At first I wondered if I was going deaf as well. The interior was as joyful as a funeral home. Most of the occupants looked as if they had just received their electric bill. When I finally achieved the optician and his ethereal chamber, he looked into my eyeballs for so long I could feel myself slipping into a trance.

Now, answering unusual questions is my speciality. For instance, I know that no surgeon worth his suture, will go near a scalpel until he knows your father's occupation or which church you attend. But his 'When did you last eat an orange?' had me completely flummoxed. I ran my tongue nervously over my lips. Was my mouth stained? Later, as he glared at my pupils in the darkness he seemed to become obsessed with the length of time I spent watching television. Not having passed the orange test, I cut my viewing time in half. He seemed aggressively dissatisfied. Perhaps his daughter was a TV personality, I pondered. When he shone a bright light in my eyes and asked again, I confessed.

Broken and dejected I was ushered into the light again and placed at a small table full of exotic frames where I selected a delectable pair of gold-rims. I was about to try them on when the assistant arrived with a pair of 'National Health' blacks. I looked like Arthur Askey in drag.

My 'How do I look' pleas were greeted with the usual enthusiasm. 'Idiotic, repulsive' and 'don't wear them when Mavis comes, please, mum.'

I had hoped to become vital, irresistible, perhaps have more control over the rebellious, but let's face it, who's afraid of Arthur Askey?

I am still an in-between and have not reached the Kenneth Kendall stage yet, not possessing the necessary courage to face the public. Of course, I am not short-sighted enough to wear them all the time, just need them to distinguish the sink from the cooker. I conveniently wear them around my neck on a cord, which means when I am not hanging myself, I gaze at the world through egg-splattered spectacles. But I admire your peerless image Kenneth Kendall and wish I had the nerve to relieve the strain in public!

Don't jump in_you might be thrown out!

ARE your children rapidly driving you out of control? Are you running out of suitable punishments? Then why not take them to the local baths! An hour or two spent under strict supervision there should soon restore the equilibrium.

But it saves a lot of whistle-blowing if you explain the rules before you go.

Swimming is allowed – within reason. There is a long list of 'Do nots' stuck to the bath's wall and for safety's sake these must be adhered to.

Then there is another long list of unwritten frivolities which are severely whistled upon by the badge-wearing guards. No nonsense here. This is a swimming bath and they have ways of making you swim. Naughty daddies must not ride offsprings on their backs - the power behind the whistle sees to that. No bodily contact is allowed with Mum – it makes the guards whistle. Yes, you can dive in from the board, but jumping in is only allowed from whichever side does not evoke a sharp blast. But there is no need to worry about the rules really, any one of four attendants will be pleased to point them out. They all have especially flexible index fingers.

I am not certain about the rules concerning spectators, which explains the neurotic feeling I get the moment I enter the swing doors. For instance, do we cross right leg over left in the sitting position, or vice versa?

Whichever position I adopt seems to depress the attendants and they are definitely not impressed with my front teeth.

Perhaps there is a law against shopping trolleys (not the supermarket version), as mine seemed to incite such alarm the moment I wheeled it in. I wondered if the dog had followed me. I know we are both slightly mis-shapen, due to excessive weight carrying over the years, but we are quite harmless. Did they think it was some strange nautical contraption I was going to sail up and down the bath in, I wondered as I tried to ignore the smouldering glances?

One poker-faced performed a mime about something that 'ought not to be allowed,' the other agreed, her whistle-hand twitching excitedly. I considered detaching the wheels and popping them out of sight in the bag. Perhaps this would bring the colour back to their cheeks. But two little boys playing hide and seek and a girl laughing and splashing soon had them whistling again.

It is amazing how infectious the abrassiveness can be. When my youngest daughter dared to emerge from the bath without permission, I was outraged! With a realistic, rigid finger impression that would have delighted any whistle wearer, 'In that bath' I ordered. When I saw her unwind her twisted legs in the shallow end I realised she had been to ask me where the toilets were.

Yes, I could see it was time to leave. After a while the atmosphere gets up my nose!

Charles Lamb wrote 'I have been trying all my life to like Scotsmen, and am obliged to desist from the experiment in despair.' I have reached a similar conclusion regarding autocratic females.

On holiday we met a lovely lifeguard. I use the term lifeguard loosely, he actually had two jobs. During the day he guarded the bathers and in the evening became an entertainer in the ballroom. Both were places of enjoyment. Although the large overcrowded pool boasted only two attendants, no lives or tempers were lost and the only overbearing obstacle was the heat.

But even this did not stop him, or us from being happy.

*

I NEVER thought I could be so disappointed at a wet St Swithin's not living up to its stormy prophecy. But this dry weather is most depressing. Although we are all water bored, it is time to face facts. We are all guilty of excessive waste. We have too many baths, shampoo our hair too often and gallons of water are flushing the drains daily as we follow the numerous washing symbols on our various fabrics.

Almost everything is washable. We are invited to use one temperature for nylon fabric, another for cottons. Don't forget to use more water to soak them in first. Most youngsters are 'hooked' on the fruit cordials that require dilution. Even after numerous warnings thoughtless car-owners and gardeners have been caught using hosepipes. A standpipe on the corner will bring us all to our senses, but I am praying for a downpour first and more sensible usage second.
*

NOW I do not want to start an unhealthy rumour, but there is a wild beast stalking near my house, and it nearly ate my small dog the other day. While I gathered the children in front of me and screamed bravely, my husband gave it a quick biff with his bowling bag. So beware! There is a slightly stunned, vicious Alsatian on the prowl. Is it mad! Well, it's not exactly pleased!

Brave the brambles and pick a pie!

'I CAN'T do anything about high food prices due to lack of rain,' Agriculture Minister Fred Peart warned housewives last week, 'You either pay the prices or do without!'

Further outlook very expensive.

Aye, Fred lad, it's a pity your plane did not land further north, somewhere near our area for instance. Then you would have seen that some of us are not going to pay the prices or do without.

With a little care and plenty of utilised bath water, gardeners up here are producing an abundant harvest, even if some can boast only a modest herb patch and a couple of frail tomato plants. We have generous friends and relatives with fertile pastures all irrigated and flourishing on soapy water.

We were encouraged last season to grow our own, remember? The last five winters have been mild and dry and the word drought has been blow around like a cloud of hot air. But what steps have you taken towards survival?

Yes, Fred, I agree it is too late to step in and help the farmers, now their crops are ruined. Perhaps with a little foresight bath water could have helped your problem. Not in buckets, but what about all the public bath water and fountains playing around this summer? How necessary is an automatic car wash? Until recently sports fields and pitches have had their quota. Where does food come on the priority list?

But the drought affects everyone. A thief stole cash from a house and had a bath before leaving!

57

In town I noticed most of the office block windows are covered in luxuriant tomato growths. We are all turning back to nature. Do not be discouraged though, if you are not within easy reach of home-growns, there is another profuse harvest waiting to be picked, and it is enticingly free for all.

It is a painful and seedy operation that does leave its stain, and often the best areas have limited access, so beware. But do grab a stick and a basket and take a nostalgic trip to your nearest blackberry patch.

I used to believe that God hearing worried mothers' helpless pleas to children not to visit distant blackberry spots, had resolutely placed them in especially precarious places. But forbidden fruit is always desirable, and a battle through swamps, nettles or rocks never deterred us.

I remember once climbing a sheer rock face to discover an unexplored blackberry haven waiting at the other side of a treacherous gap in the rocks. This perilous death trap became less noticeable after a few visits, to my sorrow. I became so adept at jumping across I forgot to point it out to my friend on her first visit. When I turned around to see look of wonder I was expecting on her face at first sight of my secluded snack bar, she had disappeared! She was lying several feet below me, with what later turned out to be a broken collarbone. And yes, she had a look of wonder on her white face. As soon as she recovered we discarded blackberrying for the most exciting of ventures, apple-picking!

There were two obstacles – the apples were in someone else's garden and, like the blackberries guarded by a high wall. We eventually climbed to the top and with unusual dexterity I jumped down first. Actually I was about to attend to a call of nature and just as I surrendered to my delicate situation, an aggressive roar interrupted me. The angry shout 'Now I have caught you' was definitely an under-statement.

With an undignified and uncomfortable dark blue patch spreading its damp embarrassment across my light blue shorts I was taken before the orchard owner's family and made to apologise. Muttering brave statements in my defence which sounded something like, 'Please sir don't tell my Dad,' my ardour for forbidden fruit was considerably dampened, and was not resurrected until I started grammar school. But that's another story!

The promise of free treats is a great stimulant. An old friend who died recently was fond of relating a tale in his thick Yorkshire brogue of a boyhood trip to Oldham in an ice-cream cart. It was a normal spring day with easterly winds biting at the ear lobes. But George, with his frozen fingers tucked in his thin coat pocket was dreaming of all the free ice cream he had been promised in return for his help at the Oldham feast.

Unfortunately, the weather was so cold that customers were reluctant to buy. But George dipped into the icy vapour with a hopeful smile. Any minute the master was sure to give the signal and he would be able to help himself. Hours later, as rain bounced off the cart roof, plastering his hair close to his head, the hopeful smile was still there.

At last the master decided it was time to call it a day. With rain and hail lashing them as they journeyed over the Standedge, George's shivering teeth were beating time with the horse's hooves.

As they turned into Marsden the proprietor glanced at George's damp little body huddled in the corner. Taking the top of the tub he pointed to the frozen mixture and invited him to 'help thissenn.' But George's appetite had been well and truly chilled.

He confessed to me years later, a tear swamping his eye at the memory. 'Do you know, I couldn't have eaten an ice cream at that minute if you'd crowned me.

Please do sample the succulent bramble harvest! With a little ingenuity and bags of sugar they can be transformed into a variety of dishes such as pies, jellies and delectable desserts.

Why not attempt the easy and medicinal Bramble Syrup, excellent for winter colds. But why not be adventurous and brew your own wine.

My recipe does not contain any synthetics advertised by wine shops, but most of my friends and a relative with delicate entrails will admit , one glass gives you the ....!

Well why not brew it yourself and find out?

Blackberry Wine

You need 3lb blackberries, 3lb sugar, 1 gallon boiling water.

Wash berries, at same time making sure there are no rotten ones, and place in large bowl. Pour over boiling water. Stir well, cover for ten days, then strain off liquid through muslin. Add sugar, stir well, cover and leave for another three days – stir daily. Cork loosely at first.

Now for the hard part – leave for three to six months.

Bag a bargain down at the 'jungle' sale

WE have been together now for over twenty years. In spite of the dark rings, the gammy leg and the indelible stains and wrinkles left by a lifetime of close proximity with intemperates, I could never bear to part with this dear companion.

I am of course referring to our oak dining table, not my other old dear, whose legs are as good as ever, anyway. We paid £10 for this oval gate-legged bargain at a local antique shop, which was closing down, the year before we married. It's still in better shape than us and looks even more attractive with a little polish and without the dead roses. More waxing and less waning would be a distinct improvement.

As I follow one of my favourite occupations, browsing through antiquities, I often see similar tables offered at more than three times the price we gave. It is that rare a commodity, one indulgence I have never regretted.

I love junk shops, the sort you can wander through at leisure, opening drawers, examining china, not the ones that forbid you to step over the threshold. I suppose it is the jumble sale atmosphere that draws me to the Oxfam Wastesaver Centre most weeks. If you have the strength to climb the mountainous stone steps, you can enjoy an exhilarating rummage without the suffocating assistance of the 'committee ladies' who usually patrol 'jumbles' in their favourite supervisory capacity, and best of all everything is VAT free. There is a promising evening dress section. But I wish buyers did not feel the need to apologise when they succumb. Most look as if they have committed something improper and feel they have to read a boring soliloquy to anyone who witnessed their 'crime.'

Actually I never feel comfortable in new outfits until they have been shocked into shape. Like Oliver Goldsmith I love everything old. Books, wine, friends, and only ask one thing, that I may be allowed to choose them.

One of the occupational hazards of owning large families are the 'relief' parcels. Old 'cast-offs' which owners are relieved to part with and for which recipients have to look suitably grateful. Spring and Christmas are the most 'relieving' seasons. But there is undeniable pleasure in choosing your own rubbish.

Up another flight of leg breakers is my favourite section, a lovely musty collection of books, furniture and other bric-a-brac.

In and among are some valuable antiques. I picked up a pretty smoked glass dish for only 20p the other day.

Another good browse for the addicted is the house clearance auctions. Everything is on view the day before and you are allowed to scrutinise to your wallet's content. The following day the lots are auctioned off. Bidding can be a little embarrassing at first. Everyone has their own eye-catching gimmick. The crowd look a twitchy, scratchy bunch, but you soon become accustomed to their craze.

The first time I dared to bid for a chair I was disgustingly eager. I raised my arm ostentatiously at the pound mark. As the price rose higher my arm dropped lower and I wished I was nearer the exit. I was just beginning to attain the uninterested look which is the hallmark of most dealers, when the auctioneer raised his gavel menacingly and demanded in his echoing Oxford accent with Holmfirth connotations, 'Madam in the blue raincoat, is your arm up or down?'

Over the years my purchases have been a perpetual surprise to my beloved, but I think it fair to admit, when the chair finally arrived, accompanied by another, their stunted legs were a puzzle to both of us. Now I confess I have suffered the 'short leg syndrome' for years, one reason I avoid bus side seats, because of the leg-swinging agony, perhaps I could use this argument in defence of my 'bargain.' But it is extremely difficult trying to sing praises to a chair which was 'made for you' with your Adam's apple trapped between your kneecaps.

Yes there are bargains for all – a three-piece suite for £5, and Victorian lustres held back because the bidding stopped at £90!

Another family favourite is the annual transport lost property sale, when all the articles left behind on the buses are sold. What a collection! Underwear, jewellery, ties, books and of course the ubiquitous umbrella. All the best sales are inhabited by the tall, so most of the objects are invisible to me. Naturally this does not deter me. I considered it safe to buy a bundle of something offered for 10p. It turned out to be umbrellas. As we continued our shopping, yes in the rain, they were duly shared out. With a brolly held overhead and a spare tucked under our arms, the five of us caused quite a stir as we paraded the Piazza. A pity we had not taken the dog. I could have strapped the remaining two to his back! It's a strange feeling really, any minute you expect a hand on your shoulder and an irate voice demanding 'Hey, that's mine!' But it wears off, especially when you have a dozen umbrellas, a bit faded and mis-shapen perhaps for 10p.

'Jungle' sales, as one daughter used to call them, often harbour hidden treasures. My mother once bought a pretty pink glass dish for sixpence, which proved to be Victorian cranberry jar valued years ago at £6. Old painting are a good buy, if you are not over-fond of sheep on a hillside, or pale females in the last stages of galloping anaemia, they are worth buying just for the frames. We have favourite family portraits in one that hangs above the dining table. Our son still finds his photograph so fascinating he often forgets to complain about the food. The morning after a jumble sale all our girls carry a handbag and all their dolls wear knickers. At our last school rummage sell out I was a voluntary patient, helping to fill up the tables. I left my old new shoes and went home in a pair which fitted me perfectly and which I still wear, unless my husband accompanies me!

There is an art in junk buying, but even if you make mistakes, it's fun and we all learn to distinguish true values in the end – don't we?

Is there a doctor in the house?

GIRLS should think twice before marrying a doctor says a leading psychiatrist.

Marriage to doctors is a risky business, the stresses they undergo in their job often leads to marital problems. Another of my illusions severely ruptured.

I fondly believed that a doctor in the house must be the salubrious answer to every girl's dream, a chance really to let your symptoms down, a marriage glowing with efficacious prescriptions.

I imagined him sitting across the table at breakfast, his strong hand resting nonchalantly on my pulse, listening eagerly as I give him an exact account of how I slept. How often have I envied the lot of a doctor's lady?

At home my symptoms bring everyone out in newspapers, books, or some just turn up the television volume. Of course they all make suitable tutting noises from behind their national fronts, but they ignore my complaints. That is probably why one winter evening found me discussing my torturous boil with a neighbour's husband over the garden wall. After listening obediently to the riveting description of his frost-bitten gladioli I treated him to a blood-curdling episode of my festering condition. This is one area where, given the right audience, I really excel. When it comes to describing ailments I have this exceptional talent. Of course it takes a lot of practice and not a little suffering.

Once when I was speaking to our doctor over a neighbour's telephone, closely watched by her small son, I described my baby's feverish chill so vividly that both the lad and I finished up sobbing and the voice on the other end sounded a bit hoarse. My revelation on the birth of our twins would probably have a greater effect on the birth rate than the pill. But that's another story that should only be swallowed on an empty stomach.

Later that night following my neighbourly conversation, there was a knock on our door. 'It's probably the chap across the road come to poultice my boil,' I joked hoping to extract a little pity from the man behind the newspaper. When I opened the door and saw him standing on the doorstep with a tin of Kaolin in his hand I nearly fainted! And I had not even mentioned the embarrassing location of my pain.

But having a doctor husband must surely make the children's illnesses less disconcerting. No rehearsing their symptoms over and over again until he arrives. 'She awakened this morning doctor with pains in her chest er . . . no she has this violent pain in her chest doctor that kept her awake all night.' Like the game of 'whispers' the end product sounds nothing like the original. Then all the tidying up and rushing to the door every time a car stops, until even the dog looks confused. When his car does eventually arrive, the patient has disappeared! It has been said that as medical techniques improve the relationship between doctor and patient sadly deteriorate. But is this just a nasty rumour spread about by people who expect too much from their GP?

I have a deep respect for mine, in fact one day I would love to have a healthy conversation, perhaps discuss his harmful habits instead of mine. The only time he lost his bedside manner was when I invaded his surgery after hours. My son had walked into a concrete post and looked as if someone had stuck a boiled egg on his forehead. Expecting it to explode any minute, I ushered him into the doctor's privacy. He told me in clipped 'How dare you burst in here' tones, his diagnosis on uninvited gormless little boys and their neurotic mothers.

'But look at his head,' I pointed to the outsize lump where his head had just been. This unleashed some querulous sarcasm. 'How long was he unconscious? Can he speak?' But fears dissolved and humour restored I apologised for allowing this catastrophe to occur at such an inconvenient hour and left, deciding a new fire engine for egg-head was not necessary after all.

Perhaps having a correct diagnosis always to hand does not lead to content-ment. What if this ingrowing toenail is actually the first stages of the treacherous Bengal Rot? Would I feel better knowing the truth? There is no doubt about it, I definitely married the right man!
*

HAVE you noticed the radiant healthy look on most parents' faces this week? They have all been transformed by those three magic words 'Back to school!' Yes, it feels great to be alive again, if we can survive this, surely we can face any crisis winter has to offer.

As our dynamic duo don their uniforms one missing item is causing much dissension. What has happened to the school satchel? Our children are developing into a nation of shopping bag carriers. The durable leather holdall we used to wear strapped to our backs, leaving hands generously free for other schoolgirl pursuits is being replaced by ephemeral 'shoppers' - canvas and plastic hold nothings euphemistically called schoolbags. When I refuse to invest in any more, until at least the satchels have been given another airing, I receive the 'stock' answer. All sensible apparel transforms wearers into the 'laughing stock,' we are up against the pervasive 'they' again.

This dissenting group has become somewhat enlarged over the holidays and now includes 'the whole class.' They are provoked to hysterics by comfortable shoes, ordinary white blouses, medium length grey skirts, and hair which stops short at the nose- end.

'They' wear make-up, stay out indefinitely and are the ultimate envy of all children with old-fashioned mothers. On parent evenings 'they' are all mysteriously replaced by replicas of my long-faced anarchists! I still don't know whether to laugh or cry when I see my two scholars stagger down the path in their thick soles with a violin or guitar and several bulky shopping bags dangling from each arm. Surely a satchel on the back is worth two bags in the hand?

Old time, old places

A RECENT school reunion celebration set a few school pals and myself a daunting poser. Were we included in this invitation?

The day I finished my 'sentence,' there was no hint of a future reunion. Teachers seemed content enough just to tear up my books. Had we the necessary courage to face a united evening, to shake the hands that once shook us? Is it wise to revive the joys and agonies – look what happened to Liz Taylor and Richard Burton.

The subjects I loved best were the boy who sat behind me and my art master. But a lot of water has passed under the bridge since then, perhaps it would be kinder to keep our illusions intact.

On the other hand, it might have been pleasant to meet up with one or two of the teachers once more. Our history mistress for instance, the one who used to stand in front of the class and gaze into my eyes with a look that could freeze chewing gum, and proclaim 'I don't like you people.'

She used to entertain everyone with rhetorical stories concerning Henry VIII's colourful past and my colourless future. I feel sure she would be relieved to know that although I never remembered Elizabeth I's birthday, I did manage to survive.

I often wish it were possible to meet up with some acquaintances again. The lorry driver who asked me the way to Meltham last week - did he ever arrive? Does anyone unfortunate enough to pick on me as a guide ever reach their destination? The evacuees I played with during the war, especially the adventurous one who promised marriage. Our old art master who decreed that all artists go mad in the end – is he still with us I wonder?

The biology teacher who confiscated a book 'Impassionate Youth' just when it was my turn to read it. If she has finished with it I'd like it back please, the unselfish biology student who cut her earth worm in three pieces when my friend and I forgot ours. Well Eamonn that should keep you busy for a while.

Years ago when we were fortunate to own a small part of history in Huddersfield, a few Christmas fairies and myself were discussing our future in an old dressing room at the Theatre Royal. We optimistically planned a meeting to take place ten years hence. With uncomfortable flying ballet harness protruding through the sequins and a mutual 'cork tip' wending its soggy way round the fairy ring, we cast our predictions for the future.

'I can see myself in ten years' time with a hungry tribe of toddlers clutching at my skirt' I said, causing a great deal of laughter among the tinsel at this prophesy. Most of our predictions concerned the opposite sex – we were going through a lean time. Boyfriends had been banned and because one naughty fairy, who shall be nameless, had been seen receiving a playful slap from a stagehand, any conversing in this direction was considered a breach of contract.

Time disintegrated our fairy band and I wonder if anyone did remember our pact? One threw away her tutu shortly after and joined a nude review, another kept in touch for a while until her family grew up and she ran off with a Greek.

I did see one of the Theatre Royal stagehands the other day though. We were both 'strap-hanging' – well I was hanging, he was leaning.

'Remember me?' I asked, wiping away the tears as a waft of 90 per cent proof hit my nostrils. He became very excited when I mentioned the old theatre. Resting an elbow on a nearby straw hat he gave us all a hair-raising description of something nasty he had just had removed there. When he started undoing his buttons I realised he was confusing his theatres! He pretended to remember me, but age and high spirits kept getting in the way.

As I left the bus he was having difficulty in distinguishing a hat from his elbow. But nobody knows a fairy when she's forty.

At least my prediction came true, although my hungry tribe are rapidly becoming hungry adults, they still clutch at my skirts occasionally. Well now I can look forward to the next decade, perhaps I shall enter into the realms of 'Grannyhood' with another hungry tribe of toddlers clutching at my skirts.

I AM surprised to read that estate agents have only just discovered that half their clients just like to see the inside of other people's homes. Have they ever tried to get a window seat on a bus at dusk, that revealing moment just before the curtains are drawn? One agent complains that some offenders live in the same terrace as a house offered for sale and only go round to see what the owners have done to improve it.

What a good idea! Let's face it we all have a curious nosey parker streak. I find it great fun living near a bus stop, from my front window I view all sorts of comings and goings. On the other hand, our illuminated address must be entertaining for the bus queue on certain occasions, especially when a middle-aged sugar plum fairy takes the floor.

On taking a cut

AS a deluge of rain from the porch roof threatened the solitary life of my husband's coveted and evergreen tomato, I sighed contentedly from the kitchen window, what a beautiful day!

The children had stopped being sick, no one with the exception of a one-eyed doll needed new shoes, the dog was not in love and I would shortly be the owner of a new hairstyle. What more could anyone wish for?

There were a few minor problems, of course, although our college student has had various offers of 'settees' and 'floors' she is still virtually homeless – but nothing that could not be swept under the table with the rest of our 'undesirables.'

Dripping with tranquillity I felt almost happy enough to start darning socks again. With a few motherly instructions to daughter on how to throw jeans in the washer, I whistled off to a new hairstyle. Yes, this is the way to bring up children – give them independence.

I could imagine the hairdresser's waiting scissors drawn, fighting for the right to stunt my growth. A friend once said a hairdresser was wildly excited when she went for a trim. 'I love to get a really bad head of hair,' she confided – mine would obviously be greeted with rapture.

My first feeling of disquiet arose when the receptionist inquired without looking up from her cuticles 'Trim?' Professionals can cut conversations down to the rude essentials. When I mentioned the complete overhaul ordered by phone she looked at my hair and quickly understood. Everyone watched through the mirror while I played 'find the coat-peg' and eventually found it concealed in a corner.

After struggling three times to hang my coat on the collapsible hook, I picked it up off the floor and nonchalantly placed it on the back of the chair I was offered.

The girl in dark glasses nodded sympathetically when I described the way I wanted to look. 'I know my hair would never look like that,' I lied. The smile left my face when she agreed. With my old hairstyle lying in a circle around my chair I felt like a rabbit we used to have. She used to pull her fur off and sit in the middle of it, because she wanted a family.

My family had driven me to it. An hour later shivering at the bus stop with white face, blue nose and naked scarlet ears glowing patriotically, I wondered if this transformation would leave the rest of the family as cold as me.

Opening the kitchen door I entered the next disquieting phase. Instead of swooning at the devastating change, my daughter never even looked up from the kitchen table. What could possibly be more interesting than my new hairstyle? On closer observation I could see she was carefully laying out the sacred remains of the weekly wash. Immaculately clean, soggy and tatty pieces of fivers and one pound notes were spread out on the table.

'They were floating on top of the water when I took Howard's jeans out,' she explained, ignoring my hairstyle.

With nervous fingers we created two mosaic fivers and one mosaic pound note, and still had enough bits left over to make half of something else.

'Take them to the bank,' our neighbour suggested, wiping the laughter from her eye corner. Usually jobs like this are reserved for the boss, but cowardice has to be swallowed in emergency.

We decided to make a clean sweep and face the bank clerk together. If we could persuade him to 'give us the money' I may yet live to see my hairdo admired.

Post Offices and Banks always make me feel deaf. The bank clerk and I find it easier to communicate by sign language. It cuts out all the 'Ehs,' and 'Pardons,' which used to accompany the cashing of my weekly cheque. He usually stamps it, raises a hand and in his Indian chief voice says 'How,' then I point to the fivers.

When I presented him with the assortment of wet paper his responding 'How?' sounded strangely emotional. Watched closely by a small queue I gave him instructions on how to devalue the pound. He wrote it all down, then came the difficult part – could anyone vouch for me? I looked down the queue, a cigar-smoking refuse collector winked at me. I decided my neighbour's name would suffice. Trying desperately not to smile we watched him transfer the stubbornly adhesive pieces from his finger ends into the three plastic bags. Then we tried not to cry when he informed us these would now be sent to the Bank of England and they would decide what to make of them.

But this day was not over yet; how to tell number one son? I was still smarting from his unsympathetic outburst the time I washed and ironed his jeans without noticing the bulging wallet in his back pocket. Perhaps now would be a suitable time to visit my sister in Australia.

Could we make a joke of it? 'Ha, ha,' you'll never guess what we've found floating on top of the washer today?' Or would a philosophical approach be more agreeable. 'Well lad, money in the bank at last (I hope). One day you will thank me for this.'

He ate his special banquet tea without comment then sank into his favourite position on the hearth rug, blissfully unaware that his future happiness was in a hundred pieces inside a polythene bag on its way to the Bank of England. When I threw him what I hoped was a motherly smile, he scornfully poked his big toe through the hole in his sock.

When would be the best time to tell him I pondered as I plucked a piece of pound note from the vest I was ironing. 'Did you pay that £16 in?' Father inquires. £16? Did he say £16?

'Where's the dog?' 'Mum my shoe sole is hanging off.' Son suddenly looks at my hair. 'What have you been doing – you look different?'

The end of a beautiful day. So what if I am not God's gift to children. The dog loves me, doesn't he? And what about my new hairstyle?

Making (d-i-y) music

ONCE the harvest has been dispersed, autumn loses its charm for me. Those autumn leaves which pass by my window may be beloved by lyricists – but have they ever tried to sweep them up? Now the family are all back at their desks, I feel as divested as the leafless trees.

Although most evenings find us draped around the fireplace in various states of idleness, there is a seasonal 'Do it yourself' spirit stirring within us. I fondly communicated this to my son the other evening when, unable to reach his coffee without moving his eyeballs, he asked me to pass it. He was almost annoyed into blinking his eyelids, 'Are you too lazy to hand me my coffee,' he demanded. But I firmly believe in a 'do it yourself' attitude.

When I was first married I could not even change a plug, but long nights sitting with a baby in one hand and a plug in the other waiting my overworked husbands' return soon had me extending my electrical education. My penknife and I became inseparable, except on washday when a sharp wallop with a rolling pin seemed more effective, until one morning found me embarrassingly hysterical on my neighbour's doorstep. The wringers on the washer had snapped menacingly back at me and had fallen to pieces.

People used to think my kitchen was an extension of the printing works next door, on wash days it sounded just like their machine room!

But it is never too late to join the independent enthusiasts. Libraries are lined with helpful books on most subjects. Rowland Parker became interested in his Tudor cottage's history; it became so fascinating he turned his discoveries into a best seller, 'The Commonstream.'

A friend of ours built his own house; another is tackling his drive and garage, all in their 'spare time.'

Television showed us a glimpse into the Royal Academy of Arts' annual exhibition of paintings. One widow whose paintings were rejected looked philosophically towards next year when she hoped to try again. All hopefully building their own dreams.

My father has always been an optimistic 'do-it-yourself' addict. No job is considered too difficult. He once tackled the marathon task of dividing a bedroom. This did not please my mother much, as he made this decision at 6.30am one Sunday morning while she was still asleep. By 7.30am she was encased in plaster and fully awake, looking more like Tutankhamun's 'mummy' than mine.

But often amateur designs have a strength their appearance denies. Last year an expertly designed greenhouse sprang up on the land behind my father's, making his home-made effort look like a patchwork aquarium. A violent storm ignored my father's and blew all the glass out of his rivals!

During the war 'do-it-yourself' was disguised as 'make do and mend.' Before my father was shunted off to Africa he was kept busy decorating rooms with a can of distemper and a rolled rag, my mother was decorating my sister and I with knitting. We were smothered in knit and purl ones, vests, socks, jumpers, skirts; we even had 4-ply slippers. One advantage of the paper shortage, knicker patterns must have been unavailable.

My friend's mother could not knit so she made do with trimming everything with fur. We must have looked a cosy couple as we trudged up the hill to school.

We spent autumn afternoons making dolls' clothes, with the aid of a 'rag bag.' I cut them out while my sister sewed them. A friend of mums called one afternoon and unfortunately placed her hat on the table. While they chatted I snipped.

By the time she was ready to collect her hat, our dolls were sporting grey felt skirts and silk lining blouses. We all searched diligently for the hat, unaware of the 'mistake.' When the crowns rim was eventually discovered she fortunately saw the funny side of the situation, but I do not remember her calling again.

I have been struggling for a while with DIY piano lessons. I started on the guitar, but someone keeps hiding it. The piano is immovable. Unable to find any music to match my unique style – there seems to be something wrong with my left hand, it only plays waltztime – I compose my own. It's easy really, I just make it up as I pom along, quickening the walztime accordingly. In fact sometimes my left hand does not know what my right hand is playing, but why should it I ask myself? At times my compositions evoke a familiar 'horror film' atmosphere, a sort of chilled expectancy, as if any minute I may break into a melody. This may sound immodest, but when our Sunday school pianist was on holiday, my rousing piano recital of 'When Mary Had a Baby' shortened the collection march succinctly.

There was none of the usual football behaviour among our primary donators. The pennies were in the box and they were back in their places almost before I had finished the introduction. Their silent obedience was a joy to behold. I feel tempted to learn the chorus. The family regard my piano playing as a mixed blessing, at least I cannot sing while I am playing . . . yet

*

HOW refreshing to hear the American Democratic candidate Jimmy Carter describe his wife as 'trusted adviser.' This is a position I have long wanted to attain. Over the years I have collected enough advise to keep my husband housebound for a week. But this surfeit of wifely wisdom remains disappointingly untapped. I naively imagined that one day my family would be clamouring for this excellent service, but all I am asked is 'What can I wear?' or 'Who asked you?'

Having suffered painful attacks of unasked for advice, especially after the birth of our first child, I decided to suppress my own advising instinct until it was called for. But I did not dream I would never be asked. After my fifth child I look forward to the crowd of eager young mums fluttering around my pram pleading for my secrets.

Our youngest is nearly seven, if someone doesn't ask soon, it will all be out of date!

On the other hand I admit our neighbour seems to be under the impression that I am my husband's 'trusted adviser.' 'Can he come?' he always asks me, when a night out is imminent. But before I have a chance to reply, their car is speeding eastwards to their oasis.

Yes, here I am, swollen to bursting point with benevolent information and no-one willing to take advantage.

Tell-tale morning egg

HOW much do you really know about the chap who cringes behind the cornflakes every morning?

For instance when he eats his boiled egg does he (a) sever it gently with little taps.... (b) remove the top with his spoon ... (c) does he give it one sharp slice with his knife? Or perhaps (d) he hasn't the strength to do either and usually asks you?

Well, sometimes it pays to notice these small foibles, especially if you want to enter the Mr and Mrs Contest shown on ITV every Wednesday lunchtime.

Perplexed contestants are regularly finding out how little they know about their mates. When one Mrs was asked this question last week she confidently informed everyone that her Mr always cuts the top of his egg straight off.

She giggled a little with embarrassment at this secret revelation concerning his breakfast habits. Her mirth was cut short when he emerged from the soundproof box and confessed, with a shy glance at his glowing egg-timer, that he always severed it gently with a few sharp taps. When he heard his wife's differing answer he looked as if he would like to perform the same service on her top. As they departed one could sense that their future happiness will definitely not be egg-shaped!

But to win the prize their answers must concur. One husband who admitted he spent a lot of time collecting vintage cars stated emphatically that his wife never wore face cream in bed, he looked shocked when she blatantly confessed she wore a 'little.' But how many of us take the trouble to notice our partner's idiosyncrasies?

Do people who take part in these televised marriage games have to rehearse rigorously beforehand? One can imagine their excitement the previous week with all the tenacious snooping into each other's privacy,

71

all that silent surveillance at meal times. Or perhaps a sneaky key-hole preview at his bathroom rituals. All's fair in love and jackpot hunting.

Does he begin his shaving at the right or left side of his five o'clock shadow? Do you know? Let's face it at that hour does he? This may sound trivial, you are sure you know all your adorable's tendencies, but he may have developed a few new tricks without consulting you. If he shaves the left cheek first, without you realising it, what else has he been up to during the last decade without your knowledge?

But after the easy week of intimate confessions the big day arrives. There stand the happy couples, hands entwined, peeping coyly at each other with that 'I know all about you mate' expression in their eyes.

Then comes the shock, he is convinced his arm goes further around her waist than it used to, when actually she knows her measurements are exactly the same as the day he married her. Oh – the shame of it! What can he be thinking of – or even worse – who can he be thinking of!

You can see by the look on her face that future embracing is cancelled. The monocled compere, a bundle of joviality, asks who would like to hold the candelabra. Four arms stretch forward eagerly and usually the wife takes this consolation, probably husband gets his share later!

Then confidence in shreds the unhappy couple sit and watch the next two reveal how much they don't know about each other. Surely we are discovering new traits to our characters all the time, is it not this which makes marriage so . . .er . . .interesting?

We had been married for five years before I discovered that apple crumble was not my husband's favourite dessert. 'Why do we have apple crumble every Thursday?' grumbled one bored young gourmet. 'Because it is daddy's favourite.' 'Who says?' inquires daddy. 'But you have always liked it, that's why I make it.'

'I eat it because you make it.' 'But it is your favourite' my voice is rising dangerously. 'No it isn't, I like jam roly-poly.' 'But I never make jam roly-poly!' 'That's why I eat apple crumble.'

End of conversation and the Thursday ritual of apple crumble which we had all been sick of for years!

I wonder what effect the Mr and Mrs programme has on the relationship of those who take part. Not long ago we had to suffer the other extreme, glowing examples of the 'Husband of the Year' with gushing heroes pouring their virtues all over Marj Proops and company. I actually felt really grateful to this programme for showing me what life could be like with a paragon husband.

If mine said he never lost his temper, I should feel tempted to spend the rest of my life provoking him. But then I never did want a perfect husband and can only hope he never wanted a perfect wife.

Dr John Hack, an American psychologist, is currently investigating the state of marriage. According to him 'The time it takes to boil a couple of eggs is all it needs to jeopardise a marriage.' Then he frightens us all into mental wrecks by pointing out the danger times. He believes that evenings and mornings should start with warnings. Breakfast and when husband returns from work are periods when your marriage is in the most danger. Monday mornings and Friday nights are also considered to be hazardous times, and Sunday evenings need watching too.

According to these calculations, Dr Hack, it seems the only times our marriage is not in jeopardy is when we are all asleep?

It doesn't seem so long since that another distinguished professor informed us not to bottle up our emotions, as this could have a damaging effect on our relationships. He advised couples to shout and bawl at each other – a great relief for pent-up tensions.

So what do we do? Start throwing ornaments or silently sit avoiding each other. I think the most dangerous threats to marriage are eminent psychologists and their interfering, useless surveys, and I for one intend to go straight out and buy some more ornaments.

Standing room only

APART from the fact that one of our children was almost locked in the Tower for the night, a packet of tablets cost me my purse and its precious contents, considering we never saw a tram stop once, and most of the hotels and guest houses were displaying 'House Full' signs by 7.30pm – yes thank you, we spent a lovely weekend at Blackpool!

As most of our children had already donated their weekend's allowance to the nearest slot machines, we merry band of parents decided to spend the first evening rediscovering the internal delights of the Tower.

With a gentle drizzle playfully destroying mums' 'shampoos and sets,' dads pointing excitedly at the fluorescent puffins and the children nagging eagerly for toffee apples, we naively joined the nearest queue.

After what seemed like an hour contemplating the empty tramlines, our deteriorating hairstyles and the children's unalluring social habits, the carnival atmosphere began to decline. Depressing rumours concerning an accident further up the line began to circulate the dripping queue. A tram had stopped and almost let a passenger on - we tried to joke ruefully.

73

Anyway as the rest of England seemed to be walking, why shouldn't we?

'Have the trams stopped running' one intrepid member of our party asked an inspector who appeared reluctant to leave his little wooden hut. Whether the question upset him or it was just the reflection of the pale green lights, his face took on an unhealthy glow. Poor man, we sympathised, life must be frustrating for a tram inspector without trams.

After an interminable walk during which we seriously wondered if the recent drought had affected the toffee apple season and doubled the distance between the South Pier and the Tower we eventually arrived.

The admission price, which put years on us, had a miraculous rejuvenating effect on the children. But the cashier had already done her own survey, she looked remarkably like the 'Guess Your Age' celebrity on the pier. Was she a relative we longed to enquire?

It sounds incredible but the Tower was populated with the largest bodies I have ever seen. One friend wondered if there was some sort of 'outsize convention.' Wherever we went these jolly-faced bouncers were everywhere - all looking as if they had just stepped out of the jolly postcards on the Promenade. It certainly modified my weight problem and made us all feel a stone lighter! While the children escaped to the universal slot machines, we watched a man struggle to play a trumpet as he pedalled a bicycle wheel in ever decreasing circles around a tiny stage. All his talent was in his feet, we applauded thankfully when he stopped.

But a more entertaining drama was taking place in the ladies' powder room. As I entered a beautiful West Indian girl supported by one of the ubiquitous corpulants was giving a realistic impression of Shirley Bassey. Tears of woe flooded her ear-rings as she unleashed her emotions to the row of 'engaged' signs. Too embarrassed to intrude, her hysterical outburst had us all glued to our seats in silent trepidation. If this continued much longer, some of us could carry its 'imprint' permanently, but after a suitable interval doors started to open and one or two of us crept out.

'She is always like this when she's had a drink,' her plump friend was proudly confiding. 'It's since she lost her baby.' My friend and I turned the corners of our mouths down and made a few remarks on 'silly exhibitionists' as we returned to our table.

One hour later I was running wildly in all directions searching for one lost daughter. With lights being switched off and doors being bolted, I sank to my knees in front of a laughing attendant, trying desperately to persuade him he had just locked our daughter in the deserted ballroom. I had almost convinced him that truth is stranger than fiction when our tearful prodigal returned on the arm of her relieved father,

74

She had gone back to the ballroom for her belt. Restraining my desire to give her another, I waited at the entrance. Unfortunately at midnight the attendants come to life and they can clear the Tower almost as fast as Joe Bugner wins fights. She was forced to leave at another exit.

The following morning had us all rushing for headache pills. The ones I bought certainly gave me one. We were idly watching a demonstrator shoot holes through her victim's ear lobes giving her 'press stud' ears, as our seven-year-old described them, when I felt as if I had been shot myself – my purse had gone!

For someone who has preached regular Friday tea-time sermons to out-stretched hands on the unimportance of spending money – my resulting performance was a big let down. We raced from counter to counter without success and finally went to lunch with the result of a morning's shopping – one small packet of tablets in my bag. The truth is spending-money takes on a greater significance when you have earned it and saved it yourself. It seems that if I am not wasting money I am losing it, when all I want to do is spend it!

But Blackpool is no place for regrets. A liberal helping of good company, good food, another hand-out from my long-suffering supporter and some liquid sustenance eventually diluted the bitterness. Selfishness came to the rescue after all, the West Indian girl had lost her baby!

The wet weather had quite an influence on the 'funny hat' trade. A group at a nearby table all had sinister, wide-brimmed black felt hats resting on their eyelids. We nervously wondered if they were Mafia members. But nothing could disguise their Barnsley giggles and we soon realised they were just protective gear.

Considering its devastating effect on transport, the 'standing room only' entertainment and general overcrowding, are illuminated weekends proving too much for Blackpool? Is she coping satisfactorily with this weekend boom?

I know one group whose future visits will be Monday to Friday and next time we plan a bowling trip to support our 'champion' I intend to spend at least some time doing just that!

A gourmet's delight

DO I live to eat or eat to live? This question is particularly haunting at this time of the year.

I find myself returning all holiday brochures to the library and eagerly searching out all the French cookery books.

75

Browsing through one of these is almost as exciting as reading a novel. Trying out new dishes is as exhilarating to me as trying on a new outfit. I wish it had the same effect on my tea-time crowd. But George Bernard Shaw was right, 'there is no love sincerer than the love of food.'

I managed to curb my indulgences during the drought, but all this surplus rain is driving me to the gas oven. Once again I have the seasonal and uncontrollable urge either to smother everything in an exotic sauce or garnish it with parsley. Food is the eighth wonder of my world.

Unfortunately a lifetime of being experimented on has made my other seven less enthusiastic. An air of lingering mistrust hangs over my smouldering concoctions. Even the dog lowers his ears and creeps under the table when I light the oven.

At the moment my fancy is lightly turning to thoughts of cabbage. Although some of my best friends are generous cabbage growers, my family is divided on its merits. Half of them refuse to darken their plates with this nutritious gift. My latest attempt at disguise, cabbage au gratin, directed a la French cookery book, evoked some interesting comments ranging from 'Don't give me any,' 'Ugh it's cabbage,' to the spectacular 'I could eat this as a main course – delicious!'

They are the sort of gourmets who will eat curry, if I omit the pepper and oriental spices and could exist permanently on roast beef and Yorkshire pudding followed by apple tart and cream. Then to accompany his coffee, our son's macabre appetite demands a banana teacake.

Fortunately, our eldest daughter shares my adventurous culinary spirit. When she is home from college we are like a couple of 'Macbeth' witches cackling over our mysterious brews.

When she goes back it's curry for two again, me and the dog, when I find him.

Our letters are full of gastronomic inquiries. 'My liver was all dry and curly last week,' 'Did anyone like your kidneys?' which often confuse the rest of the family.

During last summer we gave a small celebration dinner party. Once the serving difficulties are under control, dinners seem easier to cope with than buffets. It's just a case of keeping the guests awake between the mad dashes to the kitchen for the next course. Then stifling the indigestion this creates, as you continue your scintillating conversation.

The egg mayonnaise starter and main course chicken with almonds were easily prepared beforehand. The hardest part was buying the garlic. How does one ask for garlic? 'Can I have a garlic?' sounds incongruous as 'Can I have a lettuce?' I hung about for ages hoping someone else would purchase some. Perhaps it would be easier to ask for a pound. Eventually I solved the problem by picking one up and asking 'How much?'

The instructions were to crush one clove. I spent a long time crushing the lot piece by piece. After adding half, I tasted. When the blood came back to my lips and the fever had subsided a little, I removed as much as I could, thanking the Lord I had tasted first. A hint of garlic might so easily have become a torrid condemnation!

Boiling the rice proved expensive. The finished product looked like thick porridge. Never mind the children would eat it as a pudding after tea. The second attempt became a rice pudding for supper. It took a course at the Polytechnic to teach me that I was simply overcooking it.

We decided on a lemon syllabub for desert. This sounded easy. Just a simple marination of wine and lemon whipped lightly with fresh cream. Our connoisseur son was invited to taste the result. After a small sip his face shrank like a walnut and his eyes almost disappeared. 'A bit tangy' was his verdict. But after all he is a banana teacake man.

All the best cooks learn by trial and error. However many years' experience you have, there are still new dishes waiting to be tried and several ways of improving the old ones. After countless years of hacking like an impoverished sculpture at the stalagmite remains following a ham and peas session, I have recently discovered that cooking it in a casserole in the oven solves this sticky problem.

Oxfam is not the only waste re-cycling centre. Once when I was in the last stages of a particularly chunky pregnancy, my smock pocket upturned a grill pan of lamb chops and gravy all over the floor.

I quickly returned the miss-shapes, scooped up the gravy, added a pinch of this and a touch of that and watched my husband and son scoff the lot. They naturally put my loss of appetite down to my condition!

One of the most heart and kitchen-warming pleasures of winter is bread baking. The satisfaction gained from three pounds of dough is immeasurable. This is one lump that really improves with bashing. You can punch your way to perfection. Nothing can compare with the simple goodness of old fashioned home baked bread spread liberally with butter, and if you still have a pot of your own blackberry jam – delicious!

From three pounds of flour I make two twists, one dozen small rolls and after kneading a few currants, spice and sugar into the rest of the dough, we have some hot-cross buns to finish off with. Naturally it makes you fat! Too much of anything is bad for the figure. I try to fast a little when I am busy during the week then go mad at weekend. That is why Fridays are so exciting.

People often tell me they cannot bake bread. This is just not true. Anyone can succeed. It took me loads of heavy dustbins to prove it. During my failures even the birds stopped visiting, and I admit there seemed to be no way of using up the cement-like constructions which threatened the kitchen table (this was before modern art).

But the satisfaction achieved from your first golden crusty batch is well worth the effort. When you have mastered the muffins you can graduate to the delectable world of stolen and other yeasty delights.

Let the children dip in with you, they will play for hours with a piece of dough, before they surrender it to the oven. Then you have the extra pleasure of watching Daddy eat it for tea!

Old grey bristle test

SO PARIS hemlines have gone to our fashion writer's heads, or perhaps thighs would be a better description, once again.

We are supposed to greet this mini-skirt forecast for next spring with blessed relief.

'A long and overdue change from the wrapped up, baggy, shapeless peasant gear we have lived in for seasons,' as one columnist puts it. But what about baggy, shapeless peasants like me who have just discovered the delights of this ethnic mid-calf fashion?

Of course if we do not fancy these brief-revealing skirts, there is an alternative in cheeky little rompers. These did nothing for my figure when I was a baby. Naturally these scant miniatures will cost more! Fortunately by the time middle-age arrives most women have adopted their own uniform.

Fanny Craddock would look as naked as an undressed chicken without her velvet bow and sparkling fingers. Barbara Goalen, ex-fashion model now retired, confesses she always sticks to the same sort of clothes and caftans are her favourite for evenings. She said in one interview that she still wears clothes she bought fifteen years ago. That makes two of us.

I have just given my winter uniform its annual wash and brush up. Ignoring the usual comments, 'It's time that thing was destroyed.' 'Have it put down, it makes your head look little,' and all that scratching every time I wear it. I fully intend to sink into my old grey simulated fur once again. I can vaguely recall when it was young and fluffy looking, when people used to smile enviously and tell me how fat I looked. Certainly it moults a little each season, but who doesn't? It takes some of the discontent out of my winter anyway.

The pockets lost their bottoms during the severe frost we suffered one year. The following year dry rot got at the lining. I gave the matter of renovation a lot of serious thought, as I do all jobs I loathe and detest. Chores of this nature require more logic than the likeable jobs. But after all, I concluded, do mere hand warmers need pocket bottoms? Since the lining deserted, the hands can hang quite cosily on to my jumper welt, or trouser tops.

This arrangement worked quite satisfactorily until the day I was talking to a stranger at the bus-stop. We were just discussing the disgrace of the falling pound and rising prices, when my only button dropped off, thus allowing a sneaky blast to expose my two naked hands tucked neatly into my trouser tops. I don't know which one of us looked more surprised. Ah yes, shame is the spur, these pockets will certainly get the needle – tomorrow.

Actually given the time and the word I love dressing up. Only the other day I gave my best suit an outing. With hair parted, immaculate shoes, even a handbag on my arm, I walked into the local breadshop and out again, without being recognised. But the winter epidemic of school functions always seem to coincide with my 'Spring Cleaning' phase, which can hit me anytime between now and Christmas.

Other mothers turn up on these occasions looking as though they have just left Christian Dior, while I arrive looking as if I have just finished washing.

Last year I went to a party with my 'Old Grey Bristle' slung around my neck. During the evening I was introduced to another guest who seemed to think I was the waitress. When it was time to leave and I fetched my coat, she suddenly came to life 'I know that coat, you live in Slaithwaite!'

Yes, it's an old friend, and since I overcame the 'dry clean only' label and threw it in the washer it gives me no trouble at all.

Trying on new outfits in communal changing rooms is matey but at times embarrassingly disappointing. A tall, robust lady and I tried similar mid-calf evening skirts on recently, side by side. She looked so stunning with the gathered flounce swirling around her knees that I looked and felt ridiculous with my resting awkwardly on my shoe tops. We looked like the Two Ronnies in drag.

Then follows the fascinating contortion of dressing without revealing your ungainly assets, I suppose it cuts trying on time in half. There is none of the postulating one can enjoy secretly behind the curtain. You know, the hand on hip swagger, accompanied by the face pulling. No leaning against the wall in your favourite party pose, an inviting wet-lipped half smile resting seductively on the smeared lipstick. When everyone's looking it's just a quick apologetic nod at the mirror and off.

This is definitely our main party season, with four birthdays and one anniversary to cope with between now and January. Our children are generous present buyers. From now on it's 'Mum, can you give us some more money, please?' Thank goodness our cards are home-made. Our seven-year-old spent all her money on two choc-bars for her sister's birthday last week. Then after she had reclaimed the wrapping paper for the 'next birthday' she admitted she had bought two bars so they could share, and promptly took one back!

There have been surreptitious whisperings concerning a double party this year from our young teenagers. They have nearly convinced me of the wisdom of this, but I get the feeling that once the food leaves the oven, the party is over for dad and me. We then become a couple of redundants.
*

IN my opinion tomorrow is the worst day of the year. All that money going up in smoke makes me fume. I hate bonfires, fireworks and all the half-baked burned potatoes and gunpowder-flavoured parkin that accompanies them. Yes, you are right, I ought to be locked up with my dog.

The other night I saw a lad with jingling pockets, wheeling a Guy Fawkes away from a house. When he reached the steps the guy jumped out and they carried the cart down together!

My firework code is 'Don't buy any,' and if you do keep away from me!

But I'll give you the recipe for a tin of my chewy, teeth-gripping toffee.
TREACLE TOFFEE

1lb brown sugar, 8oz butter, 1lb treacle, small tin condensed milk. Boil together for 25 – 30 minutes. Pour mixture into a shallow tin and leave to set.

Job on the shelf

'ARE the plans complete then?' I asked eagerly when our recalcitrant handyman walked in with a piece of teak tucked under his arm.

Ignoring this sarcasm (the plans have been at the drawing-board stage for two years now) he proceeded to measure up the hall radiator.

'When you get back your new shelf will be in position' he said proudly. This proved to be a profoundly modest understatement. When I returned two hours later, our new shelf, complete with brackets, was resting on the hall carpet and a hole as big as a golf ball was gaping above the radiator. Inside the cavity was a lead pipe decorated with an outsize lump of chewing gum.

A familiar wave of uneasiness washed over me. I had the same feeling years earlier, when our neighbour decided to fix a new tap. One minute I was vibrantly entreating the washing up to 'Take a pair of sparkling eyes,' next minute the kitchen wall had crumbled and I was staring at my neighbour's Black and Decker.

'Daddy's hit a gas pipe' the children were wildly excited. 'You can't use the cooker' they said as I reached for the kettle. The next day the pipe was sealed and I was left trying to decipher some mysterious maintenance double-talk concerning 'something unhealthy' in the cellar.

Two days later the invasion began. We awakened to what sounded like a rampant army of machine guns. Our first clutter of gas men made a head-scratching survey of our cellar, and the search began.

'Will you be long?' I asked, thinking of my important spending spree which could not be cancelled. This made them laugh so much, I felt bound to join in, wishing I knew what the joke was. Brushing away his tears with his hairy hand, a man with a Rudolph Valentino haircut and a Mexican moustache said 'Go to town luv, we shall be working in the garden this afternoon.'

When I returned our house had acquired a set of flashing yellow lights and a diversion sign. A pile of homeless rose trees were lying in mourning on the mud encrusted path. All that remained of my husband's velvety front lawn was an open grave deep enough to bury three gas men.

Rudolph Valentino came to the kitchen door. I watched him grow three inches smaller as he meticulously wiped most of the front garden on the door mat. 'We can't find it' he explained. From my hiding-place behind the curtains I watched them threaten a beautiful relationship as they gave our neighbour's garden the same treatment. The following day my neighbour and I watched nervously as they stalked the path of the house on the other side.

We were highly relieved when they started filling up the gaps, until a man said comfortingly, 'Don't worry luv, sometimes it takes a fortnight, but we nearly always find it in the end.'

This 'Fabian of the Yard' spent the rest of the day happily ploughing up the main road. With their permanent 'lost a pipe and found a hole' expression we had learned to dread, three men and half the garden marched into the hall. I had a melancholy vision of myself phoning the latest developments to my anxious spouse from a deep trench. Fighting a

81

compulsive urge to throw stones at the new shelf, I suggested they call off the search, we would go electric. It would certainly be cleaner, we had accumulated enough sludge to keep a hippo happy for a month.

Grinning nervously and feeling like an Al Read character, 'Er . . have you found it?' I asked a man who was busily knocking down the cellar wall. 'Oh aye, we've found it,' my hair went straight with joy. 'But its dead,' he added. What a morbid occupation. Malignant cavities full of dead pipes!

Just as I switched on the vacuum cleaner the man who was perforating the path turned on his drill. My neurotic scream was bigger than both of us. When another tribe of boots made for the cellar, I escaped next door. We were discussing the disadvantages of radiator shelves when three men walked out of her cellar. With triumphant smiles they held up a chisel. 'We managed to pull it out,' cried one with Arthur and Excalibur pride.

I resisted the desire to repeat 'Big Socks,' our twelve-year-olds stock reply to all victories. After all, any success must be overwhelming in this unrewarding job. 'This corroded pipe would never have been discovered if you hadn't opened your wall,' said our neighbour. I couldn't decide whether this was a threat or a consolation. And still the excavating continues.

At the end of each day as our garden grows longer and the main road narrower – we look back on the happy memories of days gone by when all we had to complain about was a dark patch over the radiator. Who would have thought that a piece of teak 2ft x 6in designed to cut wall cleaning down to the minimum could transform our outlook so disastrously?

Who would have guessed that not only were we gaining a shelf – but also dedicated, drill-happy gas men in triplicate, complete with diversion signs and traffic lights – plus a new landscape which looks as if a giant mole has hiccuped all over it?

But we do have one contented dog. Although he barks incessantly if the cat next door dares to so much as peep over the garden wall, he adores strange men. I think I can truthfully forecast without exaggeration, that future outlook for our household will be decidedly frosty – and not just because we have a draughty gap in our cellar wall.

Our youngest daughter has turned her thoughts to higher planes. The other day a friend said she had just seen our travelling player on her way to school. While her small escort held the music at eye level our perpetual recorder blower was stoically playing 'God Save Our Gracious Queen' all the way to school. We ought to be thankful for small mercies, I suppose. At least the pneumatic drills are louder than her playing.

Lament on the gas pipes

ALTHOUGH the gas maintenance men are still encamped in our front garden, the first part of the week was strangely silent. The holes were still there, but where were the gas men? Had they taken their drilling too far? Perhaps they had joined all the gaps and were already tunnelling a short cut to the cellar?

On the other hand, were they like us, in the fearful grip of the 'Health Maintenance' series currently featured by one of the Sunday newspapers?

Every Monday morning since the features started, our readers have been nervously fighting cancer and heart disease symptoms. In fact we haven't felt well since. Thank goodness we have come to the final episode 'Old Age' – we feel just about eligible.

But two days later our happy band returned, having temporarily deserted their drills for a gas leak in the village, which according to one was ideally situated between two friendly housewives who continually supplied them with their national drink, strong, hot tea.

I was just pulling faces at the dog while I waited for the sausage to brown, when the most painful sentence to date was passed upon me. 'We are turning you off, love' My blood ran cold and so did the sausage.

'Will it be on for tea?' asked my neighbour, who, miraculously still visits us. 'Sure,' he said. Twenty-four hours later I was still divorced from the gas supply but madly attached to my old-fashioned kitchen range. Unfortunately my long-suffering neighbour, who had nothing to do whatsoever with the cause of the trouble – our new shelf – was the worst hit. They depend on the Gas Board for heat and cooking.

Thank goodness I did not succumb to a half-hearted lust for gas fires. Earlier in the year I was considering having my Yorkist range with the gargantuan side oven and triple hobs 'done in.' Since we were struck 'gasless' it has kept us warm and cooked our meals. What more could two neighbours wish for? But the magic words came at last. 'All done, love,' plus a salutary caution from the fitter.

'This is your new meter, and just in case your husband decides to put up another shelf – this handle turns of the gas!'

My husband rang at lunch-time to inform me we have two slates missing. Now although he can move a bus stop, divert the traffic, cut off his innocent neighbour's life supply with one single wave of his hammer, we both agreed we would call a qualified roofer.

WELL, it's 'all I want for Christmas' time at our house. Mouth-drying lists are springing up everywhere. Just in case I miss any of the downstairs display, there are several duplicates decorating the bedrooms. 'Is there anything we could sell?' I ask myself, trying not to dwell too long on my husband's tarnished bowling trophies. No wonder Jackie Onassis has finally sold her share in the family shipping line to step-daughter Christina. She let it go for half the price she wanted originally, but five million pounds should mean a lot of cream on anyone's Christmas pud.

Our hardworking, big-spending engineering son has solved his Christmas shopping problems early – he called for a postponement.

Anyway, list composing is an enjoyable, harmless pastime for all ages and at the moment ours are at their most generous. We don't start the alterations and name-dropping until nearer Christmas.

I let our children's imagination run riot for a week or two, then I start dwelling on the unpleasant side-effects of the most expensive items. 'Bikes give you bulgy biceps, love' – when their cycle-owning friends are out of earshot, of course. With a little applied psychology their insular urges can be turned outwards. They are often just as happy planning extravagant luxuries for others, the trouble doesn't start until they have to part with them.

But usually as time draws on, some of these fictions are naturally discarded and the cornflake packets start disappearing. Last year their home-made presents all had a plastic, gluey base. This year's effort looks and smells the same, but there is a small difference, it seems we are expected to eat them.

When we have paid the prices and dried our tears, the next problem is where do we store these annual surprises? One year we hid nearly all the toys in our piano. It says a lot for our resident musician's talents, no one noticed the difference in sound that £25 worth of toys made!

Entertaining adverts

HOW dare anyone suggest that television toy commercials ought not to be shown? According to one daily newspaper, youngsters are being switched on to luxuries no parent can afford, causing discontent among the tinsel.

Rubbish! Don't they realise children were tuned in to the 'can't afford' message long before the teatime gifts appeared. Banning implications always make me abrasive. As if saying 'no' was beyond our control. Any purse-bearer worth the title knows 'no you can't have it' is much easier to inflict on your own hearth rug.

It cuts out all the veiled threats concerning 'When I get you home,' which accompany most departmental visits. Toy-lovers lose their appeal much faster without the benefit of a shop audience.

On the other hand 'the wait and see' ploy can work miracles during Advent. Most children are receiving this treatment one way or another, but they still love this gift-wrapped season, looking and longing is all part of the fun. Let them loose in a toy department and watch them gallop from counter to counter, little wet eyes and noses running everywhere. It always brings a lump to my throat as I watch – from a suitable hiding place. Any parents who can't cope can always switch off, burn magazines and take up astronomy.

I once heard a lady doctor on the radio condemning the spanking of children. She would never dream of laying a finger on any of her three children. My rebels were revolting for weeks following her rebuke. Right up until I discovered she employed a nanny to tutor hers.

These paragons are almost as nauseating as those who bring out their children's 'good as new' toys every year sending us into paroxysms of boredom as they relate the virginal history of their perfect replicas. The only toys that remain intact at our house are the ones nobody likes. Most of ours have had their insides fully analysed and 'mended' by ever-curious fingers before Santa has regained consciousness!

American novelist Mary McCarthy gives a heart-tugging account of her life with a cruel parsimonious aunt in her 'Memories of a Catholic Girlhood.' Every year she was sent a beautifully dressed doll by her grandmother, which remained in its wrappings and was only brought out on the rare occasion when a relative visited. It was then returned to the top shelf as soon as the visitor, beaming with satisfaction at the 'happiness' of the orphans, departed.

I believe that toys were made to be played with. Our son's train set has given hours of endless amusement and one Christmas when dad was particularly exhausted, he even got to play with it himself!

I suppose we all have a weakness in our character. One of mine is viewing television commercials. The periods in between are sometimes a yawn, but I agree with 'New Faces' panellist Micky Most, the adverts are supremely entertaining - not to be taken seriously, of course.

A recent report from America states that even the famous Colonel cannot stomach the chicken sold in one of his celebrated 'Fries.' But I confess the latest margarine epic has affected me. After seeing all those hungry relatives grouped round a 'supermum' even the effervescent Bruce Forsyth could not induce me to use it.

Who could eat those magical chocolates after watching the man in black leap from precipitous rooftops and ford raging rivers to deliver the goods, only to find she has fallen asleep in the meantime? They just don't taste the same when they come from the corner shop. 'He couldn't do that if he worked at our place,' remarked non-chocolate buying husband.

Those rib-tickling 'Angel Mums' are my favourite. The neurotic washing crazed mother who dresses her son in a white T-shirt and then sends him out to play with a bicycle chain. Then, nothing else to wear, he has to sit and wait while she washes it, before he can go and get oiled again.

I love the martyr who crawls to the car with her mountain of shopping only to be confronted by a know-all who starts boasting about his toothpaste. Instead of sending the interfering menace or the much-filled child back to the shop – she promptly thanks him, puts down the shopping and runs back herself. It's as stimulating as Monty Python.

'Bum, by dose is blocked' says malingering son on exam morning. We all have ways of dealing with this complaint, which can strike scholars from Monday to Friday. But a sniff of nasal spray is enough to send her reluctant son over the doorstep.

We had this emotive process in reverse last week when our eight-year-old was invited to a party. 'But bum, by throat is better,' she croaked, all white faced and marble-eyed. 'Sorry love, you are not fit to go.' 'But bum' – unfortunately with no nasal spray to hand I had to resort to my regular stand by, 'Oh shut up.' But apart from the 'I can't believe it's a girdle' agnostic who sounds as thick as two banana teacakes, our family favourites are the disconcertingly familiar looking chimps. I forget what they sell, but the way they sell it never fails to amuse. It's a shame Katy the beef cube girl has retired, I used to enjoy watching her handle Phillip's moods. As long as he got plenty of gravy, everything ran smoothly.

How deeply are we affected by television, I pondered the other night during supper as a Chinese man ran across the screen with a bloody dagger stuck through his neck? Perhaps penicillin is not the only drug we are building up a resistance to.

It's nearly bargain time again

AS READERS of this column will have guessed, I am excellent at ignoring nasty jobs in the hope they will eventually go away.

But there are occasions in life, I tell myself, after hitching my buttonless trousers up for the hundredth time, when these aggravating adversities have to be dragged into the open and faced – or sewn. With all these pillow cases waiting to be filled, luxuries like mum's new trousers have naturally to be denied.

So, off comes the six-inch waistband that had been choking my handicap all through the bowling season anyway, on goes one new button plus one home-made buttonhole. What a transformation! If I ever manage to lever this button through the introverted hole – what a comfort!

These trousers are one of my 'bargains' from last year's winter sales. Naturally they are too long and the welt was so wide it evoked operatic breath control, but they were such a beautiful shade of grey, an exact match for the cardigan I bought the year before. It is so remarkable how bargains seem to lose their appeal the moment they reach the bedroom mirror. In the cramped cubicle the trousers felt quite roomy. At home, my thighs looked more like over-stuffed sausages, yet there was enough material around my ankles to make another pair. Perhaps I could wear them upside down, volunteered one family wag.

But they were a lovely colour – after I washed them. When I buy new clothes I tend to visualise the shape I would like to be, not the one I'm stuck with. It's a serious hazard.

Yet, who can resist the tantalising call of the untidy tubs or the ravaged counters masquerading under the 'bargain' labels? I love to run my fingers through them, even if I am only taking a short cut to another store. There is nothing as exhilarating as a vigorous rake from one end of the 'reduced' stock to the other and if you indulge in a tug of temperament on the way, it all adds to the fun.

But I find the best grin and tonic among the hat displays. I am still searching for a woolly cap which does not make me look as if I am about to tackle Everest, or a turban type which doesn't remind me of paint-stripping. The perky-beaked Tam O'Shanters makes everyone else look so attractive, why do I look as if I have escaped from the Yorkshire tea bag advert? The other day I pulled a brilliantly coloured outsize one, with a neb that could have sheltered all the family in a storm, down over my ears and eyelids.

Just for amusement I asked the children to lead me to a mirror. A helpful onlooker took pity on me and pulling my ears out she straightened it up, the result was a bigger giggle than ever!

Husbands are unsociable shoppers. They arrive at the 'Yes, it'll do' stage before the garment leaves the coat-hanger. Mine has the impractical idea that once you have tried it on it is a sin not to buy. I can never make him understand the logic of trying on a dress you would not be seen dead in or one that you could not possibly afford. I usually end up taking a daughter then we can cover more ground.

*

THE legend concerning the length of time it takes us to dress for parties is blind exaggeration – I proved it last weekend. 'Taxis here,' shouted impatient escort dressed in best bib and tucker. 'Won't be a minute,' I pretended, silently trying to emerge from the bath water. Believe it or not, five minutes later I was drifting through the back door on a cloud of talcum, one eyebrow immaculately plucked and a spare bra dangling from my stole!

*

THE drought has been blamed for most of the soaring prices, so not surprisingly the Christmas trees have been affected. We took one look at the cost of tree trimmings and headed straight for the toilet roll tubes and foil. Our debilitated seven-year-old has been mass-producing angels on the kitchen table all week. I hope we can find a tree strong enough to hold them. I use the term 'angel' advisedly; when they have been stuck together with flour and water paste, the drying-out process adds nothing to their facial expressions. But long eyelashes and more glitter seems to be the answer to everything. I noticed that one of our Cornish pasties had a suspicious sparkle at teatime.

'Where did you put my dish?' asked our angel maker, as I tried to chisel the table clean. 'You mean the one with the milk in?' I inquired, glancing at the dog's empty dish on the floor. 'It was paste,' she cried.

My sympathies were equally divided. But after a week of 'Do tortoises have ears and how many days, hours, minutes to Christmas?' all I can say is 'Help!'

It's party time again!

HOORAY, it's almost here! I love the festive season. A chance to display my talents at the carol concerts. If my sopranic tones are not discovered this year, I swear I shall go contralto as I am growing dangerously near the voice breaking age). The get-togetherness of family celebrations, parties, are all a big excuse as my husband puts it, to indulge in my favourite pastime – talking.

It's true I love a good old grumble around the Christmas presents. Such a change from the daily dog and plant chat and if only I can remember to pause occasionally, I get replies. Yes, I talk to anyone who will listen, and at parties, they haven't much choice.

But after a brief coffee-break glance at one of the Christmas glossies I admit there's a chilling gust of envy wafting on the air. How marvellous to be able to overwhelm other partygoers in best magazine tradition, to pause exquisitely on the party threshold watching them choke with gall, instead of hiding in sour-grape attitude behind the escort or having the door slammed in your face while everyone admires his new jacket.

How rewarding to arrive with hair in the same style as you left, face faultlessly engraved in stunning make-up, attractively painted lips succulent as uncooked liver and an up-to-the-minute creation gracing the flabless curves. It must be gratifying to have such an entrance.

My party image has not caused much of a ripple up to now. Could it possibly be a reflection on the lack of preparation I feel bound to ponder, trying to hide my latest oven scars, which stretch from the top of my cuffs to the base of my newly nibbled fingernails.

One can only imagine the elaborate build-up that precedes some of the glamorous results such as a strenuous morning under the hairdryer, followed by an afternoon reclining under the eye-pads. I was a fool to think a casual hairstyle would be easier to maintain. What a mistake! It has to be washed lifeless twice a week, resurrected with conditioner, casually glued back with a can of hairspray, and it still refuses to look 'natural' - I have to torture it with electric curling tongs. Any success with these means the hairstyle has to be lowered another inch to cover the nasty burns on my frayed ears.

Perfume is supposed to transmit some sort of message to the other sex. Considering that I bathe in male bath lotion, smother myself in talc belonging to one daughter and one with an unpronounceable name belonging to another, plus liberal dabs of something which my husband says smells like almond paste, and top it all off with a squirt of cheap hairspray – my message must be rather confusing.

If Cinderella could escape to the Ball immediately she is ready it might help. But after a desperate search for his missing cuff link, a comb with a full set of teeth, a Disprin for the insecure reluctant who always becomes feverish at the sight of anyone else's party dress and the dreaded farewell speech, my appearance tends to unravel.

'No, we shouldn't be too late,' we ad-lib gaily, trying to avoid the pleading eyes, and carefully re-arranging the bribes on top of the television. I have learned not to be quite so fluent with telephone numbers. The last time we left one to be used in case of fire, flood or an act of God, one daughter had me palpitating all evening. I was about halfway unwound when I was summoned to our host's telephone. Picturing three children (a) fighting desperately among the flames and (b) fighting desperately against the flood or (c) just fighting desperately, I waited anxiously for the message. The feverish voice of our twelve-year-old trembled over the line, 'Where is the suet?' she asked.

But after instructions to the eldest regarding the big television switch-off, another edited fairy story for the youngest and an indigenous threat of a salary reduction to the middle one, we are eventually off. Thanking our lucky stars and a certain clinic that the breast-feeding era is over and there is no danger of mother arriving in her 'off the bosom' creation at least not this year anyway!

My husband always jokes about my garrulous qualities but he fails to realise that sometimes I am so exhausted when we finally get there, if I stopped talking I would probably fall asleep. Also, when and if I ever do pause for breath someone is sure to ask 'you are quiet tonight, not feeling so good, eh?'
*

TODAY'S fabrics are certainly easier to maintain. In my 'debutante' days the layers of net and taffetta creased up if you coughed. At a civic reception I attended once it took me two waltzes and a quickstep to straighten out the crumples wrought by a taxi ride. When at last I emerged from the cloakroom, my escort took one look at the wilted pale green net and ushered me in to supper. As I entered, a large lady councillor poured a cup of coffee all down my diamante. The dress and I shrivelled up like a leaf of last year's lettuce and we left. Unfortunately the dress belonged to a friend, who was also very bravely sitting in for us.

Does anyone remember the Town Hall and Cambridge Road Baths weekly stints with a celebrity band, a bottle of pop and boyfriends thrown in, all for three and sixpence? I used to hate the precious dancing time wasted hanging round the cloakroom waiting for my 'peacock' friends. Wishing I had the courage to attack my hairstyle the way they did theirs. Then after all the grooming for the 'lads' - the haughty refusals when they asked for a dance! Well my mates shook their curls, but my gratitude was such that I could hardly reach the parquet fast enough.

During the coming weeks, party professionals will be out en force. Some searching for love, some for trouble, but most of us will be looking for a little light relief from the daily grind.

The last event I supported, one young man seemed really exhilarated by my chat. I felt ten years younger until I discovered he was making eyes at the glamorous slinky over my shoulder, just using me as a 'front.' Another conversant seemed to regard me as part of the wallpaper until his wife came into view, whereupon he laughed heartily at the tragic tale I was unfolding.

I have always had an unrequited passion for false eyelashes. If I didn't think my spouse would die of embarrassment, I would love to part the cigar smoke with one stroke of extravagantly long sweeping lashes. Once I had the pleasure of conversing with a Cypriot girl at a party – her conversation was all Greek to me but her false eyelashes were fascinating. She was obviously short sighted and had myopically fixed them a tenth of an inch above her own. The double set of upper eyelashes adorning each eyelid gave her an unusually sinister appearance that I found quite hypnotic.

But who wants to look natural, anyway, except perhaps Elizabeth Taylor? I get tired of being described as 'a scream' and yearn for some other title. What about 'breathtakingly beautiful' for a change? During this joyous season I have fallen, unfortunately, out of favour with our youngest artist. 'What a super drawing' I said the other day, particularly admiring the boat full of heroic Vikings. 'It's a bowl of fruit' was her disgusted reply. 'But is this an intrinsic trait?' I asked myself after showing my mother my party outfit, complete with black stockings. I'm still smarting from her 'We used to wear them horrible things for work!' remark.

Ready for the fray!

SURE I am ready for Christmas. Just the puddings, mince pies and party fayre to finish, a last minute race to the shops, one or two presents to rewrap and the turkey to fold into the oven, then if I can keep my eyes open I intend to be the life and soul of the party.

This week is always overwhelming for the inefficient. If the pillowcases are not full enough now they will just have to shortened!

We eat so frugally the week before Christmas, trying not to damage the festive stock that the family tends to be thrilled with anything that doesn't include peanut butter. The presents that we wrapped earlier seem to have shrunk with age. I could have sworn this doll was twice as big in the shop. But it usually turns out right on the day and the recipients often hold a 'swap shop' - sometimes agreeably.

One Christmas dawn, Santa stood frozen to his interlocks, vainly trying to persuade three-year-old son to come away from his sister's sack and investigate his own. But the minute he grabbed her miniature vacuum cleaner he lost interest in everything else. After first removing the dust bag he spent all day aggravating the guests as he vacuumed everything within reach. The only peace we had was when he fell asleep and it eventually dropped from his paw. He lost interest after a while, but he has never been able to master his aggravation urge.

My excitement this year is insurmountable. I have been given my big chance – a part in the Sunday school play. I have adored Sir Laurence incessantly through his brilliant television portrayals, gleaning every fragment of artistic ability possible – come Sunday evening I shall be throwing it all into my debut. Perhaps 'part' is a slight exaggeration, but although I say only one sentence, I believe my stage presence will be remembered for quite some time. It's a sort of 'out of character' cameo, which calls for extreme acting ability on my part as I play a mother who does not like anything to interfere with her work. 'I really don't know what you are talking about, I have my work to do.' It has a splendid vital ring to it, don't you think.

There was talk of adding another line or two but unfortunately our producer decided against it. The rest of the family is not aware of this 'star' attraction, yet, they have enough excuses for non-attendance as it is.

*

REMEMBER my 'Old Grey Bristle' article concerning my antique grey coat? After a recent service a friend tugged the sleeve of my best mock ocelot and asked coyly, 'Is this the old coat you bring out year after year then?'

Either my left leg has started growing at last or I've sewn one trouser hem shorter than the other. In order to stop myself tripping up when I'm wearing flat shoes I have to kick my feet free every few steps.

I was kicking my way to the zebra crossing when a fully loaded bus screeched to a halt and a sympathetic driver beckoned me across. Gratefully overcome by this unexpected gallantry, I naturally felt obliged to continue the kicking action until I reached the other side, and hope I remember it next time I run for a bus!

*

THE air at our house is already heavy with the distinctive smouldering odours of Christmas, burning vac-belts, smoking candles and charring envelopes.

It's surprising how certain smells evoke almost forgotten memories. I can never breathe in the acidy smell of red shiny apples without suffering a flutter of guilt, as I remember a certain December during the war. My father was considered too vital to the war effort to be allowed home leave. When he was not clearing the jungle of poisonous snakes, he was busy helping West African natives build a camp cinema, and my mother, sister and I had to make the best of it without him. Our Christmas lists, heavy with luxuries, like fruit and chocolates that were 'rationed' at that time, must have caused our mum quite a headache. We returned from school one afternoon to a strange spicy smell. After a sniffing expedition and a clamber up the cupboard door I discovered six delicious mouth-watering Mac-reds gleaming on the top shelf. We blissfully shared one there and then and repeated the treachery at intervals until inevitably only one apple remained. We had decided to leave this one for mummy, until with cunning logic, which would have done any serpent proud, I pointed out if we ate them all there would not be any evidence.

I shall never forget my mother's rage turning to bewilderment when we innocently asked 'What apples?' after the theft was realised. My remorse was such that I almost felt tempted to blame my sister, but as she couldn't even reach the door handle, there did not seem much point.

I applaud the disciplinary approach of two teachers in the news last week. Though miles apart geographically they both showed much needed originality.

One American keeps a four foot long boa constrictor in front of his class with the warning 'Upset me and you upset Charlie!' A Gateshead headmaster ordered his pupils either to pay twenty pence each towards the removal of wall graffiti or clean it off themselves. Well done!

If I could only wipe the smile off my face I would be the first to complain about writing on the wall. Reading the walls on one unhygienic town centre convenience the other day was the healthiest part of my visit. 'A merry Xmas to all our readers' was inscribed just above eye level. Trying to keep my head above water, I managed to decipher words written at ground level: 'You are now at an angle of forty-five degrees.'

Best wishes for a happy Christmas to all. If you can manage it why not join your nearest carol service and share in the true spirit of Christmas?

A special thank-you to the kind letters and cards I have received and Peace and Good Health to all.

1977
And now it's Monday!

YES, I am slowly emerging from my semi-comatose state of television, turkey and trifle euphoria, thank you.

When I have become accustomed to the changeover from continuous

Sundays to perpetual Mondays I should be home and dry with all seasonal regrets behind me.

Like wishing I had digested the article on 'How to look good before, during and after the party' in time to benefit, instead of this dinnertime. Wishing I had not succumbed to yet another recorder request, wishing I could overcome my reckless urge to surprise everyone and thereby save endless trips to dress shops for exchanges and refunds.

Wishing the sentimental holiday film 'Love Story' had not followed my illicit plunge into daughter's mascara, foiling all my efforts to disguise the deluge and adding two black eyes and twenty years to my already wilting image. Mind you this fable certainly left no tragedy untapped.

One item missing from my pile this year was the inevitable 'wrinkle-remover.' I don't know whether to feel disappointed or thankful. Did the last lot achieve perfect results or am I just regarded as hopeless? I am always being accused of not using it anyway.

The best Christmas present our son ever made for himself was a ski-bike - he made it in 1974. It spent the first year in the porch, the second year in his bedroom and last year it finally reached a corner in the attic. Unfortunately we have never been able to see it in action; the snow has never been deep enough since.

One post-Christmas effect I am blissfully thankful for is our cellar door can now be closed. In order to serve guests beer 'on tap' our willing host had to set up a highly sophisticated piping arrangement from barrel in cellar to pump in kitchen, which necessitated an ever-open door in every sense of the word. This provided ever-flowing draught beer for everyone else and a permanent icy draught for kitchen staff.

Felicitous New Year wishes have almost dried on our lipstick now and most of us are trying to pull our weight towards a healthier looking economy. Last year prophets forecast a 'Serene Britain floating on a flood of profits from North Sea oil.' What happens now the Government has started playing Monopoly using oil shares as stakes?

The drop in the exchange rate of the pound was correctly predicted and it was promised that by this time we should all be earning 9% more, rising to 17% by 1981. Unfortunately no one predicted that exorbitantly high food prices would bite caustically into most of this.

Like decimalisation the drought took advantage and made fools of us all. Potatoes became a luxury and standpipes an embarrassment. Looking back on the old year I was not surprised to discover that only thirteen of Britain's 9m working women have benefited from the Sex Discrimination Act that caused so much fuss at the beginning of last year. Women brought fifty-seven of the first seventy-one cases and only thirteen were successful. Women seem to find it difficult to pinpoint when they are being discriminated against.

I thought one of the most ridiculous understatements was the confrontation of the youthful Pam Ayres with a 'This Is Your Life' programme. Although I love her poems, what life has she experienced?

My favourite woman of the year was the delectable Angela Ripon for proving so delightfully to agnostics she not only has beautiful legs but also knows how to use them.

My future hopes and prayers go with the Ulster peace women, Betty Williams and Mairhead Corrigan, may they infect everyone with peace and stability.

I wish I could make up my mind about Jimmy Carter. I know he grins piously back at the television cameras all the time, and that he admitted to Playboy magazine that he isn't quite perfect. I know he loves his mother, and he bought his wife a new nightie for the White House – but why do I still find something about him disagreeably indigestible?

If I could have one New Year wish granted, I would hope for a change in the current educational attitudes in most schools. Now that we have an influx of highly educated teachers and professionals without jobs, perhaps mistakes can be rectified. Why not more industrial courses – with industry and commerce making their requirements and apprenticeships more appealing to school leavers? 'School leavers don't want apprenticeships where they learn a trade, they are looking for a soft office job where they don't have to get their hands dirty' says the boss of one firm. Why? Whose fault is it? Where does this idea take root - at home, school or in the factory? Another spokesman admits 'I no longer even look to recruiting youngsters – fortunately there is a satisfactory supply of married women prepared to give a fair day's work for a fair day's pay.'

At a recent school open evening a comprehensive teacher stunned a group of parents, pupils and teachers by admitting that the maths he is teaching now will be of no use to the majority of his pupils in their jobs. Why not teach them something that will? I agree with the verdict of one headmaster who said to me recently, 'We have too many chiefs and not enough Indians.'

Throughout most of last year we were haunted by two predominating questions. One concerned the matriarchal aspirations of Princess Anne, and I don't blame her for keeping 'mum.' The other concerned the whereabouts of Lord Lucan. I confess the latter still has me utterly andintriguingley consumed with smouldering curiosity. Where is Lord Lucan now?

Today is the best day

AFTER living in a prolonged vacuum of boisterous opinions, incessant brawlings provoked by petty thefts from a comb to a wine gum, all accompanied by continuous sultry mumblings from Elvis Presley, the dog and me now look like two prisoners in solitary.

Except of course we are both smiling.

I must have become so brainwashed by the sound of Elvis's voice during the last fortnight, I find myself unable to stop impersonating him. His songs have taken over my mind completely, which is bad enough, but it must be a source of surprise to shoppers and bus queues when I strike up in best 'Presley' tradition with 'All Shook Up' warnings of 'You can knocka me down, slappa my face, but aha honey, lay offa my blue suede shoes!'

I can never decide which gives me most pleasure, putting the trimmings up or taking them down. On the other hand, although I welcome the extra hour in bed that school holidays bring, there is no comparison for the joy in my heart as I wave them back to teacher.

As most people seem preoccupied with predictions I may as well join them and see what the stars have mapped out for Cancarians. Naturally I do not believe in these horoscopial absurdities – they have no influence on my life whatsoever – I just read them first because they are next to my favourite cartoon.

I have to be on my guard a little at the moment, for some reason the Moon has it in for people in my sign. 'Something unpleasant is due to arrive at any time.' Seeing as most of our bills have already taken over the mantelpiece, it must be something really nasty.

But it's the 'you are in a hardworking phase at present,' which sets my lunar 'tic' athrob. Is there some job I ought to be doing, I ask myself from the comforting depths of my sofa. 'The holiday could have left you jaded,' sounds more like it, if it was not for the rest of the sentence 'or it could have brought much-needed relaxation.' Still I suppose they have to cover everything.

No harm in casting a blood-shot eyed over my partner's future, I suppose. I often see him off to work with the bits about his 'ruler being nicely aspected with the main emphasis on business matters, etc.' No need to burden him with any of the disturbing non-committal jargon like the promise of a 'new romance' one star gazer promised him for Christmas.

You never can tell – perhaps one day this 'mooning' over the family signs may produce some profound conclusion, besides an empty coffee-pot. An accurate reading of one's future comes more expensive, of course.

A relative once wrote for her personal horoscope and received a wad of typewritten sheets. The only two bits we could decipher were the suggestions 'Your daughter will soon have a child and you will be moving house in the near future to a place near running water.' She was highly impressed by these altruistic observations even when we pointed out these facts were easily deductible from the rough sketch she had submitted – mentioning two married daughters and the fact that on average she changed her address every three years. But the astrologer did predict the running water unprompted.

One aunt lives in mortal fear of ever offending a gypsy. She would rather adorn her mantelpiece with expensive sticks of pink tissue-trimmed privet (remarkably like her own garden hedge) than risk being 'cursed.'

I used to have a regular gypsy visitor whose appearance I eventually became to dread. She was exactly my size and although I admired her good taste, she had an irritating habit of begging the clothes off my back. Until one day I got my demand in first and asked her if she could possibly have something to fit me? After a short silence and a warning that I was going to spend a lot of time crying in the future, I managed to shut the door and get back to my onion pickling. I have never seen her since.

Was it one of her relatives, I wonder, who paid me a visit one snowy lunchtime a few years later? My son and I were just about to eat our fish and chips, when she knocked on the door and asked for a cup of water. 'A slice of bread please, if you don't mind,' she then asked, until my son, probably realising it was the only way he could get his dinner, offered her a chip.

We finished up in a cosy threesome around the fire. That is until I made the mistake of telling her about my forthcoming 'happy event.' This seemed to agitate her so much I began to wonder if she had been sent by the family planning organisation. When she left she was still pleading with me not have any more. Any minute I expected her to break into a chorus of 'Don't have any more Mrs More.' Mind you when the wind whistles round the empty coal bucket and I gaze at the row of occupied chairs guarding the fire, I often think of her words.

I admit to a semi-detached fascination, but I also hold a deep mistrust for Spiritual Mediums.

Looking ever so slightly forward can jog the adrenaline somewhat, but too much looking back would give me a pain in the neck. The literature I have read on this subject concerning what are described as 'true life' accounts of liaisons with the spirit world have not altered my agnostic aloofness. People often turn to mediums following a bereavement or other personal tragedy, when their emotions are particularly vulnerable and easy to seduce. In the cruel grip of acute disorientation they grasp at any escape from awful reality that offers the 'go-between' a powerful status.

A woman turned to such a person for help last year when her sister's daughter went missing. She was informed that her niece had been strangled and buried. Strong words for a medium. The day before Christmas Eve the 'strangled' daughter rang her mother and told of her whereabouts and three years of misery were obliterated, thank God.

Somerset Maugham lived for ninety-one years believing that 'there is only one thing about which I can be certain and this is that there is very little about which one can be certain.'

I fervently try to make myself believe that today is the best time. Some people have three worries, yesterday, today and tomorrow, when actually they need only have one.

Where to this year?

IT'S no good beating about the brochures any longer; this family will definitely have to come to terms regarding a holiday decision.

Every year we gasp our way through technicolour photographs of thriving turquoise swimming pools surrounded by overhanging concrete, but we never discover anything cheap and attractive enough to tempt us across the Channel.

The glamorous bikini gracing the cover holds certain charms for some of us, but the thrills of this revealing figure are no match for the shock of black and white ones on the page marked 'prices.'

These ubiquitous blondes who spread their tantalising forms across most of the holiday landscapes always raise the same question in my mind, who actually chooses the resort? Perhaps the dishy damsels with the wider than average smile are aimed at the dads, while mum gets on with the serious small print.

This year we dreamed of a boating holiday, until we finally translated the financial columns. But £160 before food, fuel or entertainment makes me seasick before we start.

Last year our son and eight mates steered to glory down the Norfolk Broads. He tried hard to find the right words to describe the beauty and advantages of his adventure into 'boat land.' Although he can give a lucid description concerning the interiors and lubricating merits of every pub situated within crawling distance from each of their moorings the rest remains an enigma.

He has retained the indelible memory of a certain precarious trip from the deck of one boat to another carrying a plastic bucket filled with beer cans. 'The water's not fit to drink, mum.' It seems he missed his footing and the weight of the bucket, which for some reason he was reluctant to part with, dragged him to the bottom of the river. The rest of the crew never really recovered from their disappointment when he dragged himself back on board, empty handed. From all accounts mutiny was just avoided.

But what about children were there any interests for them, we wanted to know. Oh yes, there were swings thoughtfully placed in all the pub gardens, he told us enthusiastically. I tried to picture three children, ages ranging from eight to fifteen, swinging away into the darkness, while 'throwing out time' brought forth a swaying ship's captain and his mate, but it kept fading, somehow!

We did try a tenting holiday one year – the year before hot summers arrived. When you knew it was summer because people carried umbrellas above their fur hats. I remember us all following chief campers' instructions and laying all the equipment (except tent, which hopefully went on the roof rack) outside the car, ready to be packed in the boot. Without the cases of food it would easily have filled a removal van. I could imagine the relieved expressions shining behind the lace curtains at this obvious evidence of our withdrawal. In the end we had to hire a friend to help transport us there and back.

But the outdoor life can become rather addictive after a time, especially the mouth-watering smell and sound of fresh bacon crackling merrily on the outdoor Calor.

During the coldest nights I thought of all the other bodies spread out across the moist field, and wondered what we would all look like if a gigantic wind suddenly wafted all the tents away!

For a number of years all the family were content to browse around the picturesque and lazy harbour of Saundersfoot in Pembrokeshire. We could either be anonymous in a quiet little cove or join the rest of the exploring tourists in the surrounding villages or perhaps take a trip to busy Tenby. I love the unexplored, but not all the time, being content to swap stories with other visitors and natives sometimes.

Our ideal holiday plan is to spend the first weekend unwinding in solitary, idle confinement, after a hectic week of packing and planning our only thought is to get away from everyone. This feeling usually lasts till Monday when we start feeling 'matey' again. Meeting new friends is one of the interesting by-products of my holiday.

When I hear others condemning 'tourists' and 'tourist' places I wonder in what category they place themselves. Are they actually admitting 'We don't like ourselves?'

Some proprietors in Cornwall are complaining all the way to the bank because the holiday-makers they encouraged have become too many for comfort. Surely we should all be prepared to sacrifice something to share our little patch of coastal heaven.

All happiness must pay, we thought last year as we finally broke under the double pressure of children and television and consented to go 'holiday camping.' Unenthusiastically we joined what looked like a million others in the battle for our self-catering chalet key. With the sun slowly sinking over the chair-lift pylons we drove swiftly in the direction of our chalet, which according to much pointing from various traffic wardens promised to be in the next county.

With excited children in raptures over the unusual bedding arrangements – ours was next to the cooker, we bit back our tears and forced ourselves to eat. Heart-sick for our Welsh cove we read what looked like a weekly programme, and brightened up a little. Didn't look too painful, perhaps it wouldn't be a bad week. Our hopes were shattered when daughter turned the page and asked eagerly 'Now tell us what happens tomorrow!'

By lunchtime of the second day our children were fully paid up members of every club there was. Dad and I had actually enjoyed a morning together with conversation and a delicious strawberry milk shake followed by our first hand-in-hand stroll along the beach without childish interruptions since we became parents.

Feeling extremely thankful and slightly sorry for 'Uncle Jack' we wandered back to camp. 'What time's dinner?' shouted three voices from the sky, and floating in space on the chair lift were our three lolly-licking club members.

Some of our days were spent strolling up the beach to Filey where, after shopping, we often picnicked on the beautifully groomed lawns above the bay. But we really appreciated the camp entertainment during the evening. The children managed to stand beside us in the magnificently decorated Viennese ballroom for five minutes at a time, then off they dashed to the 'slots' or other esoteric pursuits, after which we all met for supper then back to the chalet for bed.

We played tennis, did some sailing, everyone except me swam in the pool and on the whole we all agreed it had been an unusually happy holiday. The biggest bonus was the fact that my man and I actually conversed, mostly me persuading him to dance but conversation all the same.

But none of this answers the pervading question, where to this year?

Tiring work, relaxing

'MUM, I don't feel like myself,' said our seven-year-old at breakfast, a change of personality some of us would welcome during the winter of discontent, not to mention demoralisation. Far from being the month of hope renewed and promise of better days ahead, January is merely presenting some of us with a cold front, whose chilling effects could be felt for quite a while.

After weeks of practice for the lead in a new show, the vivacious Elizabeth Seal, who is nearly my age, received the 'don't come Monday' treatment. Her director decided he had miscast her, at forty-two she looked too old for the part.

Queen Juliana and Lee Radziwell who always look immaculately dressed to me, were recently voted among the ten worst dressed women.

The proprietor of a body-building studio has just told Raquel Welch that she needs special exercise to slim her hips, raise her assets and correct the 'sag' in her rear. He also pointed out that Miss Welch had a tendency to 'loose-muscle' tone, which must make mine on the verge of collapse.

As if all this wasn't ego-damaging enough, while visiting the doctor the other day I received another deadly shock. While daughter was having her verucca excavated, in my eagerness not to miss anything I accidentally stood on the weighing scales, I don't know who looked the most distressed as we left, daughter or me.

Of course I blame it all on the snow. To think I once couldn't get enough of the stuff. When I wasn't rolling my friend's face in it I was eating it, sliding happily home from school with a large juicy icicle in my mouth! Now for some reason it has me in a state of semi-slumber. Hibernating animals have the right idea, they stock up their little bodies for a nice long sleep until spring. My little body is well and truly stocked but nasty people keep waking me up. All the articles I ever read on 'How to Relax' have taken their toll, smoking can't be as hard to give up as the soporific relaxing.

Night after night I can be seen dozing in front of the embers a frail picture of senility. The same two buttonless shirts shielding my knees and the same needle and thread resting in my lifeless fingers. All this easy pleasure must surely be bad for me. I know, I ought to be out somewhere learning to slim, or being taught how to stick flowers in plastic, but at this time of year I always feel tired and listless, my eyes constantly straying towards the 'tired blood' adverts.

After reading about the vicar who feels better after standing on his head for a while each morning I did reach for my yoga book again. But when I stand on my head the blood that drags itself to my brain is accompanied by ten stones of loose 'muscle tone.' But I do believe a few mornings of this treatment would alter my shape considerably. The top of my head should become quite firm and flat, the wrinkles on my neck would probably disappear – but so would my neck! I suppose everything would just start hanging the other way.

If only I had the courage of one Dutch fish and chip shop proprietor in the news recently. He persuaded his dentist to sew up his jaws with steel thread to stop him eating. He hopes to lose weight by existing on a liquid diet poured through his teeth.

Unfortunately, after one needle prick my dentist and I are not on speaking terms and he has such difficulty getting me to open my mouth I suspect he thinks my jaws are permanently locked anyway. I wonder what happens when the stitches are eventually removed. How does one keep the figure so painfully acquired? It would mean a lifetime in and out of stitches for me.

Although it does nothing for my figure I am an enthusiastic plant-watcher during the winter months. Mine give me endless pleasure. It's a satisfying, unenergetic and warm pastime and definitely beats gardening.

There is a peanut-growing craze sweeping America at the moment. Carter enthusiasts are paying £2 for a 'presidential starter kit' – one peanut in a plastic pot. But plants need not be expensive. Most of mine started from one 'mother' plant. One year I planted some green pepper seeds just for curiosity. We have never had any flowers but the glossy green leaves flourish every year and look very decorative. Fruit pips – orange, apple and lemon – grow quite successfully in a pot; it's more fun not knowing what to expect.

Apart from me in my wellies, the snow has brought forth some strange sights. Glancing through her curtains at the silently falling snow a friend was mystified at what looked like a tiny red light floating through the air. On closer inspection it turned out to be a young man on skis with a light fixed to his bob-cap!

It sounds paradoxical but I think the labour-saving age is most exhausting. I am beginning to realise why my gran was always full of interminable energy almost until she died at ninety-three.

She managed to raise a family of eight without modern gadgets I know, but my grandad didn't change his shirt every day – his stiff collars were sent to the laundry. The heavy serviceable shirts were not always in the

102

washer – nowadays men don't just change their collars, everything is washable. Instead of one weekly wash, most of us are at it two or three times. They did not have to go trampling round various supermarkets serving themselves, shopping meant leaving a weekly order at the Co-op to be delivered later. Also there was not such an exotic choice of meat and veg to choose from. The Sunday joint had to last much longer, meals were less varied and, therefore easier to prepare. So that's why we need more rest today – husbands take note!

Signs of the times?

HAVE you noticed how everyone is suffering from the 'mumbles' these days? We seem to be breeding a nation of ventriloquists. Everyone sounds to be speaking through clenched teeth or forked tongue.

Perhaps our stiff upper lips are so weighed down with inflation, clear speech is impossible – either that or I have suddenly been struck deaf.

It used to be difficult enough during my anti-natal days. Spread out on the tissue paper trying to decide what the doctor's question was and whether it would be considered too pertinent to ask 'his majesty' to repeat himself yet again. Strangely enough with only a little strain one could hear Mrs So-and-So's kidney trouble coming loud and clear through the adjoining wall. But what with the crackle of the paper at the back of one's eardrum and rising nervousness the voice booming above could have been asking me the name of next door's cat for all I knew.

It's most frustrating for a garrulous person like me having to waste valuable talking time in outbursts of 'Pardon?' 'What was that?' or 'Eh?' A bewitching smile is not always a suitable standby, especially if your mumbler has just confessed his mother is dying of leprosy.

With the abundance of expressive hand-waving and bleary eye-rolling peculiar to the occasion, our son often tries to communicate his Saturday evening adventures.

We manager to decipher a 'Marsden Soach' connection which crops up repeatedly, but the rest remains a mysterious slur. The only person who ever speaks clearly is my dentist, but unfortunately he always places me in an unanswerable position first.

Scholars have a unique jargon. 'Yeralavter gerritermorror' splutters one of ours in answer to my accusation regarding gym equipment, which seems to dwell permanently in a school locker.

We had one exceptional French mistress at our school. Apart from the fact that she liked me – an unusual trait in any teacher – she was an excellent elocutionist. We left her class with near perfect French accents, which was a miracle in itself, considering that none of us spoke English correctly. She had us all stretching and exercising our lazy lips until they felt elasticated; every time we opened our mouths she stuck a strange vowel in it. When she had finished with us even the Marsden lad who always pronounced 'war' as 'woar' sounded like Maurice Chevalier. Unlike the French we do not use our mouths enough in speech.

Mind you I am fiercely proud of my Yorkshire heritage and the accent that goes with it Not that I haven't made a fool of myself trying to talk all 'cut glass' as Dylan Thomas puts it, before I learned more sense. Trying to speak posh may round off the vowels, but it also stunts my speech – a painful handicap for me.

Twice a week I struggle through a conversation with a jovial Jamaican, who sits next to me on the bus. He used to sit behind until we got fed up of shouting our 'pardons' across the cloth caps. Although he opens his mouth wide over his nine-carat teeth, I find his accent difficult to follow sometimes, to cover any confusion I laugh when he does and he giggles with me.

But I am wondering if perhaps one could look too amused. In the middle of a hearty chuckle the other day, he gave my left kneecap an intimate crunch. I was inquiring about his Friday pursuits – like the males up our valley, did he join his pals, have a steel band rave up, perhaps? 'When he workin' day over man, he doin' no such ting. Ma parents always bring me up not to be sick for work – that's the way ah always try to be, man'

Work for him meant up at 5.30am every day except Sunday. But Saturday is big night out – vigorous pressure to my left patella here, followed by a meaningful laugh from him and a nervous giggle from me, man! He certainly livens up a dreary journey.

After a weary day it is a temptation to drift through the 'gibbers' with a blank smile and let them get away with it, sadly my curiosity will never allow this. I must know what is being said. A bus conductor muttered something as I was about to step off his bus the other night. It took five minutes of 'sorry's' and 'pardons, but to everyone relief I finally let the bus continue, with his farewell message, 'it's coming lighter now' written forever on my heart.

The joker who rang me consistently recently without answering my 'who is that please?' should certainly have my message imprinted on his eardrum.

After lifting the receiver to a silent caller three times in one hour, I eventually mustered all the power possible for my 5ft frame and screamed

104

fractiously into the phone 'IS ANYBODY THERE.' An immediate click was the satisfying response.

I have recently become interested in age concern – mine, and don't mind admitting old age holds no charm for me. But how old is old?

A recent television programme took years off me when an eighty-year-old young lady admitted that there are compensations. This dear lady said that she actually enjoyed the peace that age has brought her. With troubles all behind, her life is now pleasantly peaceful and she had a lovely expression on her face to prove it.

I read recently that an eight-one-year old granny has gained a BA degree with the Open University, fulfilling a life-long ambition. In the same London paper was a piece about the remarkable recovery of Norman Cousins (from the book 'Powers of Mind,' Adam Smith) who became dangerously ill with a blood disease. When he discovered a note left by a doctor that read, 'We may be losing Norman,' he immediately checked out of hospital and into a hotel.

There he tried to cheer himself up by watching a Marx Brothers' film and as he laughed he began to feel better. From then on he made laughter his main course of treatment and gradually he recovered. None of the doctors could find an adequate explanation. Nevertheless he was cured.

So laugh and be healthy is the message. Good news for brave people, who like me, can stand anything – except suffering!

A gap without bridge

IF I was not already up to my double chin in 'societies' I would feel staunchly tempted to form a new one, the SPCPEM – A Society for the Prevention of Cruelty to Parents especially Mums.

Any society misappropriation can, it seems, with a little help from various authorities and psychiatrists, always be traced back to parents. Yet no one notices the adversities we suffer or the cruel way we are neglected.

The pain of childbirth is nothing compared with the agony and fatigue of adolescent rearing. We are provided with Trilene to numb the discomfort when they enter this world, but are compelled to suffer their adolescence undrugged and sober. On certain painful occasions in our household a whiff of gas and air would be most welcome.

The trouble is my juveniles just don't understand me. My first mistake was not being as tall as everyone else's mum – a great disadvantage now their twitchy nostrils are higher than my parting – another twelve inches could give me more authority. Also, I am constantly informed other mums are half my age, which on my calculation means they had their families before they left junior school!

They give me too much homework for my age with no television until it is completed. They make disparaging remarks about my 'tatty' appearance but won't allow me more spending money. Yes this is a cry from the wallet. I am just an in-between, too old for the boys and too young for the joys of Metro and pension benefits (hope that there are some left when I am eligible).

Every disagreement is related to 'age' – mine. I am expected to be gripped with sympathetic hysteria at the sign of another of their 'spots' but when I mention my grey hairs they tune in to Elvis.

Everything I wear has to meet with their approval; nothing designed to make anyone look twice is acceptable. As long as it blends in with the crowd it's OK. Whenever we see their friends approaching in town I have to walk three paces behind until they pass. They often go out and leave me alone for hours never bothering to tell me where or when to expect the back, which makes me most insecure and unhappy.

If I try to confide my worries to them, they do not listen. My 'nobody cares' soliloquy, which used to even make the plants wilt a little, only makes then yawn or play imaginary violins. They giggle all the way through the sordidness of my favourite serial then sit with faces as animated as Shredded Wheat when Laurel and Hardy have me in stitches. My small efforts to amuse have them re-excavating their latest pimple. I did think the dog was on my side the other day when he sported a lop-sided grin. But when the leer was still there an hour later, although naturally flattered, I did begin to wonder.

On closer investigation I found a piece of bone wedged between his teeth holding up his top lip. Pity, he nearly had me convinced of his intelligence.

To crown all, our teenagers have started hiding their make-up. It said in my morning paper that if you wore none you are either self-confident or a nursing mother. Well I am not likely to be either this week. The next paragraph hit me right below the bulge. If you wouldn't be caught dead without your lipstick – you are probably over forty and missed out on the permissive society. 'Missed out? I am drowning in it!

'When the children get ready for bed without being told or clean their shoes or get ready for school on time – give them a prize,' says educational 'wizard' John Presland. What about giving dad and me some reward? I say a medal for bravery or better still a diploma stating that 'while under the influence of three aggressive, demanding children under fifteen you

106

did still continue to cling gamely to sanity above and beyond the call of Vallium.'

Even my dreams are invaded. There I am drifting into delicious sin with Frank Finlay when someone wakes me up to tell me there's a man-eating spider creeping about. Why do they always have nightmares in the middle of favourite fantasies? I tried three times to dream myself back to Frank but a gigantic spider kept getting in the way.

Where is this all forgiveness we tried to inject? Just because I inadvertently vacuumed up a set of plastic fingernails, one daughter showed the compassion of a bank clerk. How was I to know they were not part of the usual rubbish that lives on their bedroom floor five days of the week? In an eggshell they just don't seem to have time for us any more; goodness knows what sort of wrecks we shall become after all this callous neglect.

Fortunately, the worst pain is soonest forgotten. Time has a restorative habit of diluting the pain. Despite parental shortcomings our first daughter has reached twenty-one virtually unscarred. This is a time when only the special happiness they brought remains.

Our son did confront us one tea time with some peremptory soup-spilling views on the spoken word. His English teacher, he announced proudly, thought parents were wrong to ban swearing. He (the teacher), considered this a snobbish attitude. Anglo-Saxon language was our proud heritage. He then gave us a few examples guaranteed to resurrect anyone's ancestors. When I suggested we all start swearing at each other the moment his friend arrived, he didn't seem as fervently consumed by the idea.

Try the exotic potato

I OFTEN fancy myself as an amateur sleuth. In fact you could say I spend a lot of my time collecting clues and confronting culprits.

Whodunnit? Is a byword in our household but I confess this latest and outrageous potato scandal has me completely baffled. Not too surprisingly, actually, seeing that even the experts are getting their alibis confused. Exorbitant prices were first blamed on the rain, then on the sun. Last week I read a balsamic report that potato prices are likely to drop later in the year. 'Growers are planning to produce crops three times as big as the national record average – with the help of a new planting system called 'Blueprint.' This was developed at the Ministry of Agriculture experimental farm near Selby and simply means that crops are planted close together with heavier fertilisation and extra attention at each stage. This method enabled one farmer to harvest twenty-five tons an acre – sounds promising!

At a recent National Power Farming Conference at Bournemouth, Professor Dickson, of Newcastle University, went along with this 'Future profits depend on higher yields of crops and livestock,' he said.

Other 'experts' agreed that factory made foods were forcing farming prices down. Someone else was frightened into admitting that 'dearer farm products will lead to a drop in the amount housewives buy.' Ah, a vital clue here – so we do help to control prices, then?

Does this mean a heavier crop will satisfy everyone? You could be forgiven for asking. Just as we all start reaching for the potato masher we are then informed that someone is holding back 2 million tons in order to keep the prices high! We can expect 1 million surplus spuds at the end of the year.

A touching scene, one lot feverishly fertilising while the other lot is waiting to make a mountain out of their 'molehills.' Sounds like a load of compost to me. 'Someone somewhere is making a killing,' says one MP.

As the mother of a growing family, I try to avoid any cuts in food, though luxuries are the first to go. But it seems that the potato, once considered a vital part of our daily diet, is now a luxury we can no longer afford. In future our intake will be considerably reduced, and after seeing a tray of what looked like old pebbles half buried in the sand hiding behind a ticket marked 20p a pound in a shop this morning – giving them up is going to be easy. It wouldn't do my 'spares' any harm to cut out this starch friend altogether. But although it's 'pasta' joke I will even eat spaghetti before pay this ransom. Yorkshire puddings and savoury rices will accompany our weekly meat.

Once I could look at my bulging trolley and ask, do we really eat all this? Now when I compare the bulging cash total with my few scattered items, my temperamental outbursts must be entertaining for everyone. 'I shop anywhere, prices don't bother me,' boasted one shopper as I steadied myself against a supermarket freezer after seeing the coffee prices. Current prices would bother me, even if I could afford them.

For a good wholesome economical stand-in you can't beat home-made bread. Ignore the agnostics – believe me it is cheaper and it tastes better. Your man will adore its yeasty flavour: a whiff of hot bread has saved me from many a telephone bill explosion. It's so easy a child could tackle it. If I didn't enjoy baking it so much mine probably would.

To help wean you from the potato I'm even prepared to pass on my coveted recipe. It takes up very little time. I usually mix mine after lunch then place it   in the top of the airing cupboard to double its size while I attack something else.

When it looks all swollen and about to give birth you start bashing it about the kitchen table. Pretend it is a potato grower, knock all the wind out of it. When you start feeling better, form it into whatever shape you fancy, place on a greased tray for another half hour, then bake in a blistering hot oven. From three pounds of flour I make sixteen small baps, two elongated French loaves and two pizza bases - filled with onion, cheese and tomato topping, these are delicious with a winter salad. Or given the mood I knead a few currants, a handful of sugar and a sprinkling of spices into some of the dough for hot cross buns. With a syrup glaze on top and butter oozing out generously from their middles they make a satisfying dessert – when I am not on a diet, that is.

Bread Recipe: 3lb plain flour; 3 teaspoons salt; 3 teaspoons sugar; 1oz yeast; 1½ pints tepid water; ¼ milk; 2oz lard.

Mix one third of liquid with sugar and yeast, leave 15 minutes in a warm place. Rub lard into the flour and salt. When yeast mixture is frothy, pour into well in centre of flour and mix well. Knead for ten minutes, place in covered bowl in warm place for approximately ninety minutes. Knead again, shape, leave another thirty minutes. Small rolls in top of hot oven for fifteen minutes, loaves twenty minutes, on one side then turn over for a further ten.

Living it up 25 years ago!

IT'S a long time since we sat munching our potted meat around the television while the Queen sat waiting for her crown in Westminster Abbey.

There have been colourful Royal occasions since but none more glorious to me than my first view of the Coronation in black and white.

I was eighteen at the time, young, half-free with a multitude of delights as yet unexplored – television was one of them. Only having a wireless to turn off at that time we were delighted to take our sandwiches two doors further on, to our prosperous neighbours eighteen inch screen.

What changes have evolved during the last quarter century?

Looking at a photo of a young soldier holding up what looks like his consumptive mother, taken on our first holiday together, twenty-five years ago, I feel inclined to agree with the children, I did look ninety years old. Whether this was due to my old-fashioned clothes and hairstyle or was merely the result of the intemperate pleasures of our initial unchaperoned holiday together – I don't know.

In 1952 my National Serviceman was stationed in Germany. Every Sunday with tears dripping silently into my Yorkshire pudding I used to listen hopefully to Cliff Michelmore and Jean Metcalfe swapping record requests from Forces and their sweethearts on radio's Family Favourites. Once a week I received an account of the unbelievable atrocities taking place on a certain parade ground near Hamburg, a small paragraph revealed the loneliness and a full page was given up to pleas for another parcel of coffee – love. This granular barter was in great demand for some reason. His weekends were spent learning the language with a friendly family in the village. When he returned home on his first leave he could say 'Willhelmina' like a native.

My friends were passing round pictures of gleaming ears holding up an army beret wearing suitable lovesick expressions underneath. After persistent requests plus another parcel of coffee mine finally arrived. Although I pondered carefully over the close-cropped khaki figures grinning round a table, I had to revert to the inscription for a clue. The romantic message read 'Me behind the pint glass.' But life had to go on. Covered in Pancake make-up with ear-lobes dabbed liberally with Woolworth's scent we had several Saturday night harbours to shelter our fretting hearts, including over twenty cinemas and various dance halls.

Now that my favourite footballer was learning to 'Sprechen sie Deutch' instead of me being allowed to thaw my frost-bitten toes in comfort on a Saturday afternoon – I was now expected to accompany a claret and gold adorned father to Fartown's terrace side.

They had a rugby team then, with tries scored regularly to prove it. With a voice twice the size of his small frame dad's advice would ring out resonantly across the tightly packed supporters. Hunter, Devery, Valentine, Cooper and Banks were all given the benefit of his abundant sporting vocabulary. Because of his dark wavy hair and deceptively gentle eyes Cooper was my favourite. When I wasn't dreaming of my score with him I was watching the crowd.

Any minute I expected someone to realise the loud insults at my side were not coming from the giant in front of us. But all the bullies were sergeants and NCO's in the army, if letters were to be believed, so it was safe to argue.

Threats punctuated with 'What yer talking about, man' were thrown back and forth, but after the match everyone walked matily home, and rugby fans still do, says our recently retired supporter.

Radio highlights were Kenneth Horne's 'Much Binding in the Marsh,' 'Take it from Here' with Dick Bentley and June Whitfield (Ramsden Street connections), 'The Goons,' Wilfred Pickles and Mable at the table and Ena Sharples on the piano was urging us to 'Ave a Go.' Mrs Dale was worrying about Jim twice daily.

110

Esther Williams was swimming across the cinema screens for three and sixpence, without wetting her coiffeur. Rock Hudson and Gregory Peck were helping us to forget our soldier heroes. Elizabeth Taylor had only just started collecting husbands. Old Mother Riley and Abbot and Costello were for amusement only. The only blue jeans we saw were clinging to the horseshoe-shaped legs in cowboy films.

For afternoon tea we could tiptoe into the esoteric powder-puff atmosphere of Rushworths or follow the tantalising coffee aroma up Westgate to Fields' were a coffee-grinding machine could be seen churning the beans in the front window.

This was a three-tiered, thick-carpeted oasis where one could lounge luxuriously over the silver teapot in basket chairs, strictly for the twin-set and pearls clientele. When my mother and I were not enjoying pie and peas in the top market hall we would raise our noses occasionally and crack a cream puff there.

Another famous landmark, the Theatre Royal, was still alive and well supported. Once a year I took out the greasepaint and entered the magical world of amateur operatics. Twenty-five years ago a local actress, Thelma Piggott played the part of Grete in Ivor Novello's 'The Dancing Years.' Every night I watched her cry real tears as 'Rudy' left her for another, wishing that I could learn to develop this useful talent. Now I watch her walk down ITV's 'Coronation Street' twice a week guised as 'Mavis.' Her name has changed but time has had little effect on the rest of her.

We wore seven-and-sixpenny fully-fashioned stockings attached to our suspenders. One-and-elevenpenny Rayon turned inside out with the fringes trimmed were a cheap substitute if you didn't let the scissors slip. Tea towels were one-and-eleven each and Horrocks's pillow cases were three-and-six. A three-piece suite cost £54, a gent's worsted suit with waistcoat ranged from £6 to £12. Dr Williams' pink pills were on sale for nerve sufferers. A train journey to London cost thirty shillings and one to York cost five-and-six.

Television's one channel was uncontaminated by advertising, it started at 5pm and finished at 10.30pm. The first programme I saw was 'The Barrets of Wimpole Street.' I became enslaved, and the thrilling combination of my favourite pursuits – eating, viewing and fire poking – still has me in its intoxicating grip. That was also the year I discovered that gin tasted like paint stripper!

Birthday blues

LADY FALKENDER is not the only one with 'party' troubles. February will also be remembered as a back-aching, list making month in our camp.

I always sigh felicitously as February fades away. Icy temperatures and hazardous conditions are hard enough to bear but I also gave birth to two of our children during this cheerless month, so it means double celebrations, too.

This year our eight-year and twenty-first year parties were more than years apart. One was a happy informal affair the other an over-planned, overdressed, not to mention overwrought affectation for a dozen grown-up eight-year olds. Not only have they to be fed, watered and continuously entertained but they also expect to be returned home with gifts clutched tightly in their little paws. I don't know who started this affluent habit but I can tell you who has finally put an end to it!

The carefree days of dainty sandwiches and ice cream to finish are only memories. Food has now to come up to rigid standards – sausage rolls, patties, savoury tarts and various canapes to nibble accompanied by jellies, mousse, trifles and ice cream.

'Jane only eats chocolate marshmallows,' announces birthday girl as I spread my home-made confections on the kitchen table.

The dull bowling trophies a-tarnishing in the corner have to be shone to their original silver. I hadn't realised before now how impressive they looked when clean, and even put one on display in the front window. It was just bad luck that the cup I chose to show off belongs to a bowling friend up the road. After taking it to be inscribed I still had to return it. This says a lot for my familiarity with them.

The party invitations ambitiously forecast a 4pm kick-off, and as the clock ticked towards 3pm the first of the long-gowned guests arrived before I'd had time to clear away the baking mess and change from my working gear. The tension began. While I pick up the trail of coats, scarves, gloves, handbags and shoe bags everyone unwraps the presents. By the time I return to suggest a game before tea, the dining table is half empty.

The most important part of the celebrations being over for our daughter, her temperament is now rising rapidly and we note that her lip is showing. Once the pickles and crisps have been devoured, they stand like food inspectors looking for bacteria. One cool blonde casts her bored expression over the desserts, eventually resting on the fruit cocktail. 'Is that fresh fruit?' she snoots, turning away in disgust when I shamefully shake my head.

One rule I have learned as we survive each party is to hide the television. Once they discover this, only a hammer and chisel can dislodge them. When their dresses start bulging it's time for the games – but appetites fluctuate. With a little ingenuity some can manage to look hamster-cheeked all evening.

Children are nocturnal creatures, at their best or worst in the dark. Their favourite party game is 'Murders.' Off go the lights, then everyone has a go at being 'choked.' They never get tired of strangling each other. When everyone had been murdered at least three times, they were still at it. The only way we could take their minds off 'Murder' was to wheel in the refreshments. Mary Whitehouse would burn her banner if she knew.

Our teaching daughter read a cautionary tale to her eight-year-olds about the death by burning of a little girl who played with matches, telling them to write and illustrate this in their own words. One normally pencil-shy little boy set to work with unusual enthusiasm. After a short scribble he presented his effort. Underneath a drawing of a girl with elongated arms in giant flames was the inscription 'I like the bit were she died.' All produced a similar theme decorated with gory pictures of flaming limbs.

Another favourite is 'sleeping lions.' The carpet is covered with 'mock' dead, the first one that moves is out. With a bit of luck and a lot of 'blind eye' casting, this can sometimes be stretched to home time. One child actually fell asleep. They love anything connected with water. 'Apple dunking' is a huge success if you don't let them drown. One year parents could hardly recognise their soot-covered offspring after a sooty telescope session got out of hand.

They seem to have preconceived ideas about fun activities. Long ago, at one of my sister's parties a girl spent the time standing on her head. Nothing could persuade her the right way up, so we ignored her. Eventually we all lost interest in the navy blue bloomers hanging in the corner.

Another important rule is to lock away anything that makes a noise. Unfortunately our piano is unlockable, which means that budding Schuberts can try out their unfinished symphonies. One child who insisted she took piano lessons offered to play for a game of 'musical statues.' As soon as her sticky fingers daubed the keys it didn't take a Rubinstein to realise her deception. Nurturing a sadistic streak of my own I let her continue. I still laugh at the memory of the poor dancers trying their best to struggle on as she hit the incongruent notes rapturously, for almost thirty minutes.

Boys are much easier to please. Our son and his mates used to eat everything except the print off the table first, then retire to the garden to play cricket. When son got tired of holding the bat they all had a good fight until they were worn out and ready to go whistling home. Then they graduated to a successful 'speedway' outing. One of my happiest childhood memories is a visit to 'Make Mine Music' at the Ritz, then off home to a fish and chip supper.

We ate out this year for the twenty-first celebration. I hope this will be the start of something permanent!

It's good to have a cry

WHEN did you last let your eyelids down and enjoy a really good cry? Not just a moist, prickly flicker, but a shoulder-shaking, tension-relieving, not to mention medicinal, weep.

Although we are all slapped to tears the moment we are born, a dry-eyed status seems to be a desirable asset as we mature, as if a trembly chin and bubbly eyes were something to be ashamed of. But tears are not all antiseptic eye-wash, they also lubricate and beautify – according to an ancient keep-fit manual I refer to from twinge to twinge. I have had my share of practice but I have yet to see them enhance my appearance. Mine are definitely the ugly type, featuring blood-shot eyes and blotchy cheeks.

I notice most TV heroines not only manage to expel one elegant salt-drop at a time, but each one is perfectly trained to follow the same trail and after a gentle blot with a tissue the eyes and face resume their original glossiness.

So it gave me supreme pleasure to note the nauseating weeper messing up the screen recently. One hero had to kiss a tear-soaked, runny-nosed damsel in 'Another Bouquet.' Even when he broke away she was still unglamorously attached to him by salivary threads. As we were all laying bets as to how far they would stretch it took a certain amount of pathos out of their passion.

But all the vigorous bed swapping had turned it into a comedy, anyway. It says a lot for their acting when they manage to keep their own faces straight.

What makes us cry? We share our laughs, why not our griefs? There are enough disasters around to tremble the firmest chin; food mountains, futile deaths, hooliganism and cuts in education.

Perhaps nostalgia or sentimentality evokes our tears. Some catastrophies cut too deep to be relieved by mere tears. The sort that make you feel that someone has you by the solar plexus. You long to dissolve the tension but remain painfully dry-eyed. Our bank statement has us in such a grip at the moment.

Sometimes when I am iced to the wall at the bus stop, scanning the bleak horizon for a bus that never comes, I feel an uncomfortable bubble of rage well up from the pit of my stomach until it almost chokes me.

I don't need to ask the feminine side of our household what provokes their watery outbursts. Deep depressions and assorted tears are an occupational hazard, caused by poverty (theirs), homework, friends, washing up and my inadequacies.

What brings tears to your eyes? I asked our male element. Their answers were varied: 'Paying my board, bashing my finger with a hammer and watching Crossroads, says son. 'Onions' from dad. Men are more ashamed of showing emotion than women. Some cannot bear to face female outbursts, Harold Wilson was one – according to Joe Haines.

My family think it a huge joke if television induces me to tears. Seeing as it is responsible for a lot of my wailing, this is most disconcerting.

I am not a football fan, but I always find the Cup Final a great tear-jerker. When the victorious captain goes berserk with the cup it's impossible to stay dry-eyed. Last year when Lawrie McMenemy stopped gnashing his chewing gum and allowed his pride to show, I sniffed appreciatively. Liz Taylor has wrung a 'flood' from me over the years, and no one was more thankful than I was when Lassie finally did come home.

Witnessing another's defeat makes me cry. 'Weep with them that weep,' urged St Paul. Although prone to self- pity I do sometimes dab my eyes for others. During the showing of the Vancouver Empire Games film of 1954, when the brave figure of marathon runner Jim Peters crept into the stadium and he struggled desperately to guide his rubbery limbs over the last lap, our handkerchiefs were dripping. With the crowd screaming encouragement he collapsed, before he reached the tape. Just the thought of all that effort brings the tears again. A friend tells me she cries every time she sees the Queen. I want to mop my eyes every time I hear a seventy-eight-year-old widow friend thank God and count her blessings. She is partially deaf and recently had to discontinue her newspapers, even with the aid of reading glasses and a magnifying glass the words are indecipherable.

Oscar Wilde was jeered and laughed at by passengers as he stood in his convict's attire on the central platform of Clapham Junction. In his last work of prose, 'De Profundis,' written during the final days of his confinement in Reading Gaol, he describes his humiliation. 'For half an hour I stood there in the grey November air surrounded by a jeering mob. For a year after that was done to me, I wept every day at the same hour for the same space of time.' As if to decry his despair he goes on to say, 'That is not as tragic as it sounds. To those who are in prison, tears are a part of every day's experience.'

My son and I once spent a week crying at the same hour. He was upstairs in his cot, I was sitting in the stairs. We were following the 'Let him cry' technique, but we gave in first – setting the precedent for future evenings we placed him downstairs in his carrycot. Life brightened considerably. Every night he played with his toes until he was tired, then I would awaken my mate and we all toddled to bed gratefully. Now we sit playing with our toes waiting until he is tired enough to come home!

When crippled children were refused accommodation in a Yorkshire holiday park because of the alleged effect on other holidaymakers, it brought tears to my eyes.

Of course people are upset by the handicaps of others – so they should be – if only to remind them of their own abilities and the duties that go with them.

On holiday last year we joined a small queue of elderly people at a theatre side door. We hadn't noticed at first, but it gradually became embarrassingly obvious we were the only members in the queue who were not disabled. The rest were physically and mentally handicapped. A woman in front made the children giggle when she twined her arms round her companion's neck and kissed her.

Their excitement showed in their happy smiles that kept spreading over their faces. When the doors opened my smile disappeared. 'This entrance is for the disabled only,' said a red-blazered youth. But when I mentioned the shooting pains in my left leg he grinned and allowed us in. We saw the small party many times later and gradually accepted their deformities naturally.

Of course it is disturbing to see their hardship, but a thousand times more disturbing not to see them enjoying their right to a happy holiday as anyone else.

Spring – then summer!

NO DOUBT about it there is a balmy suspicion of spring in the air.

Our bright little chorus of crocuses are victoriously pointing through the weeds at the sun again, the call of a stray gas-man rends the March air as he drills away on a nearby pavement; delicate entrails of dust are haunting our bedroom ceilings.

Although these floating threads drive my fastidious partner spring feverish, I find they have a pleasant soporific effect on me. Watching them waft about soon has me dozing off.

While others greet this season with disinfectant, I am busy preparing my old deck chair and brochures for some serious outdoor study. Our holiday is booked, now all we have to do is save up the small fortune it will take to finance it. By the time the week arrives I should know every face in the brochure, I study them all closely for any visible signs of discontent.

Of course I do a certain amount of extra cleaning. Instead of running the vac over the hearthrug I shake it, and on Monday mornings I can often be seen searching the shrubbery with a pile of wet sheets hanging round my neck. Most of my clothes pegs disappeared with the Swallows, running my fingers through the weeds is always a prelude to the 'hanging out' season.

As I hold the ladder for my duster-happy handyman I often ponder on my unorthodox cleaning characteristics; perhaps a wash-leather earlier on in life frightened me.

It's hard to imagine life without my double layer of winter wool as it is to visualise my midriff without its excess layers of Yorkshire pudding and winter diet but if Jimmy Carter can cast his 'cardy' and jeans so can I. Jim Callaghan has already bought his Easter present for the American president. A local Kirkburton factory had some suiting made up especially for him with the initials JC cunningly woven into the pin-stripe. With the immortal 'Miss' Lilian in her personalised T-shirt and Jimmy in his initialled suit, they should make a lovely couple.

Have you ever taken a really truthful stare at your reflection? I mean without pulling yourself together first. I have – not a pretty sight! It's always a shock to see my other half anyway as my kitchen mirror only shows my head and shoulders. The other day I caught an unrehearsed glimpse of myself in full sag and realised that the best way towards home improvement was mine.

I decided to try a sage hair rinse. The resulting concoction smelled similar to chicken gravy, but I swear my hair is more manageable. Not that anyone has noticed, although the dog does lift his nose and sniff appreciatively every time I pass his basket. I am strongly addicted to anything herbal and firmly believe that nature has a cure for anything – providing you can find it.

This is not just folklore, there is a lot of truth behind the old wives' tales. Foxglove tea was an old remedy for people with heart problems. It has been discovered since, that this hat-shaped flower contains digitalis, a substance used in the control of heart disease today. Dock leaves that soothed away our nettle stings contains a valuable anti-irritant – antihistamine. With the addition of garlic, onions have a marked effect on

117

the lowering of blood cholesterol – which is considered to be one of the causes of hardening of the arteries. Researchers in 'The Lancet' admitted this a year ago. So these country remedies are not to be scoffed at, so pass the blackberry wine please!

We all have our own ways of paralysing the wrinkles. Paul Newman plunges his head in a bucket of cold water every morning. With the aid of a snorkel he stays there for twenty minutes. Not to be recommended for people like me who can barely stand a gentle dab with aired water before breakfast. Before Elinor Glin sank on to the tiger skin she scrubbed her arms and face with a dry nailbrush and always slept with her head facing North – probably it helped to cool her blood! Audrey Hepburn washes her elfin looks in Givenchy soap and water five times a day, and believes in lots of sleep, I could afford the latter.

If one cannot slim – buy a supportable swimsuit, I say. There is certainly a wide choice all with hidden assets, stout cups, firm-hold for lumpy hips, but I haven't found my type yet. I am looking for a sort of Victorian variety with bloomer legs to cover my ex-chorus girl thighs, which are rapidly going to seed. And if only I could find a bathing cap that didn't make me look like Kojak! The blossom-covered creations are pretty but I look more like a wedding guest than a bathing belle does. It's strange but although I normally shun handbags, whenever I walk to a pool, I long for one to hold – preferably an outsize one!

Now that lighter evenings are here and we start weaning the children away from television it's the usual protest 'What can we play at?' All the playing out games of our youth seem to be gone forever.

Long before the washing up rattle started we were heading for the 'lamp' in winter or the woods in summer. Anyone who hasn't played 'tin can squat' around the lamp post has missed a vital part of education in my opinion. Then there was 'hide and seek,' 'I draw a snake' and whip and top delights, ball games against the wash kitchen wall, 'When I was one I ate a plum,' if anyone saw you drop the ball, you were out.

If the company was mixed we acted out the latest Tarzan film – the lads going hunting for crab-apples and rhubarb or other delicacies left unattended, while we 'native' girls waited in the cave with wick-infested blossom stuck in our hair.

Sometimes we played 'truth or dare' – most entertaining of all. Even if you chose 'truth' with a little ingenuity it became a 'dare.' 'Is it true that if I tell you and Tarzan to (something suitably disgusting) you will?' I blush to say we usually did!

In retrospect, of course, childhood summers stretched from March to September, a blissfully endless season of discovery. Even cracking bubbly gum had its exciting moments. A friend and I used to stand hours laughing at our reflection in a neighbour's low window. Practising our largest bubbles, and designing the funniest set of pink false teeth.

We were so carried away by our amusing display we didn't notice the threatening fist inside the window until it was too late. When the owner came galloping out with a long brush however we soon got the message. You couldn't see our black pumps for dust and before long we were rolling about laughing in the long grass nearly swallowing our bubbly gum in delirium. The five o'clock mill buzzer announced dad's imminent hometime and we walked jubilantly home, our gum stuck on our noses. But after my mother and our irate neighbour-in-waiting had finished with me I confess I felt like sticking it somewhere else!

A wife in disguise!

ONE of my favourite fantasies used to be compiling a long list of luxuries I would enjoy if somebody left me £100.

I even infected the children with this make-believe. During our 'saving up' periods we have worked this 'let's pretend' in most of the stores, astonishing shoppers with, 'Is that £50 or £60 we have spent now, mum?' Naturally fantasies have to be adjusted like everything else, now £500 would be more acceptable to our immediate requirements.

I confess that spending money is one of my favourite occupations. One of the great joys in my life is to ride into town with a full wallet and spend an exciting afternoon emptying it. Of course to gain this felicitation one must first endure the interim period of saving and lusting.

That is why I sympathise with 'Big Spender' Viv Nicholson and thank God I was never unfortunate enough to win £150,000. The televised version of her book 'Spend, Spend, Spend' had us realising how rich we really are. Money could not buy her the one commodity she craved – love. Never having experienced it, she was unable to recognise love when it lay under her feet in the shape of her first husband.

Describing his slavish attentions she laughed at the way he accepted her brash ways and derided him for putting up with anything that made her happy. 'Well, that's not love, is it?' she asks pathetically. One thing is certain, Vivienne is a survivor and one day I hope she finds the answer and recognises it. Another 'Big Spender' playwright, Lionel Bart must be sleeping easier these days, he has just become a fully paid-up member of the human race again. A millionaire before his bankruptcy charge, he now faces the future with a clean slate and a new philosophy – to hang on to his next million.

I have a weakness for 'How to Succeed' books which I have never been able to master. Last week found me trying to digest Mirabel Morgan's threat to women's lib, 'The Total Woman' – 188 pages on how to captivate your man. I am only half way through which makes me a sub-total at present.

The first chapter, 'The Organisation Woman,' has had me in its clutches for three full and extremely tidy days. Being the original 'woman in a dressing gown' this was aimed right at me. For the first time in my life I have been able to say 'sit down' without doing a removal job first. For three consecutive evenings the communal meal has been steaming on the table, all the family had to do was sit down and raise it to their mouths. For the same number of evenings they have all been unavoidably detained.

I am now suitably immersed in the 'Happy Homecoming' bit where wives are advised to put new life into teatime by donning a 'costume.' Anything will suffice as long as it is different. Be a pixie girl, a gipsy or even a showgirl suggests Mirabel. Her initial experiment at home time featured a 'Baby Doll' outfit, her pink shorty pyjamas plus white boots soon had him playfully chasing her around the baked beans.

As I am struggling with a reluctant coal merchant at the moment who seems to be delivering my order via Alaska, my regular 'costume' of mountaineering socks, trousers and two of husband's shapeless sweaters would best fit the description of 'Eskimo Nell.'

While I love the idea of dressing up – 'when he opens the front door make it like opening a surprise package' coos Mirabel, I cannot help thinking the transition from Eskimo to Baby Doll may be too drastic for a start. No point in giving him heart failure before we reach the 'Fizzle and Sizzle' chapter.

Are the children ready for this costume period? I can imagine our teenage son's comment if I open the door one day dressed like a pixie.

Determined to be a dedicated student though, I did the next best thing for a blustery March teatime. After the advocated and I must say delicious bubble bath, I ignored my trouser uniform, donned a skirt, applied some make-up and combed my hair, then waited eagerly for the prophesied result. 'Your marriage will begin to sizzle, etc.'

'Where are you off to?' was the first eyebrow-raised comment from the children. After tea my captivated beloved went straight upstairs and washed the bathroom ceiling. This book should do wonders for my spring cleaning. What do pixies wear these days?

Some males are more perceptive than others are. I realised how observant mine was when I first decided to rinse out my stray greys. Days later I felt his gaze on my 'dark plume' tresses. 'Just stand still a minute love,' he said as he carefully rearranged my hairstyle. Then with a yell of triumph he pounced. 'Grey hairs' he cried as he lovingly amputated the few I had missed.

Some of Mirabel's advice has to be slightly modified like the suggestion of a phone call to the office telling hubby 'I crave for your body.' Still if my coal does ever arrive I could need some help with the spadework, so I may just be making that call.

A good job I hadn't succumbed to the pixie outfit, I mused, the other teatime when I opened the back door to a handsome young telephone engineer. 'Are you having trouble with your receiver?' he asked as he fell over the dog. I looked around our unusually tidy household – so that was it – no distracting telephone calls. Hoping it was something serious I led him in to the hall. Our daughter's doll 'Sweet April' was perched on the telephone with the receiver balanced delicately on her lap. 'Well it's the first time I've come across anything so funny.' Once again, I felt glad I hadn't found a pixie shop.

There is a distressing side to the book. All the case histories supplied as bad examples sound just like me. It's a miracle I still have a spouse.

If ever Yehudi Menuhin's wife writes a book I shall be the first to buy it. In a recent interview her violinist husband devoted his pleasures as 'having a job to do like preparing a sonata or cooking something in the kitchen with my dear wife.' As his wife left the room he whispered 'Isn't she superb?' She certainly must be. Definitely not the way Pierre Trudeau would describe his reluctant partner.

After a week of trying to be a 'Total Woman' I have come to the conclusion that what we femmes really need is an enterprising young homme to write a sequel called 'Total Man' with lots of heady advice to all chauvinists and 'how to make your wife adore you,' I'll buy that.

Rise and - yes shine!

WHAT sort of morning face do you present to the world? Are you cheerful, smiley and 'Put the kettle on,' or down at the mouth and 'Shut that door-ish.'

Can you automatically cast the sheets and head for the toothpaste without batting an eyelid, or does your plunge into the coverless need half an hour's careful consideration first?

My energetic leaping partner can bound from his hollow the second the alarm splinters my eardrums, but my unwinding process takes longer. Every morning I awaken to what feels like two lead puddings bulging from my arm sockets. However carefully I arrange my affairs the night before, each morning my 30 denier has me in its blood-clotting embrace. My body is trussed and bound in nylon like a spider's dinner and the dead weight of two bloodless arms has me pinned to the flannelette.

I have tried various styles of slumberwear in my effort to overcome this crude awakening but they all seem to grow strangling tentacles overnight. Narrow straps become steel tourniquets, half-belts give me the 'hump,' high-waisted yokes leave me with a painfully quilted chest – all necessitate an elongated recovery period, there is no short cut. I have tried releasing the pressure gradually but it only prolongs the pain. Once I manage tentatively to undam the bloodstream the excruciating tingle that slowly creeps down each arm finally to prick the sausagey fingers is enough to shrivel anyone's benevolence.

No wonder birds can wake up singing, they don't wear nylon nighties. All this confirms that I am a miserable morning person, ever searching for a mode of undress that does not feature the dreaded tangle-tingle. By some slow and painful metamorphosis all the nighties have emerged looking like fussy ballgowns and the evening dresses are beginning to resemble night-gowns.

One Christmas I received an ambitious floaty two-tiered affair that looked promising. Unfortunately during the night the top layer became trapped underneath my sleeping partner's heavy anatomy and when I turned over it split up to the first button. With my usual early morning aplomb I didn't notice the damage until I caught a bathroom occupant staring quizzically at my new cut-away front.

The slippery satin creations look divine, but I already have a sadly neglected satin housecoat, which always provokes an icy sensation of having been rubbed down with an iced lolly whenever I try to wear it. Pyjamas always haunt me with that back to front feeling.

My husband does not share this problem. No holiday counterpane would look complete without his neatly folded pyjamas. I bought them to celebrate his first illness of our marriage – before I could ring the doctor I had to rush out and buy them. I think they still retain their original creases; ah yes, they don't make them like that any more.

The only compliment I can pay the man-made fibres is that they are easily dried. They are not easy to wash, as water temperature has to be carefully controlled with only a suggestion of the spinner to dry, and in my opinion look tatty and unironed when left just to drip. White nylon school blouses are a disaster, we never had one yet that lived up to its colour after washing. Do the men who make it ever sleep in it – or on it – I wonder?

Its static properties are also a nuisance. I have a skirt that clings to my legs like a pair of tights and snaps frighteningly back at me when I try to dislodge it. I consider it an unhealthy fabric, but mixed with cotton or wool it does have crease-resistant advantages.

I saw a beautiful white cotton broderie anglaise trimmed negligee set the other day with matching mop-cap which looked reasonably priced until I realised this was only for the cap. But I long to possess it, if only I could be sure it would behave in bed. Would it change into a choking octopus the moment we hit the sheets?

Would the cap finish up dangling from hubby's aertex, like the antiquated hair-nets my mother used to wear? The caption underneath amused me, though – Women's size only. It wouldn't suit him anyway.

What I really want is something in soft, cuddly, interlock material, a loose-fitting kaftan style, something that will not make me feel as if I have just wrestled three rounds with Jackie Pallo – when I reluctantly have to leave the arms of Morpheus. You can keep the pretty lace trims, which feel like frayed wire netting on sensitive skins; stimulating male adrenaline takes second place to keeping my circulation flowing.

It's surprising how swiftly golden slumbers can kiss the eyes of the elderly. Once on holiday, a lady who I had never met before fell asleep on my shoulder as we shared a park bench. I was enjoying a few quiet seconds waiting for the children to spend up so we could go to tea, when I felt her weight slip slowly on to my shoulder. An hour later with the sun slowly sinking behind the heads of my bored and impatient sycophants and the goose pimples rising swiftly on my bare arms, I sat in the empty park racking my brains for some way to arouse the unknown sleeping beauty at my side. Eventually her own snores penetrated her slumber and we slipped gratefully away.
*

I SHALL definitely not be tuning in to morning television. A laryngitic goldfish would be too noisy for me to face at breakfast. Richard Baker's radio programme is the only contact I can stomach with the outside world at this time of day what with cornflakes being thrown into dishes, a yawning

123

dog, and screams of 'Where's this?' 'Who moved that . . . . ?' my sensitive acoustics are not ready for the onslaught of morning television. Actually the distant call of a nearby bowling green is presenting promising opposition to evening viewing, and anyway I can burn toast just looking out of the window.

But I have taken up a new position. I can no longer be described as sedentary. Once again I have become a cyclist. Last Tuesday evening – the safest time to launch myself on unsuspecting motorists and hopefully washing-up time for most of my acquaintances – saw my initial pedal-in.

Feeling a shade conspicuous with a handbag swinging under my chin and trouser bottoms sweeping the road, I pedalled as elegantly as I could up Manchester Road homewards. Thankfully the call of Hawaii Five-O proved stronger than the urge to ridicule, and my family did not witness my touchdown outside our garden gate. My exhaustion was such I found it easier to fall off than climb off. When I get the use back in my legs again, I'll let you know if it's doing me any good!

Awaiting the patter . . .

NOW we know for certain that she is definitely having a little Scorpio, Princess Anne's impetuous announcement has denied us the one pleasure we all love – speculation.

There will be no need for significant nods and nudges concerning the Royal waistline now her sweet mystery of life is public knowledge. But, understandably, first babies are too exciting to keep to oneself. I told half a dozen people about ours on the way home from the doctors.

It's afterwards when the seconds come along and you are fully aware how long nine months of answering the ubiquitous inquiries of how you feel can be, that you camouflage your new development as long as possible. As one's family increases it's surprising how long the mystery can be sustained.

As she was the only one of our babies to start life in a new pram, our fifth baby caused the most excitement in our household.

We managed to keep the secret until two months before her arrival. The clan were duly gathered together, and trying to make it sound as thrilling as the new bike Father Christmas would not be bringing again this year, I announced the forthcoming event.

The two youngest performed a frenzied dance of ecstasy, luckily we had struck a high status note here and they could hardly wait to present the news to the school-yard. Our eldest had guessed anyway, but eleven-year-old son was the most incredulous. 'Blimey!' he exclaimed when his speech returned, 'How many more are we gonna have?' A thought I confess had crossed our minds.

Being a princess naturally presents certain public life pressures, but I imagine it reduces some of the private fears, like 'Shall I be able to cope?' or 'Am I responsible enough?'

Once I had recovered from the shock and realisation that, contrary to popular belief, I was all there, my biggest worry was my lack of maternal instinct which, as it often has since, lay deeply dormant during my first pregnancy.

I was haunted by thoughts of the sub-standard mothers featured in relatives' conversation that 'couldn't rear a dog,' and 'ought not to be allowed.' I was a novice at pram talk and still imagined matinee coats were what film-stars went to the pictures in. In only four months of marriage I hadn't really mastered the 'little wife' act.

Fortunately my maternal instinct arrived with baby, in a highly con-centrated form. The realisation that this noisy red-cheeked bundle had to be fed and watered every time I wanted to put my feet up, overwhelmed me. I don't know who was more alarmed by our first meeting – baby or me. It took us weeks to get over it, night after night we cried ourselves to sleep.

Then a sadistic friend added to my problems with a saga on 'Don't neglect your husband – first baby could mean first crisis.' Leave him out? We never left him alone, he was even included in breast-feeding arrangements. I did the first stint – getting baby from cot to my place, then daddy got the wind up and performed the transfer of full baby back to cot.

It worked well for a time but it became increasingly difficult to arouse fond father and I gradually resumed full responsibility. If only breast milk came in see-through containers half the anxieties would be dissolved.

Will Princess Anne follow in mother's footsteps and have baby at home? I have experienced both and the only disadvantage in births 'in your own midin' as our family doctor used to put it, are the continuous evening feeds. In hospital mums are allowed to sleep through.

I suppose Royals also miss the advantages of the weekly 'bottle' parties. The invitation to 'attend the ante-natal clinic and don't forget to bring your bottle.' All the fun of the weekly maternity market where you wobble in feeling reasonably well then spend long hours sprawling around the corridors bulge to bulge, surrounded by science fiction on all sides, until you finally reach what looks like a tissue-lined, plastic padded shelf with no ladder provided to help you reach it. 'It took me three days to have our Fred,' one experienced mother told me, 'then I had to be seduced!'

After dying a thousand deaths wondering how swollen ankles have to be before you confess, a stranger in a white coat carelessly throws back the blanket you are modestly clutching, lifts your mini gown and starts warming his hands on your future asset. When you have both exhausted your repertoire of 'ehs?' and 'pardons' thoughts of conversation are rejected and he leaves you for another.

The claustrophobic atmosphere must affect the staff. There is a rumour almost as fiercely pervading as the stench of disinfectant that no matter how hard they try, nurses can on no account learn to love 'softies.'

So when one arrives to pump your pressure you give her a winning smile. The harder they pump the wider you smile. It's the same technique as the doll our eight-year-old had for Christmas – every time you squeeze her hand her mouth opens. But one does feel at a distinct disadvantage in that sterile atmosphere. I got the paranoic feeling more than once, that is exactly how they would like to see me.

The lovely part of home confinements is that husbands are always on hand. My first hour in hospital after mine had been whisked away without even a wave, was the loneliest I have ever spent. No time allowed to whisper last-minute thoughts that mums-to-be long to express at this time, like 'please take me home' or 'I've changed my mind.' Although I had already given birth twice in our front bedroom I was ignorant of hospital procedure.

I couldn't help feeling curious about what looked like fishing tackle hung in an adjoining cubicle, an outsize plastic mac and sou'wester dangled over an enormous pair of wellies. I hadn't been there long when a doctor promised he would rupture my membranes if I hadn't 'started' by morning.

Wondering if he had taken an instant dislike to me I consulted a fellow sufferer. It sounded even worse in plain English. 'He's going to break your waters.' She had suffered this indignity a few times and was eager to pass on the details. I never did hear the whole story, when she got to the part where Doc donned his fishing gear, our daughter was well on the way and I was spared the epilogue.

I really tried to believe in Dick Grantly Reed's book - 'Natural Childbirth,' and I read all the legends available on 'Painless Childbirth.' Between gasps of gas and air and pleas for my pethidine shot I struggled to keep the image of the natives who squat and gave birth at the roadside uppermost in my mind. Each time I came to the same conclusion, I am a registered coward.

One occasion I did turn my thoughts to an epidural, but have you seen the size of the needle?

Actually I found the relaxation classes a good help psychologically. But you can't beat having an efficient midwife and doctor in attendance and I am sure Princess Anne is assured of that.

I like the Eastern image given to mother, who is considered the spiritual heart of the family. 'Heaven is under her feet,' says the Koran, the Moslem holy book – and that's where you find most children!

Old wives – but true tales

CONSIDERING the ancient cures featured in the news recently, future hospital visiting may take on a whole 'new look.'

Instead of the proverbial grapes and orange juice, our baskets could be bulging with paw-paw fruits and do-it-yourself acupuncture kits.

A festering transplant wound cured with paw-paw strips; an inflamed hip joint relieved of pain by two matchsticks – sounds like a witchdoctor's diary, nevertheless it is fact and no doubt a lot of old-fashioned remedies will enjoy a revival following these revelations. Most families have inherited their share of folklore usually well bound in superstitions.

Regarding my vestless state as slightly immoral, my mother often relates that I owe my life to brown paper and grandmother's 'rubbing bottle,' her cure for bronchial pneumonia. From crackly brown paper wrapped around my chest I graduated to Thermogene wadding vests. Its pungent smell not only discouraged bronchitis, but also most of my friends. I only tolerated it because it added size to my unvital statistics, how I longed for them to be vital enough for me to wear a bra.

The rubbing bottle rested permanently in our hearth, a concoction of all the penetrative oils you could acquire. One sniff could cure catarrh from twenty paces. My mother's hands and a drop from this bottle were a deadly com-bination, her inflammatory massage could pulverise any complaint from a sore throat to a sprained ankle. The only organ that defeated her was my appendix.

I had an aunt whose guide to good health was an oyster bar on Blackpool sands. As a small bucket and spade carrier I used to gaze billiously at what looked like lumps of lime green slime, waiting in their gritty beds to be sucked alive into my aunt's stomach. Her proud acclamation concerning their restorative properties never fooled me. Considering she had only one kidney left and had also undergone a mastectomy, her claim 'They clear out your stomach,' sounded an understatement to my way of thinking.

In the past 'luck' played an important part in one's welfare. A lot of the superstitions sound too far-fetched to be taken seriously today, yet they had a strange habit of coming true. It was considered unlucky to place new shoes on our table. This was a fact – anyone who absentmindedly forgot, received an ear-stinging swipe to prove it!

My father's mother was the original 'old wife.' She could usually find some reason to stop us doing anything interesting. Hair and nails could never be cut on Sunday, whistling women - usually me – were shushed violently, spiders were revered, I still cannot pluck up the courage to murder one. Thankfully she never heard the one about children's weak bladders being cured by eating three roasted mice! Although I imagine it could be quite effective, I think just a suggestion of this would be efficacious!

Many scoff at the old superstitions attributing them to ignorance and the primitive. But how many of us has not said 'Bless you' to a sneeze? It was believed that sneezing forced evil spirits from the body evoking this necessary blessing. Who can resist the temptation to throw spilled salt over the left shoulder? This is where the Devil was supposed to be and a pinch thrown over the shoulder atoned for the evil of wasting such a precious commodity.

Cornelius Vanderbilt, a self-made millionaire whose statue stands outside Central Station, New York, hired spiritualists to get in touch with his dead mother when he was ill. Defying doctors he used the mustard plasters she advised and lived to be eighty-three. Although a powerful character supposedly afraid of no-one he had each leg of his bed set in salt – to keep evil spirits from attacking him while he slept.

Feel as if this winter has been the hardest yet? Take heart, more than 400 years before Mrs Dale, Samuel Pepys was telling his now famous diary, 'I am now in perfect good health, and though last winter has been as hard a winter as any have been these many years, yet I was never better in my life. Now I am at a loss to know whether it be my hare's foot which is my preservative, for I never had a fit of the colic since I wore it, or whether it be a pill of turpentine I take every morning.' Personally I should keep taking the tablets.

'Spit' is also considered lucky. We used to spit on green 'lucky stones' (among other things) and make a secret wish. Mine were mostly concerned with an evacuee who stayed next door. Unfortunately the war ended before they could all be realised.

In April, 1967 it was recorded that a substance contained in the saliva of vampire bats can dissolve blood clots, which could help thrombosis sufferers.

Since seeing a professional do it, I spit on my palms when I am bowling. I haven't noticed it brings me much luck yet, unless you count the fact that I have not had to buy many drinks since joining our bowling team. This privilege is reserved for the winner.

The ancient adverts depicting the wonders of 'Fennings' whose varying doses can cure anything from flu to diphtheria are taken from an amusing little book, 'Good things, made, said and done for every Household.' Printed in 1893 long before the Trades Description Act, the pages are filled with wallet-starving delights like 'beef steak pie' for which one is advised to 'take three or four pounds of beef steak and a pound of bullock's kidney.' All are garnished with proverbial and homespun philosophies such as 'A blunt knife shows a dull wife,' 'Too much bed makes a dull head.' I plucked this unique little gold embossed album from a dusty pile in some junk shop for just a few pence. I find it as interesting and stimulating as any novel, especially the adverts. The trouble with cookery books is I spend so much time reading them I haven't any time left to cook.

I suppose manufacturers will now be gathering the paw-paw and set about synthesising the effective healing ingredient – then having done that, trying to improve on it. Dr W Thomson the author of 'Herbs and Heal' believes this process may make it dangerously potent. He believes that some of the drugs obtained from herbs are more effective and safer than those manufactured in a laboratory.

I believe modern drugs play an important part in our lives – where would we be without penicillin? But I also consider it a duty to promote good health by feeding our bodies natural foods as fresh as possible and try not to lean too heavily on 'convenience' foods. Let us not forget the anti-infection properties of hops. I fortify myself regularly with my own herbal 'brews.' This is the time of year to start preparing your Balm and Rhubarb elixir to build up your holiday spirits – so Good Health!

Growing happiness

WITH the sunlight sparkling on her dewy gums, she mopped her eyes, blew her nose and gave the cashier a few coppers in exchange for the cube of yeast.

'Eeh a'm reight 'appy when a'm baking bread agin,' she told me, as I tried to hide my sliced loaf sticking out of my wire basket.

I watched her leave the shop, her dough-dreaming grey eyes shining with happiness – a charming example that this elusive ingredient can still be found in simple pleasures. It was recently revealed in a survey of over 1,000 people that only 5% were content with the pleasant life and 32% wanted to make as much money as possible.

Taking time off from shortening my already dwindling clothes-line to make yet another skipping rope, our youngest daughter informed me the other day, 'Mum, I forgot to tell you, I think I'm getting a sore throat, my left ear has been aching and I am starting with eczema again.' With a satisfied sigh she continued her skipping – it doesn't take much to make some of us happy.

Take our three market gardeners for instance – that's my husband, son and neighbour. Only a month ago they appeared to be leading a reasonably ful-filling existence. Tired of snoozing the evenings away in front of the TV, one had even taken to switching off and with suitably intellectual expression he now spends most evenings dozing with a book on his knee.

The other two had developed their own unique method of survival which consisted mainly of regular elbow exercising and much internal fortification ready for any threat of a drought. Seemingly they were quite content to blear at life through rose-coloured eyeballs. Then came the message that transformed their lives. A six-year dream came true in the shape of a plot of land. My enthusiast husband and semi-enthusiastic neighbour, and, when he cannot escape, our son, are desperately trying to prove 'the answer lies in the soil.'

Wrapped in furs and scarves and refusing the offer of a spade, we females were dragged from our room temperature to see how the land lay. After an initial glance my first thought was how could there possibly have been an earthquake so near without us noticing? As loud as we dare we supposed optimistically that yes there must surely be soil lurking somewhere underneath the wreckage.

But the men were besotted. I have never known such a load of rubbish to have this aesthetic effect on my husband. The sight of our living room on his unexpectedly early home-comings never affected him like this. Yet here he was proclaiming ugly little peaks of broken glass a potato patch, a pile of tin cans and wooden boxes were described as an onion bed. We girls managed to sneak away without voicing an opinion.

But I must admit we started reaping a 'harvest' after only a week. An ancient pot vase was unearthed and filled with palm it now sits prettily on the hall-stand. They also dug up an old-fashioned earthenware bread crock that now houses some of my geraniums.

The dynamic trio have literally put new life into their patch and it really is beginning to resemble a garden. They all have their different functions, the young recalcitrant believes no garden is complete without a fire and the other two have built a most impressive compost heap. All visitors act as advisers, we find. We females gasp admiringly, when it's not raining. The children spend most of their time jumping from path to path. It was only as our gardener was pointing out the newly planted seedlings interspersed between the neatly weeded paths that I realise one confused daughter was actually jumping from seedling to seedling, carefully avoiding the paths. When we arrived at the onions, there was a newly arranged 'sunken garden' in the shape of two size three wellington soles. The depressed onions seem to have passed away. Lost for words we looked accusingly at the dog, who helpfully irrigated the remaining onions.

We were duly reprimanded and released with a caution but the dog still has the death penalty hanging over his fertilising instincts. My husband probably remembers the occasion when his old gardening trousers were mistaken for a tree – while he was still wearing them.

An irate householder brandishing a broom was once giving me her views on people like me, and their incontinent pets. In the meantime mine got tired of waiting for a more suitable place and to her apoplectic annoyance and my deep red shame, illustrated her complaints admirably, just inside her gate. I still tiptoe past her house.

Something exciting happens every day on our gardening calendar. One night we were all shushed to silence around the television while a chap wearing a natty 'hacking' jacket performed a transplant operation. Up to his neck in muck and punnets he explained the drama in hushed tones as he went along. 'Oi just break the root gently away loik that and plant it here loik so.' Then like all 'show-offs' he demonstrates the perfect growth he arranged the week before, which he takes from a ledge underneath. Actually I wish surgeons could do this with us. How comforting when an operation is imminent for him to bring out a successfully recovered patient. 'I have here a lady who had her operation years ago and still speaks to me,' type of thing.

The memory of our gardeners the evening they discovered free manure will linger for a long time, especially around the porch area where the boots live.

One day I arrived home to find a frail young man struggling up the front steps with what looked like an enormous roll of carpeting wrapped in brown paper. 'Where do you want it, love?' he managed to gasp.

Looking at the manufacturer's name I realised somewhat incredulously this must be the new greenhouse. When I told him it was for my husband's allotment and surely it couldn't be all there, he looked at me with a similar expression.

I got tired of explaining to visitors that the carpet rolled up in the back yard was actually a greenhouse and couldn't wait for Saturday and the big 'build-up.' A light hurricane gaily bashing the dustbin lids about had them off to an early start. Humming what now seemed to be my regular theme song since our house had been deserted for the garden, 'Everyone's Gone to the Moon,' I filled a flask and went to view.

My song had never been more appropriate, with high winds mistaking the plastic roofing for a kite, the three stalwarts hanging on were almost moon bound. They were struggling bravely to keep their feet on the ground. But a pound or two of nails and plenty of banging had it looking like a plastic tent. They looked so happy it seemed a shame to break them off for their bowling match.

Sometimes as I sprawl across our empty settee listening to the wind tantalising the half-remaining hinge on the coal house door, I dream of the greengrocery bill I won't have to pay soon, and smile.

There's no need to starve

NO NEED to sit with full-blown eyelids watching Rich Man, Poor Man on television. It's happening all around us, not unfortunately, in glorious technicolour but in despairing shades of black, white and sordid grey.

'World in Action' reported a few distressing facts recently concerning the families of a caretaker, policeman and refuse collector, and their efforts to survive on what they considered unsatisfactory wages.

Out of his £39 take-home pay the refuse collector optimistically put 90p carefully on one side for his weekly dream of riches – the football pools. A typical meal for them was tinned soup, tinned peas and chips. Naturally this did nothing to lighten their darkness and I found it most disturbing. For the same money they could have bought, say, a ham shank and a packet of dried peas then all would have enjoyed the benefit of two decent nutritious meals, with the addition of a little flour and suet it could even have been stretched to three.

The policeman's wife complained because she could not afford fillet steak – I know that lustful feeling well. A large poverty-stricken family with an out of work father once lived in our vicinity. On the nights their members were sent for fish and chips nine times, we were always consumed with envy.

Another soul-destroying programme was featured on TV a couple of years ago about a family of five that were barely existing in appalling slum conditions. Damp paper hung in curls from the walls, water dripping from the roof, un-healthy plumbing, no gas or electricity. The atmosphere was dark and depressing, with pallid half-clad children sat unnaturally silent, not even a book in sight to break the monotony. The only heat in the room came from the glow of the cigarettes that both parents were drawing strength from continu-ously. The highlight of their week was pay-day when they all ate sausage sandwiches.

There is a vital ingredient missing from the lives of these mendicants and it is not just monetary. It's difficult to find the right word – independence, initiative, ingenuity are all near the mark, all prefixed by 'in' denoting that it comes from within a person. Perhaps we should introduce a new subject to the school curriculum, where pupils could be taught to develop their own unique brand of survival instinct.

Everyone deserves the right to earn a living wage, but ideas on this commodity certainly seem to differ. In a newspaper letter one wife admitted she, her husband and two children live happily and healthily on her £85 monthly allowance. This has to cover food, gas and electricity bills, which also includes central heating.

She buys cheap eggs from a local market and manages to keep her family content on chicken wings, roasts of brisket, knuckles of pork and hints darkly on her concoctions with mince.

An executive acquaintance was reminiscing the other day on the splendid meal he and his wife had enjoyed at an Italian restaurant. 'Marvellous cooking, but a bit pricey at £20,' he recalled. Sounds far removed from the 'sausage sarney' luxury, but I know the long hours he works and the years of studying on a near starvation diet that led to his present affluence.

Some lyricists poet on about their mother's eyes; 'It's there – in my mother's eyes,' goes the old song. I always felt the same way about my mother's stews. If we didn't get our chins down they lasted for days. Nutritious and extremely satisfying, interspersed with chunks of home-made bread one day and fluffy dumplings the next. Of course, it was never wise to investigate the ingredients too closely (these were the war years), but some looked very much like the plate-edger's of the previous day. I swear I once came across a pea-pod which my mother, with a miraculously straight face, insisted was cabbage.

She tells me that one can still buy offal and poultry giblets that make excellent soup for 10p a pound.

Pork ribs at 25p per lb are also good pot-boilers. Breast of lamb at 30p per lb is mouth-wateringly tasty, especially when cooked in a barbecue sauce, one of my favourites! With time and patience one can still provide a balanced and nutritious diet on a low income. But let's face it, we all need a little luxury from time to time. The high spot of my week is being served a cup of coffee made by someone else on Saturday afternoons, accompanied on affluent occasions by the most luscious cream cake on display.

When I seemed to have more mouths than money our regular washday lunch was shepherd's pie made from the remains of the Sunday roast. It was this delicacy that threatened to turn our eldest girl into a vegetarian. At three years old she ate all the potato but carefully decorated her plate edge with the minced-up meat. Seeing my formidable expression, 'Sorry mum,' she said 'But I couldn't eat the shepherds.'

Not long ago we saw the 'other side of the coin,' foreign visitors were invading Harrods like a swarm of hungry locusts. Grabbing everything within reach, while back home their traders were standing lonely and unwanted in their silent stores. One Arab girl was thrilled to her diamonds and knew that mummy would be, too, when she saw the fur coat she had managed to buy for less than £700. Others were eagerly filling suitcases with bargains for the rest of their families. One admitted spending £1000 in a few hours.

Greed is spreading its vice-like tentacles like a rabid virus, an infectious threat to us all. We want everything – but now, and almost most of us, I include myself in this category, eat too much – far more than we need.

If you are shopping in town this weekend take five minutes relaxation in the Piazza, sit and watch the bulging shoppers. Listen to the echoing symphony of the rattling tills as the money piles up in the surrounding shops. Count the 'chewers' – not just children but adults. It is a personal matter for individuals how they spend their income, but watching them spend it is certainly an education!

Chapter of accidents!

I FEEL compelled to report a rift in a certain relationship – my bike and I have become slightly strained.

On a balmy afternoon with flies swerving madly in all directions to avoid me, I breezed gaily down a hill at full speed. One minute I was whistling 'Rock Bottom,' next minute I had achieved one. I was on the concrete with the handlebars deeply encased in my full cup.

An assortment of onlookers all with ashen faces begged to drive me home. Naturally I couldn't miss a chance to display my brave and courageous nature, and after replacing my personal effects – a bundle of Co-op stamps and two bus tickets into my bag – I picked up my machine and carried on. After five minutes, a searing pain pierced my chest, changing my kneecaps to jelly.

The biting hurt felt like two or three broken ribs at the very least, possibly a punctured lung, with definite and severe bust displacement. Fifteen palpitating minutes later I was limping into 'Casualty' praying my damaged lungs and ruptured organs hold up until they had time to operate.

A clerk at the other side of a window was speaking in hushed funereal tones to a couple that looked as if they had both just finished donating all their blood to someone. Their diminutive son, who was giving an excellent impression of Napoleon, supported them. Trying with great difficulty not to overwork my punctured lung and fractured kneecap, I stood in the queue. Another little boy wearing a false nose and spectacles came to stand behind. On closer inspection I realised the nose was real and probably broken. He smiled encouragingly and I tried my best to smile bravely back

When it was my turn to give a potted biography the clerk's face lit up. He seemed to regard my 'accident' as light entertainment. My face often has this humorous effect on people, I've noticed it before. By the time we reached my date of birth we were almost chuckling, without moving my tender diaphragm, you understand.

Next it was round the corner to the row of stiff backs – the chairs were un-yieldingly straight, too. I could see that being a casualty was a seriously silent business. It was my first time but I soon got the hang of it. The idea is to fix your eyes on a focus point opposite and the first one to blink is 'out.' However, we did all move our gaze slightly when an elderly woman hobbled in behind her daughter and husband. The younger lady was terribly distressed, it transpired the old lady had inconveniently chosen son-in-laws swimming night to damage her limb.

I took time off from worrying about my painful breathing to dwell on another serious problem, the toilet situation. With a man on one side and a small Indian boy on the other, things looked desperately leg-crossing. I tried some lip service with the lady sitting opposite which fascinated my small companion but left her aloofly unimpressed. Finally, holding my broken body as firmly together as possible while effecting an angle of 45 degrees, I managed to get the message across my neighbour's denim to his wife.

After all that sitting around the journey to the toilet and back seemed wildly exciting, but had it been too much for me? My temperature was probably raging. I amused myself for a while with thoughts of the children taking turns to wheel me around the village.

A kind nurse eventually sorted us out and I was sentenced to a tiny cell with a door at one end and a curtain at the other. She came back with instructions to strip to the waist and get into what looked like a double-bed sized cotton sheet, euphemistically called a 'hospital gown.' Had a few moments indecision here. Should I keep my beads on? I toyed with the idea of removing my headscarf, then, remembering the state of my hair, decided I would look less frightening with it on. There was no need for a mirror – a cleaner came in and almost burst into pitiful tears when she saw me. 'You would think they could find something better,' she muttered to herself. Still, a brown and white spotted scarf and black trousers were not quite the best accessories for this 'Demis Rousses' outfit.

All this waiting could prove nerve-racking for anyone of a nervous disposition. Luckily this situation was not new to me, having read all the best prison survival stories plus Greville Wynne's compelling biography on how he foiled the KGB's efforts to brainwash him.

It is simply a case of concentrating the mind and, as Samuel Johnson remarked, 'When a man knows he is to be hanged in a fortnight, it concentrates his mind wonderfully.'

I struggled to haul my body on to the high-rise bed. At the same time a heart-lurching scream of agony tore down the corridor outside – in two squirts of a syringe I was at the door and would have been halfway home if I hadn't remembered my bizarre outfit. So that was the reason for this ugly 'get-up,' cuts out risk of escape!

Minutes ticked by and hospital sounds closed in. 'This will sting,' preached a gentle voice outside, followed by a violent yell from a profound believer. Were casualties ever forgotten? What if I was still in this 3ft x 4ft tomorrow morning, with blood bubbling all over from my perforated lungs?

I was reminded of a nasty experience I once had at a family planning clinic. After screening me off in the corner of a large room a nurse told me to strip off and lie down until she returned. She left at 9.30am and I was still there at 11am. Mind you, time passed unbelievably swiftly – the room was also being used for interviewing new clientele. After becoming so deeply involved in everyone's contraceptive history I felt it would be unwise to make my presence known. I had to wait until all was silent and then embark on my unique rendition of 'Getting to know you,' until someone remembered me.

More uneasy questions danced in and out of my mind. How would they mend me? Would I be parted from top to bottom?

Unable to stand my exclusive company any longer I pulled the curtain aside, and came face to face with a jolly clerk. He smiled appreciatively at my fancy dress. 'Er . . . I just wondered . .' I began, but a pretty Oriental nurse cut into my wonderment sternly, with an abrupt, 'stay in there please,' and shut me up again. I felt most unwanted.

Some time later with my clothes in a large brown bag and feeling like 'Orphan Annie' I was directed to another chair outside a deserted and shadowy X-Ray department. It felt as cold and silent as a mortuary. A sister startled me by wheeling in and leaving what I hoped was a sleeping body beside my chair. One foot was exposed, I had to fight an overwhelming desire to tickle the foot and make her the 'life and soul' of the party.

In the X-ray room I posed as painlessly as I could, holding my breath obediently, trying not to think of the Norman Wisdom film when they forgot to tell him to breathe out.

Felt a little foolish when the handsome young man had me bent double across the table, wishing I were better dressed for my photograph. Wondered what sort of picture I presented with my black trousered posterior poking out in full view, lifting my trouser hems just enough to reveal my husband's socks which are three sizes too big for me. Still, every job has its perks, I suppose.

At long last I arrived at my final obstacle - a cleaner who was wielding her status as strongly as her polisher - then back to the doctor once more, and he pronounced a 'bruised sternum' and I was duly released on the world to breathe easy again.

Is it painful? Only when I laugh or stop talking about it. The hardest part to bear is not being able to show off all the technicolour bruising – you just have to take my word for it – unfortunately! Unless I keep abreast of the times and decide to go topless!

It's coming out time!

HOORAY! It's almost summer! Well it is at this sunny moment in our back yard, as I sit with my trousers rolled up to my bruises and my polo neck turned down another half inch.

When this East wind stops biting the goose pimples it will be here. But already I have enjoyed one or two hot blinks under my sun hat - as soon as the sun comes out so do I. My sturdy frame can be seen distorting the deck chair stripes whenever possible.

As a friendly masochist reminded me the other day, after June 21st we start 'going back.' Only three weeks to the longest day.

But the signs of summer are all around us. Once again it looks as if a Wild West wagon train has just blown through, every time I sweep the yard. The Kirklees buses are still maintaining their abnormal winter schedule; pre-sumably the flu victims are now on holiday.

The magazine cover girls are uncovering more and more. Angular models with coat hanger shoulders are trying to tempt us all into holiday shape with much expensive preparation. 'What will another hot summer do to your face and body?' asks one. Put new life into it, I hope. Will you be ready to dash for cover after one blistering afternoon, or, like me, wish it would go on forever, or at least through the winter.

The glamorous models do not influence me, how could they? I have never seen one yet with a figure like mine. When are we pleasantly proportioned, cosily plump forties going to be featured? There are a lot of us about, you know, and we are all waiting to be served as glamorously as anyone else.

Although life begins at forty, it is supposed to be an under-cover affair judging by some of the fashion prophets. No women over thirty-five is fit to be seen uncovered, seems to be the message. Knees, arms and chests have to be hidden away. But if, like me, you have your own 'who cares' fashion rules, you can laugh in their hollow cheeks even if it means causing a few yourself.

I am still smarting from my swimsuit parade in front of my panel of judges – my family. No one could stop laughing long enough to comment. My 'stop beating about the bush – does it suit me?' fell on noisy guffaws. But whether it does or not I intend to take the late Winston Churchill' chauvinistic advice and 'fight them on the beaches' or anywhere else I feel like wearing what I want – if necessary.

'There is something very sexy about sun-tanned toes' says one beautician who obviously hasn't seen mine. We once had a tortoise with nicer looking feet than me. Covering the toenails with varnish helps, but guiding the brush over all those ridges with my feet tucked under my chin always makes me feel bilious. Actually, nerves in the feet affect the whole body, so when your feet are comfy, so are you. It makes good sense to start your summer shaping at the bottom - I mean feet, or both.

NOW that Jubilee committees seem to be taking over the country, I am beginning to dread school home time with even more apprehension than usual. Almost as soon as the school bags hit the dog basket the aggravation starts. 'Mum I want . . .' and then there's the ever-threatening cry of the marathon maniacs disturbing the purse day after day.

There ought to be a 'Sponsor of the Jubilee Year' award for hectic sponsoring above and beyond the call of 'booty.' Everything at our house is jubilee flavoured – it's giving me jaundice. Three groans for the red, white and blue.

Even our hardy planter has been infected. 'Psst,' he said from the corner of the greenhouse the other day, 'Want to buy a yard of Union Jack material cheap?' I try to visualise our gardener in a pair of jockey-type red, white and blues, but it seems we are to dress up our flagpole.

I know for a fact he has persuaded our bowling club ladies' committee into organising a jumble sale, and I heard him eagerly discussing under-canvas activities with another. Our children's rooms have been suitably cleared of junk ready for the onslaught of rubbish that finds its way back following a jumble sale.

Our son seems to be the only unconcerned member of a jubilous family. But I suspect his Jubilee celebrations will live up to its stout reputation. I do so admire the committee compulsives and their feverish back-room planning of entertainments for me to support. Events where we see the same faces and and the same crepe trimmings. But I wish we could have one massive 'meet' embracing the whole community and be done with it. This would certainly sustain me for the whole season. Or perhaps a large medieval fayre, a chance to wear up my old outfits.

*

NOW that Whitsuntide is one big flop, a frustrating confusion to most of us, why not throw new ideas to the wind and fall in behind the band again? Nothing will ever replace the joyful Whit Monday trippety skip, following the brass band around the houses. The coming together of brass and voices on selected doorsteps and the melodious double-time march back to Sunday school for a cuppa and currant bun, followed by another after tea tune-up while the children fought the war of the races. There is something highly spirit-lifting about a brass band that makes me want to tear up my sponsor forms, raffle, dance and jumble sale tickets and throw them in the air. A Whitsun walk is still as magical to some of us as the Pied Piper was to the Hamelin children.

THE most encouraging question of the week was popped to me yesterday. 'Are you going down t'nick, lass?' was the complimentary inquiry. I would like to announce to all corpulants that I have managed to shed a few pounds. No, it's not the Jubilee preparations. I have discovered a non-fail way to grow thin, which I would like to pass on to fellow sufferers. Ignore all the low calorie rubbish displayed in the supermarkets, there is only one sure way to slim and that is – eat less. Stop enjoying those delicious desserts that make life so wonderful (sob), those melt-in-the-mouth buttery potatoes (slurp), and if you still have a bulge – buy a bike! It's the only way to a flag pole figure.
*

I HAVE had an enquiry from a reader concerning the origin of the green 'lucky' stone I mentioned in my column, 'Old Wives but True Tales.' It seems we both indulged in some spitting and wishing and have both noticed this little gem does not seem to be around any more. Does anyone know if it was peculiar to our district? Has it disappeared entirely? I should be pleased to hear any information regarding this stone – before our next telephone bill arrives, please, if possible!

Mrs Dale's diary has nothing on this!

SO MPs have been banned from diary keeping. I should imagine what they don't put in diaries would prove more interesting.

Each year my daily jottings always dwindle into appointments, birthdays or gems like 'Don't forget to turn the oven off.' Some days are listed '2lb carrots and 1lb shin beef.' The 'One Man's Week' contributors to the Sunday Times appear to lead a wildly exciting daily existence. I often wonder what my week would look like in stark black and white. I managed to keep one week's sojourn for posterity.

Monday: Awakened by 1812 overture a la dustbin lids. Sweep up ashy message left by our friendly refuse collector regarding our perforated dustbin. Promising weather has me too busy feeding washer to care about whereabouts of pumps, books, bags, shoes, etc. Had nasty moment when I discovered man in my bed, forgotten it was husband's day off. By the time spinner-tangled washing is ready for the line, it's raining. Sinfully ignoring dizzy revolutions of red arrow on electric meter I push everything in tumbler. Listen to Desert Island Discs and picture plump castaway swimming ashore with record player on head. If I get shipwrecked, hope they are extinct, and there is an influx of do-it-yourself books on boat-craft. Iron midway through Afternoon Theatre, then revive yesterday's left-overs, heavily disguised them as tea. Don daughter's fluorescent orange kagoul for damp bike ride, ask coyly for husband's comment, 'Looks daft,' is the encouraging reply.

Tuesday: Awakened by wailing neighbourhood peacock, too late for comfort. Examine reluctant scholar's throat – explain her tonsils are not divided into four. Search of pockets and tins produces other daughter's £4 school trip money. Persuade another daughter, whether best friend likes it or not, her anorak is not yet ready for the jumble sale. Phone rings, strange female voice speaks, she chats on while I think of unused excuse. Her 'Love your column' has me eagerly reaching for diary. Take picnic lunch to allotment where husband is happily spending his second day off. Although abundantly soaked in sunshine, picnic area disappointingly situated between compost heap and soaking rubbish. Smoked potted meat butty unbelievably tasty. Small thud on my crown turns out to be a ladybird. Sign of hot weather or was I mistaken for a clump of grass? Add hair conditioner to shop list. Spend afternoon writing, sun worshipping and planting seedlings.

Wednesday: Seedlings still unconscious, with yet another school cottage trip to finance – immediately – I wish I was. Reluctant scholar says can she have tonsils removed? Well, can she have her ears pierced then? Recite excuse list, it's barbaric, etc. Then fall into trap and promise 'When you leave school' evoking our 'When can I leave?' rebellion. Wave her off with usual farewell, 'Wait while dad comes home.'

Decide to do something about ever-increasing mending pile gathering dust on kitchen unit. Move it into dining room. Notice strange odour that dog and me fail to unearth. Attack children's bedroom and change furniture around. After half-hour toiling, vac gets dangerously hot and develops cough.

Thursday: Rob coal-money to pay for youngest trip enthusiast. Neglect everything and everybody in order to finish 'Weekly' contribution and win tonight's bowling match with clear conscience. Excellent team spirit, perfect weather, good supply of chewing gum, can't go wrong. Opponent's green looks apprehensively smooth. Buy raffle ticket which I absentmindedly screw up and throw away when called to play. Spend a few nervous ends standing behind what must be the league's tallest bowler. Realise I am not winning because partner is standing on the mat too long obscuring my view. Ask her to move. Realise I am not winning because of the sun, the green or the flavour-less chewing gum. Score 19-11 down and I wish I were dead. Spit liberally on bowl which slips out of my hand before I can aim it. By some miracle I manage to shake hands with opponent after losing. Swallowing my wailing peacock impression I even manage to warble the old Bruce Forsyth saga 'Good game, Good game.'

Friday: Sock and hanky drawers mysteriously empty again, fill up washer and discover son's socks wedged down chair in dining room. Strange smell disappears, wash mirror and so does my tan. Thrilled about neighbour's holi-day which starts tomorrow, not just because I fancy their rhododendrons, but genuinely hope they enjoy their stay at our favourite part of the Pem-brokeshire coast. Love hearing their plans and seeing their cases lined up, nearly as exciting as going ourselves. Lovely to think our August holiday will still be waiting fresh and unopened when they return.

After buying extra bananas and luxuriously adding two bottles of pop to my order, pluck up courage to beg old onion bags for our gardener. Disappointed when greengrocer tells me they now come in boxes.

Saturday: Neglect lunch for school orchestra meeting. Wish I could learn to concentrate more on 'Matters in hand.' One unhappy parent asks why guitar group is not invited to play more often – no one brave enough to tell him. I couldn't bring myself to look as complacent as everyone else on learning that Kirklees put on a 'splendid feast' for visitors.

Buying youngster's new jacket twice as difficult with her friend invited to 'help.' Eventually met with her approval and my pocket; treated us all to 99's in the market. They shrink considerably when four knickerbocker glories were passed over our heads to table behind.

Manage to push a dish of chats to scrape on to football supporter's knee while he is under the influence of 'Match of the day,' saves valuable Sunday morning time. Read Sunday school lesson, pass last-minute preparations to daughter. Best thing I ever did taking her on as helper.

Sunday: Up late as usual, still manage to pile into faithful chauffeur's car, climb chapel steps, refuse offer to be a marathon walker and be suitably doubled up in pew for 10.32am. Beginning to regret the week we changed places with our primary pupils and let them play teacher. 'Can we be teacher again?' they scream every week. If my spine ever regains shape from the battering it received from one small teaching bully who religiously believed that what couldn't be achieved by one thump, could always be managed by three, we may try it again sometime. It did take their tiny minds off the pervading question 'Who made God?'

After lunch calculate how many expected visitors for tea? Eight plus two dogs! Cook chicken, arrange massive salad. Bake choc and walnut gateaux, rhubarb tart and raspberry mousse. Cook ready-scraped Jerseys. Prepare parsley butter with chopped parsley, melted butter and lemon juice ready to pour over potatoes. (Diet's cancelled on Sunday). Drag kitchen table into sunny corner of back yard. Sun says goodbye, so do two of our members with tea invitations. Return table to kitchen. Visitors do not arrive. Three of us decide to start without dilatory son, who arrives as I sweeten my tea. After tea dad suggests a walk that we all pretend not to hear. Turn on TV and discover that foxes look as startled as I would if someone shone a light on my bedroom habits. Then it's the order of the bath, smallest first! And so to bed.

Hurrah for the red, white and blue

YES, I had an indulgent Jubilee holiday, thank you. I even wandered away from the wonders of colour television once or twice and spent one afternoon sheltering under a bridge along our stretch of the canal with five children and two bikes. Owing to the shortage of plant sitters our gardener was sadly absent.

After ten soggy minutes of watching four snooty ducks swim up and down the water in the rain, without looking wet, we all agreed that Peter Scott's idea of 'wild' life was certainly not ours.

Convinced the holiday spirit was somehow passing us by, we defeated band of ramblers decided to paddle back home to the comforting security of a hot television.

At this decision one borrowed child became so excited she eagerly peddled her bike over a small hillock and plunged headlong into the middle of duckland, which put new life into the ducks but did nothing for the bike and even less for the rider. Shivering and wailing she clambered out on to a stone and perched there like an overdressed mermaid, unhappily out of reach.

Our number three daughter was just as frantic – it was her turn to the ride the bike next. But some squelching time later we were all gulping hot coffee, wiping our noses and suitably sprawling in front of the Queen again.

Actually I discovered that while Her Majesty and myself have many traits in common – for instance, we both wear outfits more than once, are not afraid to flaunt our grey hairs, sometimes wax sulky and don't always join in congregational outbursts – she has one outstanding talent that surpasses all – her undying stamina. How does she do it?

Imagine the coach journey to St Paul's, a service of praise, a tedious walkabout, and a somnolent sounding luncheon with speeches and without wine, another coach journey with yet more arm-lifting and mouth-stretching. And still the jubilant expression shines on. Remarkable!

On a recent train journey to Sheffield, followed by interspersed coffee drinking and shopping, then a small serve-yourself lunch, my expression was definitely past its best.

I stayed awake long enough to smile at the adversity of a couple in front who discovered too late they should have been in the front half of the train, which, to their horror, was just departing. Then I fell into a deep sleep.

My awaking expression, which could never be described as jubilant, remained unaltered until I reached my next cuppa.

I am always at my most gracious on all outward journeys, but there is a distinct pause in the graciousness after lunch, which the rest of my family have learned to respect. Without these regular pauses, life would be un-bearable – especially theirs.

One wonders how Her Majesty endures the long and tasteless variety yawns she is often exposed to.

Years ago, near the end of the war, my father's unit were stationed at Kirkham, which meant we had a dad every other weekend. Saturdays became special. First, a wander round the shops holding his hand, then a scrumptious meat and potato pie meal at Gledhill's Café in the old Pack Horse yard.

A friendly waitress served us wearing a brown and cream uniform. The white tablecloths with their water jugs and matching glasses seemed the height of luxury. My sister and I could not have filled our glasses more often if it had been champagne.

Afterwards we paid our shillings for balcony seats at the old Palace Theatre and played at guessing advert initials on the front cloth until the orchestra spoiled it all and started the show.

The first few acts held us spellbound. We were a perfect audience until the ice creams had been bought. The rest of the time we spent playing our favourite game of 'houses' in the toilets.

When uninvited guests intruded, which, to our chagrin, they naturally did from time to time, we performed lots of hand-washing at the sink until they left. Not a very salubrious pastime, but boredom can have a drastic effect.

I though the Queen presented a sincerely happy and stable influence with her delightful family in full support, which sadly emphasised her sister's mal-content and estrangement.

I unashamedly let my tears of pride flow unchecked. Amid family queries of 'What time is dinner?' and 'Not sandwiches again!' and with my friendly teapot at my side, I followed the dignified pink-clad figure all the way to the Palace balcony and felt 'proud to be British' over and over again, with repeat performances throughout the evening.

Noel Coward and Gertrude Lawrence were once peeping at an audience through the stage 'peephole' as they awaited the arrival of the Royal guest. When the party eventually arrived Gertrude Lawrence gasped in admiration: 'What an entrance!' Noel Coward replied 'What a part!'

And what a part! Aside from the violence of our times, riding unshielded at the back of eight well-fed horses takes guts and courage, even if the streets are covered in sand.

In certain areas it seems fashionable to criticise and disparage the Royal Household. She could have been forgiven for displaying a little nervousness at the outset. Thankfully she was cheered so valiantly all along the route and I feel proud to count Jubilee Day as seen from our settee, as one of my happiest memories.

In spite of her faults, England will always be my Land of Hope and Glory, the only place I ever want to live. If this sounds like a hymn of praise for the finest system in the world, however abused, then I am satisfied.

I may not have a flag flying from my window but red, white and blue blood flows through my veins!

'Life was all sore lips, hot cheeks and good-hidings'

WITH a meaningful wink at his two companions the denim-clad youth strode past our table towards the cuddly brunette opposite.

Nonchalantly placing his hands in a pool of brown ale, he waited patiently as she drained her glass. The pretty blue eyes gazed up into his and filled with tears. Obligingly, he removed his cigarette, 'How about you and me . .' was as far as he got before blue eyes exposed her sharp little teeth and sardonically advised him to 'Get knotted.'

These heavily made-up bundles of female liberation must present a daunting prospect to young lovers. A psychiatrist hinted recently that parents should not discourage their sons from 'chatting up' the opposite sex. This could cause problems of violence later on. With girl friends like this who needs discouraging.

145

I once managed to catch an earful of our son's telephone rhetoric. 'Listen sunshine, I'm not one of your local riff-raff,' was as much as I heard before he threw the door at me. Judging by the telephone bill a little discouragement now would reduce dad's violence when it comes to paying it.

Where does an experienced adolescent learn his trade? Do young suitors ever compare their sweethearts with a summer's day any more or are they inspired by the modern lyricists?

Twenty years ago, girl friends were wooed Frank Sinatra-style. 'They try to tell us we're too young,' or 'I'd like to get you on a slow boat to China,' was crooned into receptive ears on the Town Hall parquet.

As mine only reached my partner's top pocket, these advances were never made to me, or if they were I missed them. Being a reluctant sailor, I can't think of anything more nauseating anyway.

Today's pop song messages seem to be written in a different language, known only to teenagers. 'I can tell by your eyes you have been crying for-ever' sounds a shade unkind when a girl has spent a tedious hour painting and highlighting.

But we all have our own methods of projecting our feelings. Ogden Nash, the American humourist, tells his valentine:
'I love you more than a duck can swim,
And more than a grapefruit squirts,
I love you more than gin rummy is a bore,
And more than toothache hurts.'

Feelings used to be worn on hats. 'Kiss Me Quick' and 'Hello Sailor' was a couple of Blackpool favourites. Nowadays they are worn on sleeves, pockets, T-shirts, even on bottoms. But the message has altered.

I stood in front of a large lady in a coffee queue last week trying my best not to take her T-shirt slogan literally. She had the swinging message 'Touch, touch, touch' inscribed across her protruding parts. Another young woman with no visible protuberance to support her legend had 'Detroit Tigers' optimistically printed on hers.

One daughter has 'Try it, you'll like it' stitched to the back pocket of her jeans. When we inquired what it referred to 'Oh anything,' was her disturbing reply. So there is no need to be stuck for words with all these talking accessories.

Our thirteen-year-old was eager to tell me of a message she saw in minute, hardly readable, print that said: 'If you can read this you are standing too close.' But she has forgotten what she was standing too close to.

'Chatting up' seemed a sadly onerous preliminary in my youth. During term time if a boy bashed you he liked you. Later on came the kissing stage.

In those days it wasn't the way you did it but for how long. We used to hold competitions to see who could kiss the longest. Life was all sore lips, hot cheeks and good-hidings.

The next phase: A boy you adored asked you out and you spent all evening ignoring each other. This was followed by the teasing, where you ran off with his scarf – but not too quickly.

Then all too soon you reach the sweetheart stage and start speaking civil to each other. At this point mine sailed off to Germany with the army and we were apart for an eternity of twenty letter-writing months.

What we weren't going to say to each other at our first meeting? Night after night I dreamed of it until the longed-for day arrived and we were walking towards each other from opposite ends of Lord Street – just like two cowboys in a Western film. The sun was glinting on his best-bulled boots, his familiar black beret was pulled so far down it made his eyebrows bristle aggressively.

A yard before we met I wanted to turn and run. It was like meeting a stranger. All those passionate promises and all I could manage to say was 'Can I carry your bag?' A stupid question as it was an army kitbag and weighed a ton.

Teenage magazines are another source of advice. Our girls live for the magic moment when 'Jackie' and 'Blue Jeans' fall on the mat. These are full of 'true-life' experiences to weep over. 'The past won't let me go,' says one forlorn blonde, who looks about twelve. This week's edition tells us, 'You know it's not love when your parents approve of him at first sight and on second, you don't.' There's the inevitable problem page. 'Dear Clare' (says one pathetic) 'I am thirteen and really like this boy of twenty-one. I think he likes me because he said when I am seventeen I can share a flat with him.' 'Film Fun' and 'Girl's Crystal' were never like this.

There comes a time in every mother's life when her son displays signs of maturity. Ours comes home most Saturday evenings with sparkling eyes, ruby lips and his neck beautifully marked.

All our questions receive his stock answer: 'Just freelancing, Ma.' We can only surmise one facet of her personality – he is her favourite drink.

Our girls do not seem to be as frustratingly esoteric. 'I may be going out with a coloured boy next week,' announced our fifteen-year-old. Next week comes and goes without comment. What had been her decision?

147

Unable to swallow my curiosity any longer, I make tentative enquiries about her new romance. 'Oh he hasn't asked me yet!' is the optimistic reply.

According to educational psychologists, girls are mentally more mature than boys and the gap widens in the formative years. True, and if you're not careful there's a chance it could expand again in the menopausal years!

Alas, poor Napoleon

FURROWED brows are becoming a familiar sight on the home and holiday landscape now the pet fostering season is upon us.

Animal hotels and dog diners may be making their pile in America, but over here similar catering is not so hot.

We can endure the wail of the jukebox, indifferent service, but in most seaside cafes and hotels nuisances like prams, pushchairs and dogs are forbidden.

Going on holiday can present some of us with a serious parking problem. What to do with the family pets?

I look forward to leaving ours at home once a year. For relationships to survive a certain time apart is necessary, and at the moment one week is all we can afford. After all, even children receive invitations out occasionally, whereas pets are a permanent fixture.

In my opinion boarding kennels are not the ideal habitat in which to place our loved ones, much easier on purse and pet to find a friendly fosterer. Then later you can give them an anxious week in return while you take in theirs.

Most of our friends are either gathering dandelions or stalking the tree trunks with strange animals. Only the other day I saw a mysterious black beast dragging a friend around the turf in top gear. 'Our son's' was all she had time to gasp, as it whisked her around again.

Last Friday night the children and our dog waited in ecstasy for granny's pet poodle to arrive for its fortnight bed and board. A cushion was placed in readiness on my favourite chair.

With newly Afro-styled hair-do, bright red bow threaded through the diamante collar and nails exquisitely manicured, he made quite an entrance. Our regular canal-washed mongrel sniffed the white curls expectantly, his tail eagerly lashing my legs.

For a minute I think the red bow had him fooled. But with bristling moustache and snarling hot wafts of halitosis, our brown-toothed guest soon asserted his bumptious masculinity.

148

We listened to the instructions carefully; 'Won't eat tinned meat, a pill to be given once a day, no trouble at bedtime – if he can sleep at the bottom of the bed.'

The following day, after shutting our tin-fed gourmet in another room, we placed a dish of fresh meat before our guest who sniffed disgustedly, duly refused it, then wandered over to our dogs dish and cheerfully scoffed the mixed up morsels. The swap over naturally met with approval from ours.

It took me a while to get used to the patter of tiny paws which accompanies my every move. But I quite enjoy the vicious way he snarls at anyone who tries to get near me.

Pill pushing is the worst chore. I tried pushing it in sideways – it just came out the other side. Prising it through his front teeth and keeping his mouth shut for five minutes seemed the most successful until I let go and he gently spit it on my lap. Now I have the answer. I open his mouth, aim for his tonsils and with a bit of luck it hits the jackpot and I get my reward.

Sometimes there are complications with two leads on our walkabouts. Especially as they both seemed compelled to cock-a-leekie on the same tree at the same time. Consequently the smaller one finishes up with a shampoo and wet.

Actually, our pet-keeping record is not promising, which I feel bound to point out to potential pet leavers. Our front garden is scattered with our failures.

Take Harry Hamster for instance. He was a loveable little chap once I stopped comparing him with his cousin Rat. I swear I was beginning to get used to his escapology feats, but I just felt safer with him on the pantry shelf in the wash kitchen at night.

Unfortunately, he took a short trip, landed in the sink and spent the night under a leaking tap. Poor little fellow must have thought he had been banished to the cooler. In the morning his fur was all wet and facing the wrong way.

To dry him out I wrapped him up and placed him in the top of my Yorkist range with instruction to all not to close the doors. Sadly, I have an intrinsic 'shut that door' obsession.

It must have been an hour later when I remembered, but too late. The doors were firmly closed. Harry is on his back, warm and dry but extinct. I was never able to convince everyone that he would have died anyway.

I was devoted to Napoleon, our chubby white guinea pig. He always scurried to his door when he saw me coming – an exercise which sadly became his downfall.

149

One day on opening it, I accidentally gave him a resounding wallop that glazed his eyes somewhat. When I returned for our teatime chat he was doing a realistic impression of the late Harry.

Fanatical animal lovers waffle on about cruelty to animals, but, after keeping one or two (albeit for a short span), I have come to realise how merciless they treat each other. Their law seems to advocate the survival of the fittest.

My guinea pig relationship became slightly retarded when I opened the cage one morning to find two of them had half eaten their next of kin, who were lying headless and bloody at the bottom of the cage. To think I used to allow them to playfully nibble my finger!

The last time we were entrusted with a pet canary I placed its cage in the garden, not because he only seemed to know one song, but the sunshine was so pleasant.

Curiosity prompted our toddler to open its prison door for an illicit poke. By the time her frantic shouts penetrated my twitterless euphoria, yellow bird was heading for the banana trees.

My husband unluckily chose to buy a replacement the day they were only selling pairs. It seemed the hardest task in the world explaining to the felici-tously tanned young couple stood on our doorstep holding a new chrome bird-cage stand (a present for birdie) that canary had given us the bird. We have never since accepted a 'watch the birdie' offer.

But if you can ignore our pernicious pedigree – foster pets are always welcome!

Leave your worries at home

'NOT going anywhere this time,' the shopper in front confessed to her companion as they ran their fingers through a box of lettuce. 'What with the kitchen extension and Jack's new . . . .'

Although eavesdropping is a favourite pastime, I couldn't bear to listen any longer and shall never know what else Jack built. The thought of anyone being denied a salubrious waft of sea air is too depressing. 'I do like to be beside the seaside' could have been written for me. The thought of our one week's gulp of ozone is my solid support through many a gloomy day.

It's not so much the holiday I would miss but all the glorious anticipation that comes before, and the residue of memories to gloat over for the rest of the year. A week without suitcases is too dreary to contemplate. Nothing to diet for, nothing to blackmail the children or curb their spending with, no hot dogs to enjoy on the way home from a sandy picnic. A week in the back yard watching the weeds bloom is definitely not my idea of a holiday.

I blame this addiction on my parents who started me on this annual holiday trek when I was three. My husband has had to follow this tradition once a year ever since. We did miss a year when our eldest daughter was born, mistakenly believing it would upset her routine.

Four children later I realise that the younger they are the less trouble they cause. One of our happiest holidays was spent when our youngest was less than four months old. She slept and ate her way through the week in soporific contentment. Instead of pushing each other about the promenade her proud sisters took it in turns to push her pram while big brother looked on scornfully. He liked her better when her pram became his 'hurry' cart.

This year we have to take our week off in August, the last week of the school holidays. As my sanity will most likely be in question by then, I intend to tackle my sewing now while I can still hold a needle. Dylan Thomas must surely have recorded his observance, 'My children grow large and rude,' during the midsummer break.

I hope to channel some of the corpulent exuberance into sewing machine treadling. One daughter tells me they do it at school and the machines are still working. We have two ancient and temperamental machines, which work by a series of pedalling and kicking. Our eldest daughter is the proud owner of an electric masterpiece and is the only one who can drive it. At the moment our kitchen looks like a machine room. With this influx of treadling and bike pedalling I should have calf muscles like coconuts when the holiday arrives.

In between pedalling we haunt the market stalls, a copious bargain centre for home dressmakers. Sons and fathers can feel a little neglected during this pre-holiday kitting-out period. Naturally their drawers and wardrobes are adequately filled and do not require any new additions but we generously made them two new hankies each, just the same. A real bargain from one 25p piece of cotton and enough left over to make four small nose size for us girls.

One satisfied customer tells me she has made her own pillowcases for years from this hardwearing material, so our males should not need new hankies for quite a while.

Not being over fond of sewing, why sew three seams when one will suffice? All our patterns are exceedingly simple. Dress patterns are easily adapted from 'Burda' magazine and can be adjusted to fit all figures. Sometimes we sneak a Saturday afternoon snoop around the boutiques and pinch a few ideas. With a little improvisation and a lot of cursing we then make up our own, for a third of the price.

Caftan-style nighties are readily made from a piece of material twice your own length. A small slit along the fold forms the neck, sleeves can either be cut out or just a space left for arms. Children were sewing on their own trims, a chore I always encourage.

But this is not without complications, if one is not careful, renovation can set in. During a weak moment when I was in the grip of the 'Emergency' series showing on TV, I agreed to let one daughter convert a decent blouse into a 'grandad' shirt, whatever that may be.

Rigorous drawer slamming, tearing and wheel-whirring filled our evenings. Collarless blouses were springing up everywhere. More pin-chewing sessions ensued - the bathroom waste bin was suddenly full of collars. But as yet no 'grandad' shirt has emerged. Surveying the destruction, I feel it would have been cheaper to buy one anyway.

Anticipation is always a mixture of joy and trepidation. On good days I remember all our marvellous excursions, on bad days I dwell on the disasters. Holidays do not always live up to expectations but there is the fun of grumbling about it afterwards. One year we were booked into what promised to be a delightful country inn on the Devon coast. Our bedroom had a panoramic view of the sea, as stated, but the brochure photograph had not included the disused railway line, a racing track or the several amusement centres that stretched beneath our window. Every evening as we retired wearily to bed it was 'disco' time below stairs. In fact, with its pintable alley and thriving restaurant it turned out to be the strangest, noisiest country inn it has ever been my misfortune to inhabit. But even so, nothing can take away the wonderful weeks of planning that preceded this disaster.

It's a long time since my sister and I rushed down to Huddersfield railway station from the Outlane bus stop, with our three-penny bits clasped tightly in our hands and a terrible anxiety in our hearts as we waited for dad to discover which of the long queues trailing down to the main road was ours.

Then the icy cold blast of air when we were eventually allowed on to the platform and the panic rising again as we waited for our change at the bookstall.

Every minute was precious, the fuming giant could roar down the track at any moment. When the train did eventually screech into the station there was the mouth-drawing fear that we may become separated in all the pushing and jostling for an empty carriage or, even worse, one of us might be left behind.

Only when dad was happily balancing our big brown case with two leather straps on the luggage rack and smokey Huddersfield was receding into the swirling whiteness did we really settle down to some serious holiday dreaming.

Relaxing is an exhausting business at any age. Most of us look forward to a rest as much as the change, but how much time do we actually spend doing nothing? How much of our day is dedicated to sitting and staring? There is an art in leaving worries at home for a week, some people pack them in with their gear.

If you are going away this weekend try leaving them at home with the cat, they'll be quite safe – and have a carefree holiday!

On with the summer show

WHY is it – with all these extra helping hands during the school holidays – our house looks as if Oxfam have just moved in?

Strange heaps of unidentifiable objects appear to be taking over our rooms. Chairs are either occupied by musical instruments or someone's cast-off clothing. The enigmatic sign of the Black Hand is taking shape below door handles.

Semi-precious commodities like combs, hairbrushes and today's paper cannot be unearthed by threats or bribery. No one can be sure after all the 'subbing' which week's spending money is due anyway.

Late nights bring a new dimension to young appetites. Breakfasts occupy most of the mornings. The other day one child had an acute fancy for fish fingers. Idling around is such thirsty work, milk and orange juice are flowing almost as fast as Margaret Thatcher's counter-attacks in the Commons.

But the most dreaded four words in our daily vocabulary are definitely 'Your turn to wash!' 'Your turn to place your feet in hot wax' could not strike more terror. The mention of 'washing up' can turn a dining-table into a battlefield, and our dog into hiding. Instead of being allowed to snooze off his dinner, suddenly everyone wants to take him for a long walk. For some obscure reason, although no one is actually in favour of 'drying up' it does cause less distress. We thought it a good idea to start ours off the moment they grew high enough to reach the sink. But now I wonder if this was wise, we should have initiated them earlier. The clearing up process afterwards is diabolical.

They leave so many containers round the sink, soaking in grimy liquid, it looks fuller than it did before they started. Would a dish-washer be the hedonistic answer, I ask myself – but a friend tells me her children argue over who shall do the stacking.

In Greenhead Park I noticed a pervading comfort of grandads, pushing swings, retrieving balls, nursing gloomy toddlers, cajoling wailers and faith-fully leading aspiring equestrians on tired ponies.

These energetic treasures are worth their weight in coffee. Every family should have at least one, we are lucky enough to have two. While one plied us with the most swollen and luscious home-grown strawberries the other rang and actually asked permission to take three exuberants off for the day. They were on their way before the phone was back in its cradle. Hardly able to believe our luck, eldest daughter and I were on our way to town almost as quick. Throwing dietary caution to the dog we dined in style with a calorific strawberry cream flan to finish.

There are several ways to keep spirits up and boredom down. It is surprising how many youngsters enjoy a visit to the art gallery. In my opinion many parents sadly neglect this asset.

I confess the slippery floor seemed the most inviting to our son in his cap-ricious youth, but the portraits, landscapes and a strong hand from me did eventually arouse his interest.

If you are suffering from the interminable whine of 'What can I do?' why not invest in 'The Picolo Holiday Book,' an excellent forty-pence-worth of ideas on how to keep you and the children sane at this time.

One of the suggestions is for children to write and act their own play. This can be humorously rewarding for all concerned. Our children spent one rainy summer engrossed in this pastime. Every afternoon saw the splatter of grimy feet as a motley group of players retired to our attic with pens, books and paper. We gladly endured the ceiling tremors just to see them occupied at last. Then came the grand opening and command performance – we parents were ordered to attend.

The seating arrangements were not too salubrious but old packing cases and broken chairs are hardly noticeable when one is fighting the unforgivable desire to giggle.

There appeared to be a difference of opinion behind the scenes and the two moth-eaten grey blankets that served as curtains trembled dangerously. At last a pair of black-rimmed eyes glared unerringly at us through a large hole and conveyed the message 'They've come' and after a lot of tugging the 'curtains' were torn off – the show had begun.

We could perceive immediately by the macabre costumes and the hideous make-up – it was to be a horrific epic. Although the attic temperature was at least 80deg, for some reason most of the cast was wearing fur coats and hats over several layers of clothing. Our youngest, in her black tights and leotard, was obviously a creeping beetle, but we couldn't help puzzling over the reason for her incongruent pink bathing cap.

The heroine looked a feverish picture in our eldest's fur coat and her mother's fur hat worn rakishly over one eye, the whole outfit smartly offset by father's best suede driving gloves.

The plot was confusing. Why did black beetle languish speechless throughout on a pile of rags in the corner? What was the reason for the curious stooping gait of the rest of the cast? Had the layers of clothing taken their toll, we wondered? In between the five acts we were gratefully allowed downstairs.

All was revealed later. Unknown to the audience there had been a change of title. We had not been witnessing an adaptation of 'The Three Witches' as advertised. Owing to difficulties with the youngest member, and her inability to memorise lines, and her threat to withdraw her fur hat if she couldn't play, they had no choice but to give her the leading non-speaking part in a Brer Rabbit extravaganza called 'Brer Rabbit meets Tar Baby.'

So they were all disguised as animals – naturally we realised this as soon as it was pointed out!

No one was brave enough to inquire about 'Tar Baby's' pink bathing cap – it's still a mystery!

Wish you were here in the rain!

'IS THIS an indication of our future weather?' asked one bikini-clad daughter as we sat sunning ourselves during that scorching afternoon in late May.

Unfortunately the heat-wave we were hoping to become accustomed to has not arrived – yet. The colourful bunch of sundresses that optimistically filled the stores in early spring are now wilting sadly on their hangers.

The postcard scribblers have had to change their style this year. According to most of England's soggy holiday outlook, any hint of 'Wish you were here' could be bordering on the vindictive.

We have facsimiles of sun-baked sand dunes, washed by turquoise seas and voluptuous saucy maidens pinned up all around our kitchen sink. Glorious technicolour miniatures depicting how beaches and belles ought to look during this season, but the side facing the wall paints a somewhat duller picture.

However, some stalwarts are dedicated to 'having a wonderful time,' whatever the weather. 'It never kept us in,' I heard one compulsive nose-wiper inform a bus conductress as she guided her cap and scarf-hidden husband off the bus with their luggage.

A postman friend delivered two cards bearing the same Blackpool postmark to one house, but the messages bore little resemblance. 'Having a super time, weather not too bad,' reported one; the other was slightly more succinct, 'Weather rotten – fed up.'

But are these 5in x 4in's designed to carry home true holiday confessions? Which sounds worse, a spurious, light-hearted cover-up attempt or a ruthless reveal-all?

My pep talk to our holiday-departing son concerning the necessity for a sentence or two to apprehensive parents regarding his arrival must have been keenly digested. The promised card arrived home before him, for once. But I feel less explicit tidings would have sufficed. He sent us a view as requested. The picture showed what was left of an ugly piece of rock, being bashed unmercifully by an angry sea. His message ran: 'Have just been severely rep-remanded by hotel management for being too noisy last night. Food good, rained every day – played golf – red hot.'

A friend tells me his teenage daughter's message home described 'Rotten weather, a bilious sea crossing' and concluded 'having a super time.'

There is no doubt at certain ages kind weather does kindle the holiday spirits. There's a lot to be said for the professional 'aunties' and 'uncles' working the holiday camps who earn their rewards entertaining youngsters so mums and dads can sneak off and learn to converse again. At least that's what I tell myself as I send off this expensive deposit which dispels our youngest daughter's favourite delusion, 'And it's all free,' she loves to boast to friends. If this inclement weather continues, they will certainly extract our money's worth.

It doesn't help to read in the morning paper that the temperatures in New York are blazing so high, apartment walls are starting to crack with the heat.

But if this 'back-end' weather is tarnishing our holiday brightness the horticultural harvest is thriving profusely – without the sun. Every evening our gardener returns in hand-rubbing exuberance, his lettuce-filled pockets dragging the holes in his cardigan down to his knee patches. Yesterday he crept in with a small bundle cradled affectionately in the crook of his arm.

We gathered round to learn we are the proud co-owners of a cuddly, crumbly, baby cauliflower!

While we femmes swap symptoms arising from TV's 'Medical Story' (I wish the BBC would invent some fictitious diseases that didn't need surgery and could not possibly happen to me) gardening terms are floating back and forth among the weeds. 'We'll 'ave plenty on, but nowt in 'em yet,' boasts one, evoking a subtle comment from another concerning his 'swollen trusses' and the remarkable size of his beans.

I just wish there was another way to serve the ever-increasing lettuce that seems to be taking over and what a pity tender juicy young peas have to be ruined by twenty minutes of boiling water.

Garden tips are flowing like fertiliser. One advocate discovered a unique way to cure depressed lettuce was to cover his open cold frame with netting. Marvelling at this unusual deduction I felt bound to ask what difference this made. 'It keeps your mother's cat out,' was the altruistic reply.

It is a shame that at this crucial time on the gardening calendar one wife tells me her husband has been struck down with the dreaded 'bad back' syn-drome. But he still tries to help in his own way. Only the other day he called her away from her spade to his deck-chair. Telling her she looked exhausted he fished into his top pocket and gallantly offered her two of his glucose sweets to be sucking while she worked.

Naturally I try to play my small part in the scheme of things. I prod pro-fessionally at the pea pods, gasp at the size of his onions and last week I was actually allowed to hold the hose for a few minutes while our expert turned off the water. I have learned to stop asking what he uses to make the tomato leaves curl up so glamorously – it would have little effect on my hair anyway.

*

IF ANY of you are feeling Garbo-ish and tired of being the school holiday centre for distraction, really yearning to be left alone – why not try a large and crispy helping of garlic bread?

Not to be recommended before bedtime unless you are a twin-bedder or have aspirations in that direction – but scrumptuously delicious, if, like me, you are a garlic lover, and worth testing even if you are not.

Besides its efficacious properties the distinctive aroma can also keep the family away for hours.

Just cut a medium sized cob into three, length wise, spread each slice liberally with garlic butter (a mixture of crushed garlic and butter). Press back into original shape, wrap in foil and place in a hot oven for about 20 mins. The result is hot, crispy, and extremely tasty. I had to travel to

Bradford market in my search for garlic, though. For the uninitiated just a hint of garlic is enough to start with, but do try this savoury change, it peps up the palate and is said to be 'good for the heart.'

Really, chaps, it's not cricket

IN THE act of lifting a lettuce leaf from the tea-time salad bowl my spouse yelped in pain and dropped it as if he'd been stung.

Well, perhaps I had washed it a trifle hastily after my afternoon date with a lengthy patch of sunshine. However, this was no reason for him to frighten the rest of the family, two of whom refuse to approach my salad teas without benefit of reading glasses anyway.

His furious comments and subsequent retreat into the living-room was, in my opinion, carrying this aphid phobia too far.

Apparently I had no need to air my views on lettuce cowards, as a sneaky batsman currently playing to an empty living-room had provoked his unsociable oaths. It seems our addict had been seated opposite this still-life cricket scene most of the afternoon and while he slipped out for a sandwich some ball had actually made contact with a wicket.

I cannot think of anything more frustrating for a non-cricket lover like myself than the antics of a cricket freak and son, in the throes of the season. Our family philosophers delved into the subject of frustration very deeply one evening, during a Parliamentary broadcast.

We decided that nothing could be more frustrating than trying to eat a jam doughnut without being allowed to lick one's lips (try it!). I had forgotten about the boring sights and sounds of televised cricket.

But last week the memory came yawning back by courtesy of the Test Match.

There pose our two addicts, maddeningly hypnotised, while all I can hear are rankling crowd noises of subdued conversations and restless coughs. Not that I haven't tried to rattle up a squirm of interest in this action-less pastime, but there is a limit. How many times am I expected to watch a chap roll a dirty ball up and down his clean trousers before he gallops madly down the turf, turns himself inside out, hurl the ball down and then prepares to set the whole tedious process in motion once again.

To add to the aggravation we also have to endure the dreariness of the commentator explaining what we have just seen not happen for ourselves.

As if this was not disconcerting enough, he then asks another bore to des-cribe it all over again! Sometimes they wander off into unexciting regurgita-tions from past matches – here they become quite animated. 'Yes,

I remember it quite clearly, old Don was wearing his pullover back to front that day,' hearty chuckles all round. 'Was he really,' says a voice. 'Most remarkable,' chants someone else.

At this point something usually happens on the pitch. Then there follows a 'Guess what's happened' pause in transmission. 'Er, yes, well something's obviously happened here at Nottingham – John is smiling, what do you think, Fred?' 'Yes, I would agree with you there, Peter, that's definitely a smile.'

Old cricketers never die they simply fade away to the commentary box.

I shall never understand why Fred Trueman failed to make it as a comedian. His stunted announcements during the televised dart and elbow contests have us all in stitches. His expressionless monotone sounds as interesting as this week's shopping list and is even more costly. How often have I told our cricket zombies 'I would not be paid to watch this slow-burning rubbish,' during a match - but this is not strictly true. In fact, it is the only way to watch – talk about 'money for ham.'

One good thing about this season, it cuts out fancy meals. If I served devilled tripe on horseback our supporters would not notice. It's the same with conversation. Their glazed eyes look at you, they even nod occasionally, but underneath the hair, their ears are crickety twitchy all the time and just when you feel you have convinced them of your distaste for all things cricket, 'Quick, hurry up, you'll miss it,' whoops a besotted voice from his TV position at silly mid-off and you are expected to wax mad with him.

Some are more chauvinistic than others. I read recently of one cricket fiend who not only hogs the TV set, but he turns the sound down and listens to the radio commentary at the same time. Mind you John Arlott's rhetoric takes some beating. His dark rich voice is one of my favourites. 'And as a toffee paper floats across the deserted pitch, we say goodbye,' I heard him once recite at the close of play. He could make a funeral sound entertaining.

Beware of the supporter en repose. This is cricket worshipping at its most savage. Before risking the big switch over, do make doubly sure the eyelids are securely fastened down first. These hooded monsters may look unconscious, but many's the time I have tried, without moving the rest of my body, surreptitiously to tickle the other channel button with my big toe, only to be frightened into convulsions a second later by the dreaded spine-chilling 'Hey – leave it on!' or words to that effect.

Understandably, perhaps this is one sport that demands diligent concentration – who knows, something may occur unexpectedly. I did become

159

extremely keen during a match one year, when I looked up from my book to see a delightfully proportioned Adam impersonator skip gaily across the turf. My cricket instinct immediately aroused, I closed my book. As my concentration improved a policeman offered his helmet to help the disguise but it looked out of place. My interest in books wavered slightly for a while after this.

Thankfully, cricket has not reached the wide screen as yet. We have suffered boxers, mountaineers and motor-racing, but who could possibly sit through a three-hour epic on cricket, apart from the you-know-who's. I could consider it, if a happy ending was featured, perhaps. These seem to have fallen into decline of late. I don't care what adversities the hero has to overcome or how many wild beasts have to be shot to bits, just as long as there is someone left to walk hand in hand towards the sunset before I go to bed.

Yes, I know that cricket on the village green is an important feature of the English landscape, but there's always such a good film on the other side. Let's face it, without the necessary accessories, the smell of hot tea and tobacco, mingled with the sweet aroma of grass clippings, a splintery seat attached to one's tights and a neighbourly voice at my side telling me the juicy saga of 'Our Mabel's Ernest' – televised cricket is just not my scene.

In a world of their making

'YOU pretend to be daddy,' the persuasive voice of our eight-year-old pseudo housewife drifted in from the porch that was all cheerfully decorated, jumble sale style.

'You go out every day and at the end of the week you get paid' she went on hopefully, but her friends' sulks never lifted.

In their idyllic childhood world of fantasy it seems that everyone wants to play 'mum.' No one is interested in playing the 'father' figure. Apart from the fact that he usually comes home every teatime, eats a gargantuan meal and brings home the money on Friday, no one seems quite sure what function 'daddy' is supposed to fulfil anyway.

But even so 'mummies and daddies' with the latter playing an unseen 'noises off' role in the background, is still a favourite game. At least daddy is still included in the family scene!

The television programme 'Horizon' gave us a short glimpse into the behaviour of nursery-age children at play recently. Some appeared to be leaders, sorting out the small offenders, some were happy extroverts, content to bash the nearest head to hand and unfortunately one or two were easily dominated introverts. Naturally these characteristics were all traced back to, and blamed on the behaviour of parents.

So it was with great interest and not a little trepidation that I did a spot of eavesdropping on our youngest and her friends at play. Who knows what colourful shades of me might emerge from this experimental adventure?

All dressed vivaciously as their idea of a 'modern mum' with brilliantly painted eyelids, Boris Karloff eyebrows, and each featuring two rollers on top and a matchstick cigarette stuck in their mouth corners, these liberated 'mums' enjoy an active existence.

Smacking their 'offspring,' changing them frequently, visiting friends, complaining about their respective husbands' wife-neglecting hobby – it's difficult to conclude what gives them most pleasure.

Household routines are delightfully flexible. 'Yes, of course I can come round for coffee, love,' coos one into my sacred geranium-come telephone. 'I never do any work in the afternoon anyway,' displaying a well-adjusted balance of priorities!

Listening in on these charades one can often pick up a household tip or two. 'I don't need to vac up' confides one phantom housewife, looking the diminutive image of Elton John in an outsize pair of Polaroids which she has some difficulty in keeping on her nose. 'I just turn the carpet tiles over.'

They can happily 'set up home' under any conditions. In the process of throwing some dirty sheets at the washer one day I discovered one 'family' had taken over my wash kitchen. It took me quite some time to find the washer, which with the aid of two soiled bath towels and another sacred geranium, was heavily disguised as a sideboard. Two dolls were sleeping peacefully in the sink, another was perched upright with pants around her ankles on a saucepan and 'mother' was about to tuck into an ashtray filled with chopped dandelion leaves. Bedtime is a pitiful sight.

Demolishing these 'homes' is heart-breaking. The ensuing homeward trail of 'homeless' and bedraggled evacuees each pushing their bundle of household props and families, all silently chanting their violent thoughts on heartless interveners who have shamelessly turned them into the street at a half hour's notice – are poignant to behold. When this drama is particularly uncontrollable we are many times touched deeply enough to allow their dwellings to remain unscathed – until weekend anyway.

The situation is certainly becoming a little easier to control since this weekend we are off on holiday. The 'If you don't behave we shan't' blackmail sequence is now at its peak. Yes, we have started the big countdown to blast off. At long, blissful last we are down to the last three sleeps before our holiday proper, with some of us wishing we had counted our pennies as conscientiously.

It always amazes me when fictional heroines, before making a hasty escape, throw a few dainties into a beautiful looking case and wave off gracefully to their retreat. Our farewell bonanza is somewhat different. For one thing we can never remember who had the decent case last, or where we eventually hid the others. When we finally unearth them, we have to find homes for the des-pondent looking articles which have rested there secretly since its last journey, ie someone's bikini top, three Marks and Spencer bags, a belt and two coat hangers which no one owns, and a tin of foisty talc.

I can never muster the courage to throw anything in a case without consulting one of my five lists first. All packing has, of necessity, to be performed needle in hand. I always make it a holiday rule to replace all noticeably missing buttons.

Our three suitcases, the good, the battered and the indifferent, lay open mouthed in the front room all week, until everyone has played their hysterical scene about not having a thing to wear, then I sit on top while our strong arm tries vainly to make ends meet.

But the clothes-packing trauma takes second place to the endless bouts of coin counting, concealing and bitter defamation of characters. Every money-box session is concluded by accusations; 'There's 10p missing from my pile' or 'I know I put my purse on here – who's taken it?'

Tears gush so fast and furiously the eve before departure that by the time we are all scrambling for window seats in the car the morning after, we must look as if we have been struck by some debilitating disease. The children all swollen-eyed and semi-drugged, me with my tension showing, our driver pale and weary as a result of all the case-lifting and patient refereeing, we must definitely look in need of a holiday.

The next step is to belt up the motorway as fast as we can. Not just to avoid traffic congestion, but also to beat the junior travel drugs so hopefully administered, once they wear off – we all get sick.

Sadly, I have not yet taken a driving test. After all, I have only been learning five years. One day of course, I hope to be allowed out of a cul-de-sac and eventually attain second gear, until then journeys continue to be a strain for me. My husband could one day give me the wheel and take over the back-seat monsters for a while – that is my dream.

I suppose the secret is to keep them occupied, with a little ingenuity we can sometimes get a competition going. If it is early morning and we are well deep in wild country 'The first one to see a supermarket' is a good starter for ten. Or 'look for a man carrying two brown poodles under his left arm' can keep eyes down for a mile or two.

We used to make up our own lyrics to familiar tunes until the super imagi-native among us waxed a shade scurrilous – but however arduous the journey with a bit of luck we shall arrive amid the heather in time for tea – so just giggle among yourselves until I'm back again; be with you in a fortnight!

Good morning campers!

ON OUR return from holiday I invariably have just enough energy left to see me to the nearest armchair and just enough elbow power to lift next year's holiday brochures.

This year we had the additional excitement of a watery chase through a monotonous motorway build-up and a mad dash to church to attend a friend's wedding at 2pm on the afternoon of our return home.

Unbelievably, we made it and were all shivering in our summery outfits at least half a second before the bride arrived. We made up for this by being first at the resplendent buffet table, but missed the wedding gift perusal. After my husband had parked the car he promptly fell asleep, awakening just in time for the evening festivities.

Our Scottish holiday brought forth some unusual incidents. We all gasped as we sped down the 'electric brae' and our driver freewheeled – upwards. Because of the lie of the land - whatever that means - although you appear to be driving downhill you are actually going up.

In the pretty town of Girvan a kilted assistant actually recited the ancient words, 'A pleasure to serve you, madam.' Admittedly the children were absent at the time.

In the same town we noticed a small black-bordered card in a butcher's shop window. Leaning against a batch of black puddings it cordially invited everyone to attend 'My brother's funeral.' We noticed another butcher with a similar request set amid the black pudding to 'My sister's funeral.' Must be catching. We thought it wiser to buy our meat from one without a card.

We were awakened on our first morning by what sounded like a dozen highlanders dancing a fling in hobnailed boots on our chalet roof, but on investigation turned out to be two seagulls and a rather depressed-looking pigeon. All I can say is they must have suffered from flat feet.

Last year on our initial visit to the holiday camp world we became sitting supporters of the olde-tyme dance movement. So once again we eagerly consulted our maps to pinpoint the Regency Ballroom, home of the waltz and valeta lovers, and set out early to capture a front seat.

It was situated next to a bar called 'The Continental.' We peeped in but could only distinguish a noisy blanket of smoke and quickly ushered the children past and into the rich plum velvet and satin elegance of the Regency.

Curiously we were the first arrivals and enthusiastically spread ourselves across five ballroom edge seats. Half an hour dragged on, then a drummer and organist took their places on the raised platform - it seemed the band had arrived. Another hour passed, the children had tried out all the seats and were waxing restless. Where were the rest of the campers? We listened enviously to the raucous yelps of gaiety wafting in from next door. At last an official-looking elderly couple, both wearing identical red blazers two sizes too large, came in and struck an aristocratic pose on the ballroom floor. Obviously the camp commandant and his wife.

Madame wore red sequinned pointed shoes, 'Just like the wicked witch of the North in Wizard of Oz,' as one child tactlessly remarked.

This dynamic duo wove in and out, he miraculously missing her pointed toes while they performed intricate patterns of half-turns and side-steps guaranteed to baffle Victor Sylvester himself and intensely fascinating to all nine of us watching.

After a salutory skip round they stood in their supervisory capacity and scrutinised two brave couples who dared to impersonate them. A while later he turned his aquiline profile in our direction. Understandably, I suppose seeing as we were the only other people there. Throwing us a 'We have ways of making you dance' glare, he strode over to the microphone and shouted 'Everybody dancing' then an even louder 'please.' I tried to look deformed and he approached the mike again. 'Have you come to dance or not?' he snarled. We pretended hyper-interest in the two stricken dancers on the floor.

The 'band' struck up a bright little foot-tapping number. 'A quickstep' I whispered with relief to my partner who was buried in the cricket scores. Nearly tying their feet in knots to the beat of the quick tempo the two MC's did their act again, then cruelly left the floor to the other two couples.

After a struggle one partnership lapsed into a quick-step. Madame was on the floor like lightening shaking a cautionary finger. 'This is a dinky

164

one-step' she announced. The offenders smiled sheepishly and continued their illicit quick-step. This was Captain Red Blazer's cue. With a face to match his coat and his voice rising above the 'Continental' din from next door, 'If you want to do that,' he sniffed in disgust, 'Go to the Stuart.' This was the best bit of news we had heard all evening and we all beat a hasty retreat to where it looked as if the rest of the camp were awaiting us.

Here was a vastly different scene. The ballroom floor was crawling with infants all 'doing their own thing. A two-year-old sliding from one end to the other via his T-shirt front, another gang of extroverts playing cops and robbers, a guitarist surrounded by a serious-faced group of twelve-year-old lads all breathing down his plectrum, was crooning something inaudible. Mums, dads and aunties were sitting around the plush seating having a relaxed natter about the occupants of the chalet next door.

In this 'Children rule – OK' atmosphere we soon forgot about the Regency SS, although I did visit the adjoining restaurant for a quiet read and a coffee once or twice. The only dancers were the two red blazers and a couple who looked like their parents.

I could not summon much interest in the ubiquitous competitions, a favourite pastime for some. We all want to be loved and admired, I suppose, some more than others do. The prelude to these occasions was mildly entertaining. Disguised accordingly, the same people competed in each event!

All were to be seen occupying front seats, preening and painting themselves for each competition, one 'Glamorous Granny' finalist turned up in a mini-skirt to win 'Miss Lovely Legs.' The entertainment came when entrants were invited to come forward and collect their number. At this point the lovely ladies underwent a much-displayed personality change. Their cleverly shaded lids were lowered demurely as they came over all shy and negative. The only way to get them on stage was over a steward's shoulder.

'Over your red body' seemed to be their slogan. Then comes the unbearable part, each entrant is asked in turn to name her favourite TV personality – my signal to retire – yawn, yawn.

Manners maketh man

THE headmaster of a Dorset comprehensive school said recently that good manners are to be added to the school curriculum.

Pupils are to be instructed in the gentle art of saying 'Please' and 'Thank you.'

Good manners were a compulsory part of my school life; if these were evident other shortcomings were less noticeable, I found. In spite of this strict endorsement of politeness, I notice that in some areas of adulthood charm and courtesy have undergone a sad decline. Perhaps this subject should also be introduced into the field of adult education.

It has been my misfortune to come into contact with many potentials who would benefit from a refresher course in good manners.

Like the snooty assistant who pounced on our diminutive fifteen-year-old as she was diligently selecting the correct batch of 'Key Notes' in preparation for her GCE exams.

'You won't be taking those for quite a while,' she sniffed, snatching the notes from my embarrassed daughter. This assistant's powers of observation must have been lying especially dormant that day, because she also failed to notice diminutive me browsing through the paperbacks opposite. Fortunately what I lack in stature I make up for in assertiveness. Suffice it to say we left no 'Key Note' unturned and I made certain my daughter had seen all the cards before she selected the one she required and we swept out.

These superior dignitaries who keep the sight of their front teeth a secret between their mirrors and themselves are becoming a silent feature in some establishments, where the 'We aim to please' has been replaced by a 'Get Lost' attitude.

Journalist Lynda Lee-Potter visited a London boutique recently. Her daughter, unable to make a decision, said she would look round first then come back and try on the £39 coat again later. 'Don't bother,' was the salesgirl's helpful hint.

In one town centre chemists an assistant tried to blame us for her low IQ. Two daughters and I were choosing a bikini. Our buxom thirteen-year-old was trying to persuade me to purchase what looked like three small triangles and a piece of string. 'It's been reduced a lot,' she coaxed. Reduced! It looked to me as though it had been demolished. In my poverty-stricken opinion the price of £1 a triangle seemed grossly exorbitant, even if she could squeeze into it.

We were in the middle of this debate when a burly till-pusher turned on us and rasped 'Will you be quiet I can't reckon up.' With such a handicap why take a job involving cash? I was careful not to ask, as she was rather a big girl for her impediment.

Serving food can have a disastrous effect on good manners. Some friends decided to treat an elderly parent to dinner at a regal country pub about seven miles from town. Although months previously this had been booked and confirmed later by phone, the manager had no record of it. After making

166

them feel like confidence tricksters out for an easy table he finally, after much dragging about of chairs and other ostentations, led them to a secluded table, away from the 'registered' clientele. After an hour they realised it must also be secluded from the waitresses. At last they attracted the attention of one who condescendingly asked what they wanted.

By this time most of the items were 'off' and she made it quite clear she was hoping to be the same – as soon as possible. When asked what kind of soup she had brought, 'I don't know,' was her amazed reply.

Not wishing to make their elderly guest feel more unhappy than she already was they paid up and left without throwing anything at the manager. But they told all their friends who told all theirs – so it is likely this establishment will have less business to confuse in future.

Although some of my best friends are hairdressers they are not immune to this bad-manner cult. I had the ill-choice to be overpowered by one on holiday. In her voluminous caftan and faded jeans supporting an Afro hairstyle she looked like a curly Demis Roussos – from behind.

But the front view cancelled any frivolity usually associated with corpulence. Her lips were folded into a tight narrow crease. A lifetime of holding hairgrips between her teeth had obviously taken their toll.

Giving me a Humphrey Bogart grimace she spoke the only four words of our alliance, 'How dya want it?'

My hands were trapped beneath the salon cape at the time, which caused me some amusement as I fumbled about trying to free them to describe my 'casual flick back.' These antics seemed to depress her even more, but I had no choice but to keep uncharacteristically quiet for the rest of the time.

I left wearing my highly bouffant, stiffly lacquered hair-do like a new hat, taking the long way back to the chalet in case the children saw me before I had time to dismantle it. Actually I was pleasantly surprised how manageable it was once I had tamed it.

*

PERIODICALLY, top-level studies are made on the effects wrought by television. In a recent survey Dr Belson discovered that screen violence could upset and disturb young children. The crunch of fist on jawbone seems to upset me most in our household. But what this research failed to report is the cruel discomforting embarrassment some TV relationships evoke in the not so young.

I think most of us are willing and able to exercise our imagination to the extent that we take it for granted once the naked duo reach the sheets they are not about to start making the bed.

167

So why do we – and at our house late viewing includes two impressionable teenagers – have to squirm, shuffle, reach for a newspaper, when what promises to be an interesting drama sinks into another excuse for an excessive grope and panting session – which no channel seems to be complete without.

This detracts from the plot in more ways than one. How do the camera team keep straight faces? What do their 'real-life' partners think about this 'perk' in their mate's occupation? I find my mind is pondering at this time. Once I used to watch horror movies through a gap between my fingers; I'm almost reduced to watching the passion wallowers the same way. During one sizzling performance I asked our son's feelings on the subject, 'Ssh,' he replied. I suppose all occupations harbour their own stresses.

*

'DO you think you look beautiful or ugly?' asked one of ours the other break-fast time as I threw my kitchen mirror a charming smile. Answers to these sort of posers have to be prepared carefully – one can so easily be trapped. 'Ugly,' I lied. 'You're right' she said.

If music be the food of love . . .

WITH over 400 courses listed in the adult evening class programme, it takes an evening to study it.

'Gardening Under Glass' sounds interesting, but uncomfortable. Perhaps the 'Chinese Language Culture' would improve the quality of my life; it would certainly brighten up my take-away visits where conversation to date is limited to 'Number 7 please.'

The subject that strikes me as being most enlightening is the 'Musical Appreciation' course. This could be vitally important in this music-orientated age – when we all are being manipulated by its continual drone from breakfast to midnight. But why should advertisers be the only ones to appreciate its advantages?

We have three radio channels that malign the air from 6am to midnight. Car radio enthusiasts can alternate with favourite cassettes in the meantime. Call in the supermarket for another blast of pop music to help loosen our purse strings and suitably relax us for a spend, spend, spend.

Buying a new outfit? Here in the semi-darkness with whispering back-ground beat that teenagers adore, all monetary inhibitions are drummed away as mum is persuaded to buy less and less for more and more.

Our gent boasts he can choose a suit from the shop window and be in and out in ten minutes. So what! His outfitter is musically uncontaminated-as yet.

Meanwhile in the front room the children are tuning up for another punishing hour on their freely hired instruments. When you have endured the much repeated sample of their free tuition for longer than you thought possible and refrained several times from hopefully suggesting they take on leather-craft, you are then invited to hear them play en-masse at the school musical evening. These instruments are unbelievably well made and never wear out.

Even my dentist has succumbed to the pound of music, he does all his cavity clearing to the twang of guitars. Whether any patients complained this was causing more pain than the treatment, I don't know, but one day he turned it off. On my last visit the weird music had been floating across the ceiling by the aid of a projector and slides. It took me some time to decide whether they were red blood corpuscles or just spots before my eyes. I admit they had a slight hypnotic effect until one appeared evilly to devour the others.

It took my mind off my latest fear of having a heart attack during my treatment. When I wasn't feeling neurotic about my eyesight I was desperately fighting off cancer fears. Actually my dentist's kind face and restful voice are all the tranquillisers I require, plus the six-inch spear he thrusts into my gum before each session of course.

Manipulating with melody is not new. The shepherd boy David was one of the first to discover its hidden potential, when he harped on to King Saul and soothed his savage breast. But where will all this musical directing lead us? Shall we eventually rebel at being continuously tuned-in?

During last summer a well-advertised brass band concert took place one Sunday afternoon in the pretty pavilion in a blossom-decked corner of nearby Marsden Park.

Flowers were blooming in the sunshine as we took our pick of the many empty seats at the corner of the plush bowling green. The band struck up its rousing overture and two small children wandered in to stare in surprise at the smartly uniformed musicians and their twinkling brass.

We spent a happy hour gazing across the magnificent Marsden landscape to the accompanying lilt of a Strauss waltz. Before we left I counted six people and two dogs. Such a colourful setting, a carefully chosen and excellently played programme – pitifully wasted.

Switch on ITV and ears are titillated again. It seems we will buy almost anything that activates our sound buds. Blending the right music with the desired social class image, the selling machine casts its spell. Forty-year-old housewives present the most profitable bait to advertisers.

Tunes from the Fifties, recreating the exciting atmosphere of the first romance, that first reach out for freedom are all aimed at softening us up for the supermarket.

Our minds have been well and truly motivated by the bright, suggestive visual aids and now the strains of music are creating an even more portentous impact. Even the newly-born can become impassive on hearing certain sounds.

A Japanese recording of a mother's womb sounds, which is said to put a crying baby to sleep, is a best seller at the moment. Some farmers are successfully serenading their cows into a more generous milking mood with the aid of the Beatles.

My dog is also affected by the tonic-sol-fa. One croon from me and he's begging to leave the room. But if music hath such charms why couldn't some-one introduce a little into my maths set? We have rapidly progressed since the cheery voice of Bill Gates introduced 'Worker's Playtime.' A half-hour lunchtime show geared to entertaining factory workers in their canteens during the war. 'Music While You Work' was another half-hour recital of popular songs that revolutionised working life and transported bored workers into new spheres of conscientious diligence.

We have come a long way since then, the Big Brother world of George Orwell's '1984' may be nearer than we think. But even the best advertising ploys can misfire. Most of us were more interested in William Franklyn's act-ing than the 'You know who' soda water he advertised and I suspect more people were clamouring for a bloodhound like Clement Freud's Henry rather than the morsels he used to frown.

It strikes a raw chord with me when manipulators start strumming on my own insecurities, and I confess the fact that I am in the much-sought-after consumer group definitely makes me feel 'kneaded,'

I demand the right to choose freely, even if it's the wrong choice. I refuse to be coaxed into buying something I don't need or cannot afford. Nothing can alter the fact that quality is the best selling power and, anyway, not even Beethoven himself could persuade me that margarine tastes better than butter. It's time we consumers did our share of manipulating.

When the leaves fall . . .

ABOUT this time of year something happens to my bed. Although its mag-netic pull is the daily bane of my workaday life, suddenly it feels even more comfortable; the sheets appear invitingly warmer and softer, the pillows stay at just the right slant.

Each morning our parting become more acute – a condemned man could not enjoy the luxury of an extra five minutes more than I. For twenty-three years I have struggled to become adept in the art of being the first to leave it, but as yet I only manage on birthdays and holidays.

These are all signs that the pleasures of autumn are descending upon us. The 'back end' season of fires and toast, chips instead of salad, succulent stews and butter-filled crumpets are with us once more. Our kitchen is brimming with wintry sounds even now.

The sizzle of wet teabags on hot cinders mingled with the welcoming-home cries of 'shut that door!' followed by the dreaded rattle of an empty coal bucket heralding its answering chorus of 'I filled it last.'

A much-enjoyed winter's afternoon treat at our house is home-toasted marshmallows. For the uninitiated all you need is a packet of marshmallows and a long fork each. My children use my old knitting needles. Stick a mallow on the end, hold in front of the fire, preferably coal when it's nice and red, until hot and gooey, and then eat. One packet lasts twice as long and they are lip-smacking tasty.

Now is about the right time to bring your gardener in from the cold, replacing his spade with a paint can and brush, of course. During this 'season of mists and mellow fruitfulness' I have dutifully 'ploughed the fields and scattered' my sopranic intonations all over school and chapel. I love the rousing harvest hymns, second only to the Christmas Carols. It is such a relief unashamedly to exercise one's arpeggios. For some reason I only feel able to do this fully when drowned by the sound of other voices – or the sound of my vac sometimes sets me off.

On the odd occasion I do give full vent – unaccompanied – someone always intervenes. In the middle of one exceptionally sensitive rendering from my 'Madame Butterfly' selection I was supporting myself dramatically on the fridge door as I peered into the distance at my audience – the dog. 'He comes,' my voice held a tear, 'Can you guess who it is . . . can you guess what he'll sayyyy?' I was almost sobbing, when a brusque voice from behind me grunted 'Parcel missus.'

I have tried all my life to understand my mother's aversion to all things hymnal. The inspirational vocal efforts repeatedly performed by my sister and I with intermittent bass and tenor harmony from my father only brought forth her walking coat and a fond farewell, 'You put years on me.'

Having attended harvest functions for many years with young toddlers, it was a feeling of relief that I eventually went solo. It gives one a certain power to be able to sing from a hymn sheet held the right way up, without a dead weight in one arm and a writhing escapist on the other.

The smell and sight of all the untouchable fruit seems to have an adverse effect on the young, mine had to be trained for a week in advance.

The pleasure of my first lone appearance was slightly marred by the unnerving stare of an overgrown baby hanging over the shoulder of his mother in front of me. His fat little pulpy features were disfiguringly plugged by an outsize dummy, which amazingly remained intact until the final Amen.

His bottom lip was in constant danger of overtaking his plastic rim, and most disturbing for my debut. Instead of letting go I found myself whispering – he seemed just as horrified by my singing as I was with his sucking.

He had sucked it so vigorously, when mum finally removed it he still bore the scar and looked as if he was still sucking it.

I had a nasty shock at one harvest, someone had removed all the schoolchildren! We adults were left to fend for ourselves. With no one sure when to stand or kneel.

We spent the first half bobbing up and down and the second half seriously divided. One half stood the other half sat.

The recent bread strike nearly provoked me into breaking a Commandment. At one festival there were only six inches and the glare of the preacher between me and a golden crusted home-baked cob.

Incidentally, although it's autumn my dog is still airing his springtime instincts. Nonchalantly untouched by the sad fate of Victor the giraffe, he is still trailing home after hours wearing his sultry Marlene Dietrich expression looking as if any minute he will howl into a husky version of 'Falling in love again, what am I to do – I can't help it.'

Although now in his thirteenth year his rampant condition shows no signs of wavering, whether this is due to his daily diet of left-overs or the occasional supplement of marrowbone jelly spliced with thiamin, I wish I knew.

It was the televised dog food advert that had a serious effect on our son's career aspirations. He was all set for the fire station until he heard an advert mentioning thiamin. After watching for a while he burst into tears. When at last we managed to comfort him back to speech we asked him why he was crying. He told us they had started putting 'firemen' in dog meat!

*

AS the nights wax colder I shall be taking a rest from dietary caution. Most of my bulges will be well covered in winter weights anyway, so I shall not be buying the new gimmick currently tempting American housewives, called 'Diet Conscience.' This is a small box-like gadget that can be fixed to the fridge door.

Every time it opens a salutary voice yells 'What are you eating again? No wonder you're so fat!' It sounds too much like my husband, son and daughters - they give me the same advice - free!

*

IF like me you don't care anymore and you became hooked on dough-bashing during the recent strike, why not save a piece of dough for a delicious 'Lardy Cake?' Just roll out into an oblong as for puff pastry, dot two-thirds with small pieces of lard, sprinkle with spices, fruit and sugar, then fold bottom up, top down and repeat the process three times. Leave it to rise again, criss-cross the top with a sharp knife and bake in a hot oven for about thirty minutes. 'Scrumptiousness divine' as one of our addicts puts it.

On the receiving end

'DO YOU buy presents to please yourself or the person you are buying for?' asked our budding Magnus Magnusson as we tried to decide on a friend's birthday gift. Mm-er-pass.

I suppose the honest answer is, yes I do choose presents I like and just hope my impeccable taste is shared by the recipient.

At our house we share a zest for the mysterious, and love presenting sur-prises. If these well-meaning eyebrow-lifters are to be fully appreciated, an auto-suggestion period is necessary beforehand.

We are about to enter this phase now. There are exactly twelve hinting and hoping weeks before Christmas and early 'dropping' takes much of the shock out of the unwrapping. Stops one overdoing the 'more blessed to give' bit.

Receiving gratefully is an art we could all cultivate. On receiving a gift recently, a relative branded one of our children a 'naughty girl' for spending some of her precious holiday money on her.

Accepting pre-school gifts is an uncomplicated affair. Just a case of finding enough spare time to unravel the mysterious looking bundle of string and brown paper and possessing a stomach strong enough to digest the couple of well-sucked toffees you eventually discover.

When they are older and their spending money and your loose change has been sacrificed for weeks in order to buy something you really need, the correct acceptance expression is all important when they present you with the glass bear filled with bubble-bath liquid.

At children's parties all the agony is in the giving, as anyone who has witnessed the nail-biting crew of present-bearers will verify. The much-labelled and lovingly wrapped gifts are roughly torn open, fleetingly examined, then thrown on the sideboard.

During the war I sent our leading-aircraftsman father a tie-pin for one birthday. It was slightly rusty and had probably been in the gutter - where I found it – for some time. Embedded in the top was a jewel which could only be a diamond and I had to go through a lot of heart searching before I reluctantly took it from my school tie and pinned it to the letter. I could well imagine the envy it would evoke when my dad turned up on parade with this twinkling jewel flashing from his dark tie.

But the passing weeks brought no mention of promotion for smartness on parade. Then a letter arrived with a photo of my dad in his West African uniform of khaki shorts and open necked shirt, I was disgusted. Although the pin was mentioned in all my foreign dispatches until the end of the war, it never arrived.

Although money gives mouth-drooling pleasure to our children, I am wary of giving it. An aunt in a moment of desperation (we were avidly listening in to another scorching episode of her character scarring) gave my cousin and me a shiny sixpence each.

In two darts of a snake's tongue we were in Mrs Green's shop across the road and I was asking for the never-before-seen sixpenny box. 'Are you spending it all at once?' said my cousin, aghast.

But I was busy turning over the luxurious boxes. What a feast! I chose a box of fruit pastilles and, too eager to wait, dashed off to sit on our front steps and attack the full flavour.

I was about to 'press and tear off' when the grumble of voices from inside the house became noisily high-pitched and clearly audible. 'All of it?' – my mother's voice was loudest. 'The greedy little . . . where is she?' was all I needed to hear. Quick as a cat I scraped a hole in the soft damp soil and hid my prize.

'I still have threepence left,' gloated my cousin. And I was filled with regret. I should have buried her and kept the sweets.

Months later I was burying a dead frog when I unearthed the soggy sweets I had forgotten. All that remained were one or two coloured blobs and some sticky syrup.

This incidence had a crippling influence on my personality. After a long struggle my natural generosity fortunately prevailed. Today there is no trace of the old reluctance to spend up. I think my husband would support this statement.

Without exaggeration I can truthfully say I was presented with my most unexpected gift to date this July, a day before my birthday. It was an average end-of-the-week afternoon. My tired body was hanging fretfully over a deck chair in our back yard as I tried to summon enough strength to turn another page of my keep-fit manual.

Was an imminent coronary, hypertension, or varicose veins slowing me down? Two faces peeped around the corner and grinned. A minute later my husband and son wheeled a brand new bike over the dog's tail.

After a short speech of acceptance – 'What on earth? Oh no – not mine! Why?' – I pulled myself together and gratefully looked forward to another twenty years' cycling. What had I done to deserve it? Come to think of it I had insulted my old bike and complained of cyclists' knee occasionally.

But new bikes have their drawbacks – they never wear out. The intricate gears have taken some mastering, but I can change them now without stopping first. I wish lorry drivers who whistle at my back view would learn to hide their disappointment more endearingly when they arrive at the front.

I am still not sure what will happen when I stop. The other day I squeezed the brakes, swung my legs elegantly into position to greet the kerb, but when I stopped the bike didn't. We fell in two untidy heaps in front of my greengrocer.

One day I prepared to disembark and found I had suddenly been struck paralytic. My anorak was hooked over the back of my saddle and had me pinned in an immobile position before I finally collapsed in another untidy heap in front of my greengrocer, who has taken to enquiring about my health every time we meet.

I can now return pedestrians waves without riding into the nearest garden. 'We passed you on the road the other day panting and blowing,' giggle some of my friends. 'You were on your bike,' they add, splutter splutter. I could not cause more amusement if I galloped up Manchester Road on a hippopotamus.

The most embarrassing part is taking a corner. I feel so ridiculous with one arm in the mid-air and the other trying desperately to control the handlebars.

All presents lovingly given are surely acceptable, especially the home-made ones. I remember the light-as-air sponge brought to my sick bed by a kindly neighbour, the hand-sewn Mothers' Day apron embroidered with 'mum' from our hard-up student. The countless Christmas cards and gifts so lovingly made and presented over the years.

175

I only hope Liz Taylor's diamonds and Jackie O's millions give them a third as much pleasure.

A trip to the 'lights'

IT'S overcrowded and scruffy, there is a pervading air of horse manure and fried onions wafting along the tram-lined promenade, everything has to be queued for and takes twice as long.

So what exclusive ingredient draws the crowds, not to mention their £50m to bawdy Blackpool from Easter right through to Christmas?

And in spite of the inclement weather and the incessant queuing, why does everyone look so matey? Blackpool must boast the hardest worked landladies in the business. After a few short recuperative weeks in Majorca, they are back in accommodating mood once more busily dividing their partitioned bedrooms yet again to take in even more visitors the following year.

Last year besides hotel and other novel expenses Blackpool cost me a cherished purse and its contents. As a result our relationship felt well and truly severed. I only supported our Sunday School illuminations trip on Saturday out of a sense of duty. But when their feverish voices were announcing hysterically 'I can see it – it's there' my indifference deserted me and I was straining to see the Tower with the rest, my infantile joy dribbling all over my cheese teacake.

Rigby Road bus station was bursting with empty buses as we embarked. The day-trippers, easily recognised by their uniform of T-shirts, jeans and fancy sombreros resting on their pierced ears, occupied the rest of the space.

We pushed with the rest of the crowds towards what we hoped would turn out to be the sea front. Trying to curl intransigent fingers of six to eight year olds into a controlling hand-clasp in the midst of Blackpool exuberance is not easy.

Feet occupied every inch of promenade. The roads were blocked with traffic. With a hair-splitting gale rattling our teeth we decided the emptiest part of Blackpool was the beach. The wind was blowing waves of sand at the raging sea as we descended the wooden steps. A donkey man was galloping across the sand with his animals, after a long season he looked more like a donkey than they did. 'They know just how far to go you know, and won't go any further' he told me. For some reason this seemed to upset him.

In the meantime our young adventurers, in a most undonkeylike manner were belting up the sands towards the delights of the Pleasure Beach. Taking big gulps of ozone through the spaces in our scarves and looking like wander-ing Arab extras from a Desert Song film-set we did our best to pursue them.

At 12p a time donkeys must be the cheapest form of travel in Blackpool, the shortest tram journey has shot up to 18p.

Some of the more observant among us couldn't help gawping at the promenade scenery as we passed. One couple were practising passionately for an X certificate in an open shelter, successfully keeping out the cold and other embarrassed would-be occupants. A large mother appeared to have small faces sprouting from everywhere, in her pockets, up her sleeves, under her feet, all contentedly buried in fish and chip papers.

At 5.30pm we reached the South Pier and the children's spirits suffered when someone pronounced the Pleasure Beach suffocatingly full. With only an hour left to unload their stuffed purses they naturally panicked. But the clink of falling copper from the pier amusements brought the blood back to their cheeks and the pungent smell of coffee lured me in with them.

Moving a pile of soiled plastic cups, which the overworked staff hadn't had time to clear, I tried to bend my small well-padded frame into the six-inch space provided. Like the landladies, café proprietors are infected with the double-up bug. If this continues what will happen to the larger person. Will Blackpool only be fit for streamlined dwarfs?

To say our groups were scattered about spending their savings with a speed that would have brought a tear to many a parent, our knees were sticking in our necks and our fingers were shrivelled visibly under the hot plastic cups, we adults did enjoy a second or two sipping the cream coloured liquid.

'Has anyone seen Carol?' soon revived our day trip mood.

With only forty-five minutes to bus time and an ever-increasing toilet queue to master, we waited for last-minute rock-buyers, lost another two members and finally trundled back to the bus station.

But that carefree 'Golden Mile' feeling was already throbbing beneath my fur collar, as we passed the crowds battling there way back to their 'full board' and 'luxury' flats.

Headscarves were lashing the life out of new perms. Dads were carrying youngsters in one arm with their other wrapped around mum. Teenage twosomes were huddled together behind prams. Everyone seemed to be keeping time to some inward rhythm of content.

177

Strangers nod and smile and suddenly you have an insatiable urge to stop and down a plate of salty mussels, or nip into Ripleys and 'believe it or not,' you also long to test your powers of recognition in Tussard's Waxworks.

Madame Tussard's, the place where during one hot summer patrons queuing in front of us were chokingly offended by the acrid smelling atmosphere, putting it down to the odious effect of heat on painted wax.

In fact I was in a position to confirm the pungent aroma was actually a combination of landladies' haute cuisine and my uncle's delicate gastric system.

Is it the sea air, the universal camaraderie or just the feeling that we are all 'in it together?' Whatever the reason it always affects me this way and I am wishing I could stay a while longer.

Perhaps it's nostalgia, a longing to return to the seaside dreams of childhood. During the war, big-spending, gum-chewing Americans took over the horse-drawn landaus. I used to watch them ride past the Tower with a blonde wrapped in each arm, shocking most of the civilians. I longed for the day when I could wax disgusting in a horse-drawn carriage with a 'Yank,' but the war ended leaving another dream unfulfilled.

At exactly 6.30pm our children's fingers were pressed against the bus windows in gleeful anticipation of the highlight and the reason for our trip to the 'illuminations.'

By 9pm we had moved about a mile up the road towards Squires Gate – the gateway to all our afternoon dissertations.

With three full lanes of traffic feeding into the main promenade stream and no driver displaying any intention of 'giving way,' mutiny was rife in our camp. After another cramping hour one desperate member left the bus and approached a motorist. Pleading a bus full of Sunday school scholars longing to see the 'lights,' she threw us on his mercy. Our prayers were answered and he let us in. We quickly wakened the children and ordered them to wave and cheer as he dipped his headlights at us.

Alas, we never saw him again. But at last we faced the twinkling cascade and dazzling shapes that made up Blackpool illuminations.

What a pity all the painstaking work and detailed planning that goes into creating this electric showpiece is frustratingly ruined by the stop-starting, waiting and gear grinding, not to mention the spurt of poisonous fumes, one has to endure in the process.

Our driver was particularly long-suffering, not only had he to endure the trials of brake-pushing, but he was supervised closely throughout by three pairs of mascara-daubed eyes staring down on him from the back window of the bus in front.

178

A youth driven insane with desire climbed up their window and was rewarded with a face full of cigarette smoke. Our driver, contrary to advice from behind did not 'Ram 'is 'ed in.' The lucky children who managed to fight off Morpheus voted 'The Gingerbread Factory' at Bispham their favourite. The luminous sight of a tram 'dressed up as a boat' overcame one child.

When a plastic bucket was produced for toilet arrangements, small-boy chauvinism was well to the fore, little girls were too modest to insist on equal rights and big girls were not invited.

Jammed on the inside by buses filled with snoring passengers, some turned their interest to the enticingly lit lounges of the sea front hotels and a hamburger kiosk caused some anxiety.

Looking like an old friend the elegant dome of the Winter Gardens rose impressively from its cramped position between bars, bistros and seaside novelties.

At 2.0am four of us were sat clutching our Ovaltine and telling our stay-at-homes, who had stayed up for us, about our eventful day.

'Did you enjoy yourselves at Blackppool then?' we were asked. The answer was a unanimous 'Yes!'

Like the crazy distorted images that stare back unbelievably at us from the 'Hall of Mirrors' – this cannot possibly be you - but giggle, chuckle, it makes you laugh. That's Blackpool.

Chips and everything

ONE of the most pleasurable habits to develop from my dilatoriness is our Friday lunch ritual of fish and chips.

I didn't slip into this easy living without a fight, of course as being seen in the fish shop queues in the early days of married life made me feel as guilty as a baths attendant caught smiling.

I made up all sorts of fictitious excuses, 'the cooker's collapsed,' or 'our kitchen's full of workmen,' to anyone who saw through my disguise.

Now, blatantly and without shame, I confess to all – my dinner is cooked most Fridays either by a besmocked lady or if I am in the mood, not to mention funds, an Oriental gent does the honour.

I was promoted to Friday fish-and-chip carrier in my teens while working for a printing firm. Although tedious it had its perks. I could spend a jolly half hour away from workaday strife among the wits in the composing department; here my girlish outlook on life was considerably broadened and if I was quick enough my queuing coincided with that of another apprentice fish fetcher – whom I fancied nearly as much as the fish and chips.

A change from my usual pop-star impersonating boy friends, this lad was the image of Jesus. His hair, beard and blue eyes looked exactly like the Sunday school pictures I remembered. From my lowly nose-on-counter position I worshipped him religiously for about four Fridays.

Then one day he wasn't there and the assistant dropped the bombshell: 'He committed suicide.' The smell of fish and chips lost its allure for months after that. I spent a long time pondering on the sad-eyed youth.

Earlier recollections were all connected with the cinema. A gang of evacuees and myself used to spend an evening watching Tarzan and Jane until we were eventually turned out into the misty musty air for the trolley-bus. The lure of salt and vinegar perfume from the wooden hut by the bus stop had us weighing up the choice between a ride home or a three-hayporth bag of chips and a long walk through dark fields.

'To eat now, or wrapped up?' had us fighting for a turn with the vinegar bottle, then out into the cold to face the walk home. When I think of the evenings we walked through those lonely fields and never had any nasty encounters, truly amazes me.

Today I dare not let our children cross the street alone after dark. But during my youth the most able-bodied were busy attacking Germans.

I don't know whether the secret of bought fish and chips is in the ensuing soak of salt and vinegar or the esoteric 'Examiner' wrapping, but I have never yet been able to capture the same delicious flavour with my frying pan.

I can manage the chips – but my battered fish look exactly that. Instead of the tongue-tickling smell of golden crispy fish lumps, our kitchen is filled with a deathly blue haze, which hangs about for hours. And, of course, there are no bits. At today's prices I always ask for my share of these crunch-ups and I give the condiments a good shake-up.

I shall never forget the fish shop an aunt sent me to one suppertime. All the way there I practised the fascinating French accent I was playing around with at that time. It worked wonders with strange assistants and was always worth a few extras. At that time foreigners were a bit of a novelty.

The fish lady was really impressed. I was just getting warmed up to allow-ing her a sentence or two more 'Thankeeng you er vairry much, sil-vous-plais' when my aunt's neighbour, a workmate of my father walked in and spoiled everything. 'Ello lass, 'ow's yer dad?' It made me wish I had stuck to my broken leg act. This was guaranteed to soften any chipper's heart, as long as I didn't get too cocky and forget which leg was injured.

Watching the crispy chips pile up only to be shovelled on someone else's order can have a malevolent effect on the appetite, which can be embarrass-ing. Watching for fallen chips, I once darted my hand forward, but the treasure was snapped up by a lady in front – we exchanged guilty smiles.

The old-fashioned noises have disappeared along with the ornamental enamelled ranges. The white tops on vinegar bottles which had a sort of delayed splurt when you shook them; the crunch of naked potato being executed as the guillotine handle was brought down on it and the chips fell into the bucket underneath.

Our chipper was such a gasbag it's a miracle we didn't have chip fingers. He always left his hand holding the potato until the very last second – a terri-fying sight.

Our Friday lunches were especially enjoyable when we had a baby and even had me waxing poetic. I used to sing this song to the children as we prepared for our shopping trip.

Catching my excitement they used to join in:
'My best day is Friday, shall I tell you why?
We all have chippy charlies, and the baby doesn't cry!'

And she didn't. Friday was her day for a tin of strained food and, it says a lot for my cooking, she was especially contented. My euphoria evoked by the thought of someone else preparing dinner and no washing up, infected us all – except the dog. Left-overs were in short supply on Fridays.

Good batterers are in danger of becoming extinct. But there is one or two still frying. We have a favourite eating place in York. A certain square over-shadowed by the ancient Minster has two excellent fish and chip takeaways.

Wooden seats and strategically placed baskets are thoughtfully provided all around the square. Shoppers can sample our national dish in the open air – it's quite matey and cosmopolitan.

In my opinion outdoor fish and chips eaten from paper are unbeatable. It takes a while to master the feeling you are doing something faintly illegal, a hangover from a school rule, 'No eating in the street,' but worth it when you do.

Health experts have voted them the top take away meal, safer than curries or Chinese delicacies while re-heated foods like kebabs and hamburgers are con-sidered the most dangerous foods on the market. In an annual report restaurants and take-away food shops were blamed for the increase in food poisoning last year - so fish and chips are actually one of the safest foods, health-wise.

At 32p I consider them more expensive than they ought to be. No one has yet given me a creditable explanation why they always increase early season, but never decrease when potatoes come down in price.

NB: Consumer analysts MINTEL published a report on December 17th, 2004, which says over £25bn will have been spent this year on eating out. Fish and chips came out on top, with over 50% saying it was still their favourite take-away. The price however is now £2.60 - WB

The bathroom terror

WHO would dream that one small creature, barely two inches long, could plunge a robust household of seven into such frenzied jeopardy?

Who could imagine the fear and trepidation wrought by one small breakfast announcement from son; 'By the way I met a mouse on the bathroom corridor this morning.'

Undeterred by my nervous collapse, he rambled frighteningly on, 'He was just ambling cheekily along the edge of the carpet not even hurrying.' Just our luck to get an adolescent-type mouse. 'Wwwhat did you do,' I managed to blurt, after persuading my heart to 'keep going you fool.'

'Oh you would have laughed,' he chuckled, as I grabbed a handful of Co-deine. 'I stuck out my foot and he just walked over it!'

In two twitches of a mouse's whisker, coats were donned, bags slung on shoulders, doors slammed and I was . . . alone. Well, just me, the dog and our wild beast in the bathroom.

All morning I kept near the dog, quaking and jerking at every sound. Then during one stoic spell of fortitude, I had just endured five minutes of Tony Blackburn, and if I can stand that surely anything is possible, I told myself. So, grabbing the reluctant dog who, by this time, was sitting with his legs crossed looking hopefully at the door, I forced him up the stairs and dragged him towards the bathroom.

We peeped gingerly around the door, nothing. All was silent except a syncopated metallic click that turned out to be the effect of my heartbeat on the good luck charm I wear around my neck. When the rise and fall of my chest became less noisy, I bravely thrust the dog's head into the cylinder cup-board and waited. Again, nothing.

Had my son been joking? I pondered as I listened to our mongrel's urgent sniffs. We surely couldn't have a mouse running, I mean strolling around, and not observe other give-away signs? At this hopeful point in my conclusions, the dog started some non-stop sniffing in the area why my nightie normally curls up. 'Good dog! Find it lad!'

182

This was quite exciting. My primitive instincts were impressively aroused for all of two heartbeats. Up until the moment I happened to turn my eyes towards the other corner and perceived a diminutive brown velvet form creep out of a wool sock and dart towards me.

I didn't stop until I reached the safety of the kitchen door, with the dog panting at my heels.

Some hunter he turned out to be! All that showing off with the next door's cat.

I spent the rest of the morning fighting hysteria and looking through house sales. I screamed when the milkman opened the door and when a letter dropped unexpectedly through the letter-box, I picked up the poker.

Even my shopping trip was mouse-miserable. It was so depressing seeing other carefree shoppers hurrying happily back to their pest-free homes. All able to visit their bathrooms without initially performing a hearty clog dance on each stair. It's not that I minded him living with us really, I rationalised – if only he would learn to use the bathroom last . . after me.

By tea-time everything had become mouse-shaped and I was gasping like a puncture. That dark patch on the curtains, the crease in the towel . . . was it? . . . could it be . . ?

The previous afternoon I had lounged felicitously in a silky warm bath up to my neck in tranquillity and Yoga breathing. Little did I realise small eyes were watching and planning a big take-over. All the promise of Yoga ruined in a day by three ounces of mouse flesh.

'Did you catch it?' was the optimistic tea-time greeting. Never before have I welcomed a table full of school clutter so gratefully. We decided, after a brief conference, no one was going to bed until father or big brother had done his duty.

Spider-addict son now turned mouse lover was aghast. 'Kill it! Kill a harmless creature . . . What harm has it done?' he asked as I filled the sugar basin with scalding hot tea. But wielding charm and promises of no coal fetching, eventually we persuaded him into the bathroom with orders to 'just carry it outside, then.'

We sat quietly planning who should sleep where, using my age, authority and nervous twitching, I bagged the dining-room settee. Our big white hunter entered briskly in a clean shirt, minus the day's grime, sporting a toothpaste smile. With a cheery 'Lend me a quid – see you,' he was off. Never even mentioned 'the you know what.'

It would have to be father. I hesitated to disturb him. Just having completed an epic kitchen paint job he was now busy painting all the buffets. It would seem strange to see him without a paintbrush.

Still, priorities had to be preserved. Which would he prefer, a mortified wife or a glossy kitchen stool? It transpired he wanted neither. The call of a TV football match proved bigger than both of us.

Son arrived home unusually early, raising our spirits slightly – until he took his place beside other heartless fan.

Nothing for it but to try the dog again. After much searching I eventually discovered latter crouched behind piano. This time we shut him in the bathroom and ran away. His cries of anguish echoed downstairs, even drowning the ecstatic yells of our football fanatics.

Between shouts of advice to the referee, son playfully threw small furry objects at anyone who stopped twitching long enough. Small daughter, who only yesterday was on her knees begging me to take in school gerbil for holidays, was now a mental wreck at the thought of being first to bed. A useful time to mention my gerbil doubts. She reminded me this is a cage-dweller – I'm beginning to wish I was.

She was eventually persuaded to dole out goodnight kisses and ran her finger nails up the back of my neck just for a laugh. I burst into tears.

At 11pm I prepared my farewell speech. 'What sort of son is it who will not kill a tiny mouse for his mother? St George tackled a fire-spurting dragon for his.' Husband turned up volume and I noticed for the first time that his face has a distinctly unhealthy pallor beneath the mushroom paint.

'Look, it's only that size,' he tried to convince me at bedtime, as he placed his clothes on top of the wardrobe then locked the bedroom door.

But thanks to a sprinkling of wonderful, peace-bringing rodent poison, our household has now returned to normal. I followed the instructions on the tin, tried to ignore the children's 'Ooh! Come and listen mum, it's great! You can hear it crunching.'

Tried to ignore eldest daughter's remarks about their college mice going berserk for three or four days before finally succumbing to death's blessed release.

Since our son triumphantly carried one small, strong smelling corpse to the rose garden, I have stopped tying our dog to the bedpost when I make the beds. He trembles so much he makes me nervous anyway.

But uneasy questions still pervade. Where did it come from? Was it, hopefully a bachelor out for a night on the tiles? Or, heaven forbid, has he a wife and family tucked away . . . somewhere?

Impersonators at large

'IS HE the real one, dad?' asked a small voice full of disillusion. Dad looked embarrassed. Giving Father Christmas another surreptitious glance he patted his offspring's wilting head and confessed, 'No son, he is probably one of his helpers.'

An excuse we parents pour out year after year when children come face to face with the pathetic ludicrous figures that fall far below their beloved storybook image, impersonators who mistakenly imagine that children are instantly appeased by the sight of a red dressing gown and a touch of cotton wool.

The scene was a Huddersfield toy department where an earlier than ever Santa had eventually settled after his long journey. Another small infant clutching a much-cuddled teddy wasp pushed on the dais where the beaming figure was holding court. One look at the bewhiskered face and the tiny teddy-clutcher collapsed in terror, which was not surprising as this year's Father Christmas was sporting . . . two moustaches! This must be a record even for him, definitely not a pleasant sight.

His bright new outfit, complete with boots, his friendly patter guaranteed to inspire the toughest agnostic, the merry eyeballs were all in vain – the whole bewitching effect was ruined by his phenomenal whiskers. The false moustache, a feature of most Santa's, had been severely displaced by a heavily aggressive home-grown one that refused to be disguised. This double layer gave him a sort of out-of-focus, double-dimensional appearance and had one wondering about double vision.

Consequently his beard was a little misplaced. There was a piece of chin sticking through the mouth gap and his beard was trailing round his Adam's apple, as if someone had held his beard down and given him a facelift, proving once again to young believers that Santa neither sleeps with his whiskers under nor over the sheet, but hangs them on the bedpost.

Kitting out Santa is no easy task, when his figure fluctuates so much each year. But let's give young imaginations a little credit. Even a three-year-old can see through a three-inch gap between false beard and chin. The idea of visiting without charge is most commendable though, and I hope this trend catches on – but please, Santa, shave off one layer.

Over the years I have paid to see some whimsical sights. Some with beards pointing due West, some with outsize moustaches almost growing out of their eyeballs, some whose spirit of goodwill had left a telltale stain along his whiskers and ignoring my negative expression promised too much too soon to one small boy.

After one expensive consultation one child (probably noticing the tatty outfit) marched out, demanding like an irate husband 'What does he do with all his money?'

Our son was miserably disappointed on one occasion to discover Santa wore dark pin-stripe trousers beneath his gown and wanted to know why he wore brown pointed toes instead of Wellies.

The toy shops are tantalising places to be now. Watching the pre-Christmas dramas unfold can be fascinating. First the family group stroll in holding hands. Mummy and daddy watch proudly as junior darts in ecstasy towards the invitingly packaged boxes. The mum gently drags him to one side while she checks the prices. Next dad starts prising off the cellotape to peruse the contents, he winds all the winders, tests the mechanical objects, flicks through the annuals; mum cuddles a doll or two, pulls the strings tugs the curls. Toddler waits anxiously in his non-seeing position below counter, until he decides it's his turn.

His groping fingers and tentative selectings do not go unnoticed. The extra Christmas staff swoop down brimming with motherly advice. 'Don't touch. dear.' Reminded of there responsibility dutiful parents scold naughty little boy and while mum drags wailing recalcitrant away dad makes his secret purchase. All exit, with youngest dying for the day he will grow up and become a toy-toucher, like dad.

I think it's safe to admit this now my children are older. When they were in their early 'I want' stages I used to dump them in the nearest toy department and with orders to 'stay here while I collect you' I let them loose on unsuspecting assistants while I disappeared for half an hour.

On my return they were either sitting on the steps scowling with a newly appointed 'heavy' patrolling the entrance or nowhere to be seen – according to their powers of subterfuge.
*

WE parents are now entering what must be one of the most harrowing seasons of all. Christmas loaves to mix, puddings to boil and all the green tomatoes to use up in home-made chutney. This is the sum total of my culinary efforts until the week before Christmas anyway. Every year I promise to make mincemeat of the Bramley's but have never made it yet.

Of course, if after all the power cuts you are still supporting a freezer, you can start wearing yourself out earlier, and prepare your entire Christmas menu during November. Then when the time comes all you have to do is switch on for the big warm up. Instead of a kitchen heavy with delicious vapours of frizzling turkey and bubbling savouries on Christmas Day morning and the usual bustle from oven to kitchen table – you are free to spend extra time with the family. Free to listen to all the old stories on their umpeenth airing or you can spend an enjoyable hour waiting for your turn at scrabble – as your pre-cooked delicacies thaw out on their own.

I am old-fashioned I know, but my Christmas Day kitchen has a perfume all its own, I actually enjoy cooking dinner on Christmas Day. My reward comes afterwards while the others are washing up and I am left with the chocs.

For any other old-fashionds this rich fruity Christmas pudding is an ancient family recipe (not mine) dating back to about 1713 and should be made now.

Ingredients:

8oz flour, 8oz suet, 8oz each sultanas, currants, raisins, peel, 1tsp mixed spice, 8oz grated carrot, 8oz brown sugar, grated lemon rind, 4oz chopped almonds, 1tsp grated nutmeg, small peeled raw potato grated, 1 large wineglass rum or brandy.

Method:

Mix together, put in basins, cover and steam for eight hours and store in cool place. Steam for another three hours at Christmas.

Back to winter food

I MANAGED in summer, but now there's not as much of me on display I find I am slipping back into my contented, delectable eating habits once more.

Will I ever kick this vocation I have for enjoying my food, I ask myself. Will my stomach ever get used to receiving only half of what it asks for; will the noisy protests it subsequently transmits between small portions ever be silenced?

Getting rid of the pounds is easy compared with the eternal struggle to maintain one's loss.

All you need is a bike, galloping harassment from family, hard work and a baking decline – 'I can't face baking and a diet' is my excuse. It helps if you can throw in a yoga crash course. Well that's how I have come to regard my weekly yoga class anyway. Every time my arms are asked to support my body – it's crash! If I try to heave my weight on to one leg – it's crash! But one day I hope to achieve the cross-legged position for at least two groans.

These classes really help to keep your bulges down, everyone else's leotard looks so unstretched – it's embarrassing for us tubbies.

We fat-fighters could do without a recent newspaper article boasting the attractiveness of bulkiness. 'Times' writer Hugh Tompson waffled on about a village in Nigeria where a girl is packed off to a stuffening farm the minute she gets engaged A fat wife is a figure of esteem for the African husband, a hint of his great wealth. Apparently a bloated wife indicates a bloated wallet.

Then there was the tantalising piece informing me that older men love vol-uminous partners – a longing to return to the fleshy enveloping womb – says Freud.

It's enough to evoke a serious bout of non-dietary logic in a semi-slimmer like myself. If I start eating now I could one day be just the cuddly sort of dumpty my old man will desire. But I desperately want to think thin.

Judging by the recently publicised divorces we all know what type of damsels attract the middle-aged ramblers. In last week's blow-up Bruce Forsyth looked all the forty-nine years he admits to after his 'in at the birth' ordeal, with the unwrinkled Anthea looking younger than ever. Good luck to them, I feel bound to say, although unlike accomplished divorcees I find it difficult to erase the memory of their previous marriage partners.

I couldn't help wondering how ex-wife Penny felt to hear Anthea cooing 'I have never seen Bruce look so happy.' Hair-tearing stuff but excusable, I suppose, considering she wasn't there for the three previous happy Forsyth events – probably she had just become one herself.

Actually I am at the most trickiest stage of my diet. If the family miss a day without a slim comment, I sulk sensitively.

Non-eating would be easier if I could mix only with the thin. It's no help to be reminded by contented non-dieters, that Anorexia Nervosa is just around the corner.

You eat because you want to be loved, say psychiatrists – I do, I do – but can't we eat first, please?

Would a fat in winter, thin in summer condition be more suited to my temperament? Winter food smells are so inviting, simmering stews spreading their appetising message all over the diet sheets, beefy casseroles with fluffy suety dumplings boiling their juices all over the oven – mmm – pass the bread, please. Then of course (another bout of non-dietary logic emerging) if I continue to keep wasting, the family is deprived of one source of amusement.

'Mum, Julie's come to look at your legs,' our youngest said one teatime, while her giggling companion lurked in the doorway. Friend had come for a demonstration of my thigh-dithering act, part of the previous evening's mirth-inducing designed for family viewing only – but it seemed my fame, like my thighs, was spreading.

There are only one or two useful tips I don't mind passing on to other sufferers. I find if I wear a skirt occasionally, such a change from my daily smock and trouser outfits, someone is sure to notice I have a dent around the waist area and comment on it.

Always weigh in at your emptiest. If the arrow still points in the wrong direction try: cutting toe-nails, eyebrows or stand on one leg. The verdict still depressing? If no one's looking try leaning - just a little – gets rid of the surplus a treat.

When life seems just one long stomach noise, dieting does often bring out the despicable in one. I pile my youngest daughter's lunchtime platter twice as high as mine, then when she's not looking I find myself pinching great forkfuls. When preparing supper for the family I cram my mouth to choking   point with biscuits when I am alone in the kitchen. Then I face the family martyr-like with my pot of sugar-less coffee. Sometimes I even wax mean with the dog, making him wait another hour with his empty dish.

Face watchers can be a deadly hazard. 'Have you been slimming?' they demand, making you feel like an alcoholic caught sucking wine gums. 'I thought so,' they nod bloatingly. 'You've lost your face.' Your hands fly to the place where your features are fast disappearing from and you dash home to the mirror. And yes – you look quite ill and gaunt – pass the cream buns.

When a doctor gave a friend of mine a diet sheet he told her 'All your friends will say you look better – never mind the others,' so I tell my friends this.

Last summer I thought I was winning when I bought a suit one size smaller than usual. Surely this would keep me on the straight and narrow. But summer's over and woollies can stretch so far.

If any of you are fighting a two way stretch this verse by Frances Cornford should help you to contract a little, especially the title.

To a fat white lady seen from a train
Oh fat white lady whom nobody loves
Why do you walk through the fields in gloves?
When the grass is as soft as the breast of doves,
And shivering sweet to the touch – missing so much and so much.
But if beauty is only skin deep – does it matter how much skin there is? There goes my non-dietary logic again!

189

The day of the stork

CONGRATULATIONS to Captain Mark Phillips. Anyone facing that delivery room without due qualifications deserves a rosette for valour.

What perfect timing! They cantered up to the starting line with plenty of time to spare. Time for him to retire to another room and nod through the labouring preliminaries, then he was fully alert to enjoy watching the main event and, tantivy! tantivy! It's a boy!

Not like a husband in our household who had his wife speeding towards hospital in an ambulance two minutes after she complained of backache. When disturbed wife rang home later to tell him a false alarm had been diagnosed, she learned that anxious father was starring in an all-important darts match.

On another occasion my man was discouragingly brushed out of maternity like a swarm of bacteria the moment my back was turned. No one asked him if he wanted to stay and watch, I can imagine the colour he would have turned if anyone had. To tell the truth I could have done with a blindfold and earplugs myself.

But my first hospital appointment coincided with an unfortunate drama. A hysterical sixteen-year-old had suddenly changed her mind. She had decided that giving birth was not her scene. As I entered the ward two hefty Sisters were trying to reassure her. While one described in detail the inhuman tapestry of stitches dissident mothers could expect, the other hinted at the dangerous effect this agitation had on unborn babies. It wasn't doing much for me either.

My teeth rattled together like a castanet accompaniment to a flamenco dance. I tried to remember what time the next bus was – thank God I hadn't unpacked. Looking around I noticed for the first time three other silent lumps protruding from the beds opposite. They must be either drugged or dead, I thought, either state seemed infinitely more desirable to me as I reluctantly allowed the nurse to ungrip my fingers from my small case handle.

As most pregnant ladies realise, one can only leave the 'receiving ward' via the 'delivery room. In receiving you part with everything except your baby. After the exacting enema this is about the only solid you retain. When you are bathed and clean shaven your pasteurised body is wrapped in what for everyone else resembles a shrunken shift – but in my case ample covering – you are ready for Sister's talk. 'Take these,' she says, crossing your palm with capsules, then a short click and you are plunged in darkness, alone with your ante-natal exercises.

Did Princess Anne attend anti-natal classes, I wonder? These are excellent propaganda for pregnancies. The one I attended gave us all an exciting preview of what we could expect when eventually delivered. We all became expert breathers. I, for one, left believing that if you could breathe in and out while slowly counting to ten, no labour pain was insurmountable.

So when the time came for me to meet my baby I was totally unprepared. Instead of a delivery room brimming with anti-natal conditioned staff waiting to count me peacefully into motherhood I was faced with two masked nurses who gave me the impression they had left a kettle boiling somewhere. Mind you, counting and relaxing were the last two thoughts on my mind, anyway.

Stretching a hand out for the gas and air mask was the only exercise I fancied. But my chance to show off came when one of them ordered me to 'pant!'

Now I cannot speak for others, HRH must be made of sterner stuff, but this 'panting' exercise takes some nerve to perform in front of hospital staff, never mind husbands. One feels so foolish lying there undignified with bent knees, ludicrously panting in and out like an overheated animal. But I followed the instructions to the best of my ability. Perhaps a little hesitant for a start but after the first apologetic coughs I really entered into it, doing a lifelike impression of an Alsatian I once knew, aptly named Randy.

However, as time dragged interminably on, my breaths flagged somewhat. How long was I suppose to keep this up? Unable to carry on panting any longer and live, I whispered in a barely audible rasp 'Can . . . I . . . stop . . now . . . please?' 'Stop what?' said a voice from a distant corner.

As memory came flooding back and she remembered who I was she apologised and handed me a bloodshot bundle as a reward.

Next to ward orderlies who have the all-important duty of bringing in the bacon, besides bedtime cocoa brewing, Sisters are the highest form of maternity hospital life, highly regarded by most mums. During my five confinements I regarded some more highly than others.

One Sister was a super efficient drug deterrent. Administering the sleeping draughts was one of her duties we came to dread. Her descriptions of poison-saturated blood streams left our minds festering with neurosis all night. Her nightly cry of 'Who's for poison, then?' could clear a locker top in two seconds. Only the large and the brave dared to take one of her sleeping pills. 'Good girls,' she would smile at the pill-less on her way out, leaving a trail of anxiety as she left. Were we breast-feeders slowly poisoning our off-spring? Was the soporific contentment we fondly adhered to our rich home-grown milk actually the deadly results of last night's sleeping pill? Until by morning we were praying our babies would still be alive and crying.

Once I heard a Sister whisper a blood-curdling sentence to my neighbour, 'Tomorrow we are going to take some marrow from your breast-bone, dear.' Her voice sounded so matter-of-fact she might have been saying 'Tomorrow I am taking your shoes to the cobblers.' I didn't like the 'we' bit, how much marrow were they going to take if it needed two to carry it? A short sentence but enough to shatter a newly-delivered.

One is at their mercy after all, once you cross that threshold there is no limit to what they can remove. You go in voluntarily hoping to have your baby, but if they fancy taking anything else you're in no condition to refuse, anyway.

'W . . . hat for? H . . . ow?' asked the now simpering wreck in the next bed. Sister sat down. I could see this description was going to be in detail, but I still eavesdropped. 'Just a needle into the bone.' That was enough. There was only one question in my mind now, whatever that girl was suffering from, was it infectious?

I sincerely hope the Phillips' enjoy their first baby, babies smell so much sweeter than horses, and you can dress them so much prettier.

Everything will be all right (I hope)

'BEST days of your life!' a stranger once confided to me in the middle of Woolworths.

I was about to swipe our three-year-old son with a loaded shopping bag at the time. He was doing his spider act all over the floor, entangling the legs of unsuspecting shoppers in the web of his shoulder reins, while his sister and I followed frustratingly behind, at the end of his tether.

Temporarily postponing my fury I craned him up to eye level to be looked at. Not quite the punishment I had in mind, but it reduced him to tears and I felt more amiable. The stranger tickled his chin and avoided a nasty side-kick, 'They aren't babies long enough, are they?' she smiled and left me pondering on the profundity of this remark.

Children seem to have this irritating habit of wringing platitudes from strangers. 'What a good little boy, and so quiet,' said one onlooker as I pro-duced our son from underneath a bus seat one day. His face was decorated with cigarette ash and his mouth full of bus tickets and I had just discovered this was the only way to travel with him – peacefully.

As a result of re-pagination after the colour section was printed some of the references made to text in the picture captions have had to be amended

Pictures of dancers (now page 359)
Enid, baby Heather and William (now page 314)
Saundersfoot harbour wall (now page 99)
William's allotment (now page 277)
William and Enid's wedding (now page 236)
Dirker Roods wedding (now page 247)
Dragonora Hotel (now page 238)
Whit Monday in Slaithwaite (now page 236)
Decorated lorry (now 236)
Whit Monday sing (now page 139)
Watching TV (now page 367)

Enid, aged nine with five-year old sister, Marlene

Enid, third left, with little sister Marlene and cousins Christine and Doreen In 1943 at Rhyl.

Enid's mum Emma, extreme right with group of mill girls about 1945.

Jack, Enid's dad front left during his RAF days in West Africa 1942 (see page 22).

DANCERS

Connie Hallas	Cynthia Crowther	Marjorie Abbot	Marjorie Evans	Pauline Morgan	Mary Hoyle	Gloria Lacey
Jean Whiteley	Audrey Spencer	Maureen Scara	Enid Jagger	Barbara Walker	Brenda Buckley	

(above): A group of girls from the Norah Bray School of Dancing 1949. Enid is the third from the right, front row (see Page 363).

(left): Two lovebirds. William and Enid at Middleton Towers Holiday Camp 1953.

Enid, baby Heather and William in their Lewisham Road home (1956). Heather looks as though she can't make up her mind about Veal knuckle bone broth. (see Page 318).

With mum Emma relaxing at Primrose Valley, Filey. Expecting Melanie at the time (1961).

*Heather, Emma,
Howard and Enid
making for the
Beach at Filey
(1961).*

*Louise, Melanie,
Amanda and Enid
at Saundersfoot
1974 (see Page 100).*

*The family
enjoying a
camping break at
Acaster Malbis
near York, 1975.*

*Just as Enid said 'weed free and all in straight rows.' One of Williams allotments
(see Page 280).*

*Paul Marshall, Chris Squires, William, Denise Bottom, Pat Taylor
and Enid bowling for charity 1992.*

*Receiving trophy at
Marsh United BC
after winning
mixed pairs cup
with William
(1993).*

Almost there! Runners-up in the North Ainley £1000 mixed pairs competition in Oldham.

Linthwaite Hall Ladies. Winners of Division II 1980 (Enid back right).

*Doing what she really enjoyed...
eating. Sampling a pastry in France
(1994)*

Typical baking day. Making apple pies with George in 2000.

(above): Enid at her happiest – playing with her grandchildren, Oliver, Emma, Tom, Jack, and Lucy in 1984 and below with George in 1998.

Enid's four 'little monsters' now all grown up.

With Howard and Amanda at one of Enid's Boxing Day parties.

October 25 1980

Dear Kay Bennett,

How very nearly right you are! But it wasn't quite
'good manners' that predominated but a healthy fear of
injunctions which put the brakes on my turn of phrase!
Not so much in this country, but in Italy. Sadly, if left
to my own devices, I would have omitted all that
happened after my mother brought me to England.

I shall take note of your constructive criticism (although
I make no excuses for revealing only my own sins).
The word I shall cling onto though is 'readable'
because, having been bitten now by this writing bug,
I would very much like to embark on a novel which I
would be able to lace with more spice than sugar!

I am grateful for your astringent review because I shall
learn from it.

With all good wishes,

Yours ever,

Katie Boyle

Letter from Katie Boyle following Enid's review of her book
"What This Katie Did" 1980

(left): Showered with confetti. William and Enid on their wedding Day 1954 (see Page 237).

(below) In the pink. Donald, Eileen, Enid and William at Heather and Michael's wedding reception at Durker Roods Hotel, 1979 (see Page 249).

(above): In the pink again, but a different outfit for Howard's Wedding reception at the Moorlands Restaurant 1981. (Below): Nice hat! Reception at the Dragonara Hotel, Leeds. Celebrating with daughter Heather (left) and guests 1980 (see Page 342).

This time an olive green outfit on the occasion of Melanie's marriage to Chris 1985. Note the new hairstyle.

Looking very happy in pink and grey for daughter Louise's wedding in 1989.

Tan and cream this time for Amanda's Wedding in 1995.

Lilac suit and nice big hat for Howard's second marriage. Pictured with William and granddaughter, Rebecca at reception at Hey Green, Marsden, 1997.

Whit Monday procession of witness making its way through Slaithwaite 1968 (see Page 238).

A typical Whit Monday scene (see Page 140).

Decorated lorry with primary children (see Page 238).

Leaving Slaithwaite Centenary Methodist Church.

Watching themselves on Television 1981 following Enid's accident (see Page 374).

During rehearsals for 'Family Fortunes'

My family are all off the reins now, their ages ranging from eight to 21 years. They are still inciting the aphorisms but with a difference.

Now it's 'They'll soon be out of the way,' or as a bus passenger put it last week, 'Growing up nicely.'

'Yes,' I lied, thankfully my three daughters squirming aggressively for their individual right to the front window seat, were hidden from view.

I have seen children grow outwards, upwards and even change shape alarmingly, but in my experience they never do it 'nicely.' All ages bring their own growing pains. One can never sit back complacently with that 'we made it' glow. Even if you manage to steer one child through a reasonably painless adolescence, this is no indication that the same tactics will be successful on the next. There is no universal panacea that guarantees good results every time. Unfortunately each masterpiece has its own intrinsic way of not 'growing up nicely.'

When two are approaching their fourteenth and sixteenth birthdays together complications can develop. Each year they threaten us with talk of a double party. Fortunately as they never agree on anything for longer than a mealtime, negotiations usually break down and celebrations are postponed. This year, however, there is an unbelievable air of goodwill pervading their conspiracies.

With only a week to 'blast off' and the party planners still on speaking terms, I am beginning to feel desperately uneasy.

This situation is slightly aggravated by the fact that their gala night falls during the same weekend as our eldest daughter's graduation ceremony. Father, graduate and I were planning a weekend in Reading and a little frivolous indulgence of our own. A breather I was especially looking forward to as our last escape was four years ago.

'Just think, mum, you can enjoy your weekend off and when you return everything will be back in its place.' But where will everything have been? I feel too sensitive to ask, and can they assure me that the young Samson who accidentally pushed his boot through their friend's lounge wall is definitely not on their guest list?

Other snatches of conversation are wafting about as they complete their plans. 'We don't want her!' says one disgusted voice. 'Why, is she too rough?' asks big brother optimistically, throwing me a grin. 'No, she's too good looking – all the boys will be after her,' comes the reply. So only the undesirables are invited? And what's this 'all the boys' business?

Food, which naturally has to be prepared in advance by mum, presents a problem. Potted meat sandwiches and jelly and ice cream have now graduated to a sophisticated fork buffet.

My suggestion of various savoury rice salads - in my opinion a good table and stomach filler - is loudly laughed upon. 'Oh, no, don't bother, they'll only throw it all over the carpet,' and they collapse into a giggling frenzy.

With only two days to breakdown, I mean countdown, I decide to play my ace and bring in a pair of grandparents. This news is greeted with unsophisticated panic. 'No one will want to come,' sobs one, which does lift my depression slightly. 'We are not babies,' cries another stamping off to her bedroom.

I suggest that grandparents can make their entrance late evening and their grief becomes less noisy. Next I have to talk my father out of the cosy idea of him watching television in one room while teenagers party quietly in another.

Children eventually persuade me that all teenagers conduct unchaperoned parties until midnight – all the time. Now all I have to do is convince grandparents. Have you ever had the feeling you are starring in a third-rate play where the badly written script is ruining your performance? Reversing the original Fairy Godmother instructions, I beg parents not to leave home until midnight. 'But we go to bed at ten,' says grandad.

It doesn't seem so long since that he was lecturing me on my late-night record, now here I am pleading for my children's extension. But gran promises them faithfully to restrain grandad until the witching hour.

I suppose everything will turn out all right, but disturbing images keep invading my mind.

I see a tired couple drowsing quietly in front of television only to be swept into teenage bedlam at midnight - the small lonely face of our eight-year-old unfortunately not on the guest list and banished to friend's house for the night.

Wait a minute, is that me tucked up luxuriously in that hotel bedroom, dreaming of a full English breakfast, and what about that delicious smell of freshly roasted coffee beans – pass my case.

Worth every VAT penny

FORGIVE me if I break out in parented pride, but my mate and I are still dripping with swank after watching our eldest receive her BEd degree last weekend.

One minute I was up to my frustrations in party-pastries and floor polish, composing last-minute notes on fire-precautions and overcrowding for our stay-at-homes, and the next being eagerly waved off and speeding towards Berkshire College.

194

I discovered it was ignominiously easy to leave the rest of the family behind and my energies were soon transferred to adjusting the car heating system and the anticipation of the graduation ceremony. The four of us, daughter, fiance, husband and me, had a whole weekend to ourselves and I intended to savour every second.

Life has this habit of jogging one along in neutral for weeks on end, until you feel to be suffering from over-exposure to the ordinary – times when the only change in routine is a day when it just rains during the morning, or an unexpected visit from next door's cat. Then suddenly you can be swept off your slippers into a totally revitalising experience.

The swell of applause and eyelids as the graduates and diplomats marched down the centre of the college hall clad in their 'Will Hay' outfits of best 'blackout' material, certainly brought out the handkerchiefs. Whether it was due to the hearing of the speaker or just a cute way of keeping us awake I don't know, but the name of each student was mysteriously announced twice, once as they mounted the platform and again as the certificate was presented. This meant that each degree and diploma-carrier had to be double-clapped. With a winding trail of over 100 graduates this was no easy feat. However, each pair of ecstatic parents donated their rigorous contribution that helped the rest on nicely.

If the students looked embarrassed and slightly in the power of their fickle headgear, not so the parents. The hall was a-ripple with proud noddings and winkings – after all, this was the culmination of many years of hard work.

Naturally, the burst of applause reached its height when the 'B' surnames were called. But I generously shared out my claps, awarding everyone seven slow counts. If you include applause for choir, organist, harpist, college principal and speaker this totals over seven hundred clashes, not to mention the exasperating handbag juggling which goes on at the same time.

While everyone was being seated the organist played everything composed for the organ – twice. Music was non-stop until I decided it was time to unwrap a particularly adhesive boiled sweet. This was the signal for complete non-activity from everyone else and the particularly sensitive microphones picked up my fumblings beautifully.

Assembling the dignitaries and parents took time, but there was much to be observed in the meantime; the delicate lace-trimmed undies of a stern-looking female official who obligingly sat cross-legged on the raised platform, the flicked-up hairstyle with ends curling like chrysanthemum petals over the tasselled mortar-board of her companion.

Self-control is a necessary ingredient when attending these ceremonies. Although it took all the restraint I could muster – I did not turn to the pin-striped on my left, to the Jaegar knit in front, nor indeed to the fake fur behind to announce that the attractive brunette basking in the luminous glow of what must surely be the principal's sincerest smile of the day – was mine – I mean ours.

And I also did not add that we had another three daughters and a son at home.

After the buffet scramble and a glass of wine, surrounded by 'awfternoon tea' accents and raised little fingers, I could easily have exchanged a few confidences with a friendly tutor. He told me that his son had been struck shiftless since he had gained a place at Cambridge. 'Been in bed since last June,' he divulged. I was bursting with son sagas of my own, but the other three dragged me off.

As we left it felt rather disquieting to take a final peep at the unfamiliar looking buildings that had been our daughter' home for the past three years.

Our next stop was a seventeenth century coaching inn, nestling quaintly in Thomas Hardy country – Dorchester-on-Thames, just around the corner from the dignified old abbey. My thoughts did wander to our motherless brood back home as we picked our way through the treacherously cobbled court-yard, our noses blue with cold. Had they heeded my last-minute fire precautions, 'If you don't put coal on, it goes out,' I wondered? But once through the entrance and the glimpse of a crackling log fire calling invitingly from an open grate, I was deeply overcome with self-preservation.

'Would you like a meal?' asked our friendly host as we signed in. We dare not look hungry until we had seen the price list. Quick as a conjuror, he produced a menu the size of a paving stone. We all swallowed in unison, and being the first to recover I said we'd-er-think about it.

Next thrill on the list was our bedroom investigation. The first thing I saw after the radiator was a welcome tray of cups, saucers, tea, coffee, cream and an electric kettle. From then on I was a pushover. One glorious coffee with cream and I was back among the hot logs ordering our evening meal.

An hour later we were iced to a pew trying to appreciate a musical evening in the Abbey. Just entering the ancient building took one's breath away – it was like stepping from a fridge into a freezer. The five electric ribbons of heat were decorative but inadequate. Spirals of frosty white breath were flowing mistily from gaps between coat collars and hats. Yet despite the chilling atmosphere, by 8pm the pews contained their full quota of fur coats and red noses.

Bach's organ toccata could not have enjoyed a more resonant setting, and the youthful orchestra, choir and soloists performed their items excellently. I did almost slip into a coma once or twice when my thoughts hovered celestially between the bliss of a hotel bedroom, where a certain nightie was draped on a warm radiator, and the smell of a crisply sizzling duckling being carefully basted with pineapple sauce for my delight at 9.30pm.

On retiring I gave the bedside Bible a thumb-through. The bookmark was placed in Ecclesiastes and I read: 'It is God's gift to man that everyone should eat and drink and take pleasure in all his toil.'

When we received the bill for our extravagance this was a great consolation. It was worth every fiver – even if my faith in self-catering has been destroyed forever. In future it's definitely VAT plus service again for me and mine!

Christmas shopping

YOU can easily calculate the number of Christmas shopping days left by observing the speed of the crowds.

As Christmas Eve draws nearer they move that extra spurt faster. Last week-end the Piazza looked like a clip from an old Keystone Cop movie; with everyone whizzing frantically along in top gear, dads buried in parcels and mums waving sweaty scraps of torn paper. All pondering on the seasonal poser 'What shall we buy?'

One is never too old or too young to join in the Christmas parade, and we all have our own technique for getting rid of the pounds.

There are the 'I've got a little list' types who have been studying the market since last August and know exactly what they want, where it is stocked and the most competitive prices. Like the invincible who sat opposite me in a snack bar the other lunchtime.

As I plunged the knife into the soft pie pastry, we both watched the rich brown mess gurgle forth. My mouth watered in anticipation and I was glad I hadn't chosen the potato pie.

'I wish I'd known you were having that, I could have warned you,' was her opening gambit.

'You should have ordered the meat and potato – it's proper meat.' I tucked in bravely to the tasty improper morsels, cunningly disguised as steak. 'I re-member when my husband and I had that,' she continued. I noted the empty seat next to her and hoped she wasn't a widow, 'neither of us could eat it.'

My face was so contorted with pie I found it difficult to look sympathetic, but I obligingly left three peas, which I trust would redeem me.

She was too busy studying the contents of my bag to notice. Doing a perfect impression of Nicholas Parson's 'Sale of the Century' swagger, she then proceeded to give me a run down on what I could have bought if I had any sense. She finally let me go when I promised to buy the rest of my shopping from a nearby supermarket – where she worked on the checkout.

Although I have spent countless hours and bus fares on shopping trips, more often than not I return empty handed. I have this unfortunate handicap which interferes with my plans – I am an avid listener, particularly when I am not being addressed. Tuning-in to others can be quite educational, the public at play on Saturday afternoons are fascinating to observe.

There are the indecisive buyers who always shop in twos and never pur-chase anything without benefit of counsel. 'Yes – I think she'd like that – go on I'll take it – no wait a minute.' She consults second opinion. 'What do you think Elsie, would Marjorie prefer it in blue?'

While sales assistant breathes out aggressively, Elsie can only see Marjorie in pink and when this is sadly extinct they sweep out in a huff.

Next door two customers buried deep in Family Trees stand blocking the store entrance. 'Our Tom has three now, you know,' boasts one, ignoring the heavy breathers waiting to get in. 'Our Phyllis is having another,' says her mate and they're off, tracing the genes back to the tasty subject of their own confinements.

Some shoppers like to preface a purchase with a short quiz: 'Now if our Janet is four that means our Frances must be six – which makes our Joseph two-years-old – so how old is our Fred's youngest?'

One of the most difficult impositions is refusing an unacceptable offering, especially when the kindly sales assistant has gone to great trouble to help you decide. How does one make a polite refusal and tell her you really fancy the gift across the road?

This is why I always keep mobile in the book-shops. But on Saturday from my position behind a large atlas I saw an elderly gentleman make a re-markable exit. He was up to his moustache in books of all dimensions – all kindly proffered from every corner of the department by the friendly best-seller. Surely he dare not leave empty-handed – but he did! 'Well thank you so much for your help,' he beamed benevolently, as if someone had just presented him with a 'long-service' medal. 'You've given me

198

plenty to think about.' He raised his trilby and made a dignified exit. I can only imagine the flabbergasted expression of the salesgirl, as you couldn't see her for books.

If you intend buying a new outfit, trying on is more frustrating than ever in some stores. There is a bizarre rule that you must try more than one outfit – but not more than three – and only one person allowed in a cubicle. I had to parade my new suit past two grinning schoolboys, one embarrassed husband and several other intrigued glances in order to achieve my daughter's opinion. When shorties like me trail back and forth, with supposedly mid-calf outfits scraping the dust, their opinions are not for public airing, I might add.

'Come 'ere,' shouted a cockney voice as I walked long the Piazza. He threw some black velvet over a hastily erected table and commenced his patter. Placing a gold plastic bracelet on the plush and patting it affectionately he beckoned us forward. 'Nar this aint gold ladies,' he said for the benefit of the blind. 'No – I'm being honest and I'm gonna treat you.' We surged forward. 'I'm not going to arsk you for £2.50,' we stepped back two paces. 'I'm only arskin' one pound.' He dipped into his case. 'Nar look at this,' he said to a passer-by who blew her nose and walked on in disgust. He draped a chain around the bracelet and turned his attention to me. 'Nar fer the two of 'em' he lowered his voice 'and I'll even throw in this.'

I couldn't wait to see what else he had to offer – and neither could he. His mate who was standing on a nearby wall let out a shout and in the flash of a patrol car – they were gone.

But there is a spirit of goodwill – here and there. 'Can we give you a lift, love?' I saw a burly navvy and his mate ask a slim longhaired blonde in a duffle coat, who was struggling to haul a pushchair up a flight of steps. 'No thanks,' was the gruff reply, and we all realised she was a man!

Discipline has necessarily to be mixed with generosity. Sometimes we have to say 'No' like the fatherly voice I heard outside a sweet shop. 'No, son, you cannot expect to have something every time we go in there.' I only hope his dog got the message.

This is the season when my generosity has a rash habit of exceeding my purse. I have a disconcerting habit of promising too much. As if some fantastic Santa Claus will fall from the skies and grant all my wishes. But without a little fantasy wouldn't life be too phlegmatic?

I felt sorry for an ageing grandad who was tempted by a shoe display. 'There's a lovely pair here for me love – only £9.99,' he said to his wife.

'Nay, what's point i' buying them at your age?' she growled pushing him outside. 'Tha'll nivver get thi wear out of 'em.'

Present giving is one way of expressing our love for each other – and after all it beats ski-ing down mount Everest in the nude with a carnation stuck up your nose.

What a pantomime

THIS Christmas as you sit sparking criticisms at the seasonal extravaganzas on stage and screen – spare a thought for the line of dancers hidden somewhere at the back, that decorative row of stocking-fillers who occupy the stage while the stars slip into something more expensive.

Their complicated routines take hours of choreographing and weeks of re-hearsing to synchronise their movements. Often this effort only evokes a cursory glance from toilet-trippers or sometimes it's the signal for ma to put the kettle on. Having served an arduous apprenticeship as a Christmas fairy, I have some idea of the punishment that goes into a festive production.

Yes – I have waved my wand o'er woodland glade, diced with death on the highflying ballet wires, I've done my share of 'ooing' and 'aahing' as a villager. I was once swept off my feet in Cinderella's ballroom by 'Buttons' – being the smallest sunbeam had its advantages – if you can call three months of enduring two rows of brass buttons being pressed into your chest twice nightly an advantage.

Shambles Lane and our beloved Theatre Royal may have been malevolently destroyed, but for sometime-retired fairies the memories linger.

One dream I had never materialised – unlike a lot of the Theatre stalwarts I never saw the interior of the Bull and Mouth pub on the corner. Being of short stature lying about my age was a pleasure that had to be deferred.

But I was a fully paid-up member of Lindon Smith's fish and chip shop. After the show we had a regular three-pen'orth to warm our hands and innards all the way through the Pack Horse Yard to our bus stop.

On Saturdays – 'treasury day' – we enjoyed a teatime treat at the Kingsway Café up King Street. If we had enough time we sometimes went higher up to the basket chair euphoria at Heywoods.

Fed up with seeing girls with long curls and ten out of ten on their blue books monopolise the school stage, I answered an advert for 'twelve-year-old dancers to train for stage work.' Ignoring the dancer bit – after all I was the right age – I took my place in the audition queue.

Watching the waiting esoterics unload their various dancing shoes, I had my first uneasy stomach flutter. Would a Carmen Miranda impersonation which amused my mum paralytic, plus the desire to be the centre of attraction, be enough to sweep this dancing mistress and sycophants off their feet, I asked myself. Half-an-hour more watching these pirouetting leg-stretchers adjusting the ribbons on their pink satin shoes and I was wishing I had re-painted my old holiday sandals tucked in my coat pocket.

When my turn came to see what was on the other side of the dark brown door I was toying with the idea of sticking with the Girl Guides another year. But the pianist struck up and I faced the three supercilious expressions opposite and crooned in my South American accent 'I like you vaary mooch.'

If they looked away I sang louder and revolved my eyeballs even faster. As long as the pianist played I sang. We were all blissfully relieved when her strength failed and she stopped. There must have been a shortage of stage-struck twelve-year-olds that year, because after complaining about having to 'drag the talent' from me the unsmiling principal said I was accepted.

Her parting threat 'Once you start there's no backing out,' makes my ears go hot even now. Our chief fairy's technique ran on the same lines as my school tormenter, he could make a tadpole dance. All he did was throw stones and shout 'Dance!' Teacher wielded the same power without the stones.

I tried every way I knew to back out during the painful weeks that followed. Twitching, weeping, promises that my parents would have a dead dancer on their hands for Christmas, but neither they nor I had the courage to tell teacher about my change of heart.

The moment we started rehearsals in the theatre life picked up. Not only was the distance between pupil and teacher greater, but we actually brushed shoulders with real life professionals. This fantastic ephemeral world was far removed from ordinary classroom existence. We longed to look 'theatrical' and copied every ostentation possible, exaggerated gestures, tied-over hair in coloured scarves.

We were all transformed from 'Hey you' to exquisitely pronounced 'Dears' and 'Darlings.' The exciting journey twice nightly from dressing-room, along a draughty paved corridor, up the stone steps past the hot water pipes to our favourite seat on the old prop basket, was a magical transition to the showbusiness world of make-believe.

During one pantomime we were endowed with an imperious looking male dancer – straight from Sadler's Wells – whom we all fell madly in love with. Every time he approached, our thirty-two-inch bras expanded another two inches. He never showed the slightest interest.

When he came on stage in his Genie of the Lamp gear our desire reached fever pitch. His body was covered in gold paint and he had a sort of shiny tasselled nappy girded about his loins.

His dance in the magic cave was the climax to the first half of 'Aladdin.' While he sat cross-legged on a pedestal with a lamp on his beautiful knee we had to glide around him in silent worship. He arranged the sequence, teaching us all to drift and bow our bodies submissively, a feat that came easy anyway, when he was around. When we eventually lie at his feet – his eternal slaves – he would creep slowly down from his perch and perform his exotic solo. We were so besotted we counted it an honour if he accidentally trod on an outstretched hand or foot, which he usually did.

From the auditorium this 'Cave' looked magnificent. Giant sheets of coloured tin foil were crushed into raffia tubes to represent jewels. Painted with glittery clusters the scenery sparkled magnificently under the concealed spotlight. Our costumes were most erotic, like transparent pyjamas with certain areas subtly covered in sequins.

One night as we crept on stage to the eerie cave music, my partner's flimsy trousers became attached to the corner of the 'jewellery.' As we floated seductively forward so did all the clanging contents of the raffia container.

The more she tried to shake it off the tighter it clung. Everywhere she danced the 'tin crocodile' pursued noisily. We went into a spin and the monster bound us together. When the time came for our submissive flop we had no choice but to drag it with us. To make matters worse we all got the giggles, even the audience sounded amused. In fact Genie was the only granite face to be seen.

When the curtain fell we were ordered to his sacred sanctuary, the smile was duly wiped from our faces and our lust was completely banished. Who needed him anyway – I was already on winking terms with a trombonist.

I often recognise panto pals on television. Peter Drake of 'Everyman' series was once a friendly Grand Vizier along with Phillip Locke the actor. Lesley French was once a much respected Widow Twanky. Would they recognise me – I wonder?

But show-business smiles cover a lot of heartaches and I am thankful for me it was only a hobby. I lacked the stamina to make it a career. 'If

you're looking for a life of adventure and excitement with excellent pay –
join The Royal Marines' said Radio 4 the other day. But I'll settle for my
Christmas tree, family and a comfy fireside, accompanied by the glow of
a certain wine to bring out the flavour.

I wish you a happy Christmas too, don't be lonely, invite someone
round – if you haven't a neighbour, ask the milkman in for a drink!

1978
So that was 1977

THIS is the time when most of us take a shifty look over our shoulder at
the mixture of events that made up the past year.

Some of us even break out in a rash of improvement plans. Actually to
spring-clean in the spring, buy a new pan scrub, stop making a floor rag of
the dishcloth, be kind to the head of the house and start treating the dog
like an animal.

'What is your wish for the future, love,' I ventured to ask our middle
daughter. 'I wish there was only me,' she sighed, giving me a Greta Garbo
look. Another daughter has decided only to make resolutions she can keep
easily. She has 'to keep breathing' is at the top of her list. Our milkman
made one a fortnight ago but tells me he can't remember what it was.

I suppose I ought to make a vow to organise myself better. The trouble
is that although I am the world's most disorganised person, I do get there
in the end. It's the trail I leave behind that rankles the rest of the household.

It was their disparaging comparisons that drove me to take a City and
Guilds cookery course. My children were always dropping hints about
their friends' mothers who were all the type of Cordon Bleau cooks who
used a sieve instead of a hammer to rid the lumps in their icing sugar.

Week after week the course irked me, although my completed
concoctions were up to taste, I lost marks because my prep table looked
like a dustbin and most of the time I was in trouble because the basins
everyone else was search-ing for were in my sink. I never did master their
'wash as you cook' rule. All the adjudicators had the same curious marking
habits. It didn't matter how delicious your food tasted, if your rolling pin
hadn't been washed you failed.

Sometimes I wonder if ante-natal classes let me down. This is where I
first learned to relax. 'The most conducive time to rest your body is
immediately after your midday meal' preached our midwife. I never forgot

her advice. Others breathe easy when the work is done, whereas I relax better when there's plenty left to do.

Although my after-lunch siesta presents a crazy picture of confusion – me dozing by the fire in the shadow of the unwashed pots – I consider this habit has been my salvation in times of stress. To anyone who finds letting go difficult, I would say that a full stomach, a coal fire and, in my case, a full sink, are definite assets. Since entering the yoghurt (my mother's word for Yoga) world of transcendental meditation, however, the habit of post-meal relaxation is rather a hindrance. After two minutes of deep concentration I start snoring. But I am working on it.

Of course 1977 will not only be remembered as the year of my new bike, but also as the Queen's Jubilee year. We all retain our special memories of this. 'She is a marvellous person and a wonderful mother. She has a marvellous sense of humour, is sensible and wise,' confesses Prince Charles on a jubilee record of speeches and reflections concerning Her Majesty.

I can't wait for our son to reach the age when he will make recordable com-ments about his mother. 'Do you think you could possibly wash me a shirt?' was his last.

I'm afraid last year's summer never came, and if it did I missed it.

In spite of the Jubilee Celebrations, 1977 will always live in my memory as the year I lost a stone in weight, and the year I enjoyed our team bowling events so much we are now relegated to a lower division.

Thank goodness fashion writers are not really prophets, and the predicted mini-skirts never materialised. When they were fashionable I was too fat. Now my kneecaps have surfaced, I'm too old.

We had Princess Anne presenting a Jubilee grandson for the Queen. She also set a new fashion for mums-to-be with her old anorak, baggy sweater, and her long hair tucked into a flat cap to complete the casual effect.

Then we had the pleasure of seeing newly Christened Peter on TV. While his mum held him aloft, like a Bishop about to crown someone, and tried to straighten his beautiful Victorian gown, he did an impression of a rag doll with a broken neck. Then proud mum slung him saddle-wise over her left shoulder and baby surprised no one by sobbing all through the ceremony.

On the home front, our eldest daughter obtained two temporary teaching posts. Our mutual vegetable patch burst forth and multiplied. We munched our home-grown tomatoes, boiled, fried, chutneyed or straight from the stem, while the front lawn went to seed and the cellar door and front gate came off their hinges.

Virginia Wade won at Wimbledon, Liverpool won the European Cup and our son won the Carter Cup at our bowling club.

I have never been a Jimmy Savile fan – his language usually sticks in the craw – but during his Christmas 'Jim'll Fix It' programme I was impressed by the thoughtful and inoffensive way he announced the death of a participant.

The elderly lady had been granted her dream of dining in the stately home where she had once been employed. Although she had died since the show was recorded, her relatives granted permission to show the film on television. Jimmy Savile had the difficult task of announcing this and his words were something like this: 'Mrs ——— died shortly after realising her dream and is now in heaven.'

I like the matter of fact way he made this statement, and the thought that our loved ones are in peace without pain does help in the struggle of coping with the grief of bereavement.

With all our successes and failures behind us it is also a time to look to the future. This is the year I am about to become a mother-in-law. I hope this will also be the year when a certain lower division women's bowling team will flabbergast all by winning a certain cup, and what about our Top of the Pops, the Brighouse and Rastrick lads? Every success to their new record in 1978.

Perhaps if I could make one earnest New Year resolution it is that I may never be 'too busy.'

Good health to all and best wishes for 1978.

A wonderful discovery

APART from my red nose and bloodless cheeks, there's not a lot to smile about in January. It could never be described as the merry month – it's more a pull yourself and your bank account together month.

If the dreary weather and dark teatimes aren't depressing enough, there are plenty of sale warnings to gnash your empty wallet on.

Even the Christmas anecdotes 'When our Claude said this' and 'When our Fiona tried to . . .' become unfunny after a time.

But we drag the guffaws on as long as possible at our household. The merry quips that fell from the mouths of babes and inebriates during our festive cele-brations are still evoking slight smiles.

Like the occasion when our eldest member was disgustingly jolly and rheumy-eyed one minute and prostrate in a deep coma the next. He convinced no one the day after that his green tinged appearance was due to the recurrence of his old liver trouble and had nothing to do with the small glass he was never without all afternoon.

One five-year-old's quizzical greeting to a relative 'Are you trying to grow a moustache, auntie?' will no doubt entertain our household for many years to come. Some of us will wisely keep a discreet distance from the scrutiny of youth in future.

Then there was the popular party member who couldn't undo his shirt buttons fast enough when 'games' were mentioned, hinting hopefully 'I hope we don't have to undress.'

In a bread queue one lady with a streaming nose enthralled me with a description of her front room décor, which she had covered in Anaglypta, 'Now we have that eucalyptus paper everywhere,' she boasted.

My mother invented her own language before I was born. We often take her euphemisms for granted and forget to translate. She never could remember Lena Zavaroni's correct name and now we all think of her as my mother christened her – Lena Macaroni, Bobby Crush the pianist has become Bobby Brush   At Christmas she refused my offer of white wine with a shudder saying it had 'too much of a pang' for her taste. The other day she complained about the arrival of two 'Jofia's Witnesses' on her doorstep.

A funny thing happened to me on my way to the bus station the other teatime. As I zig-zagged my way through St George's Square, a starling dropped its slimy message on my parting. When I looked upwards with an insult I received another in the same area.

On reaching home I combed through the rigid patch and was elated to see new body and bounce spring into my hair. To think I have spent pounds on thickeners and revitalisers that never worked and all I needed was two minutes in St George's Square. If two blobs can produce a khaki tint, what would five minutes attain?

Perhaps I should patent this wonderful discovery. 'New Starling ingredient – straight from the Yorkshire lime field of St George's – gives fibrant new colour and body to dull hair,' or what about one simple word? Would 'Dung' have more impact? Or perhaps something more Oriental like 'Dung-phew' would sound more exciting.

Sounds too fantastic. Look what horses have done for roses, horse's faeces, what's the difference? What the bees have done for Barbara, perhaps the birds will do for me. Who knows? Perhaps it comes in two colours!

Anyway if you are doubtful, why not try it. Have a flutter – it only takes a second. Some of us would go to any ends to make a fortune.

Whatever fashion dictates, I had a new long skirt at Christmas and I intend to wear it as often as I feel like it, whether fashionable or not. Apart from the bicep coverage it gives me, I feel dressed up and different in ankle lengths. As my shoe buckle has an irritating habit of catching in the hem, I probably look different – I usually enter a room on one leg.

There are one or two rules I take delight in not conforming to. I like my coffee and tea steaming hot and all other liquids including sherry and wines chilled. White wine is a special favourite of mine and I don't care what colour of meat I eat with it. Red wine at room temperature tastes like poison, whereas an hour in the fridge transforms it into a refreshing tonic.

Naturally I never dictate how other people should dress or enjoy themselves. Why should we all have the same tastes anyhow?

The skateboard enthusiasts have all my sympathy. I think they are exactly what children need to exercise their natural exuberance and no more dangerous than cycling or roller-skating.

They can't skate on the street, there's no room at home, so where are they to go? Instead of wasting energy banning this pastime, why doesn't someone with the power and sense to match, open up one of the old buildings that are fretting away from disuse – we have two or three in Slaithwaite.

It would be a drastic transition from pulling things down. Who knows? It might catch on.

January is the signal for my book binge. You can keep your diamonds – books are definitely more precious to me. Charles Chaplin considered friends to be like good music – all right to listen to when you're in the mood. I agree, but books are satisfying whatever the mood.

One at the top of last year's list which for some reason I never bought, is Dr Raymond Mordy's 'Life after Life,' which includes the statements of fifty people who brushed with death. The lucky ones who were brought back to life again after being pronounced 'dead' by their doctors.

Their descriptions of this suspended state, between life and death, have an amazing similarity and should make interesting reading for anyone intrigued by the subject. I must confess that wherever I'm going I like a glimpse at the brochure first.

But for husbands who haven't had a straight look at their wives this year, I say . . . beware. Behind the broody eyelids throbs new hope. A strange world of vibrant colour is taking shape – and it's only a paintbrush and a pair of stepladders away.

So dig out the overalls chaps – the New Year starts now!

Holidays and dreams

OUR butcher is wearing his 'I know where I'm going' expression early this year and informs me his summer holiday is signed and sealed. The original tour a relative planned was fully booked and they had to take a second choice. So it's 'make your mind up time' on the holiday front and he who hesitates may be left holding his deposit.

Naturally, with a summer wedding on the horizon, we are playing down the holiday enthusiasm this year. It's not a question of 'Where?' – more a case of 'Can we?'

Deciding where to go is usually the best part of my year. I collect as many fantasy brochures as my bag will hold, stoke up the kitchen fire, pop on the coffee, then turn the pages and spin my dreams. Where would I go if . . .? Every year I plan: a tour of the Greek islands, a safari trip, self-discovery in the Tibetan mountains or, say, a mingle with the natives in a colourful Moroccan market. Then our bank statement arrives and we head for the nearest coast.

But one place I long to visit is America. I know it's pushy, the cab-drivers are rude, but I want to see for myself the world that spread its enchantment before me as I sat in a fourpenny cinema seat thirty years ago. I yearn to take an elongated Greyhound bus and sit chewing gum while a Brooklyn accent describes the extravagant movie stars and their monumental residences in Beverly Hills. If I could only wander around the old Metro-Goldwyn-Mayer movie sets – see the famous cement footsteps, cringe at the sordid sights on the Bowery and gasp at the wonder of Disneyland. Yes, it's far away from my deck chair and at £1,700 for two, a little divorced from our holiday allowance.

Most of my holiday desires are connected with films gorged on twice weekly in my mis-spent youth.

'South Pacific' had a powerful influence on my brochure staring. I can just picture my beloved and me sitting cross-legged – well almost cross-legged – draped in blossom beside a pool, indulging in a spot of finger-lickin' 'Happy talk' being egged on to gnashing passion by a grinning Bloody Mary.

My earlier yearnings were all connected with Elizabeth Taylor, a dog and the Scottish hills. This was before her Queen of the Nile excursions, which took her to shores beyond my reach.

It was Virginia McKenna's bush adventures with Elsa the lioness which initiated my under canvas tendencies. A few years have passed since our first camping holiday, but it will ever remain a blotch on my memory as a sort of Noah's Ark adventure for six. I remember our front room up to its pelmets in improvised camping equipment, as we waited excitedly for our chief camper to arrive home from work with a borrowed tent strapped to an old Morris van.

Cramming the furniture into a corner, to make room for our 'kit inspection' I felt quite proud of myself. One half of the sitting-room contained our sleep-ing bags filled with giggling children. No matter how I shrieked they stayed firmly lodged in their feathery lairs. I had sewn everyone's eiderdown along the sides and bottom to form a bag. They certainly looked inviting, if a little bulky. The rest of the room was piled up with 'necessities' – pans, cups, food, chairs, tools, we had no room for clothes.

When my husband arrived, instead of joining in the excitement, he started behaving like a Customs officer. When he'd finished censoring, our display was reduced to six eiderdowns, one pan, six cups and the food box. I felt totally bereft of property, at least I would have if most of this equipment hadn't to be packed around my body as we travelled. The back of the van was stuffed to choking point with eiderdowns. Between these and the roof we managed to squeeze four children, who said they were going to sleep most of the way, luckily. Whether it was due to lack of oxygen or simply exhaustion, they fell into a deep coma immediately and we sped silently towards the Lakes.

We had a heavenly peaceful drive with blue skies painting an aesthetic backcloth for the flying ducks I wanted to point to, if only I could have disentangled myself from camping tackle. I had a vision of myself ruddy-cheeked in shorts and T-shirt frying bacon in the outback; other holidaymakers mistaking me for a seasoned tenter, begging for advice.

It didn't start raining until we were about a mile from our campsite. When we reached our garden gate four days later it stopped. We waded about the crowded site in a gushing cloudburst looking for a patch of space. I tried not to look covetously at a row of stable-looking caravans. At last we found a plot of empty grass at the bottom of a slope. It was handy for the toilets and shop we couldn't think why others had missed it. When we awakened surrounded by everyone else's drained-off water next morning, we understood why.

But blissfully unaware we struggled to erect our tent. Here was a mystery that would surely have baffled the adaptable Virginia McKenna. It appeared we had three tents in one. Looking at the other tents securely keeping out the rain did not help, ours was unique. The kids and I grouped underneath the canvas, obediently pointing poles to the sky, according to instructions, while our chief scout got wetter and more baffled outside. Eventually we had it stood up, in a crooked sort of way, and tied down.

With circular turrets at each end and a large square in the centre, it looked like an 'Ivanhoe' reject. The sort of pavilion one usually associates with lances and suits of armour. Any minute I expected a plumed rider to come charging forth. Although the turrets rose imperiously above the rest and could be seen for miles, when other campers enquired which was ours, I just pointed vaguely in the distance. I notice the children always called at the toilets before slipping in through the back flap.

Our chief didn't move much, just sat watching the water rise. The following day it seemed as if all the fiercest monsters of the Lake District had come down from the hills to see our tent. Horned chunky-legged beasts laughingly called cows by my husband surrounded us. We spent most of the day waiting for water to boil, but soon got used to eating luke-warm meals. At intervals a dejected Scout and disillusioned Girl Guide begged for mercy and four walls, but the children's unanimous wail was 'No.'

One night we had a welcome interlude from the moo-ing serenaders, our son became on hooting terms with a friendly owl. Every time he hooted it answered. 'I wonder what it's saying, mum,' asked one eager camper. Sounded like 'Goooo-hooome' to my damp ears. Suddenly the hills were alive to the sound of thunder and lightening. The following morning father popped the question that had been on my mind since we arrived: 'Who's for home?' The children's pleas were pitiful. 'Please - oh - no – don't.' But I had already unearthed most of the tent pegs.

'What ivver are you doing, lad,' asked a man who looked as if he had just stepped off a North Sea trawler. 'Packing it in,' grunted my husband as our borrowed tent collapsed helplessly in slime.

'Nay, nivver,' the stranger shook his head slowly from side to side. As the water from his sou'wester gushed down the inside of my mates wellies, he explained we were making a ghastly mistake. Apparently one must never dismantle in the rain. We realised the wisdom of this when we spread our tent over the back lawn at home, where the sun shone brilliantly as soon as we arrived. It was beyond recognition and looked as if a troop of cavalry had galloped all over it. I don't know where my holiday sandals will lead me this year, but I hope I shall be sampling someone else's cuisine, wherever it is.

Art and the artist

I HAVE every sympathy with the late Lady Churchill and her demolishing habits and only wish I had the same courage and powers of concealment. To destroy some of the family howlers that are kept in my mother's photo box has been my intrinsic desire for years.

Me at the age of thirteen, wearing a garter for a hairband – so tight I could only wear it for an hour, if I wanted to stay alive. The photograph must have been taken at five to the hour, judging by the row of white blisters forming at the base of each root. The one showing me in a bathing suit at the age of ten, my posture suggesting an impending pregnancy – or the photo of my sister and I taken when I was seven and she was three, her smiling sweetly and all melt-in-the-mouth, me at her side showing my ugly doorstep teeth in a sickly leer.

I never mastered the knack of smiling when I was not enjoying myself a cause of much suffering during dancing class days. 'You,' our teacher would shriek giving my thighs a fingernail prod that made the eyelids prickle, 'smile.' Quick grins are easy but dancers were supposed to leer for ten minutes at a time, which seemed impossibly idiotic to me.

For one photographic session I decided to stop forcing inane smiles, why not surprise everyone with a natural expression. Unfortunately the day of my appointment dawned drizzly grey. When I removed my headgear the carefully coiffeured hairstyle had disappeared. In its place was a head-hugging Rudolph Valentino affair.

I sat on the stool with my driest side facing the camera. The photographer sighed impatiently, 'Give me your best side, please,' he begged. 'Er – I don't think I have one, I'm a bit wet.' He seemed to agree with this and after a lot of posing he decided to risk his camera. Collecting proofs is always exciting. When I looked at mine I was reminded of something my mother used to be fond of saying when I was younger, something about her being able to sit on my eyebrows and 'that bottom lip.' What had become of the dreamy eyes and the hint of amusement I had allowed to play around my lips? This was a picture of a consumptive depressive with haunted eyes pleading 'let me die, let me die.'

'Don't open your mouth when you laugh, mum,' I am usually advised during family photographic sessions. 'We can see your fillings.' On one family portrait, I was fifteen and hoping to pass the result on to a boyfriend. My father had us grouped in the corner of a local park rose garden. Impulsively I pulled a rose branch close to my face. 'Where are you?'

211

asked my mother when we examined the developed film. I was the headless body with the foliage face.

The only portraits I ever had painted were done by our children, who all saw me as a large circle with a red triangle in the centre, two black eyes and as much black scribble as the paper would allow, for hair. Perhaps there's some significance in the fact that children never seem to draw fathers. Is this because they are harder to draw or please? I wonder.

It is only with the utmost self-control that I have not done a Lady Churchill on some of the bizarre ensembles sewn by our enthusiastic teenagers during their needlework sessions. But the thought of cost can slow down the mutilating instinct in some of us. When our middle child stepped into the dining room one evening with her pinned-together, wide-legged culottes swinging at half-mast, spirits rose considerably. Trying to swallow our honesty, we managed to keep silent. But unable to bear the suspense she eventually prodded for comments.

No one actually got around to saying anything. I feel deeply ashamed at the part I played in the stomach clutching and rib shaking that ensued. Seeing as the material had cost me £4 I don't know what I had to laugh at anyway.

Thankfully we dreamed up some suitable compliments and she did wear them consistently for a week.

In an interview last year Graham Sutherland said: 'Only those without physical vanity, educated in painting, or with exceptionally good manners can disguise their feelings of shock or revulsion when confronted for the first time with a reasonably truthful painted image of oneself.'

Well, speaking for myself I wouldn't have minded a few extra curls added to old photographs or a few front teeth extractions.

Of course what appeals to one doesn't always have the same pull for another. I have a floral effect on my kitchen wall, a dried flower arrangement glued on a brown cork plate, which I think looks most effective, even if our son does say it looks like a flower-trimmed beefburger.

I suppose one advantage of a surrealist portrait is that no one can ever confront the artist and say 'I think that middle eye is a bit low,' or 'That hole is in the wrong arm.'

All artists are inclined to be sensitive about their work. Looking out of the window just now, I saw our dog add his liquid contribution to the snowman just completed by our youngest, who has just been puzzling over the deep yellow stain blighting her creation. We all have to suffer for our art and it looks like the dog is next.

All a matter of habit

WE HAVE just received a disturbing school circular. Not only is the annual bulb show evening to be held in two weeks (just when one of our hyacinths has developed a hump), but an epidemic of nail nibbling is sweeping through the school.

The eyes are considered to be the 'windows of the soul' but always in my opinion hands can reveal all. That's why I always wear gloves.

Whenever I am introduced to strangers my eyes go first to teeth, then to nails. You don't need Romany connections to read between the lines. Jagged nails and washday reds tell their own story. During a recent TV play I noticed with disappointment that Julie Covington has a set of fingernails to match her hairstyle.

It's a constant battle to keep my nails on at the moment. I have two bendy thumbnails and four fingers that are presentable; the others are still recovering from detergents. My daughters have spent hours searching the vac bag for their false variety, an expensive menace for busy mothers who let their vacuums eat anything they can get hold of. These flyaway pieces of plastic are useless anyway – they either come off with your gloves or lean back with a huff if you touch them. The viscid stuff provided to glue them on sticks like chewing gum long after the nails have died. Apparently it will stick to anything except plastic.

It's a well-publicised fact; all nervous habits can be traced back to either parents or teachers. Naturally adult stress signs – denture rolling, sniffing, trouser hitching – can be traced back to children, which proves we all get on each other's nerves. I try hard to subscribe to the maxim it will go away if you ignore it, which is easier said than done.

One of our children has a mind-shattering pre-exam habit of clearing her throat every few minutes. Listening to what sounds like a spade being dragged intermittently over gravel all evening can have a diabolical effect on the other family traits.

'We all have nervous habits,' pointed out my smiling doctor, when I mentioned some of ours that were fit to repeat. 'I have one or two myself.' When I drew my chair up eagerly to enquire for more details, he reached for his prescription pad and clammed up – ours is such a one-sided relationship. I am expected to confide my most intimate secrets to him, but mention his and I'm pointed towards the door.

Children are avid twitch collectors. My one aim in primary school life was to acquire one. Spasmodic winks and jerks seemed a definite asset in my opinion, but unfortunately they only appeared to infect the intelligent.

213

I had one friend with a particularly studious-looking habit of pulling her top lip down - she topped all the exam lists. I practised various nose-screwings and eye fluttering until I found one that suited me and probably would have become quite adept if my mother's right hand had not intervened just as I was almost jerk perfect. In those days the psychiatrists couch was reserved for film stars; a short swipe to my left ear worked just as well.

One afternoon we had a visit from an old family acquaintance whom I soon realised had a magnificent action, which far out-twitched anything featured in our schoolyard. He gave the impression of being worked by hidden wires. Every so often his head would jerk to his shoulder (and he could do it equally well either side), then he would climax the whole fascinating performance with a neck-stretch, chin-up movement. I could see famous potential in any of these actions. But as usual my mother was one step ahead. More furtive side-swipes quashed that idea permanently.

Of course I developed other nasty habits that I try to keep a secret, here's a disquieting thought, though – do I? Clicking my one denture in and out of position is so relaxing – when I'm unobserved – but am I?

'Have I any irritating habits you can't stand?' I asked my husband who is sitting at my side for the first time this week. 'Of course not, love,' he replies, one eye on the clock. 'By the way – er sorry but - I'm off again tonight – another meeting, won't be late.'

Perhaps my son who can afford to be truthful on pay night will be more forthcoming? He says 'Lots' but thinks the most aggravating is my ignorance and the way I stare dreamily into space when asked a question. And I'm not too wild about his perceptiveness either.

Even the best of us have them, some endearing, others exasperating. What may be a loveable trait to one, may spell 'taboo' to another. I know a couple who are afraid to eat in a hotel because of the husband's eating habits. 'He always puts sugar on his lettuce' she sighs. It would take more than that to make me forfeit a meal out.

Our youngest daughter has an aversion to greens. As tact and persuasion yielded no result, I resorted to my secret weapon – force. Spoon by spoon I cleared her plate. Her cries and chokes were heartbreaking to behold, but more upsetting were the full plates left behind by the rest of the family, who were too sickened by my efforts to face their own dinners.

The loveable traits that originally evoked the passion in our beloved breast can often become the characteristic that crushes it. 'Darling I love the funny way you wrinkle your nose' often deteriorates to 'For God's sake straighten that face,' after twenty years. Like the amorous husband

214

who welcomes his wife into his bed with an affectionate 'What is it my petal?' when she stumbles over his shoes, then brands her a 'Clumsy idiot' when she does the same on leaving it in the morning.

It always brings out my nervous tic when people say one thing and mean another. The 'Can I help you?' which thinly disguises a 'Take your filthy paws of my merchandise' attitude and teachers who say 'Your daughter is a very popular member of the class' meaning 'She's a damn nuisance and never stops talking.' Certain white-coated assistants who are consumed by the conviction that patients should only be ill during surgery hours.

In our village we have a shopkeeper who labours under the misapprehension that he is the world's greatest comedian; that his cheeky little gimmicks make him a bundle of fun. But I'm pleased to his wallet about his latest jokey ploy – I loved the way he surreptitiously sneaked my full purse from my basket only returning it when I raced out in a panic, with knees like cotton wool screaming 'My purse . . .'

'I just wanted you to see how easy it is to pick pockets,' he explained. Thanks for pointing it out. If ever I take up burglary as a career, yours will be the first shop on my list . . see how you feel.

'If my dad was a vicar – would it change your life?' asks my youngest – now you know why I stare into space before answering!

Pointers to a career

FROM time to time, especially on Monday mornings when schoolchildren and I are highly inflammable, I lapse into the unforgivable habit of prefacing all conversation with my, 'When I was your age . . .' rhetoric.

I bore them all purple with my half true descriptions concerning my father's cruel black leather belt, with its brass buckle and what he would have done had I displayed half their cheek.

In reality it only left its trousers once, in my presence anyway, when I rebelled at not being allowed an ice cream wafer. These were reserved for adults, children had to be content with penny cornets. One day I returned with two wafers and two cornets and taking the wafer I had already started licking I dispensed the others accordingly, handing my dad a cornet. This outrage was greeted with another quick swap by my dad and an unprintable curse from me that roughly translated as 'You greedy beggers.' That was the beginning and the end of my relationship with the black belt.

My present outburst was created at a school 'careers evening.' We received a long list of golden opportunities all represented by an enthusiastic team of informers. All were eager to share their knowledge on working conditions, perks and wages and qualifications needed, the only drawback being the present lack of vacancies. But most include a training period with grants to apply for – which hopefully may keep them occupied until prospects are brighter.

After perusing the list, one of our dissidents, whose ambitions have fluctuated between becoming a librarian, a designer or hairdresser during the last month, has made her final decision. 'I want to be housewife,' she declares.

Teaching them the art of self-respect and the importance of being earnest is not helped by the example of State spongers.

In my schooldays – when I was your age – I never heard anyone actually confess enjoyment in their work. Satisfaction came at the end of the week in a small manilla envelope. Work was something my father left his bed for at 5.30am. With his 'jock' in his pocket he tramped the two miles across the valley towards the roar and grind of textile machinery. His day ended at 6.30pm when his clogs and his whistle rang in my ears long before his figure turned the corner of our fold.

Buses were considered a luxury when you had a pair of good feet. Although he hiked daily from Golcar to Lindley he was never late. As for enjoying work, there was no time to indulge in such fancies. The facts of life were simple: if you worked you were paid, if not you starved. He counted himself lucky to be one of the worlds' employed. Like many others of that period, he was desperately struggling to shed the bitter memories of the Thirties 'slump.'

The question: 'What's your dad doing these days?' took some answering. Anxious never to be out of work again, he cleaned windows, delivered fruit and veg with a horse and cart, was a painter and decorator – he even helped out three nights a week in a fish and chip shop at one stage in his career.

I loved walking down the cobbled mill yard to pull aside the grumbling, sliding door and step into the rattaty-rat world of worsteds. Past the stone sink with its hot smells of scalding tea-leaves and fish and chips, its row of pint pots waiting to be filled then into my father's shed where the grease and fluffy stuffiness of warm wool seemed to sink into your pores.

The noise was deafening, huge belts lashing round and busy looms beating back and forth seemed to create a menacing rhythm in their race against time. Clinging tenaciously to my father's navy-blue overalls, I tried not to cringe as the steel-shafted shuttles whizzed their cargo from end to end.

Because of the noise voices were unnecessary, just mime with the lips and hands. Even when the noise stopped the conversations were unintelligible to my ears. 'He's up at t'perch. 'Will you twist in a bit?' 'Are you ready for downing yet?' It was a foreign language to me. Whenever I mentioned my girlish ambition to follow in his footsteps, he always shook his head emphatically. He summed up his reason in two words, 'too hard.'

Only recently I discovered he nursed a secret dream during his youth – to become an archaeologist. A dream which today's adult education classes could probably realise.

Youthful desires take many forms – which all have to be filled in. At grammar school we regarded career forms with the same awe as a chemical equation – far removed from reality. Nobody actually became what they put in the space marked 'choice' – did they? As years and exams waxed and waned 'choice' fluctuated accordingly. Once I optimistically wrote 'Vet.' Consider-ing I could never face cow, horse or pig without benefit of a six-foot wall – this could have been a rather limited profession. Finally with mind solidly fixed I put 'film star.' Work experience where students spend a day trying out the type of work they fancy is a good idea. I once spent two days in a biscuit factory, but it only took me one to realise, when it came to the crunch, this vanilla flavoured Utopia was not for me.

First a lady in butterfly specs brought another girl and myself two white coats. They were so stiff she stood them against the wall with instructions to put them on. When I stood beside mine it was three inches taller. After a pers-piring fight we managed to overpower them. I put the belt around my waist and pulled as much skirt as I could over the top. This shortened it but left me with a rather pointed 'hangover.'

We tied on our blue turbans, thoughtfully provided. I arranged my curls, prettily pulling wisps forward at the side and front. My partner with hair out of sight and Alice in Wonderland bow pulled well over her forehead – well, I didn't want to be unkind – but with those pebble glasses! Madame personnel came back and with a few efficient strokes altered my headgear to match my partners.

Without being given a chance to approve we were whisked away to our department. I think she was short of exercise and had decided that very morning to take us the long way round, either that or she just wanted to spread a little happiness. After we trailed through department after department in our long smocks and bizarre headgear – we certainly left them smiling.

217

My seat was at the end of a long conveyor belt. There were three girls in front and we all had empty tins before us tilted for action. A bell introduced the next load of biscuits. Four long ribbons of shortcake came heading rapidly towards us. The idea was to gather them in rows of approximately twelve and transfer them neatly into the tin. With the efficient group in front expertly lifting line after line, would any ever reach my tin I worried? My fears were drastically groundless – the biscuits in scatterings of fours and fives arrived with a vengeance. When I attempted to push them into twelves they catapulted to my feet. 'Leave them,' was the order. Meanwhile the rest of the dissident digestives were already rounding the curve to fall in heaps on the floor. I found the quickest way was to scoop them from the belt in piles and throw them into the tins indiscriminately. At the end of the load, while everyone else placed lids on their beautifully packed tins, I battled despairingly with my mountains of mutinous biscuits.

After dinner a supervisor moved me on. This time all I had to do was lift packets from another moving belt, weigh them and stick a label on. This was easy enough but the perpetual movement of the belt had a hypnotic effect. With eyelids half closed and feeling like a junkie on a 'trip' I struggled through the afternoon.

Personnel were so relieved the morning after when I confessed my inabilities. They told me I could leave immediately and even presented me with a small manilla envelope. Still that's the way the cookie crumbles!

An attack of the yawns

'AN Annual General Meeting is to be held' – this announcement always brings a squirm of apprehension to my corner.

While other enthusiasts indulge in the ensuing rush of handbags and diary flourishing, I only want to crawl to the nearest exit. In fact it's a mystery how I ever became elected to the half-dozen committees I am aware of.

I am definitely not an asset to any of them. For years I have had to struggle with my intrinsic aversion for all things planned, whenever I am called upon to attend. The only contributions I ever add are loud, long yawns. When I am in the mood I can infect a reasonably alert group to inertia within five minutes. Two or three spontaneous gasps from me soon have the rest of them dabbing their eyes.

Suppressing my output can be just as distracting. Trying to yawn through a closed mouth is possible, but the facial contortions; the nostril dilations and the disdainful lip-shiverings, which have to be performed until the danger is passed, must look less than enthusiastic to the onlooking chairman.

My powers of concentration are so vigilant on other occasions. For instance I can often repeat other people's conversations on buses when not directed at me, word for word – but at meetings, no matter how hard I purse my lips or chew my pen, my mind shies from reality like a capricious truant. Although I return home with a diary full of frightening, surrealistic caricatures I have no actual recordings of anything translatable.

If the agenda has been particularly long drawn out, the drawings all have beards, extra curls and usually flowers growing out of their ears. Trivia, like dates and events evade me.

Stuck for a model at one church meeting I drew our minister in full regalia. The minutes – so aptly named – dragged on forever. I shall never understand why we have to endure each meeting all over again via this wretched recording. As time dragged on I was compelled to add various incongruous items to his uniform. A wide-brimmed hat trimmed with chrysanthemums, high-heeled shoes, a sword in one hand and a shopping basket in the other. I was about to hang two diamante eardrops to his lobes when my model leaned forward to enquire about a certain date. I could see by his expression that he preferred my yawns.

My winter habit of wearing men's socks must also prove distracting as I also have a habit of crossing one leg over the other, thereby revealing several layers of brushed wool below my frayed trouser bottoms.

The dignified language used at these conferences adds a slight touch of the ridiculous, the pompous exchanges between officials 'Thank you madam chairman er lady,' 'Now I call on madam secretary' sounds a shade whimsical when the people concerned are normally on first name terms.

When two members don't 'get on' it can have a powerful effect on concentration and is often a remarkable cure for the yawns. Women's meetings would be tedious without them. One wonders how many St Paul attended before he wrote his salutary message 'Women should keep silent in churches – if there is anything they desire to know, let them ask their husbands when they get home.' Hear, hear! Let husbands attend all the meetings while we wait at home. Carried unanimously.

The exception to this rule, of course, is the lady bowlers Annual General Meeting. I wouldn't miss this, not even for Melvyn Bragg and I'd deny myself most things for him. Last week I duly attended ours.

Female bowlers of all shapes and sizes, their elbows eagerly pressed on table tops as they suck their filter-tips, gather around their chairlady and her entourage each year to – well what they actually do remains an enigma.

On a raised platform, their shampoo and sets fresh from the dryer, their moisturised cheeks glowing healthily under the spotlights after their winter rest – sits 'the committee.' These matronly stoics armed with long sheets of trembling foolscap and a menacing pair of scissors in place of chairman's gavel line up their ball points for the start.

While other tables of members obediently perused their agendas, we, having mislaid ours in the rush to be first at the bar, had to make do with a menu sheet (for a future dinner) thoughtfully included by one member. We passed last quarter's reading along by studying whether to vote for sirloin, scampi or farmhouse grill and swapped a few jokes about what we intended to wear for the celebration. Then quite naturally conversation turned to the nocturnal habits of one member who after more refreshment delighted us all with her explicit account of how to remain impregnant. Loud scissors banging rudely thwarted our collective suggestions on this fascinating subject.

'Ladies this is a bowling meeting – order, please!' We obediently ordered another round and with diaries purposefully poised, weighed up form, noting any useful changes in our opponents. Points for future reference were: One member had had her hair permed, another had regained her original weight, we said she looked much better and privately hoped it would affect her bowling adversely and the chairlady had been practising her delivery.

With one superb bowling action she knocked her drink for a six and without so much as an eyelid flicker she continued speaking, skilfully wiping it up with her neighbour's agenda. Well bowled!

After a lengthy chit-chat on something we didn't quite catch as it coincided with a ribald recitation from a team mate, our commander dangled her spectacle chain threateningly and ordered us all to vote. This sounded easy enough, the only problem being, what for? A whispered enquiry to the next table confused us even more. 'Do we want it rescinded?' We repeated the question among ourselves, took a drink on it, savoured the expression – but no comments were forthcoming.

'Well, or we for or against?' demanded our half of bitter. 'I'm not voting for it anyway' announced a lager lover, 'for one thing I don't know what it means.' 'Isn't it something to do with being cut off?' A bit drastic for lady bowlers, we all pondered, which brought forth a splutter during which we all agreed if it meant anything like it sounded, viz, 'Re-sinning' we were all for it! More head throwing and rib-clutching followed by urgent scissors banging.

'Ask them,' I was pointed towards an educated looking lot behind, 'To cancel' I was told. 'Do we want last year's ruling cancelled?' That seemed straight forward enough, why not say this in the first place – and er what was last year's rule?

When everything had been voted in again I decided to attend to any other business. In the toilets, conversation was jolly. 'I wouldn't miss this for owt,' giggled one, applying more lipstick before she hurried back. My husband called for me last time and he didn't want to leave. Better than the Palace of Varieties, he said.

In the corridor one or two hefties were flicking their bowling arm on the sophisticated gaming equipment. Eventually we wove our way past the rows of empties towards the exit with matters in hand well and truly discussed, voted for and carried.

We all decided unanimously on fillet steak!

Preparations for the midsummer madness

IT seems only a few weeks since we were cooing about having a small summer wedding in our front parlour–a dream I've had since I saw Spencer Tracey walk Liz Taylor down the family staircase in 'Bless the Bride.' The idea of performing a marriage in your own home, with the minister coming to you, always appealed to us. That was until we compiled our first guest list and discovered how impossible it would be to plan a small family wedding around an outsize family.

I mean how can we invite these and not include them? What would they think if we left out their so and so?

With only twenty weeks to go to our midsummer madness, the excitement in our camp is mounting. Our two males are not showing many outward signs yet, except perhaps a few shudders from the elder.

The younger is still at the 'When did you say it was?' stage. Unfortunately his St Tropez holiday falls just before and he is still in a financial coma over this. He keeps assuring me he will be back in time. But I ask myself, wearing what?

Meanwhile there is no lack of feminine fervour as each week brings a new adventure in espionage. Secret missions to eating establishments to find suitable food in congenial surroundings; then the mysteries of VAT and service to unravel.

We have discarded our first flush of fantasies – 'Let's hire a boat and float our guests down the canal' or 'Let's copy the Zulu custom and spend the evening insulting each other.' Relatives sit around ridiculing each other until everyone falls about laughing. Knowing the wild streak intrinsic to our natives, I can only visualise the evening ending in a punch-up.

The parts I really enjoy are the weekly visits to our surrounding cities and their fashion houses. Riding the escalators to the thickly carpeted dress depart-ments has become a favourite pastime.

We have become quite adept at dodging the more zealous assistants – the ones who take our pleas of 'just looking' as a personal insult. While 'our gang' keeps them occupied playing hide and seek among the racks, we can browse in comfort. With a bride, three bridesmaids, and a bride's mother in our regular entourage, tempers do often become frayed.

We have also compiled our Good Taste Guide to economical eating. After our travel expenses it is necessary to cut down on luxuries like food.

Shoppers with children may be interested in our findings, even if Egon Ronay isn't. A glance at the set lunch on the top floor of Lewis's starting at £2.50, and we were soon on the downward glide to the basement cafeteria.

If our youngest, who only eats chips anyway, did a share job, we calculated the bill at £10. So we decided to risk the serve-yourself where everyone can see before they eat.

Here, a substantial 'home made' steak pie, chips and peas, plus drink and a piece of cheesecake for greedy gourmets, cost about 80p. The eight-year-old was very happy with her plate of chips and peas and carton of orange juice.

When eldest daughter and I managed to sneak away on our own to Manchester one weekend, naturally our feasting took a different course, we chose the Danish Food Centre.

The colourful fillings spread on the open sandwiches enticed us into their restaurant. All the waitresses were adorned in outfits of pink and white gingham, waiting to serve.

I pointed to a scrumptious looking chunk of fresh salmon and a dainty lettuce frill and topped with mayonnaise, then a delicious looking triangle with a trifle-like base covered with a layer of fluffy custard and iced sponge, oozing with calories no doubt, but my kind of dessert. I flashed a fiver at my daughter, big spender that I am, and went to claim a table.

'How much do you think your sandwich was?' she smiled as she placed our goodies before me. When she told me it had cost a pound, I said 'What is it – caviar?' 'Yes,' she giggled.

So the dark brown specks I pushed to the side of my plate were actually caviar. 'Poached salmon with caviar,' said the menu. Keeping the small specks that looked like birdseed until last, I ate them slowly and with feeling. At least I can boast of having a caviar sandwich and, believe me, I do.

As we devoured our slices of luxury, a smiling waitress walked around the tables refilling coffee cups. I beckoned her over eagerly: 'This is the sort of service I could grow to love,' I whispered. Just to be polite I asked the waitress 'How much?' – merely a gesture of course. This must surely be a gift from a grateful management. Her 'twenty pence' left me speechless.

On a visit to Leeds we discovered a new eating style, tucked away in the basement of a large store – a take-away. Especially recommended for a family dine-out, or perhaps a quick snack for city workers and shoppers. A chip 'butty' bulging with crispy golden chips cost 18p, Cornish pasty, chips and peas is very satisfying at 27p. Cartons of hot soup and cans of pop are also available. Our youngest could enjoy her favourite diet – a tray of chips for 15p. Afterwards we indulged ourselves in a sit down coffee in one of the more comfortable coffee houses.

On these excursions we use British Rail and their services have proved excellent. I particularly compliment Huddersfield on their homely buffet, where individual cups of coffee are brewed at just my strength and can be enjoyed in clean cosy surroundings.

A bit on the old fashioned side, reminiscent of the original refreshment bar in Noel Coward's 'Brief Encounter,' but this adds to its charm. There's even a television in the corner.

I could definitely become addicted to this lifestyle, tripping off every weekend trying on gowns I can't afford. What shall I do when summer's gone is a question I try not to ask myself? Still, with another three daughters grow-ing up, the novelty could wear off.

Masculine shopping trips are swift and sure, a brief pop in to be measured and home again for the football. We don't invite them on our excursions.

My husband's style of buying has not improved over the years. 'What do you want? What size? One here,' and that's it. I am expected to march home with the first thing I try on. On occasions I do admit I buy the first one I try on, but only after I have compared it with everything else in the district.

Not all men are like this of course. In a milliners' recently I watched one husband describing in detail the sort of hat he wanted for his wife, while she stood meekly behind him. 'Something soft,' he hinted. To match his wife no doubt, I secretly concluded. 'To match this dress,' he added pointing to the floor where his wife was rummaging through her shopping.

The assistant, becoming unusually versatile at the sound of his long vowels, produced several wobbly brims, but he shook his head. 'The colour is right, but too harsh looking.'

One eventually met with his approval and he nodded so enthusiastically, I half expected him to try it on first, but after examining it he handed it to his wife who dutifully put it on. His expectations were short-lived. 'Take it off darling,' he sighed, dramatically, 'You look like a mushroom.'

Yes, it's a full-time glorious occupation looking round at all the exotic, glamorous creations one could buy if only . . . .

For a fleeting second I wish I had been born rich. Being a natural spender, I could have had so much pleasure. But then I realise a lot of the joy comes from all the saving and doing without that is necessary first.

If I were a rich man I would have been denied the ecstasy of savouring my first caviar or the bliss of seeing the culmination of our big spend one day in July – wouldn't I?

From March, 1978 the format of the paper altered and Enid's column was reduced slightly. There was no heading other than the Kay Bennett Column.

SAY 'Hello,' I often had to urge our unsociable son in his toddling days when he refused to acknowledge anyone who didn't offer a sweet. 'I wouldn't talk, would I?' he said once, coming out from under his eyebrows after a particularly unresponsive session with an acquaintance.

Daughters, too, are often on the sulky side. 'Show your pretty teeth to the lady,' would sometimes instigate a pursing of the lips most unbecoming in a two-year-old. Then, just when their personalities are beginning to blossom into chattiness with all, we have to reverse the process.

'Don't stop to talk to anyone,' we instil into schoolchildren, and, 'Never accept lifts from anyone,' we anxiously warn our teenagers. 'No, not even if you know them,' we feel bound to add these days.

But learning not to trust is difficult, especially when one has been brought up in an excessively friendly environment. I come from a family where any one who crossed the threshold was automatically entitled to a cup of tea or a dish of water, in the case of animals.

This tea making etiquette caused me a lot of anxiety during our first few years of marriage. When the coal merchant left his first load, I stood behind the kitchen door in an agony of embarrassment wondering which to give him first – his tip or his tea.

When my first workmen arrived to set up quarters for a week while they replaced some gas pipes, I stood talking to the door handle half an hour before I dare open it. 'Er, do you take . . . ? Perhaps 'Can I offer you . . .? sounded more experienced. Actually I needn't have worried. Dead on ten o'clock the door opened and a friendly voice said: 'We've connected the cooker first, so you can put the kettle on, love.'

Asking intruders to produce their credentials was another agony, especially when the house and its contents still didn't feel to belong to me. Understandable, I suppose, considering half of it didn't. A stranger once knocked on our door and asked me how many light bulbs we had. This certainly had me stumped. How many were you allowed? At the time I was a 'Candid Camera' addict and, just in case Jonathan Routh was lurking round the corner, I giggled photogenically.

'I'm from the Electricity Board and I want to see your light bulbs,' he said sternly. I looked at his soiled mac, the small black case, the pencil behind his ear, but having never seen a light bulb inspector before anyway, what was one supposed to look for? I thought about asking for proof but 'Show me your credentials,' sounded a bit cheeky as he was twice my age. So cowardice to the fore, I asked him in.

We stood together under each light while he wrote something in his notebook. After he examined the lights downstairs, I led him upstairs. All the time he observed and scribbled a horrible suspicion grew inside me. And, as there was our baby growing there, I felt pretty choked. At last we were downstairs and almost at the door. Then he made a derogatory remark about my bloated appearance, which I did not find amusing, as it was true. In two minutes he was in the street.

Later I discovered through a neighbour, who had the sense to ring the Electricity Board and check before letting him in, that he was an impostor! They had never heard of him and no one had been sent on such a survey. This was my first lesson in keeping strangers on the other side of the door.

The second came a few years later when we were just discovering the disadvantages of living on the main road. As usual I was pregnant and immersed in my regular occupation of ironing clothes. I was just in the process of scraping the remains of a nylon vest from the iron when a man walked through the open door and asked for a drink. Uneasiness did not really hit me until I was returning with the glass. Walking steadily towards me, hands outstretched, was a tall red-haired stranger, dressed in a smart navy pin-stripe suit and immaculately blancoed plimsolls.

He took the water eagerly, then reached into his top pocket. But instead of an automatic complete with silencer, he produced a sheet of paper. I managed to decipher the words 'Hospital' and 'Manchester' before he snatched it back. Ironing the scorch mark on the ironing board cover furiously, I tried to look interested as he described a cartilage operation and even found strength to shake my head when he started rolling up his trouser leg.

Next he limped professionally round the chairs. Then, hovering discern-ingly like a dog selecting a suitable tree he eventually sank into an armchair.

'I've just walked from Manchester,' he sighed. 'Why?' was the only word I could manage. It sounded stupid even to me, especially when he answered logically 'No money.' How much would he take to disappear I was beginning to wonder? My father's entrance – he had been working in the garden – put new life into our visitor. He was off down the road with remarkable dexterity for a man recovering from an operation.
*

HAPPINESS - that elusive, perishable, sought after state – is what? Until last week for most of us it was probably a warm television on a miserably cold night. But in one day happiness suddenly became sun shaped.

Yes – whether it shines again or not, for one whole idyllic morning our porch was covered in sunshine. The birds were peering in short-sightedly through the dusty windows, the spiders were preparing for a hasty house move as I reached for the long brush and I daringly unfastened the top button on my suede jacket. Life seemed to be perking up again. That was Tuesday – on Wednesday it rained again.

But happiness means different things to different people. Wordsworth saw it in daffodils, Da Vinci captured it in a woman's smile. Quentin Crisp is con-tent in his uncleaned flat, 'Dust isn't noticeable after a year or two.' Erin Pizzey, battered wife protector, has found new release in not ironing clothes anymore. She believes that creases fall out as you wear them. Liz Taylor, once ecstatic with diamonds, finds she is now happier with the money. Albert Einstein's theory of relativity means little to me but I love his rules for living, he believed in doing what he wanted when he wanted.

This morning I achieved something that would have driven me wild with triumph in my schooldays, but now only causes me pain. I longed to be the owner of a black eye or burst nose, great status symbols in our area. These assets escaped me until today. I was innocently removing a sweater when a 2ins long brass point attached to the end of a drawstring, whipped agonisingly up my nose and stuck there until I found the courage to dislodge it. What a sad sight – blood gushing everywhere and no witnesses. I ran hopefully next door with the rich, red liquid flowing impressively – but they were out. With no visual evidence my tender beak won't even evoke a second glance when the family arrives home.

When we were newlyweds happiness was reading the newspapers in bed on Sunday mornings. Now I'm lucky to see them before Monday. But time alters one's desires - nowadays it doesn't take much to lift my spirits. Three magic words from my dentist 'nothing to do,' a cottage trip which promises to take our volatile adolescent to Wales for five days or 120 hours sounds longer, a 'nothing to pay' smile from our librarian – simple pleasures often bring the most satisfaction.

Last Saturday all members of our household were basking in deep-seated elation for at least an hour. 'I feel almost carefree,' I cooed to hubby. 'At last I can sleep,' sighed one daughter. We sat in our armchairs and breathed deeply with no groping under cushions and no door or drawer slamming. For forty minutes at least we were all on beaming terms with each other. The reason? Our daughter's homework assignment had been found at last after an exhausting search that had been performed on a twice-nightly basis for weeks. The usual places; bread-bin, piano, sock drawer, brought nothing. Eventually, along with other missing treasure, two library books and a homework diary, it was finally unearthed from under son's bed. Our unknown trespasser strikes again!

The end of winter and herald of spring can leave one feeling as ravaged as the countryside looks. This is my signal to reach for the Balm wine recipe. My gran's ever-present hip flask of rum, which she laughingly referred to as her 'medicine,' when she laced her cups of tea with it, kept her fortified for ninety-three years.

Do you ever indulge in the luxury of your own amusement at your own pace? Think about it – then do it. I did the other day. When everyone had left for school and work, I slipped back to bed for one glorious illicit hour on my own. The luxurious bliss of it!

But perhaps the ancient philosophy of Boethisus sums it all up most sagac-iously: 'Nothing is miserable unless you think it so; conversely every lot is happy if you are content with it.' Yes - I'll drink to that.
*

'I AM not in the habit of lying,' I often snap at my family – which is not strictly true. I slip into the gentle art of prevarication more often than I care to admit. 'Too small,' I lied to a shop assistant when a dress made me look ugly. 'Mm, lovely,' I sighed when confronted with my back view in the hairdressers' hand mirror and all I'm wishing for is the sanctity of home and a hairbrush.

But my best 'romances' were woven at junior school, when imagination was dangerously fertile. My mother's maxim – 'I'd rather have a thief than a liar, you can always get to the bottom of a thief,' had little effect. I was fast becoming equally proficient at both.

At one stage, I was leading a doubly deceitful existence. Each morning I went to school with a bundle of 'presents' tucked under my arm. My mum's glass animals, jewellery, scarves, anything I hoped would not be missed. These were doled out in order of imminent birthdays. I had this terrible fear of not being invited to parties.

Our party host was busy 'bulling' his buttons in the RAF, ready to fight the Germans somewhere, so our party giving had sadly declined. I was beginning to realise that people who throw parties never invite those who don't. To make sure of being a regular guest I hit on the present giving idea and spun this yarn about 'Fairies' leaving these gifts behind in our wood. But one sceptic was unmoved by this charity. She didn't believe in fairies, even if they did come up with glass Bambies, etc.

Seeing as her birthday was next I had no choice but to sit with her on top of the wall which enclosed the wood and wait. While I was promising God the impossible if he made something magical appear, an old man who kept hens in one shady corner approached a tree just below us and, with a shifty look from left to right, proceeded to irrigate it personally. My friend's enthusiasm was sadly dampened.

As I walked her home past the largest, most impressive mansion in the district, my first social-climbing instincts stirred within. 'My gran lives here.' I was pretty desperate now, determined to be on her list before bus time. She paused to admire the outsize orchard (my gran's Corporation house would have been lost in the garden hut). The smirk on my friend's face spurred me on. With the confidence of a born liar, I marched up the endless drive for a 'visit.' In full view of the impressive French windows, my well-being evaporated – I fled. Outside the big gates, when breathing allowed, I explained; 'I'd forgotten she goes to whist drives on Wednesdays.'

The invitation came on Friday. My come-uppance followed on party day. Watched by sardonic birthday girl and grinning friends, I had to answer her mother's question: 'Does your granny still live up at t'Nook?' truthfully.

When other children were boasting about their father's strength, my son was making up stories about my health. He told some beauties, especially if he was left pram-guarding outside a shop. 'She's been rushed off in an ambu-lance' was his answer to enquiries of 'Where's your mum?' The symptoms varied according to season. 'She's been stung by a wasp,' he told one 'In both eyes,' he added, when she didn't look impressed enough.

I became accustomed to greetings like, 'What was the operation like then?' and 'You seem to be walking better now.' I could have understood lies about my age, but lying about my health? Was it wishful thinking?
*

AS the easterly gales whip across the immaculately tailored plush green squares of bowling turf, strange, scarved, behooded figures, shaped like Easter eggs, can now be seen, gently flexing their embrocated knees for the start of the crown green bowling season.

Excuse me if I burst with joy, but as last – 'They're open!' 'Get wet, on your marks, we're off!'

Mutinous murmurs can be heard in some male-order regions. 'Women ought to banned' one chauvinist bore confides every time we play at Meltham. Some men believe a lady-member's place is behind the tea urn, others curse the day they ever lent 'the wife' their set of bowls, others are just plain scared.

'Never bowl with women,' they tremble when asked to join the pairs competition, a contest between couples - usually husbands and wives – brave enough to stand the pace, normally played early season while male egos are still at their peak.

Not all are timorous; lots of husbands would not miss the chance to shout at their defenceless wives – even for a brewery trip. Their stoic cries spur us on throughout the season. 'Rubbish' they encourage. 'For God's sake come off Elsie,' they say and make helpful suggestions like 'Take up clog dancing.'

During the winter months knitting needles and crochet hooks have not been idle. It's been a long winter for some judging by the length of various jerkins. We usually start in full ceremonial Arctic gear. Three layers of knit-one-purl-one, topped by husband's hippo-shaped waterproofs. Not much shouting from supporters at first, it being difficult to discern who is actually in that bundle tied up like rolled brisket. If a gust of wind did ever manage to penetrate all that plastic the occupant could be blown to the top of Holme Moss before a chap could shout 'Don't be short, Phyllis.'

My 'uniform' varies according to what our teenagers are casting off. Some-one has to wear these expensively bought items now only considered fit for middle-aged tramps. But I don't mind, really, in fact it makes me feel – different!

Take today for instance, I am wearing son's straight-legged jeans thoughtfully provided by his firm. Not for me of course, but specially designed

229

for waistless, pot-bellied engineers with pipe-cleaner legs. I always did fancy straight legs, half an hour in these jeans and I look like acquiring them.

For shoes I have a choice between a totter on the toenails in big-dipper wedges, or Eastern comfort in flick-up plimsolls. I could wear suede boots with a zip that refuses to mount my calves, under my trousers, but I look as if I've sprouted angel wings, a sort of cycling Mercury the Messenger.

One can wear almost anything on a bike but having to land on earth and walk around the Co-op occasionally is slightly inhibiting.

Our main bowling rule this year seems to be 'Behave' and 'No giggling on the green.' We have pledged not to enjoy ourselves as much after our relega-tion and plan to reach new heights as soon as we've learned to bowl again.

Besides the obvious ones I have one big handicap, even when an opponent has been given the point after a measure I still cannot believe I am not the nearest. I want to call a second opinion, a third, even a fourth if necessary, until I find someone with perfect judgement like myself.

Marsh Ladies have beaten us to the spring cleaning, I hear, completing it straight after Christmas. Mine has sadly been postponed this year due to illness. The dog has been poorly and one daughter had a hacking cough that had to be dealt with immediately, if bedroom plaster was to stay intact.

The dog crawled in one night as if his legs were made of string. He looked so horrible I wondered if he had spent the night with son in Marsden.

But the vet assured me he was just like the rest of us – dog-tired and beginning to feel his age. Now, those wedding invitations can wait a while where's that chewing gum, spending money, lipstick and, oh yes, the bowling bag. Happy Easter folks!
*

THERE'S a certain hairdresser's shop window in town which I always have difficulty in passing. Observing the row of male chins pointing skywards like nuclear warheads while their locks are being fed and watered in the basin behind can be riveting entertainment. I am almost as hypnotised by their reflections as the exquisitely groomed staff are by their own.

I count myself really fortunate if a completed coiffeur comes out while I am there. These chaps – all tongued-and-grooved leaving a trail of aftershave smouldering behind – certainly present a different picture to the one I remember when I used to drag our son to the barbers. 'How do you want it?' customers were asked. Whatever they replied, the resulting short back and sides all looked the same anyway.

Whether it's because they have to stand alone such a lot in discos – no hiding behind partner in today's style of dancing – men can beat some of the women at grooming. However grotesque they look, twitching and jerking to the noise, at least their hair stays put. Perhaps one day they won't even bother asking us to dance – as soon as the music starts they will be out on the floor with the spotlight glinting madly on their rinses.

Even Alf Roberts the coy councillor in Coronation Street had a crimp for his wedding to Rene Bradshaw. What first attracts us to the opposite sex? Is it physical, hair, clothes, or does the magnetism come from within?

Footballer Brian Wilson's girlfriend, Anne Nolan, the singer, confesses she was attracted by his Geordie accent. 'The way you do my hair,' could be Lulu's theme song, since she fell for her hairdresser. My daughters prefer good conversationalists, judging by the phone bills. Middle daughter says her boyfriend has one endearing quality she can never resist, 'He likes me.'

Our youngest girl, aged nine, still thinks there is nothing to compare with two penny blackjacks.

I once asked my spouse what scintillating factor drew him to my side, but he deliberated so long we both fell asleep. When I ask 'Why did you marry me?' which I am inclined to do if I think he owes me a favour, it's always the same response: 'Felt sorry for your father.'

'Looks aren't everything,' my mother was fond of repeating, when we both noticed my nose was spreading non-stop and I'd have to give up laughing in company. Judging by the hairstyles advertised in magazines today – she was right. According to them the way to bewitch your man is to plait hair from top to bottom, then comb and fluff it up till it resembles steel wool. I've seen healthier looking hair on dead cats.

I watched a school production recently. 'Those two are sweethearts in real life,' whispered my daughter. As the pretty-faced teenager burst into what could never be described as song, we realised he could not have been attracted by her voice. 'There's a place for us' she droned, while we all secretly agreed.

According to my parent's description, their first meeting must have been the main attraction in Huddersfield that week. 'He was wearing his father's trousers and his brother's jacket,' remembers my mother scornfully. 'She was the only one with a coat down to her feet,' laughs my dad. It must have been love at first sight – and what a sight!

NOW the children are back at their desks – I can start my holiday. As this first break comes to a close, the children become all relaxed and slovenly and I seem most prone to my attack of the holiday 'snaps.' My conversation is reduced to 'Stop doing that,' or 'Louise stop looking happy, see!' as son once perceptively put it.

One of our holiday rules is – make your own bed if you want to lie on it, so it usually takes me a day or two to find each bed again. Removing the assortment of love letters, mugs of stale coffee, green and silver teaspoons, plastic cartons of sour paste and orange peel that have congealed beneath them usually takes another couple of days.

Just a solitary sit and think feels luxurious when the children – not forgetting their best mates – are not around. Only the distant cooling-off sighs of telephone and television, or the sound of next door's dog re-stripping the kitchen door, gives one a chance to wonder what life would be like if the house was permanently empty. Would I turn into a never-never, like the lady I heard talking to her friend on the bus?

'How are you luv – is Elsie alright?' she was cheerfully asked. 'Never seen her since bowling started' was the emphatic reply.

'Doesn't she stop in when it rains?' 'Never,' was the reply again. 'Then she wonders why her neck aches.' Friend tried another topic. 'Er – do you get out at all luv?' 'Never – I can never understand folk who can't be content in their own homes. I go to our Sid's of course, and he always brings me back – otherwise going out never bothers me. Bringing her back must be the highlight of Sid's life.

Some television viewers know all the answers, but only one question. 'How do you feel about . . . ?' In a recent comparison between our health service and the American insurance system, one was disturbing a young woman at the end of a long hospital 'Medicare' (the equivalent of our Welfare) queue.

'How do you feel about waiting here?' he probed. She had already described her state – no husband – no money – children to support – an unpaid operation behind her and more treatment needed. In sickness or in health, life looked bleak. Her eyes were beginning to glint dangerously, so he tried another inane question. 'How do you feel about insurance!' A pity we had to leave then. One could imagine her bashing him over the eyeballs with the nearest patient and asking him 'How do you feel about that?'

'This is my last day,' a hospital Sister announced to me recently as she held what looked like a fire extinguisher to small daughter's ear. In her mid-fifties and squeezing the syringe with almost frightening strength, she looked so fit I was bound to ask why. 'I'm staying at home to nurse my mother. With all the fully-trained staff waiting for jobs you'd think they'd be pleased – but they hate anyone to leave – everyone's worked here for years.' People like her deserve a special award. Like the voluntary worker in a Queen Street café who told me: 'Coming here stops me from being bored and you don't feel as if you are depriving youngsters of jobs.'

On a bus the other day a small boy walked to a spare seat at the front, while his mum sat with two other children on a side seat at the rear 'Mum,' he shouted after a while. Harassed mum transmitted a few 'belt-up' signals without moving her lips, but he was determined. 'Mum, if my dad's working tonight, don't forget it's my turn to sleep with you!'
*

WE'VE been feeling a bit choked in our corner of late, since a neighbour started sandblasting and re-building an old cottage. Everything around is covered in chalky deposit, like our bathroom on Friday nights when our talc happy teenagers have finished their disco preening.

Apart from this aggravating dust fall-out and the perpetual hiss of the blasting gun – his house is also beginning to look smarter than everyone elses.   Noting the place looked deserted last Sunday, I decided it was time to pay a neighbourly call. There is a limit to what you can see from behind a net curtain. With the family's farewell singing in my ears – 'I don't know how you dare,' and 'Oh, you are nosey,' I crept surreptitiously up the side wall in best commando style. After first cocking an ear at the corner I took my inquisitive instinct in both feet and stepped into the front garden.

'Come in,' greeted a man in shining armour pointing what looked like a deadly ray gun in my direction. When I stopped trembling he took off his blasting equipment and indicating the floorless, windowless, roofless walls asked if I would like a walk around.

As we stood tree deep in wooden planks he described his future dream home. This large draughty gap would become the lounge, we looked upwards through the ceiling beams to a large space above which he assured me would eventually be the master bedroom. Very impressive, but the most inspiring structure of all was perched just inside the front door. On a protruding brick a mistle thrush was sitting patiently on her eggs. Throughout the banging and blasting she had continued her vigil with never a complaint or cough.

Heartening to know another mother shares my instincts, a shelf above the front door certainly has more viewing potential than my peering point behind the curtains.

The same day I gave my philanthropic tendencies another airing along the canal stretch in front of our house. Our walk coincided with a young fisherman's hook of a lifetime – a writhing perch which was truly 'that length.' It was a magnificent catch. He laid it reverently on a piece of clean rag while he searched his knapsack for his camera – proof to all rod-holders that this was no tall story.

His equipment was spread meticulously on the grass, he was the neatest angler I had ever seen, even his maggots were writhing symmetrically in parallel lines. His camera looked like ours did when we first saw it in the shop window. A flash in one compartment, a film in another, camera in another.

*

By the time he had fixed the bulb, dusting all carefully, the fish was beginning to look depressed and distinctly unphotogenic. 'Hold it in the water a minute I suggested,' as is my way when faced with situations I know nothing about. But he obediently took my advice – then I think he said 'Damn' as the naughty perch pushed off. I didn't quite catch his words, but I know he looked quite sad. Perhaps he could fish for it again I wanted to suggest, but my husband dragged me off so quickly there wasn't time.

Neighbours can be wonderful people and I thank the Lord regularly that we have such lovely hard of hearing ones. The other evening our two middle girls came downstairs with shining eyes. 'We shall have to sleep downstairs,' they beamed. 'Amanda has locked us out.' It transpired their younger sister with whom they share their Presley-lined pad had sulkily locked the door then fallen asleep. The solution was simple, she would have to be awakened – but gently – I warned.

Ten minutes later after continuous knocking, screaming – and threatening, there was still no response. We concluded she was either dead stupid or . . . ? My imagination was already calling an ambulance as I threw myself down and pushed my lips under the door. 'Open this door' I commanded as authoritatively as I could, with splinters in my lips and posterior pointing upwards. More silence.

Feeling like The Sweeney I gave the order – break the lock. Easier said than done, but after my husband had tried all his cursing vocabulary and nearly dislodged his backbone the door shivered then gave in.

As we all tumbled in – Amanda continued to sleep peacefully!

*

HOWEVER much wedding dresses and ceremonies differ, I'd like to bet one thing that never alters – the look of relief on the face of the bride's mother when everyone reaches for the sparkling toast.

234

Marriages may have been ordained in Heaven for the propagation of mankind, not so the bride's mother can thrust a household into six months of 'operation wedding,' as my husband is fond of popping out of his greenhouse to repeat. But there are so many arrangements to make one cannot help it.

Anyway, I have finally finished baking the wedding cakes, and what an operation! When friends enquire 'How many tiers?' I feel like answering 'bucketsful.' All I have to do now is find the courage to present them to the unsuspecting icing expert who consented to decorate them. I can't decide whether to leave them on her doorstep with a note or soak them and me in brandy and throw us at her mercy. The trouble is that instead of three flat-topped perfections I had promised, two have definitely risen above their station. Perhaps we could have a sort of upside-down creation with the small, stocky one at the bottom and the large frail one on top?

It will certainly be a refreshing change to shed my old outfits and wear something new again after saving like Scrooge. My only fear is that when I am eventually dressed from head to toe in wedding gear, no one will recognise me. 'Who's that fancy piece hanging round the bride's father?'

Having bridesmaids in the family can be a frustrating experience for any bride and her mother, especially when their ideas of what the best dressed attendants should wear, and their figures are so different. Pinning up and trying on is like trying to manacle a revolutionary. When it comes to the 'Stand over there' bit and we stand back to examine our handiwork their reluctance is pitiful. The three dejected maids with drooping shoulders and funereal expressions smouldering discontentedly above the pins are enough to pierce any amateur couturier's composure.

Their remarks do little to reassure. 'What's this supposed to be?' 'I feel daft,' and the inevitable 'Do I have to be a bridesmaid?' No, my daughters, you can each become a mummified body wrapped from scalp to toenail in best Terylene lawn.

When the battle is at its height this is usually the signal for our happy hunters to return from the world outside – then it's all hands to the hiding of the evidence. Dresses quickly snatched and scratched over heads, all scraps of material whisked out of sight so that when our males enter all that remains of our activities are three miserable pin-scarred daughters plus two glowering dressmakers.

Recently I took a few peeps at our wedding album, trying to recapture the nerve-racking thoughts of that afternoon in December. There's my mother looking smart and terrified, whether this is because she is loosing me or the live cork-tip clenched in her right hand – I can't tell. Hard to realise the young boy standing to attention with three youths sporting convict hairstyles was all of twenty-two. My father and I look particularly happy on the church steps. Apart from this being the end of a long courtship (five years) we had just been informed that the bridegroom who had collapsed at the altar was in fact from the previous wedding.

Another shows the blissful couple, both bearing up bravely under the weight of what appears to be an overgrown rosebush, but was actually what the florist described as an American spray bouquet. A bit difficult to discern my facial expression as I try to master the flowers, as one of our toddlers discovered both a ballpoint pen and our wedding album on the same day, and on most of the photographs I have a large blue spider crawling down my nose!

*

FOR the first time this year I am actually bearing signs of sunburn. My mottled arms and kneecaps are living proof that the sun shone all day last Wednesday. Sunshine always makes me nostalgic especially as Spring Bank approaches. My husband has always to sort out this holiday confusion and tries to explain each year where Whitsuntide and Whit Monday have disap-peared to. But if we can't look forward to Whit now, we can always look back.

It used to be easily recognisable. Hail, snow, rain or shine, Whist Sunday meant going to church in our new summer clothes. Underneath our thick woollen coats we wore our thin 'best' dresses and held on smartly to our straw bonnets, while we dropped suitable hints as to what we would be wearing for the most coveted event of all – 'The Whit Walk.'

Fine or not, you wore the brand new 'washing frock,' my mother's name for the cotton print dress, white ankle socks and pumps, all these courtesy of the Co-op dividend or a cheque that was paid for by weekly instalments.

The Whitsuntide advent had its anxieties, this was no time to be churchless and I was a shameless advocate of the Easter, Whit and Christmas trinity; or I could be found lurking in the congregation when a Baptist concert was imminent.

A week or two before Whitsun I usually mingled with the Anglicans; their recreation ground was the largest.

The excitement of marching on, arms swinging, behind the brass band is an experience I shall never forget. As our procession joined the others, pride and loyalty welled inside me. I always felt fiercely attached to whichever church I had temporarily joined; vowing that it would always be mine. This euphoria would take me through at least two sermons before the call of a tadpole binge with the rest of the secularists overcame my righteousness.

236

But at the moment of marching nothing could beat the rhythmic fellowship as we blazed our way down the main road, spirits soaring as high as the royal blue and gold banner which two youths struggled bravely to master.

Mothers who had spent all morning coaxing children and taming husbands were pushing prams blissfully down the crowd-lined streets, morning troubles long forgotten. People were hanging from windows, squashed together in doorways, the call of the brass even charmed pub occupants out of their saloon corners to wave their pints gaily at us as we passed.

Then on we went to gather at a garden gate where we all sang full throttle until an elderly church member, too frail to attend services, found strength to open the door. After the initial surprise the drooping white face would come alive for a few moments as verse after verse of a favourite hymn was sung.

Next, the most longed for treat of all – double quick march into the school-room where a feast of potted meat, currant buns and steaming hot tea awaited. The tongue salad was reserved for the band which had more blowing to do after tea. Afterwards more fun with races, pop and crisps in the field.

My own children started their Whitsuntide in style – on the wagon. A lorry kindly lent, glowing with flags and streamers for the primary scholars and their teachers. As I spent the first half of my married life being pregnant I was usually included. Now Whitsuntide passes by almost unnoticed – no one to witness to – too expensive – instead we have a service and a schoolroom cele-bration, which hardly causes a ripple. Walking out with the band, the joie de vivre, the mighty feeling of matiness and church solidarity which accom-panied this has faded – but what have we replaced it with?

*

I DON'T often look in the windows of gent's outfitters, but after spending a riveting ten minutes outside a particularly exclusive men's shop in town, I couldn't help noticing a new dimension had been added to their plastic dummies.

My daughter and I had stopped to admire a pair of white translucent swim trunks that were clinging like a surgical transplant to an exceedingly life-like male model. I am not usually so fascinated by the frontal area of men's sportswear, not without sunglasses, anyway, but on this occasion a certain built-up area had my daughter and I exchanging stunned glances and collapsing in giggles.

237

After a time we realised the glowering expression raging above the collar of a towelling robe was actually alive and belonged to an unamused shop assistant – who looked as if he might fetch a copper if we didn't move on. Reluctantly we left.

So, women's lib and the fight for equality has eventually reached the world of plastic. If feminine models come complete with curvy contours why shouldn't their male counterparts? Even the toy kingdom has gained a small addition to boost sales.

In America boy dolls endowed with an extra inch of pink plastic which squirts water to order, are competing favourably with the female potty fillers. Who knows, realism may eventually bring forth hairy chests for Action Man.

I wish a little more realism had been practised in the situating of toilets in Huddersfield. Why are conveniences always so inconveniently placed? Why aren't the larger shops better equipped? They are either hidden behind furniture, just under the rooftop, or in some cases not there at all.

We had spent what seemed hours of leg-crossing in one large store, desperately trying to muster enough control to reach the nearest 'Ladies' out-side. When one daughter turned a delicate mauve and her blood vessels started to swell, I asked an assistant if we could possibly use their toilets. 'Is it urgent?' she enquired distastefully, sounding like a doctor's receptionist. My daughter, last seen racing round the fuller figures, with bulging eyes, was pointed out to her and we were ordered to follow down the steps.

Near to bursting a main myself I was reduced to doing my hunchback impression of Quasimodo. We were ordered to stand outside a door while she found a key and by the time she returned our little dance of diminishing control had attracted quite a crowd.

Another occupational hazard for ladies with weak plumbing like myself are the toilets equipped with attendants – a sheer waste of humanity, it seems to me. They are either guarded by ex-ATS sergeants who have you standing to attention in straight lines and your penny in the centre of your left hand or the over-possessive nanny type, who escort you to the door, open it, run a cloth around the seat, then take it personally when you lock them out.

I like to feel this is one job I can manage unaided, thank you, given the facility.
*

AS I write the sun is piercing its way through my camomile and we are about to spend our first day of the year in the countryside.

238

Yet who knows, when this goes to print we may be in the depths of winter again. I have just managed to adjust the radio to the children's choice of No 1 when we arrive in Harrogate. We park our car under a cloudless sky alongside the beautiful multi-coloured flowerbeds that always seem to welcome visitors to this resort. With the scent of horse-chestnut blossom titillating our nostrils we climb the short rise to the elegant town centre. Inside the shops the air is heavy with accents – outside a chauffeur waits obediently beside a gleaming Rolls Royce.

Harrogate is a tonic of old and new. It always gives one the impression of an impending Royal visit. Everywhere looks so smart; even the joggers look spruce. The Spa dome and stately gardens lend a Victorian aura to the lower half, but this could never be said of the fashionable shops that line the upper half. Tempers flared dangerously as the sun reached its hottest. One daughter accidentally stepped on another's big toe. I step in to administer peace via two sideswipes then we pack ourselves into the suffocating car to drive a mile or so up the road to a small pub for lunch.

Their draught bitter is excellent. After five minutes in the cool, oak-trimmed saloon bar I felt quite sociable again. We peruse the menu, or should I say prices and order. While our children change each other's minds about what they ordered, father and I happily continue to drive out the Northern thirst. Everyone becomes friendlier and friendlier, or is it the combination of the hops and me?

Other people's children sit quietly looking well brought up as ours start guessing the tomato ketchup ingredients and protest about the age limit on the 'bandit.'

During long waits family conversation tends to wax personal. 'Don't you ever feel like pulling your nose down?' one child asks me. They all spend an earnest five minutes discussing my facial discriminations. Eventually, an extraordinary pale waitress approaches with a tray. Two steak pies, one haddock, one sausage and one toasted cheese sandwich soon disappear. Apple pie and fresh cream for four and ice cream for one, plus coffee and cream for two followed this. The home-cooked pastry was melt-in-the-mouth crumbly. All plates were returned empty – total £4.50!

Everyone except me remembered to visit the toilets, we then drove towards the riverbank at Otley.

No Harrogate cut-glass connotations here, the language is strictly back-yard 'Cumere,' 'Geroff' type. Clothing inhibitions vary. A man has just walked by wearing a grey worsted three-piece suit, a collar and tie, wool socks and black leather brogues. I managed to note this as he did his 'If I have to speak to you again' act to his three equally well-padded children in front of my seat.

Summery conditions certainly evoke some quaint sights. Pretty rear views often turn into ancient ruins when you reach the front. To my left there's a heavily-built hulk wearing too tattoos and what appears to be his son's jeans. It took him quite some time to persuade them into a sitting position.

We ate our picnic tea in a sweet smelling velvety green corner surrounded by bowing laburnums and pink-tipped hawthorns. After tea, half an hours snooze in the shade until I felt as if all the spiders in the world had invaded my body, then a peep in my mirror to survey the damage.

The usual after-picnic fright stares back. Others look attractively tousled, while I look like one of the oddments our dog digs up and deposits on the lawn from time to time.

As the sun disappeared behind a trough of low pressure and fork lightening danced on the car roof, we splashed our merry way homeward after a truly memorable day.

*

THE first coffin I ever saw was from a fourpenny seat at our local cinema. I was about seven. Three extra large ones were being carried from a building in the moonlight.

'Where are they taking all those sideboards,' I asked naively. The answer was smothered in giggles. 'They are not sideboards stupid, they are coffins!' Not quite sure what this meant, I presumed there was a touch of humour somewhere and joined in the chuckles.

During the last couple of years I have attended nine funerals. I have seen the bewilderment and shock that relatives have to wrestle with. I have experienced the dull ache of inadequacy, when struggling to find appropriate words to convey my sympathy.

But, worst of all, I have stood around helpless – barely able to conceal my anger and frustration while certain members of the clergy have repeated meaningless jargon in a supremely detached voice, gleaned from an open book held throughout the ceremony.

At one service the only personal note came when the name of the deceased was substituted for the word 'Brother' printed in italics. There was no handshake afterwards – no personal message for the bereaved.

'Anyone could have done what he did,' someone remarked bitterly afterwards. 'Blessed are they that mourn, for they shall be comforted,' says the fourth beatitude. Sadly, in my experience at some funerals, very little of this comfort passes from pulpit to public.

What message there is becomes obscure when recited from the pages. Christ himself, the greatest communicator of all, knew the value of simple language. His simply worded family prayer 'Our Father' is one of the most beloved and popular prayers today. Reading from the scriptures is an integral part of any religious service, but the most impact surely comes when reading from the heart.

On this grief-stricken day sufferers want to hear a message of hope not an indecipherable 'piece' which passeth all understanding. I have seen the difference a little preparation and an eye-to-eye confrontation makes when a representative of God performs the job he chose, with love and concern, realising that to reach people you have to come down to earth occasionally.

At my aunt's cremation we were deeply comforted to be told in plain language that our dear one is now 'Free from pain and care.' The minister spoke to us with his arms folded comfortably across his prayer book. We deemed it a privilege to shake his hand in thankfulness afterwards.

I have seen other preachers bridge the void of grief equally inadequately. But this gift unfortunately eludes many Church advocates who imagine repet-itious chants are all that is required.

It could be argued that there is a difficulty where the deceased has not been a Church member. Certainly this must entail more preparation – but surely the need is the same, if not greater?

Death's mysteries will be solved by us all one day. In the meantime we do look to religious teachers for comprehensive inspiration. Author Roald Dahl and his wife, film star Patricia Neal, have had their share of tragedy. Besides the long illness of Miss Neal, they also suffered the death of a child, closely followed by the death of the child's favourite dog.

Granted an audience with a High Church official the writer discussed his problems. At the end of the discussion he mentioned something which greatly troubled him. Could he hope that animals went to heaven too? He liked to think of the dog and its youthful mistress together. He was answered by a cold look of disapproval and a signal that the interview was ended.

Although some of us plan our lives to the last detail, we shy away from arranging our farewell. Unhappily we cannot plan the way we leave. I would like to slip away peacefully, surrounded by friends and family, perhaps a shade mellow, but not yet, you understand. Call me morose, but I have already planned my funeral.

In my drawer is a sealed envelope, containing the plans for my last exit, which I hope will lie there for another forty years. I have picked my spot in the cemetery up the road.

The envelope has been sealed and re-sealed. I change my mind a lot – usually when I've been to someone else's funeral. But I fancy my mourners having a last sing-song to my memory with plenty of flowers – by request.

241

I like the idea of the chap who left instructions for his cortege to stop outside his favourite pub, while everyone popped in for a last drink on him. Perhaps a touch of humour can be introduced, after all. In the meantime let's all get on with some living.

NB: It's rather ironic that Enid should have written an article on this subject. Following her untimely death we found several notebooks containing what we, as a family had to do in the case of her death. These included hymns to be sung, prayers to be said and a certain CD to be played at the funeral service.

Unfortunately she didn't manage to live the forty years she referred to but a mere 26. WB

*

WE nearly had to cancel our first school trip. How could our seven-year-old possibly go without a waterproof coat? No, not an anorak – a waterproof coat. On the list of clothing suggested, it was there in black and white – like every-thing else listed, as a guide. To small minds it is law.

When she saw me reach for the flask, she had more hysterics. 'You can't take that, no one has to take a drink. Teacher is taking some orange juice,' she screamed. We arrived at the safari park to find I was the only mum without one – so thirsty I could have dived in with the hippo.

On these occasions children undergo a metamorphosis – the quiet ones go mad and the mad ones go berserk. It's great fun. Mothers not present would be surprised at the challenges their children often aspire to.

'Who is a good swimmer?' a dolphin tamer asked our group of seven-year-olds. We all looked at the giant overstuffed dolphin swirling the deep waters dangerously and mouthed a silent prayer for those in peril on the sea. 'Me,' said a timid voice, and the shyest girl in the group walked forward.

Next minute she was being dragged around the pool in a pathetic-looking dinghy by this exuberant mammal. In its anxiety to speed there and back for its fishy reward, the dinghy was tipped at a menacing angle of 45deg. While the rest of us closed our eyes and thought of home, the child clung desperately to the sides. When she was safely on terra firma the reward was duly adminis-tered accompanied by a juicy kiss – we were all so relieved we could have joined in.

In pouring rain last Thursday I went with 40 children and eight adults to the delightfully situated Wirral Country Park in Cheshire. We embarked at Liverpool docks to take the ferry across the Mersey. It took us three minutes to sail across the khaki-coloured water, during which time one boy lost a pound note and another found it.

Only eleven o'clock and I'm dying for my cheese sandwich. Surely one of them would start nagging soon? 'Make Eric your butcher' says one shop and Eric's pork pies and pasties pass enticingly by. A lad who believes in living dangerously read the café menus as we drive along. 'Cheeseburgers, beef-burgers, steak pies, chicken.' I am the first to reach for my duffle. Halfway through my snack, the bus stops and we are given permission to eat.

Once out of the coach we hit the Thurstaston Nature Trail. Down the 50ft of cliffs, left by ancient glaciers, to walk along the deserted beach, adjust our storm gear and search for seashore treasures. In the depressing weather conditions, walking with bowed head comes natural. The children excitedly collect shells, pieces of boulder-stone, and dogfish egg cases that look like little toy cameras. I couldn't help looking underneath for the 'Made in Hong Kong' sign. When I ran to teacher with my remarkably unusual species of delicate green seaweed, she smiled kindly: 'It's a plastic flower, actually.'

Walking head down against a gale with a plastic flower does become tire-some after a while, but someone remembered the film show which awaited us back at the centre. 'Yippeee,' was the chorus. 'Sooner 'ave a jar of mild,' muttered an adult at my side. Next stop the sweet shop where the kids could all release their pent up spending money. The first bought a football for 65p.

When the queue of pound notes had subsided, I bought two liquorice sticks for my daughter and I which a bossy man tried to snatch as we entered the film show. 'No sweets allowed in here,' he snarled. But we didn't let that spoil our day. After a diet of chocolate, crisps, pop and travel pills, and a ramble along the disused railway track, we travelled happily homeward – this time through that marvellous tunnel.
*

AS I write this, the sounds of summer are all around me, a crackling fire dancing up the chimney, truculent raindrops battering the windows.

One day I am enjoying a blistering face-shrink in what feels like tropical sunshine, next I am shivering at the edge of a sodden bowling green watching players (men, naturally) paddle out to their woods, looking more like a lifeboat crew wading ashore, than merit bowlers.

Conversely, yesterday was one of those old-fashioned, balmy sun-filled days when you could leave the door open and allow the summer to drift gently in. One of those heady days when the birds' songs sound so humanyou get the unnerving feeling that impressionist Percy Edwards is lurking in the bushes.

We have a robin nesting in our ivy (sounds as if a relative is being taken advantage of). At first we were so thrilled, watching Mr and Mrs Robin build their nursery, we could not understand why our neighbours denied themselves this pleasure by giving their ivy such a close shave earlier on. After days of flying to and fro with their beaks packed, activity ceased and we had a short silence. Then four tiny mouths appeared and the symphony began. The din was such that daddy bird slipped out for a drink one night and never returned. The only time the incessant squawking stops, is when Mrs Robin throws in a worm. They start again the minute she leaves. If she doesn't teach them to fly soon I'll do it myself.

*

LAST week was blood donor week. You could either take your place on the bed provided or mingle with the vampire midges on our bowling green.

I love washdays when these nasties cling to the washing and I can sadistic-ally iron them all out. This is also the time when busy little blue-bottles start dropping their babies everywhere. I am re-learning the art of murder. Fly sprays are OK but swiping them with a rolled Examiner is more satisfying I find.

'Oh come and look at this,' said one daughter the other day after I had served one a deadly blow which knocked over two cups of coffee and splattered the sauce bottle contents all over the sugar. She likes to give a running commentary on the death throes. 'Its proboscis is hanging out but its legs are still moving.' More furious swotting, fly not in good shape but one leg still alive. 'Dying like flies' has taken on a sinister new meaning in our house.

*

MEANWHILE sister May is keeping her end up in the garden, doing all the cabbages in. Our gardener returns with an air of doom about him. Has he seen my supplementary wedding guest list I ponder anxiously? 'Three more gone,' he manages to tell us when speech returns once more and we hold a short sulk for the dear departed.

Leaning against the wash kitchen wall the other morning, my usual washing position since the miracle of automation, I had a slight shock. A shiny black beetle crept from behind the dustbin carrying a piece of spaghetti! I never did discover where he was taking it or what he intended to do with it because I inadvertently let my miracle of automation overflow and the poor chap disappeared down the drain with the water leaving his dinner behind.

'ARE we all becoming teleholics?' asked a newspaper headline last week. Had I not been so preoccupied with Wimbledon and Bette Davies I would have read on.

What a neck-jerking fortnight the tennis winners and losers gave us. Even the rotten weather could not defeat them; I enjoyed every nail-biting minute. The snappy fashions, pretty necklaces, coloured hair bands, flowing locks – and that was only the men's singles.

But for once the male element took second place. The majority of us were more intent on viewing Virginia to victory again. Sadly she was outplayed by cool hand Chris. Fashions were not to disappoint us, lace frillies were coyly revealed below the ever-decreasing hemlines and hairstyles were as bouncy as ever.

Sue Barker's haircut should look attractive when it's completed. At the moment it looks as if her hairdresser was called away to India in mid cut.

It's the animal-like personalities behind the rackets that I find most fascinating. Virginia Wade with her snarling panther-like crouch with all her hopes and fears shining in her eyes and Chris Evert whose bland expression reveals nothing. Her winsome stroll onto court reminded me of that doggy star of 'Lady and the Tramp.' Billie-Jean King is exactly like a rabbit we once had who used to pull its hair out when it felt broody.

Why is Wimbledon so special? 'There is no other tournament in the world for which players prepare so thoroughly, making it the most difficult title for anyone to win,' admits Viking Borg. Peak condition is vital as Evonne Cawley discovered when she tried to ignore a leg injury. Of course the £19,000 prize money has a certain appeal.

One of the attractions for me is the chance to dream myself into a kind of wonder woman all-winner. I do mean dream. A sort of 'if only' feeling. Given the correct accessories, a cute outfit, bouncy shoes, streamlined racket, plus the Wimbledon atmosphere – how could I lose?

In between watching matches I perform fantastic volleys on our coal house door. Yet when I stand on court it takes on terrifying dimension. My normally tall number one seed silhouetted on the far horizon looks more like one of the seven dwarfs.

Naturally look plays a prominent part. Take the easy way the stars bounce the retrieved balls back up on to their rackets, a simple flick of the wrist and it's there.

I've attempted this many times but my balls refuse to play, instead they remain truculently attached to the ground. Bouncing the ball before service is another trick I never mastered, I never could catch with my left hand. Apart from this – why my Virginia Wade service makes my spouse feel so

245

fed up, I can't imagine – I feel truly wonderful as I throw back my head and shoulders, my eyes squinting upwards at the swirling white speck. Who knows, one day it could even land within hitting distance?

My holiday cry of 'Who's for tennis?' can empty a holiday chalet in one minute. Fortunately my husband's reflexes are not what they were and he usually submits.

Chris Evert's double-handers can certainly strengthen one's backstroke. I tried this last year and the ball shot out of court into the clouds and was last seen heading for a roundabout in a children's playground nearby.

With planning and perseverance players like me could easily be accommodated. All we need are half-size courts, longer arms, bionic legs – Oh, and a comfortable chair for me to sit on while he fetches the ball. Yes there's a lot to be said for crown green bowling.

*

'IT must be awful having birthdays at your age,' one of our daughters sighed pitifully, as I proudly placed my cards on the table. 'Nothing to look forward to, doesn't matter what you wear, no one's really interested are they?' Before they wheel me into the cemetery I must say I could do with a little less interest in my apparel.

Last Saturday I decided to take more care dressing for our local garden party and even went to the trouble of tying a gay, red neckerchief around my throat (Vidal Sassoon's wife writes, this is the ultimate in smartness). 'You're not wearing that' was the first incredulous remark. Ignoring daughter's horror I waved son a cheery farewell.

He who never casts a second sneer when confronted with my normal gear, father's shirt and baggy pants, now asks in the same glowing tones he would use to point out a toad on my shoulder, 'What's that around your neck?' I explained that a famous hairdresser's wife wears them all the time. 'They probably suit her,' he says. As their giggles turn to guffaws I must confess she was right in saying 'a scarf brightens up the dullest outfit.'

Some birthdays ago, a friend told me 'you don't act as if you're forty.' This could be another way of saying 'act your age,' but I regarded it as a compliment. Here I am, middle-aged already, yet I still feel the same immature dope inside. At the moment, with a nine-year-old, two teenagers and two adult children I have become a sort of three-dimensional mum. To the youngest I am 'Oh you . . .' the middle girls refer to me as 'her' or 'she' – 'She doesn't understand,' etc. But the eldest two who are now in the category of best friends are calling me mum again.

'Don't you wish you were young again?' cry the younger ones. But when I see some of the youthful expressions drooping over the morning muesli, I think - as I always have – the best is yet to come. 'I can't possibly wear these jeans again for the disco moans one, throwing aside the spaghetti-shaped trousers that were going to make more impact than John Travolta's hip joints, a fortnight ago.

'No one likes me,' sobs our nine-year-old on school mornings. Yet after school there is a continuous trail of dusty pump bags plus extra chairs for tea.

People 'my age' are not supposed to bask in the sun anymore, it encourages wrinkles. Mine don't know this, they came anyway. In middle age one should eat less. But as I work harder than ever and cycle daily – I often ignore this. We need less sleep. I am still catching up on the nights I spent walking the floor with a baby attached to my chest – some days I even have a nap for dessert.

Theologian Selwyn Hughes has the right idea. He believes 'a person is as old as his attitudes not his arteries.' Sunlight does aggravate my eyes more than it used to; I had to wear sunglasses at a bowling match last Sunday.

Searching for a toilet I wandered into a large clubroom where a couple were doing a Come Dancing act. 'Excuse me, could you point me in the direction of the nearest toilet,' I enquired. 'Over there,' said the female half without altering her chasse. The gallant gent took one look at my dark glasses and came cantering over best Victor Sylvester style. Beside himself with apologies he gasped 'Oh I'm sorry love, er, I didn't realise, here let me take your arm.' It seemed a pity to spoil this beautiful moment but I had to confess 'These are just sunglasses,' I smiled. 'I can see perfectly,' and I trotted briskly across the floor – straight into the gents' toilet.
*

THE bride looked enchanting, the two mothers, having made a pact previously to remain dry-eyed at all costs, were firmly controlled throughout. The bridesmaids were charming accessories before and after the pact.

Yes, I'm back and after our 'event' last Saturday, I'm brimming with wedding views. It surprises me in these days of equality how left out the males are in the wedding write-ups, so I intend to remedy this. Our bridegroom looked divine in his three-piece suit of fine wool in a subtle caramel shade, with toning tailored shirt of brown and white poplin. His collar was held in place by a matching tie of pure silk.

The best man wore a worsted three-piece in dark grey, which was still at the cleaners on Friday morning, with white accessories. He didn't tell his mother, but I discovered the empty coat hanger on Thursday morning. Apparently during the four hours he wore it a month ago, it had become soiled enough to warrant a secret trip to the dry-cleaners. He arrived home late Friday with a brown parcel under each arm – one contained his suit and the other his sister's wedding present.

It has been a bit of a 'come down' this week, climbing on to my pedals after posturing around in a chauffeured Rolls. All the wonderful sunny wedding scenes have been floating through my mind ever since. After what seemed an age of planning and spending, once we donned our new outfits everything went double speed.

Conversations linger on. 'Don't I look lovely, daddy?' our youngest bridesmaid announced when attired in her regalia. During the break between reception and the evening party we missed her and a call to the hotel discovered her enjoying a shower in her big sister's bridal suite.

'You look nice in pink,' remarked my mother when she examined my outfit 'but isn't your hair a mess.' The day started off so sickeningly – I awakened with the feeling that someone had siphoned off my innards. My sister rang from Australia-£3 a minute and all I could manage was a sob. An hour before the wedding three of us were trying to remove a hairbrush I had hopelessly entangled in the bride's hair. By 4pm we were miraculously sipping sherry and mingling with guests on the hot turf in front of the hotel.

In the elegant drawing room atmosphere, we had a first rate reception com-manded by Vito, a gentle unassuming head waiter who must have spent years restraining himself from strangling brides' mothers. The champagne corks exploded obediently, the food looked delicious but unfortunately my stomach was not accepting solid contributions at that time. So many sunny memories which, if anyone missed, my father has captured on 'film.' 'I have a marvellous shot of the long stretch of cars outside the chapel,' he enthused.

One moment I shall always treasure – the few minutes my husband and I stood hand-in-hand during the morning, when we went to check the floral arrangements in chapel.

Everything was still and seemed to be standing on tip-toe, the empty pews, and the air cool and heavy with rose breath. 'I think everything's going to be all right, love' he said, and squeezed my hand. It was, including the best wedding present of all – a day of sunshine.

*

BOOKIES are offering odds of five to one that it won't stop raining for more than 48 hours at a time and weathermen are warning that to take up the offer would be a waste of money.

What caused this prolonged soak? Did the ash beat the oak? 'The earth

248

is going through one its wobbly periods' is one explanation being expounded. Apparently it tilts on its axis from time to time, which presumably shakes up the elements and wets us all through.

Other scientific experts who don't know either are also blaming Canadian ice floes. No one seems to be blaming 'the bomb' I notice.

Over optimistic York health officials must be feeling sick after splashing sun warnings all over the city. 'Expose your skin in small doses' and 'Don't let the sun ruin your holiday' are now being hurriedly removed.

Those of us untouched by the continental sun are beginning to look a bit mildewed. Thank goodness for my waterproof hairstyle – frequent watering gives we curlies extra bounce.

Knitting and sewing addicts can carry on regardless, but how do the rest of us cope with this grey outlook? 'Just ignore it' was one tip at our last bowling match, as we sploshed our woods across a rising lake that used to be a bowling green.

One can indulge in a 'What's the point?' routine. This damp excuse can cover any job you don't like leaving the fire or a good book for, like polishing furniture, cleaning windows and steps – and it's no good turning out the bedrooms, they are full of children sheltering from the rain.

There's a constant rumble of dissent from mums during the summer break, especially those who are no longer available to share their offspring's leisure hours and who consider it an outrage to have them plonked on their own doorstep to become their sole responsibility for six weeks.

Whatever the weather, I could not survive without our week away. Paris couturier Pierre Cardin confessed recently 'I travel a lot but holidays are a nuisance – I prefer work.' Hard work brings satisfaction, but a change is necessary from time to time if one is to function properly.

Without my break I should go bananas. I am looking forward to a long weekend in the Lake District, which cannot come soon enough. Last night I called our daughter's new father-in-law Dorothy three times, instead of Donald.

During our family's younger days we always managed a holiday even if it meant just a change of kitchen sink. In my opinion, the family who go away together – stay together. This year we hope to bask in the semi-luxury of bed and breakfast. Awakening in someone else's bed, to the crackling of someone else's cooking, is the acme of gracious living for me.

On one occasion when our children were younger we did put all our savings into a week of full board. Our Blackpool landlady was one of the best, catering especially for families. This was in May, but if the evenings

249

were chilly the days were sunny and warm – lucky because spending money was almost non-existent after putting aside the board money.

When the children were tucked up in bed we looked forward to a free and easy chat in the cosy lounge and the informal tea and biscuit supper round the fire, but our hostess had other ideas. 'Come on, off you go, I always baby-sit for parents. Get out and enjoy yourselves. Take a late key.' Gazing covetously at the glowing embers, we were forced into a choice between a battle with gale force winds on the front or a draughty shiver in shop doorways.

Another advantage of away days is the chance to meet new friends. One year we met Peter and Nellie. She was in her early sixties, rather sedate in her white crocheted beret and Victorian shoes. 'Pe'er,' as her Scottish accent christened him, looked younger with his denim cap and twinkling eyes. A diffident pair, they were often still sitting on the same garden seat sharing a newspaper when we returned to 'the front' after lunch. What did they do all day? Did they ever move off that seat? One evening we found out.

Despite our gallant protests, we were persuaded to visit 'this little place round the corner' where in between pouring the hard stuff down her throat like it was going out of fashion, Nellie told us that besides being her favourite railway porter, Pe'er was that terror of the bookies – a racing expert!
*

DID something today, I'm ashamed to say, I haven't done for ages – made a rice pudding without using a tin opener. With great effort I threw a handful of rice into an earthenware dish, softened it in the oven with a covering of water, added a pinta and a grating of nutmeg, and two hours later that delicious smell of ambrosial perfection was pervading our kitchen. It transported me back to my courting days when my husband's brothers and sister were fighting for the right to 'scrape' the last remains from the family pudding tin.

Today when meals can be prepared so quickly a slow-oven seems a luxury. Instant dinners are convenient but that long-simmering, mouth-watering period beforehand which stimulates young appetites to fever pitch is cut out also. When roast beef and Yorkshire pud are frizzling in the oven the 'How long before dinner?' starts straight after breakfast. Even the dog sits guarding the oven door.

The sounds and smells of something bubbling in the oven, cake tins crammed with home baking, fill me with content. I suppose it's a fall out from the war years, when our staple diet was stew. I can stomach my own stews, but other peoples' always bring to mind the C Fox Smith army poem:

'If you've lost your 'aversack, your kit bag or your pipe,
Your 'ousewife, soap or oily rag with which you clean your pipe,
Your belt or second pair o' socks, your lanyard or pull-through,
Oh do not be dispirited – you'll get 'em in the stew!'

In those days reconstituteds all had the same flavour. Will anyone ever forget that sulphur-like taste peculiar to dried eggs? Then, one had no choice - now when fresh food is in abundance everywhere, supermarkets are doing a boom on dehydrated meals in a packet. With a drop of water you can reach hitherto unconquered heights of culinary sophistication. An enriched sauce can transform a roast beyond all recognition.

Sunday dinner with full family presiding is the event of our week. Our large dining table fully extended never seems big enough now they are older. Yet our standards appear frugal compared with Sunday lunch for two, Samuel Pepys style. His 1662 diary records 'a fricasse of rabbits and chickens, a leg of mutton boiled, three carps in a dish, a great dish of side of lamb, a dish of roasted pigeons, a dish of four lobsters, three tarts, lamprey pie, a dish of anchovies and good wine of several sorts,' with bicarb to follow I presume.

Most households have tasty supper standbys that rarely come from a packet. One gardener tells me they often enjoy a cauliflower cheese supper – in season. A daughter's quickie – by the time she's gone back to close the door, dashes to the toilet, thrown her jacket on the floor, it's cooked – is a savoury omelette. My late night passion is garlic bread.

I discovered a tasty quickie when I spent an evening perming a stranger's hair once. My mother has this habit of never saying 'No.' 'Yes, my daughter would love to,' is her stock phrase. Due to this trait and the invention of home-perms, I was at one point reluctantly putting our local hairdresser out of business. She had met this woman on a bus who was desperate to be curly before morning. With an address but no name I finally unearthed the living image of Tessie O'Shea, without the giggle. 'Come in love, take no notice of them,' she told me, flicking her bleached tendrils behind her ear rings. 'Them' were two large sons and a small, moody husband. 'He doesn't like the idea,' she pointed to her husband glowering behind a paper. That made two of us. Watched by 'Them' and feeling like a TV brain surgeon, I attacked her locks. Amid encouraging comments like 'What a stink' and Is it safe?' I surreptitiously covered the white burn on the dark polished table, where some solution had dribbled, and battled on prayerfully.

'Stop gawping and make some supper' one lad was persuaded, with the aid of a sharp kick, as I wound up the last curler and thought of a suitable antidote for baldness. Soon there was a distinct aura of fried onions mingling with the acrid stench of ammonia and we were all sat munching the most delicious fried onion teacakes I have ever tasted. The sort that makes your hair curl! Thankfully hers did.

*

BOB MONKHOUSE made a fortune performing his smarmy duet with one on the Golden Shot. The BBC even considers a live broadcast of some chap spluttering indecipherably down one to a studio altruist – entertaining.

What a marvellous piece of invention the ubiquitous telephone is. A voice can be heard from the other side of the world – clearer than across the valley.

In my youth the only telephone owners I knew were film stars, and our landlord. The nearest public telephone was half a mile away – a cosy box which became a bus shelter on wintry nights. Being without one never bothered me, whom would I phone? Liz Taylor was far away and the only thing I had in common with our landlord was the rent book and his patch of missing pansies.

When the corner shop was closed once, my friend and I did indulge in two pennorth of verbal excitement. Choosing a number at random she dialled and when a bossy female voice demanded 'Who is that?' the receiver was handed to me like a hot potato. I stood there speechless. A black cat stared in curiously from the wall outside. 'Er – have you last a cat?' was all I could manage. She soon got the message. 'Put that receiver down before you land in serious trouble.' I thankfully obeyed and fled.

I have never been able to take the telephone seriously. It always seems ridiculous, being expected to stand and talk sense to an instrument. I still feel slightly uneasy when I do. (Not uneasy enough, my husband would probably like to add).

Sadly our family do not share my inhibitions. During holidays our phone is permanently mid-air. Urgent requests - 'What time? What are you wearing? Etc' tweak consistently.

Ours rang one night awakening me from a deep horizontal hold. I knocked three cups over on the journey from rug to phone, to hear a cheerful voice say 'Forgot to tell you, it's my turn for a party, can I bring the gang back?'

Such a boon in a crisis, though. Our 14-year-old made three successive calls recently – one to a bowling club I had just left – one to ours I had not yet arrived at – and one later when I had - to ask if a friend could stay overnight.

A quick dial and all manner of information is at our finger tips. 'What colour of knickers are you wearing?' was an inquiry I received recently. Now, I have since thought of ear-scorching replies I could have given. Or perhaps a Marge Proops' 'Now lad, what's your problem?' or possibly an aggressive 'Who wants to know' approach. But on a Saturday morning in the middle of preparing lunch, let's face it this is the last question one expects to be asked by a stranger with asthma. 'Why didn't you sing?' was a deterrent suggested afterwards. Totally unprepared I simply followed my instinct and replied 'What colour are yours?'

From then on I gave him tit for tat till eventually utterly thwarted, confused and cursing he rang off. A police chief told me since two or three sharp blasts on a whistle has the same effect.

Yes, a marvellous medium – when you know who's on the other side!

*

YORKSHIRE landlady Barbara Fletcher has ordered her bar staff not to serve customers who don't say 'please' or 'thank you.' A commendable action, but in my experience 'staff' must take some of the blame for public discourtesy. It appears to me that the more ill mannered and rude customers behave the better the service they receive.

Wax docile, proffer large helpings of p's and q's and you are often either ignored or indifferently served. Display aloof, over demanding tendencies with a bristle of bad manners and the 'staff' are humbly at your service.

Look at the way Frank Sinatra's behaviour draws the Press and fans to his entrances and exits. I wish I could have seen his face - with my earplugs suitably adjusted of course – when he discovered an airport VIP lounge inaccessible recently. Pardon me while I smirk – politely, of course.

Unfortunately this diabolical attitude is infectious. The other day the rest of a bus queue and I witnessed the touching farewell between a couple of leather clad lovers. He had parked his bike in a pub yard and decided to have a walk with the rest of his mates until opening time, but female pillion riders were not included, even though they protested noisily. 'Get lost,' was his parting invitation.

On holiday at a country inn we waited patiently for coffee. Our waitress was busy explaining to a long vowelled show-off why the sweet trolley, a couple of feet away and clearly visible to all, was necessarily stationary in the diminutive dining area. Show-off had to be escorted personally to it. None of the four varieties of cheese was big enough for him, then his side plate was not clean enough.

253

In her place I would have been tempted to present a whole cheese 'to match your mouth, sir.' But the waitress flitted enthusiastically from kitchen to table, even presenting him with an off the menu vintage port. 'It's 65p a measure, sir,' she apologised, while we tried to draw her attention to our parched coffeeless throats in vain.

Human nature is so paradoxical. A display of ultra politeness often evokes contempt. 'Everybody worships me – it's nauseating' is the way Noel Coward summed up this superiority complex.

Some of the waitresses at a beloved, now extinct, town centre café were notorious snobs, avoiding by me at all costs. 'I'm not having that lot with 'no hands' on my tables,' one in particular would crow whenever low tippers entered her kingdom. She would then pretend her tables were reserved, which indeed they were – for her 'handy' regulars.

A friend who worked there for a number of years tells the story of one awkward customer they renamed 'horseface.' She was a noted culinary fad. My friend served her with carrots one lunchtime which she refused to eat and demanded they were sent back. In the servery my friend, greatly annoyed, made a statement which was laughed over for years. 'Huh, it's the first time I've known a horse refuse carrots.'

At another esoteric haunt in town I once witnessed the supreme belittling of a couple of fellow diners. Every request was met with a supine sigh. Anything was too much trouble for this waitress. When the broken pair had eventually crawled out, I heard her announce loudly to one of her purple-haired pastry eaters, 'Anybody comes in here nowadays.'

Yes, I have come to the conclusion in many establishments – not all – it is that unmistakable aura of wealth that brings the staff to life and nowadays, sadly, courtesy can be quite costly.

*

MRS A WILCOX, a 27-year-old mother, sits down in a lounge at her local sports centre, unfastens the top two buttons of her dress and proceeds to breast-feed her infant son. In marches supervisor, who orders her to stop or leave, someone has complained. Stoic mother feeds on then leaves when she's finished.

There seems to be varying opinions on the subject of breast-feeding in public. If your name is Esther Rantzen, you can feed baby wherever you happen to be. She says she has even done it at the pool side in the States without provoking objections. Barbara Cartland feels that blatant breast-feeding in public is carrying things a little too far. 'There's always somewhere a mother can go,' she pontificates, 'even if she's in a park, she can hide behind a tree.'

254

Screen nudity pays box office dividends, but apparently some members of the public are not prepared to tolerate the reality of a few square inches of a feeding mother's breast.

This narrow-minded attitude reminds me of the time we took our first born on a day trip to Southport. All went well until feeding time. Unable to find a hiding place, we resorted to a draughty, but empty station waiting room. Just got daughter comfortably 'plugged in' when train arrived. Within seconds disapproving eyes surrounded us. 'Hmmm! That's one way I suppose,' a woman muttered to her companion.

Lucky enough to have breast-fed all my five children, I believe doctors are right to prophesy that breast is best. But, I confess overcoming embarrassment is the most difficult part, and the unrealistic false modesty shown by some people does not help. If more mothers followed Mrs Wilcox's example, perhaps this attitude would alter.

My absent-mindedness incurred many a bashful moment. In my haste to return satisfied baby to pram, I often forgot to button up. I was on my way back from a friendly chat with a refuse collector once, when a gripping east wind gave me a cold shoulder, followed by hot cheeks when I realised the second half of baby's ten o'clock feed was still showing.

This form of feeding has a curious effect on older brothers in the beginning. 'Is she going to eat all that? When she's finished that does she eat the other one?' But after the initial shock, they accept the natural simplicity of it. Quick to cash in on any status booster, they even bring their mates around to watch. I like the statement made by a seven-year-old in Nanette Newman's book 'Lots of Love,' a compilation of children's remarks. 'Mothers can feed babies from their bosoms, but they only do milk.'

My first two children were born at home, under the supervision of an excellent midwife who set most of her 'mothers' on the path to successful suckling.

When I eventually spent a week in a maternity hospital, I was not surprised to find that in our ward of 12 mothers, 10 were bottle-feeding. At feed time it was curtains for my bosom friend and me.

'Cover her up, the doctor's on his way,' a nurse shouted, when my curtains were once left open. I felt like the proverbial parrot being hidden from sight when the vicar was expected. No one is in the least offended when a mother brings out baby's milk-bottle, why disparage the most endearing sight of all - a baby being fed naturally?

TO GET the best value from a Lakeland weekend – it helps if you are nearing the end of school holidays, your sanity in shreds – with a touch of that joyless post-daughter's wedding feeling an accurate description of me as we drove towards Keswick last weekend.

One minute you can be almost trampled to death by hiking boots at Amble-side, next you can be up the creek in crowdless calm just a mile further on. Signposts boast delicious sounding names like Buttermere, a lush green soft-centre sandwiched between the tranquil Lakes Crummock and Buttermere.

Keswick was busiest and coastal Maryport the scruffiest. But the hills and lakes radiate such a superior majestic quality anything man-made appears shoddy by comparison. The peace felt, as I lie prostrate on a rug at the foot of a mountain while 'our lot' disappeared out of sight – is indescribable.

One of Cockermouth's main attractions is Wordsworth House, birthplace of William and Dorothy. Stepping over its threshold cost us £1.40 adults 40p, children 20p. Once through the portal, two silver-haired matrons pounced so quickly, my husband had no time for his postponement tactics.

One kept us talking while the other took his money. When we had crossed her palm she took me aside, cocked a gnarled finger at a portrait of a grey faced man who looked as if he had been up all night and whispered mysteriously, hand over mouth, 'Visit the Astronomer's House when you leave here.' Feeling like Humphrey Bogart about to crack a 'case' I whispered 'OK, OK.'

I managed to shake her off eventually when the other lady, who was the image of my old school headmistress, ushered us into a small study. Interrupting her potted history I asked the question 'Were any of Wordsworth's original furnishings on display.' Deeply offended at such a presumption her veneer faded slightly. 'Many people imagine that poets leave things behind when they move house.' She smiled at the naivety of such thought. 'But he probably had a chair just like this' she mused. 'These' she pointed to shelves filled with China tulips 'have nothing to do with the writer, but aren't they pretty.' Almost as an afterthought she then admitted to the escritoire and the books locked inside had actually once belonged to the poet. Shades of writer Dorothy Parker's request to have chiselled on her headstone in very small letters the epitaph 'If you can read this it means you are standing too close.'

A tiny peep around another door revealed a spacious dining room where yet another madame sat knitting. 'Sorry, you cannot go in here – private. But do notice the marvellous carved ceiling.' she said as she shut us out.

Upstairs we were given freedom of the elegant drawing room, even allowed to 'wander lonely as a cloud' ore the inkstand where the famous pen once hovered, and to ponder over a pair of ugly candlesticks which Dorothy bought for someone, presumably some objects were easy to leave behind.

We also had complete run of the garden, rather unwisely, with pears and apples ripening abundantly at child height.

Cockermouth's other attraction was a confectioner's window. As we drooled over the calorific pastries, what looked like a giant tarantula heaved itself out of a cream-horn. The children were ecstatic and would have run inside and captured it as a present for spider-maniac big brother, if I hadn't restrained them with 'Where will it sleep?'

It didn't rain so I never discovered what happens then.

*

BLUE BLOOD doesn't run through our family's veins, but blackberry juice has certainly stained them for many generations. I come from a long line of blackberry pickers. My father has shifted tons in his time, indeed during this last week his protruding posterior has become a noted landmark in one area.

Although he is an enthusiastic gatherer, my mother does tend to wax sulky as the season progresses. After you have made wine, jam and countless pies, there is a limit to what else you can do with them. Still the bucketsful multiply, but once acquired, this habit takes some breaking. It is no good hiding containers, I have seen him bring home two or three pounds in his cap.

My mother's less than enthusiastic greeting 'Don't bring any more here' falls on deaf ears as he presents his regular daily harvest.

Yes, the hedgerows are glistening with their clusters of black diamonds, a temptation to anyone with an afternoon and plenty of sugar to spare. The damp summer has not done much for us, but it has certainly swelled the blackberries. Luscious lobes of mellow fruitfulness are just sitting there waiting to be plucked. A basket, old togs, a pair of gloves (prickle protectors or in my case spiders) are all you need for the exercise. A stick helps – not just to keep the troops in order, but it's true the best are usually hiding underneath. Alone or accompanied it's fun. If you take the family be prepared to keep mobile. Their shout of 'Ooh quick, come and look at the size of these' is one call of nature that cannot be ignored.

The other call of nature presents a different problem requiring either supersonic control or well-shaded solitude, both elusive on a long canal stretch. It's times like this I wish I hadn't listened to the one about the lady and the stoat.

Children don't take it seriously at first, a jam jar with string handle is an ample container for the half a dozen that don't finish up in their tums. When they have washed and devoured a dish or two their jars fill up quicker.

Considering all the unwashed bounty I have swallowed over the years it's a wonder I haven't been eaten alive. In our roles as twelve-year-old native girls awaiting our turn to be Tarzan's Jane, there were three of us and only one Tarzan, we prepared a communal diet of garden fodder. Rhubarb, crab apples blackberries, granite-hard pears, and when anyone could manage it, a sprinkling of sugar, all mixed together on a dock-leaf.

Blackberrying always transports us back to those childhood summers. We may not have had John Travolta's hips to hypnotise us, but Tarzan's war cry set a lot of young blood on fire. All the lads tried to imitate his call. As most of them were at voice-breaking age it sounded more like Fanny Craddock in-stead of the virile Johnny Weismuller. Children have become sophisticated, I wonder how many spend the hours we did building secret 'dens' and dragging bits of carpet to grassy hollows in the undergrowth?

But whatever else has changed, I can still gather blackberries in the same spot, watch the same canal flow murkily onwards, sit on a clump of couch grass and gaze at the willow tree I spun my youthful dreams under 20 years ago. That counts for a lot today.

So if you've a couple of hours to spare off you go. No need to spend hours cooking up exotic recipes. Just cook them gently with a few apples, sweeten, cover with cream and eat, mmm - delicious.

*

HAVE you noticed how the nights are growing longer, and how Saturday nights seem the longest of all? Not only has Bruce done a bunk but also 'Match of the Day' is in full lurch again. As soon as I've performed my little jog to the only catchy thing about it, the signature tune, out comes my book or down goes my eyelids.

'Watch, watch this,' pleads my sporting partner, blind to my boredom and fully alert since he has snored his way through my scintillating early evening commentaries. Reluctantly and without altering my 'get lost' expression, I painfully raise my lids. A man with a gleaming shoulder length perm and immaculate white shorts, favouring a sexy seam-slit, selects a suitable place in the grass and spits on it. Marking time with his chewing gum he jogs rhythmically down the field backwards way.

I was reared on a claret and gold diet of 'props' and 'hookers' cheering on giants with such unlikely names as Meek and Valentine. Footballers certainly look prettier and tidier nowadays, with their clinging shorts and

258

tousled curls. 'I find this style much easier to manage, a perm is much less bother, I have to wash it every day during training' one frizzy-head cooed on TV recently.

Of course all that water with daily baths and showers must present a problem. Some enterprising make-up manufacturer could probably earn millions plus the players' undying gratitude by introducing other useful products. Moisturiser to smooth away all those wrinkles caused by having to peer short-sightedly at the goalmouth that is always in the wrong half. Hand-cream to repair the ravages wrought by excessive ball handling. Strong polyurethane based varnish for fingernail protection during all the exuberant mate-lifting following a goal.

'Well wasn't it a deliberate foul?' asks my distressed supporter. Aren't they all deliberately foul, but no need to tell him, my attention has wandered, he's not really talking to me anyway? This conversation is just between him and an unseen assenter who sits on his shoulder during all sporting events.

I can hear him talking to him while I make coffee. 'See, watch that left foot, what did I tell you!' he rambles on while the BBC produces another miracle – a television replay, during which some eager sidekick shoots and, it's a goal! which naturally is replayed again, and again. It doesn't matter if you miss it, Jimmy Hill is paid to hold another inquest and we can have the same confusion once again.

Instead of becoming redundant at the onset of televised matches, announcers are rife in the field of sport. A ubiquitous commodity, they are there to point out everything you can see, things you don't want to see and some can even give potted biographies about players you have never seen. With practice they often become masters of understatement. 'They're having to leave themselves exposed at the back' one cried last week, which I confess quickened my pulse slightly.

'Look, Roger's gum shield has slipped out' remarked another as champion Conteh's opponent sank limply into oblivion after being lifted off his feet by a knockout swipe to the jawbone. Announcers never die, they simply laugh their way through the aqua-fairyland atmosphere euphemistically called 'It's a Knockout,' where they feel quite at home pointing to scoreboards and holding a microphone.

So through these dreary months my sports lover and I agree to achieve our kicks separately. Me to my books, he to his box. We have even learned to exchange pleasantries meanwhile. 'What do you fancy for supper, love, a ruptured elephant or a grilled snake?' 'Yes love, anything,' says his lips but his glazed eyes tell a different story. 'Blast, he's missed again!'

259

EVERY year when it's time to decide on next year's holiday we go through our nautical phase, at least, I do. 'What about a narrowboat on the canal?' I have cried enthusiastically more than once. I might have been suggesting a tour of Milnsbridge for all the interest shown by my crew.

In Skipton recently we managed to indulge a sneaky peep inside just such a boat, moored beside others along the canal. Through the small windows we could see a tiny ship-shape kitchen to one end, a long sitting room in the centre, complete with bawling baby and busy television. More windows to rear, probably bed and toilet facilities and a cute little seat-lined, open-roofed, triangular area at the end.

Even my first mate was impressed. When a saucy-capped female stepped ashore, he plied her with questions. We learned it was a six-berth equipped with bath and shower. I couldn't wait to hear her adventures. 'First we went to Burnley,' she said in a thick steak-pudding accent. 'Then we came back and went to Bingley – yes it's very nice, but the locks are a bit nerve-wracking.

Bingley? Burnley? Not exactly names to set the seagulls a-quivering. My husband's interest flagged slightly. So it was with undisguised enthusiasm that I put my name on our annual Sunday school trip list, which included a journey by barge up the Leeds-Liverpool canal, and with similar feelings my spouse did not.

We were helped aboard at Rodley by a suitably bearded and kagouled bargee, whereupon the heavens opened and parents climbed below, while children clambered on deck like happy seals.

The old vessel looked as if it had seen plenty of action; as the engine trembled into motion and we shuddered towards a swing bridge, my spirits were as high as the water lapping just below the windows. We chugged sedately past a small boy fishing – how kind not to go full speed and disturb the fish! 'This is full speed,' I was told. I could see my Wilko mints and chewing gum were going to be a Godsend.

As we sluggishly crawled away from Rodley, a voice above described our rural surroundings, also the small refreshment bar below. The deck cleared immediately, while our matelots plundered the rich cargo aft.

We nearly had an 'incident' when someone locked the exit and several sub-mariners immediately decided they wanted to come in from the cold. 'What about throwing someone in – give you something to write about,' but no one offered. 'We sometimes see a train pass,' said the voice over the mike. What a tease he was.

'Two locks ahead,' someone shouted, and parents pushed to the rails. Following the snail pace, it gave one a strange sensation, not merely in the

260

kidneys, to see all that khaki water come thundering down the sluice gates with frightening force, lifting our vessel quickly from its slimy green prison to what appeared like the top of the world again.

Another uplifting experience occurred when we saw a plant bearing weird fruit – which on closer inspection proved to be a discarded bra. At last we turned around and were homeward bound, but the crew waxed mutinous. Bottoms disappeared through windows, anoraks flying everywhere, hide and seek in the hold.

Suddenly we stopped. We shouldn't have noticed, but a man said something was caught in the propeller. We counted the children. Captain, who looked as if he was ready for a land job, ordered low profiles. 'Wouldn't want to see them decapitated by low bridges,' he says. His expression belied his words – he was probably dying to splice a few mainbraces.

The journey back seemed twice as long until someone courageously ordered a sherry and some of us followed suit. Captain graciously helped us back on muddy land again. 'Heavens, is it only that time?' I had longed to spend a week canal cruising, after only two hours I felt as I had. But the best was yet to come, our fish and chip treat at Yorkshire's largest restaurant. A lovely afternoon, children loved it, best we ever had, now where's that hotel brochure for next year?

*

I STOOD gawping at the loaf and four currant teacakes waiting to be paid for on the counter. Had the assistant really asked for 60 pence?

Did my usual conversion – that's twelve shillings – a ten bob note and two bob piece in old money? For one loaf, euphemistically termed 'large' and four current teacakes, which appear to shrink every week. At one time my weekend bread would lift the lid off the bread bin, nowadays the same order doesn't even reach the top.

If I take a bus to town with my three schoolgirls, our fifth former is now classed an adult – the fare there and back costs us £1.68 or in old coinage about 35 bob – for two and two halves.

A pensioner tells me if she buys a packet of flour, a packet of sugar and half a pound of butter, that's one pound note gone, straight away. Was there ever a time I rode the trolley to Huddersfield with half a crown tucked in my mother's big leather purse; feeling like Lady Docker because my instructions were to 'bring me a cake and a quarter of tea from Collinson's you can spend the rest.'

'Are you prepared for decimal currency?' ran a headline in December, 1970, two months before D day in February, 1971. Only seven months after, the price of our weekly food bill had risen by more than 6 per cent.

Eight years ago almost, yet I still revert back to pounds, shillings and pence when I'm feeling particularly fleeced. Then I could buy flour, butter and sugar and still have change from a ten-bob note. You could even buy a jar of coffee and pocket the change from five bob.

We all slipped quickly into the decimal vernacular, it's only when you stop and do a change-about that the gross expense hits you – painfully. Yes, we have had pay rises and galloping inflation. A pound's only worth ten-bob – I mean 50p – but I can never get rid of the uneasy feeling we were all 'conned.'

I have a feast of old penny memories, worthless now of course. Penny drinks of health at Dr Dan's in the old market hall, penny cornets dripping with raspberry vinegar, and penny comics to be laughed over. Sitting around the wireless on Sunday nights listening to Albert Sandler from Palm Court, trying to soothe away the 'night before school' ache with an everlasting toffee lolly, price – one penny.

I don't ever remember buying a penn'orth of chips, but I can remember three ha-porths. If three of us walked home from the pictures our three half-pennies – bus fare from Salendine Nook to Oakes (I wonder how much it is now?) – would buy us a bag of chips to share.

For sixpence we had a real treat, so we imagined. A four-penny cinema seat (first six rows), penny bus fare and a penny left for sweets or a dip in the communal chip bag.

I remember my uncle sending me for five Woodbines with a silver six-pence. Waiting my turn at the Co-op with a shiny black notebook, singing our check number to myself over and over again, so as not to get it mixed up with my Air Force father's LAC number, only to find the assistant had written it down without even asking me, anyway. Then the excitement of the delivery van on Thursday, dipping into all the bags with open tops before my mother came home from work.

I hope I never forget the pleasures we enjoyed for a penny. When my children reach forty, how many will they recall for the same price? Anyway, I've done my share of listening to the 'When I was you age' saga – now it's their turn.

*

MONEY isn't everything – but it's a great improver. Mrs Betty Ford proved this after her recent facelift at 60. Everyone gasped with delight as she attended a star-studded gathering without her wrinkles. 'She looks 20 years younger,' said the ever-young Paul Newman. On her photograph she did look radiant, but, with or without wrinkles this lady has guts. Didn't she bravely publicise her mastectomy operation plus a drug and drink addiction? Good luck to her.

I know I could never face a surgeon's knife while enjoying good health. Women courageous enough to do so deserve to look younger. Dental trips every six months are all the pain I'm willing to stand for the beauty stakes.

Then there's the price. New York plastic surgeons charge from £1,250 to £3,500. Yet experts claim the cheaper offers should be viewed with suspicion. Naturally, cost depends on how imperfect one has become. 'I'm absolutely delighted my husband agreed to it,' gurgles Mrs Ford. Mine would need a second mortgage.

Having my face lifted would be like wallpapering a room only to discover how shabby the furniture and how faded the curtains now look. All my other defects would be cruelly exposed. I could do with 2lb slicing off each thigh, and my body stretching another 6in, which could reduce my weight problem slightly. On off days there's a certain tattiness of hair to contend with. Yes, it's all very uplifting being made to look young and vigorous externally – but can one live up to a younger image.

Another point which rankles – it only lasts four years, then has to be repeated. How much stretching will skin take? If you start at 45, by the time you are 60 your face could be almost see-through. Imagine - a transparent nose! Beauty comes from within – but literally!

When Peter O'Toole had his nose chopped his eyes seemed to move closer together. I liked Cilla Black's the way it was. Tom Jones' throbbing hips drove fans wild, but at the height of his fame he bought a new nose. Most film stars achieve fame because of their looks, when money starts pouring in, they flee for a face change. Marti Caine gained a new profile, then lost her husband.

Gladys Cooper had her share of wrinkles in later years, but they didn't disguise her everlasting beauty. Age even enhanced Dames Edith Evans and Sybil Thorndike. I'm living in hopes it will do the same for me.

But you don't have to be good looking to survive. I don't feel neurotic about my grey hairs. I prefer to spray them with silver and make a feature of them. Good carriage helps. 'If a woman walks smooth and free it produces a happy figure,' Cary Grant once said. My children can always tell the difference between dad and me as we walk past their bedroom doors. 'We can hear your tights swishing together.' I've never been able to lose the infernal 'swish.' There's too much of me concentrated in one area, my face is shrivelling at the edges, but even if I could afford a cosmetic miracle, it would be a waste of money.

263

One hour with 'my lot' and the wrinkles would come sagging back. I once complimented an old friend of 76 on her unlined face. She was furious, 'I hate to be told that at my age, I've had plenty of struggles whether it shows or not,' she fumed.

Remember Samuel Johnson's words: 'A man is generally better pleased when he has a good dinner upon his table than when his wife talks Greek' – or looks eternally young, he might have added if he'd been presented with a face-job bill!

*

'LET them eat cake,' was Marie Antoinette's advice when the bread-starved French peasants revolted.

Our situation could never be described as desperate as theirs – but nevertheless some housewives are particularly revolting. Take the neurotic bread-snatchers that cleared all the town confectioners' shelves in a panic – before the dispute even started. Thank God our village has maintained its sanity and bakers have supplied their normal output.

Between strikes some dough-bashers have let their home baking talents lapse. Well its time to throw that white pulpy mess on the table and start knocking the wind out of it again.

Its seems inconceivable that housewives who can concoct all manner of exotic dishes often wax weak-elbowed at the mention of yeast cookery, when actually there's nothing to it. It's as easy as putting the old man to rest after a work's trip. Just rub in the lard, pour in the yeasty liquid, massage deeply and leave to rise. What could be easier than that?

Even if you live alone 1lb of flour can return a delightfully edible harvest. Use half dough for plain teacakes, stick a few currants and a sprinkling of sugar in the other half, and you also have a couple of currant teacakes.

As I say often to anyone who will listen it is a most satisfying hobby. No matter how horrific the result, it still smells wonderful. That hot yeasty aroma will still tantalise your neighbour's nostrils, even if it takes two to carry the first attempt to the dustbin. There are so many other delectable spin-offs from the main dough. My mother kneads extra lard into the last lump, a la puff pastry method, to make a crumbly golden, mouth caressing pastry she calls 'oven bottom cake.' It's worth getting steamed up for and with all the heat and thumping, your temperature rises faster than the dough.

There is no truth in the rumour that an unhappy wife makes sour bread. I made my last batch after I had just taken an honest look at myself in the mirror following a reckless scissor-happy five minutes with my hair. The scissors were just lying on the table and my fringe had been trailing up my nose a bit of late.

264

Yes, I would describe the result as unhappy. Suffice it to say, compared with my toothbrush-like fringe even my stubby eyelashes look straggly. But everyone complimented me on my bread, when they had stopped laughing.

A bite of hot muffin – your family will be putty in your hands. Don't let the nostalgic cries put you off. 'We had to be up at six, mam and me, cleaning out the fires, a quarter of a stone of flour and all that tear-jerking stuff. Who eats a quarter of a stone anyway today? I suspect the majority goes into dad's lunch box. There are other suitably healthy substitutes, crisps, savoury pasties, fruit, crispbread – all excellent stand-ins.

Panic buying is an understandable fall out from the last war when food was really in short supply. I bet some 'squirrels' still have a bulging sugar hoard from the last shortage. In our present affluence these habits seem to me to be verging on the rapacious. Rather like the 'in case someone comes' store cupboards, where row after row of tinned pork, salmon and peaches lie rusting, waiting to greet the unsuspecting visitor.

These ought to be sold with the Biblical Health warning, 'Do not lay up treasures on earth where moth and rust consume.' And like it says 'Consider the birds' the shortage hasn't affected them, they're all eating cake – or the height of bread-dispute luxury – nuts!
*

HEALTH chiefs have discovered a new threat to hospital patients - visitors. A York hospital has published a list of recommendations, which is given to all visitors. It appears they cause 'tennis' necks by sitting either side of the bed, evoking extra head turning for patients. They also bring the wrong food, say the wrong things and stay too long.

Apparently longer visiting has its shortcomings. I have been very fortunate, apart from baby confinements I have only been a hospital case three times. When Tony Bennett left his heart in San Francisco I left my tonsils and appendix in Huddersfield Royal. I also spent three weeks in St Luke's isolation unit. Visitors were only allowed to ogle at us through glass on Saturday afternoons. Being nine years old we were never quite sure whether this was because we were spotty or naughty, no one ever enlightened us. Both infirmities seemed beyond our control in any case.

But I shall never forget the nightmares between visits. It was wartime and I had this terrifying recurring dream that the Germans had captured my mother and sister; I was never to see them again. After that experience, regular visitors have always seemed harmless by comparison; wherever they sit, whatever they say or whatever they bring.

Perhaps patients could also be issued with salutary leaflets on 'How to treat visitors.' For instance is it necessary to place those succulent grapes and that sparkling orange juice in such a light-catching position. It's most exhausting for we fully-dressed, who are already fighting a drink problem with the chrysanth water. When we ask, out of politeness, 'What's she in for?' does the answer have to be quite so detailed? All that talk about bladder tubes and doctors' merciless gropings up her 'back passage,' is so unnecessary, not to mention ulcerative, for non-patients.

Do the sick have to flaunt the day's menu with 'roast chicken and salad' ticked off so blatantly? Also pointing out the delicacies they couldn't eat, while you hungrily search your fillings for the remains of the cream cracker you managed to snatch as you rushed out.

Do they have to wear those glamorous, cool and lacy bedjackets, making us tuck last year's perm more tightly under our caps, realising what a mistake the sheepskin jacket was in this desert heat, but a necessary cover up when you hadn't time to change underneath. A sweltering scruff in sheep's clothing.

Do patients have to describe everyone's symptoms so realistically? The moment I enter the sterile world of hypodermics, see tubes dangling from nostrils and other orifices, and picture all those defenceless organs waiting to be explored, my pains start. Paradoxically when I entered maternity once, about to give birth, my pains stopped. When I begged for my clothes explain-ing my painless situation, 'That's what they all say,' said unsympathetic Sister.

By the time I reach patients' bed I am already having an imaginary consultation with my doctor. 'How long have I got doc?' Patients may not always feel better after a visitation, but have you ever perused the agony column pouring through the hospital exits after visiting time. The haggard faces tell their own story.

Staff are naturally concerned for the patients, but why do their reprimands make visitors fell as if they've dropped off a coal wagon. 'Don't do that,' a nurse commanded distastefully when I once rested a weary buttock on an immaculate white counterpane. I know it was cheeky, I shouldn't have, but it was my first offence – I didn't mean any harm, honest!
*

'PLEASE mum can we have one? Do let's have one, they're so cute.' This blood-curdling plea is rampant just now when juniors, imprisoned by dark tea times turn their affections to pets. At the end of the cry comes the oath, 'I'll look after it myself,' emphasised by their stock plea, 'honest.'

Naturally we want them to learn to care for something else besides next week's spending money. But I find it difficult to love some of their pets.

Our son, now twenty and still an addict, adores spiders. At present he has two 'Williams,' and one 'Right Fast Nigel' as he calls them; bloated mottled specimens that hang menacingly from opposite corners of our porch. This hobby never interfered much with my life when he was younger and more active. He just hopped on his hurry cart and drove around inspecting spider's webs in the front garden.

Age, other energy-reducing exercises, and of course he no longer has a cart, necessitated moving his creepy crawlies nearer, to the back porch. Fed regularly with protesting flies by him and his sisters, they grow sickeningly indolent and swollen-bellied.

Recently I watched flabbergasted, when my husband, an avid animal ignorer normally, casually threw a bluebottle in a web while passing.

I have this ghastly dread that one day the family will come home and find me hanging up there, gagged, bound and dressed for dinner.

Keep this to yourself, but one afternoon I tried an experiment of my own. After courageously stalking a nasty looking wasp, then trapped it successfully alive in my duster, with the aid of a stool I climbed up to 'William's' lair and threw my struggling quarry to its death.

Unfortunately, my aim never accurate went awry and the hysterical wasp dived back for revenge. The shock nearly finished me, it certainly sapped any spider interest I might have had.

Animal love is certainly blind. How can anyone love a predatory ferret and keep it imprisoned in a living room?

A lad once called at our house with one hung loosely round his neck. In my ignorance I thought it was a fur collar. It was only when we sat in the kitchen and he removed his pet, begging me to give it a home that I fled for the brandy bottle.

Goldfish are the least trouble, but we never keep one alive long enough for me to learn to love it. We had a snake, but I could never forgive it for eating those sweet little baby frogs while they were still alive – so slowly.

We bought our son-in-law the black cat he longed for as a birthday present. I hope he won't hold it against us, such a gentle loveable little creature when I took it – now a wild beastie. When it is not hanging from the new curtains, it's scrambling up the clawed remains of the wallpaper. It eats anything – tights, plants, even the newspaper. Every time we visit, the furniture has been moved to conceal more cat damage.

Once I was sitting by their window when the curtains behind me parted slowly and a small black claw reached out playfully and tore the skin off the back of my neck.

It's becoming increasingly difficult to lie convincingly about 'how lovely it's growing.'

Dogs are different of course. Apart from Alsatians which I believe should all be on police duty and a certain sharp-faced Doberman, that once became attached to my solar plexus – these animals make excellent pets, especially little black, sandy-pawed, loveable, scruffy looking mongrels like mine. You can't lick 'em.

*

ONE of the pleasures of my day, now the rest of the family is off my hands, is my solitary lunch. Just the birds and the dog to feed and the rest of the time can be shared exclusively with my library book and my plate. It's amazing how much food I can get through when no one is watching – and frightening.

Ever since Christmas when my beloved presented me with a surprise – a new jacket, size 12, I've been meaning to diet. There's a healthy Audrey Hepburn inside me screaming to get out, but food keeps getting in the way.

This snow has me reaching for inner comforts, but Dr Jonathan Miller almost had me reaching for the lettuce after his final Body in Question series.

He and a pathologist colleague were eagerly setting out the contents of a corpse they had just emptied – like two butchers arranging their Monday offal. After extensive probing a few slices were removed for further microscopic examination. After seeing that dead body helpless on the slab, I had already reached my conclusion. 'Help! Keep going you fool,' I tried to persuade my own innards.

Roy Castle has been jogging around our screens for weeks, inviting us all to be healthy but on Sunday teatimes we are too full of Yorkshire pud to care. Until I tried that heart beat test, the one he attempted but abandoned, after two minutes. I dutifully climbed on and off a buffet for three minutes. Believe me the result was not a pretty sight and the buffet did its share of suffering, too.

The trouble with exercise, it accelerates the appetite. Once I get my breath back, mine becomes uncontrollable. This is a bad. When practising Yoga I tried to overdo the relaxation and fell asleep. I wish diet sheets didn't carry that insidious warning 'See your doctor first.' This is exactly what I am hoping to avoid.

Fashion dictates a thinner and thinner female form. In the Twenties and Forties women were much more rounded. Men seemed to prefer 'cuddlies.' But even today corpulence has its fanciers. 'I love a good bum on a woman,' sang Jake Thackery when I switched on the other night.

One asset of this Siberian weather is that we're all wrapped in so many layers you cannot discern the thin from the fat – or in some cases the faces from the hats. I saw a woman recently with what looked like next door's ginger tom coiled around her head.

Wash day seems twice as long. Everything is thrown to wash in triplicate. It takes ages to part the layers. School blouses still wearing their sweater and pullovers and tights with two pairs of dad's socks dangling from their feet. Very often jumpers disguised as shirts find their way into the washer and become over agitated – to their ruin and mine.

I'm still smarting from my son's outrage when he eventually found his mauve jumper that I had washed and hopefully 'put away.' The one with a waistline three inches above his navel and arms trailing on his sock tops. It's the weather, you know!

But if you can leave the diet a moment, I have a panacea guaranteed to warm up the sheets. Try a tot of medicinal whisky in a glass of milk. I take mine chilled straight from the fridge or doorstep. If you prefer, drink it hot with a teaspoon of honey. You'll soon feel the benefit. Make sure your partner joins you – or your snores may keep him awake!

*

THROUGH our kitchen window I can see a plump little robin doing a first class picketing job on the bird table. Fighting off all the timid sparrows that have to be content with any crumb old greedy guts accidentally drops.

This weather put paid to my usual Saturday shopping trip. 'Only fools go out in this lot,' a passing Balaclava warned as I cleared our path. So, instead, I splashed my £1 bus fare on half a pound of chocolates, added a bottle of my favourite wine and built up the fire.

Munching mis-shapes and sipping tipple could have proved a satisfying substitute if it hadn't been accompanied by husband's excruciatingly boring TV football match.

Holiday brochures bring a spurt of sunny relief on these occasions. One resort praying for a long, hot summer must be Bridlington. If permission is granted this bracing haven is about to cash in on the 'cast off clothing' urge. Egged on no doubt by the recent television programme which displayed the bare facts concerning naturist's camps on the Continent, they are planning a special cove for the uninhibited.

Bridlington, the home of salty-faced fishermen and the Yorkshire Belle could be in for a change of scene. With boatloads of naked bodies rowing all over the horizon, it could look more like 'Sanders of the River.'

'We don't say nude, it rhymes with lewd, rude and crude, said a saggy-chested matron, who faced the cameras without a twitch, after being filmed taking a naked stroll around a supermarket.

A surprising element of the film was the amiable way that children accepted family nudity, not so much as a giggle. Yet whenever I bring out my one piece swimsuit there's an anguished plea of: 'Oh no! Mum, don't,' as if I was about to inflict some terrible torture.

I imagined undressed holidays would be restful. Surely anything more energetic than walking would put either sex in a flap, but no, one voluptuous foursome treated us to a bouncy game of tennis. All they wore was a serious expression.

No one mentioned problems, but early morning bacon frying must be a hazard. Sitting around unprotected by underwear seems less than hygienic to me. Wooden seats could make quite an impression on the back view, as skin is not crease-resistant.

Naturally, packing is no problem, just a change of fig leaf for the special occasion – or if you were Bridlington bound perhaps a bush would be more suitable. Those East winds can be a scourge even when you're fully zipped up.

I suppose upbringing governs our modesty. 'They ought to be locked up,' was the adult way of looking at nudity in my youth. I admit I prefer to present a firm, controlled covered up look to the world. Although I get some strange ideas, I have never had the desire to expose myself to strangers – even on holiday.

The delightfully young 95-year-old Commissioner Catherine Branwell Booth said last week to Mike Parkinson: 'It doesn't matter how much your knees tremble, as long as it doesn't show.' These were her father's words, which helped to overcome her shyness. How true, how true . . .
*

THE Forties look, with wider padded shoulders, narrow skirts and nipped-in waists is forecast for this summer. Described as 'the film star look,' this is one period I remember well. But the memory is rather painful and mostly junior.

Shirley Temple was the cult figure for my age group. She had everything I hadn't – dimples, curls, talent, money, clothing coupons. At our cinema we had two larger-than-life cardboard cut-outs either side of the stage, one was a dark, befringed Jane Withers, the other was Shirley Temple, whose curls I prayed for twice nightly.

They eventually arrived by courtesy of dad's Air Force pension and a perming contraption run by the local hairdresser. My form teacher, who didn't realise I was now the image of Miss Temple and halfway to stardom, almost gave me a hundred lines for 'ruining that lovely straight hair.'

Her disgust was such that I now prayed to go straight during school and curly for weekends. This was the make do and mend era. Money was useless without the necessary coupons. When they ran out you did without.

Clothes came in three categories – children, junior and adult. No swinging boutiques geared to the teenage market, then. When you grew up you dressed like your parents. Sometimes you didn't have to wait till then.

My mother and I took the same size in shoes when I was ten years old. I often spent the hour between hometime and the time she came in from work dancing around our 'flags' in her new high wedges, savouring the grown-up sound of cracking high heel on stone.

Then came the day I was compelled to wear them for school, either that or another weary walkabout in my old perforated soles. Tears fell like rain. 'No one will be looking at your feet, silly,' my mother consoled. True, they would probably be more interested in my new knitted cardigan.

My mother was an excellent knitter, but her co-ordination left a lot to be desired. If I turned the left sleeve up twice it matched the other, but nothing could alter the fact, the left front was longer than the right.

My friend was waiting at the school gates. I opened my gabardine to show off half my new cardigan and pretended I hadn't seen her. 'Are those your mother's shoes?' she shouted.

Another Forties fall-out hanging around today, are the snappy suspender belts. My teenagers are so hooked on these, big brother bought his fifteen-year-old sister a racy-looking black and red affair for Christmas.

Unfortunately she inherited the dwarf-like legs that run in my side of the family and apparently these elongated expanders were designed for legs that start at the armpits. Hence the rude off-putting guffaws when she lifted her skirt to reveal two black nylon concertinas drooping unladylike around her kneecaps.

These tortuous accessories are sadly over-rated. I never seemed to possess a complete set. More often than not I coped with one suspender per leg – usually held by safety pins. This held the flesh in sort of slings, which clapped together when you moved.

Running for a bus once, one gave way. I sneaked my hand through a hole in my pocket just in time to grab the descending stocking top. But I had to pretend I was a hunchback for the rest of the journey, in order to hang on to it.

I learned my lesson though – be sure your 'pins' will find you out! Wear tights!

*

DESPITE the glacial conditions, sturdy little shoots in our garden are already pointing at the roof icicles. According to the calendar it should be spring.   This heralds the stirrings of new life, etc, a favourite season for some.

But mine starts with summer, I mean Wordsworth's everlasting sort, 'Sweet childish days, that were as long as twenty days are now.'

I hated school and always associate summer with an eternal dawn to dusk freedom and the hot, sunbaked cornfields at the back of our house. This embryonic season not only starts the birds twittering early, we have our own built-in dawn chorus of 'I've nothing to wear' echoing above the perpetual record player at our house just now.

According to an article I've just read, we should all be experiencing a certain restless surplus of energy just now. I have a half-stripped bedroom waiting to do justice to just such a mood, but it hasn't struck yet.

A lecturer in psychology, Dr J Nicholson, states that spring is the natural 'flirting' season, not only for the unattached, for he also believes marriages are improved by it. Partners become more attractive to each other, when they've had a flirtation with another.

I could see it drawing husband and me closer together - just close enough for him to club me with his spade or me to crown him with my frying pan.

The professor believed flirting to be a throwback to cave dwelling days. After a long hibernating winter, primitive Nog and his woman bounded from their hollow ripe for a round of socialising. It seems this feeling has lingered on.

Presumably this is when spring cleaning first evolved. Mrs Nog seeing the glint under her Noggy's eyebrows starts making the first paintbrush, probably using Mrs Nextcave's hair.

One way to throw off spring fever is to indulge in your favourite fantasy. Masculine daydreams usually flutter around the opposite sex but I suspect women would surprise their mates if they confided their inward desires. I must be a frustrated entertainer because all of mine are connected with applause – other peoples.

There I stand covered in spotlight exhausted but radiant after my compelling performance, smiling sympathetically as my audience goes berserk with adulation. Sometimes I work my fantasies out at the piano.

I play 'chopsticks' as if I was Beethoven in the grip of his 'fifth.' Pounding up and down the ivories with my eyes shut, resting my nose on the keyboard occasionally like all best concert pianists. The people standing in the bus queue opposite our window must be fascinated.

To show my versatility I often jazz it up in my syncopating elbow flapping style, briskly plucking at the notes like a dog digging out a rabbit. Nodding my head furiously in a bouncy eight-to-the-bar finale. This technique has taken years to perfect. It looks most professional, but, thank God, no one can hear the racket that actually does emanate from my poor offended piano. At least it's harmless, although for some reason it always sets the dog off scratching.

There is a certain male influence when I'm in my Saddler's Wells mood, because I perform only with Nureyev.

Anyone who ever dreamed of being captured by a sheikh must have followed our Queen's televised Arabian adventure with envy. Who can blame Her Majesty for being angry when Royal protocol forbids her to mingle with adoring Arabs who had been waiting in the hot sun for hours.

I wonder if Queens ever indulge in fantasies? Perhaps they dream of living in a semi opposite a bus stop, with a piano in the front room. Who knows?

*

THIS week I have had to chase our ten-year-old around the kitchen table four times a day with a spoonful of antibiotics. It looks like strawberry syrup, but she says it tastes like poison. Once you've caught the patient and administered the magic potion it's miraculous how soon they recover.

Being ill was a considerably lengthier affair when I was a ten-year-old. Any suggestion of a 'temperature' meant straight to bed and stay there. Fortunately a child in a sickbed is becoming a rare sight today.

We had to suffer many indignities to keep the doctor from the door. Never would we have been allowed out after August with an inch of goose pimpled midriff showing, like a lad I saw recently.

The fear of doctor bills was rife in our area. Tribal chiefs used to dress in hideous costume before they danced away evil spirits. We were adorned equally scandalously to frighten away bronchitis – the family curse. It started with one mother innocently trimming her daughter's pixie hood with fur, then the idea snowballed until we all walked to school looking like a band of fur trappers.

Winter brought another chest development for me, in the shape of a dreaded Thermogene vest. Two pieces of peach coloured wadding impregnated with a smelly oil, which my mother taped together to form a sort of 'Mae West' life-jacket. Worn under my blouse, it added incredible bulk to my non-existent bosom and produced enough fumes to clear all our form's sinuses.

At bedtime out came gran's special seven oil mixture, which was rubbed into our backs, fronts, sides, legs, depending on how much there was on mother's hands. For a change we sometimes went to bed in a brown paper vest covered in goose grease. Some friends used to sport a camphor necklace – a block on a piece of string – but I never succumbed.

Every week our hair was washed in Derbac soap and rinsed in a solution of Borax and water. Shampoo was for film stars and those not afraid of being handed a white card on the school 'nit' parade. I lived in mortal fear of being singled from the herd in the school assembly hall. In extreme cases card-holders had to forfeit all their hair. I came close to this once when I was in hospital with a skin disease which, I was careful to tell no one, had spread to my scalp. At bath time it took all my vanity not to flinch under the comb.

Then there were the poultices. 'Gatherings' or sceptic sores were drawn to a head with almost anything that had been boiled and wrapped in a cloth. Bread and onions were great favourites. Toothache was eased with dash of clove oil and a hot salt bag held to the pain. If a cause or name could not be found for what ailed us, out came the aperients. Senna pods, fig syrup, cascara liquorice powders, or my favourite, a chunk of black Spanish shaken up in a bottle of water.

Camomile tea and other herbal teas were often on the 'brew' simply because 'they did you good.' When we weren't being treated for an illness, we were in the 'protection racket,' drinking preventive potions to keep well.

Each district had its own remedial figure, usually someone's gran, who was always sent for before the doctor. They often had a special gift for healing and could even lend a hand in 'laying out' the deceased.

Fresh air was used more. When my sister's whooping cough persisted we were advised to take her for 'a blow on Lindley Moor.' I remember sitting beside her, watching her cheeks go bluer, while the wind played tunes with my teeth. As soon as we got home she started to recover.

274

I probably took my first steps running away from a fever mixture. Parish's food could spark off amazing energy – one clink of the spoon and I was half way up the road. We chewed gentian root, which tasted like nail-biting repellent, to settle stomach gripe. In fact, if and when you eventually could afford a doctor, his medicine tasted most pleasant!

*

'GOING OUT' – ie: tearing oneself away from a warm television when it's 30deg outside – is a grossly overrated pastime after 8pm.

I know other women share this aversion. 'I couldn't move,' a yoga absentee explained when I queried her nights off. Was she sick, a broken ankle perhaps? No. 'I love my fireside too much these cold nights.'

I haven't noticed the bad weather affecting our male element yet. In fact pressing appointments at a certain bowling club appear to increase during wintry spells.

My socialising can be handled from my armchair. Mondays and Wednesdays I pop into the Rovers Return. I've been switched on to Coronation Street ever since Mrs Dale closed her diary, and can never understand why there hasn't been a special award created for the superior acting and script-writing throughout this long-running series.

Naturally, like most figures one becomes familiar with, some possess aggravating habits. I try not to notice the way Elsie Tanner pouts her bottom lip in an effort to look coy and only succeeds in looking more middle-aged. I make excuses when Stan Ogden talks like a ventriloquist. Ena Sharples has eventually mastered those teeth – bless her hairnet. There was a time when her 'Osmond' smile looked ready to spring out and attack her nearest victim. Annie Walker must be a scriptwriter's dream. One of her supercilious sniffs can register more emotion than half a dozen Noele Gordon's splutterings.

Some members of our team are still at Crossroads Motel, in spite of the lifeless tariff. My husband protects himself with his 'Examiner' throughout this and Little House on the Prairie, which floods our living room with un-checked tears each Thursday teatime.

But I love to curl up with a good television serial especially on Fridays. The rest of the family is out. The bathroom, the best corner seat by the fire and television are all mine. When I have wallowed in unoccupied bathroom, soaked up the silence of the cassette-less atmosphere, I turn on the Flambards and tuck into an hour's adventure with William and Christina.

At first the ear-shattering background music threatened to drown the characters. It sounded like two horses playing a duet on a piano, while a girl called for her mom and someone else carried on whistling. But the cast is so refreshingly natural, the camera work excellent, I'm learning to live with the noise. Like eating fish and chips with custard, it's different.

I wonder if other serial freaks have noticed that Sarah in Thomas and Sarah wears Christina's tweedy cardigan.

Yes, I love my languid little rut, at least I did until I read about Mrs Florence Sephton, aged 80, of North Wales. She has just graduated in History with the Open University. Sophie Tucker was wrong. Life begins at 80 – if you're willing to make the switch.

*

OUR soggy front lawn looks as though the moths have been at it, my backyard flower tub would float down the path with the rest of the rubble if it wasn't so waterlogged, and in five weeks and a day we go to Cornwall on holiday.

I am finding it harder and harder to believe the rumours I keep circulating concerning the blistering heat-wave due to start May Day and torment us for at least a fortnight. Who was it that said the air near rushing water contains health-giving properties? Probably some frog.

Depressing? Not really. I may be overweight, my head may look a lot smaller since undergoing what a hairdresser euphemistically called a trim, I have the shrunken head, all I need now is a shrunken body to match, but I have not lost my one redeeming feature – optimism.

Through all the years of self-catering family holidays, flats, camping, caravaning and seaside bungalows, I dreamed of the day we would take our family to one of those exclusive, whitewashed, cliff-hanging hotels, complete with ballroom, pool and waiters. At last it's almost arrived.

In the meantime we had to wait so long – one daughter got married, another reached the boyfriend stage, our son became a wage-earner rising to a position he describes as 'skint,' he donates his holiday pay to a certain brewery he is helping to finance.

So our hotel clientele has dwindled to four and a friend.

Breaking in a new landlady again will feel strange, though. We did venture into a 'Private Hotel' when our son was a baby and our daughter two-years-old. The proprietress made it quite clear to me when, tired of waiting for dinner, my baby stamped his feet and howled: the 'children welcome' sign only applied to those without voices and feet.

A couple of years later we cruised around Blackpool's back streets, our luggage, plus another baby piled in the back of our old Austin van, until we found a homely board residence with scrubbed steps and clean curtains.

We lined the children up respectably on the doorstep, removed son's battered cowboy hat again and rang the bell. 'I could push you in the attic,' said an unsmiling bespectacled matron. At the end of a week of home cooking and pristine comfort we had become good friends, returning another three times to the two pretty bedrooms we came to love.

In my opinion three meals prepared and washed up by someone else takes a lot of beating – rain or snow (I hope!).

And this year I intend to sample all the chef's culinary delights, to shake a 'crafty clog' each evening, have a daily dip each morn, enjoy a glass or two of my favourite wine in the company of my favourite spouse, even if it's fur coat weather outside.

*

THE delectable Sophie Loren is in town to boost sales of her biography. What can there be left to relate to a film star's life, living as they do in a constant beam of publicity? Enough to attract hundreds of buyers apparently.

Her favourite food is pasta, she often has to wear hairpieces and pencil in her eyebrows, the result of a vitamin deficiency in her youth and she peers around myopically when not wearing her glasses, so why does she look so absolutely gorgeous?

*

THE current party political broadcasts have added a new dimension to my husband's allotment – me.

I don't usually attend his vegetable plot until it is time to take a basket and gather in the harvest. This is one (he would probably say the only) area of his life I try not to interfere in.

Our son's cultivating talents transpire once the rubbish has been burned. He cannot imagine what there is left to do when the seeds have been planted. 'Where's dad?' he often inquires on balmy, bowling-type evenings. 'Oh, yes, don't tell me – he's on at the allotment waiting for a weed to grow so he can pull it out.'

Whenever I do visit, it fills me with a certain uneasiness to see the trim edges, neat paths and seedlings sprouting obediently in long straight columns. His meticulously kept greenhouse with balls of string all the same size sitting neatly on the immaculate shelves. I try not to compare all this uniformity with the easy-going lifestyle he has had to endure with me as housekeeper.

I am not an enthusiastic gardener – my excuse being settee too comfy. But my potted plants manage to survive on their erratic diet of drought one week and flood the next.

It's not the digging and planting I mind, but all the accompanying aggravations, like putting the lawn mower away when you've finished and you have hardly the strength to lift your brows, or shifting the pile of heavy sods leering from the barrow.

Reminds me of the stray dogs that are sometimes locked up in the police station next door. When they are confined their anguished yells pollute our peaceful atmosphere and that is when they become a nuisance.

Gardeners are a special breed. An old friend once spent two minutes introducing me to her family, gathered en masse for a christening, and the rest of the morning presenting me to her front garden.

'Frank and I picked this cutting from a garden in Scotland, this pretty little climber came from our hotel,' – and so on. There was a look of acute tenderness in her eyes when she spoke. But it's like that with plants. I once saw the sturdy Percy Thrower almost choke with emotion over a geranium's root growth. You'd have thought it was his wife's hair.

A kind gentleman I was introduced to only a week before our daughter's wedding offered me the pick of glorious rose bushes for the church floral decorations, and would accept no money. We filled a dozen vases with sweet smelling blooms.

One occupation I do put a lot of energy into is my herb growing. I have basil growing in a pot in my porch, mint and parsley under the kitchen window and my husband has given me a small patch where I have planted chervil, thyme, marjoram, caraway and chives. Apart from their distinctive flavourings, herbs also have curative properties.

I look forward to making up my own little parcels of bouquet garni. My daughter presented me with a herbs cookery book and I can't wait to do full justice to recipes like Tournedos zoia with herbs fried potatoes.

I love one of the book's salad suggestions. 'Sprinkle a few rose petals plus additional marigold petals on your salads, you'll be surprised at the flavour' – but I don't think my lot are ready to eat floral arrangements, yet.

If any readers suffer from insomnia, take my advice – go out and dig. When I had completed my couple of hours, and eventually reached my unearthly comfort of the sofa, I fell into a deep coma, thereby missing – an introduction to daughter's new boyfriend, a fish and chip supper, the final farewells of the rest of the family and – a film ending.

But if you want to become a hardy perennial – hang on to your sense of humour, it's the only part that doesn't ache from over use!

*

MY favourite hospital status is 'just visiting' and I've done my share of queuing outside the swing doors under the 'No Entry' sign.

The only private hospital rooms I ever entered were by courtesy of TV, attended by the inimitable intern, Dr blue-eyed Kildare. His naked sunburned elbows have raised my blood count unbearably on countless Saturday nights.

Depending on how ill one is, of course, private rooms sound a little isolated. Or so I thought until I recently endured the long playing voice in the bed opposite a patient I visited. Compulsive chatterers have their value, admittedly. Had I been ill her voice would have had me on my feet, ready for home in no time.

This week I had a chance to sample the esoteric atmosphere of a private nursing home, where a friend underwent a minor operation.

As our car entered the unlit drive at an angle of 45deg (snow has no priorities) the dark building with its drawn curtains looked quite small and insignificant. Inside the silent foyer, with its picture-lined, immaculately scrubbed marble staircase, well-groomed plants were blooming healthily. A smartly dressed receptionist greeted us, not a nurse or uniform in sight.

On the way to Yvonne's room we could see small supper trays set out on the sparkling steel in an empty, equally silent kitchen.

Her room was like a diminutive hotel room; colour TV beside telephone buzzer, toilet facilities through a teak door, wardrobe through another. Reminding me of gangster films where the brave 'tec grabs his clothes as soon as nurse's back is turned.

We greeted our patient through a haze of tears, she was inhaling under a towel at the time. It smelled quite poisonous, but the fumes cleared eventually. We dried our eyes and enjoyed a refreshing breathe in. While the three male visitors swooned over Kevin Keegan as they gathered together on the cocoa-coloured bedspread, we gentler sex perused some Christmas party photos, where ladies were dressed as vicars, and men wore tights and dresses.

It seemed strange not having to hide when nurse answered the buzzer, but three a bed does not apply here. We were even invited to coffee, which before I could open my mouth husband politely refused.

Not having a row of beds opposite cuts out the opening gambit, 'What's she in for?' There was the usual hospital-type radio – no sound and on the locker stood a vacuum flask of iced water.

A typical dinner menu was mushroom vol-au-vent, jacket potatoes, green beans, carrots and rhubarb crumble to follow.

Speaking as a fully paid up member of the NHS, it does make one realise what it costs to keep a patient in hospital, 'not to mention a prisoner in prison,' as someone else added.

Money does buy priority, it does shorten the queue, but when you eventually reach the National Health bed, one consolation is, although it may be noisier – treatment is just the same!

*

'PLEASE go with me,' pleads our seventeen-year-old, 'You can explain how I want it.' Well it would be a pleasant change to watch hair falling instead of snow – especially someone else's.

We rehearsed my part all the way to town 'Not too much off – but fairly short at the sides.' Once we enter the salon my act is drastically slashed to 'Sit there and don't say anything – please.'

A sulky lass comes out from under her hair and leads daughter towards the row of washbasins. Opposite my seat, a lad with a delicate air is discussing styles with a wet-haired youth in a chair. His locks are pushed forward until he resembles Li'l Abner. He grins and shrugs his shoulders sardonically as the hairdresser goes into a creative trance. Males seem to have this 'You'll never do anything with this lot, mate,' unlike the feminine approach, 'You'd better do a lot with this.'

Meanwhile a worried looking matron in a headscarf creeps in and proceeds to thumb frantically through a pile of glossy mags. 'I am going curly,' she explains.

Do these photographic models ever run a comb through their own hair I muse, or have to face unexpurgated family opinions when they do? Is one born with natural good looks, as Raquel Welch confessed she was. Or does beauty come expensive?

Our eldest had a pre-wedding set and shampoo – a rehearsal for the big day. She put her waist length hair in the hands of a recommended stylist. Unfortun-ately, once it was shampooed he couldn't do a thing with it. He tried everything - when hairspray failed he tried prayer.

Neither sprayer nor prayer had any effect. He called his mate over for an estimate and they let her off at half price.

We tend to believe the advertisers legends – the right style could transform our lives. Town centre salons have another occupational hazard. 'I know my appointment is for tomorrow,' a young mother bustles in, 'but seeing as I was passing – perhaps you could do it now.'

The old helmet dryer is being replaced by that coward's curse, the scalp-scorching hand dryer. I had a dread of being left under the old type, a forgotten rissole in the busy arrival/departure world. Either that or sometimes when my small head was buried in that claustrophobic dome, I might get electrocuted. My mother never had this problem, when she's had enough she lifts the top and removes her own rollers.

In this particular salon shirts and jeans have replaced nylon overalls. Big chief curly-top wears a draughtboard check shirt and blonde linen trousers. He's a bundle of fun, miming to the background pop music as he snips. Very amusing to watch if you're not under the scissors.

A completed customer, who has just spent 45 minutes being tongued and blown, gratefully admires her straight locks. I can tell by daughter's tragic eye signals that it's her turn to be cut. The stylist is a true artist. Sitting here with the warm windy breeze tormenting the weary-looking remains of my last perm, I wonder if perhaps a bouncy bob would be the answer. I'm still looking for a style I can live with longer than a month. Sometimes I think it would be simpler to have my face changed to suit my hair. Ah, pay time at last - £3.80 please. Daughter beaming her thanks while I beam the money. 'Yes, a trim in a month.' She is madly in love with her new look, right until we close the salon door.

By the time we reach the bus, her head is bowed low under the burden of her ruin. We all know whose fault it is – of course. 'Why didn't you say something, it's horrid?'

*

SINCE I gave birth to our five children, it astonishes me how anyone, let alone a male, dare tell others how to bring up their children. Dr Spock tried it forty years ago – years later he had to rewrite it.

Surely coping with our fifth must be easy after the other four, 'experience is the name men give to their mistakes,' as Oscar Wilde said, but I haven't felt myself brimming over with parental confidence yet. In fact does there ever come a stage in their development where you can step back and say to your partner 'That's it love, our job is completed,' then resume your own life again?

'Whether children grow up to be lifelong optimists, warmly loving or cool, trusting or suspicious, will depend to a considerable extent on the individuals who have taken the responsibility for a major portion of their care in the first two years,' so prophesised Spock. In other words another way of blaming parents when children 'go wrong.' So providing both parents are perfectly balanced, loving, faultless characters, they have nothing to worry about. But how many of us are?

'There is no such thing as a bad child,' I heard Spencer Tracey say to Mickey Rooney in 'Boys Town' years ago, and I believed it for a long time. After studying characteristics in young and old alike, I now believe, although mum's and dad's are responsible for a large percentage of their children's personalities, there is another essence of something, call it what you will – that shapes their ends.

For example the child from squalid beginnings who rises against all odds to become a great success. Charles Chaplin spent his early life trying to scrape a meagre living for himself and his mentally ill mother in a London slum, but he became a genius. Conversely – reported in the Press recently – a glamorous and wealthy young woman from a loving and secure background drugged herself to death.

I always found the advice on telling small offenders you love them even when you're feeling violent hard to swallow, and confess I never managed it.

I could not say 'I still love you although I'm belting you,' to a child. When the rebel has reached an 'I won't do it again,' mood, the loving comes naturally. I'm waiting for someone to write a book that does not automatically assume that once you give birth you become a paragon of unselfish perfection. A book, which accepts I wax neurotic occasionally and am not always in the mood for humour, when a swipe would be quicker. One with some words of wisdom to tide me over that 'I don't care if I never see another child again' period.

'They don't owe us anything,' some parents are fond of excusing their off-spring. Whatever mistakes we have made in our humble efforts to produce five respectable members of the human race, I believe my husband and I are entitled to one thing, if nothing else – respect. I shall always demand it!

*

WHY does it take ladies so long to choose new outfits? This is a question usually asked by men and followed up with a smug description of how quickly they acquired their last purchase. 'Saw it in the window, tried it on, etc etc.' You know the sort of implication, as if this is all there is to it.

What they fail to realise is that women actually derive pleasure, not to mention fun, from the exercise. That's another thing with us, buying is an actual exercise. Like anything else, women put more energy into it. Also, women are great improvers, always eager to go one better than nature, given the appropriate outfit. It takes time and effort.

I had to repeat this evidence, in my defence, after a trip to Manchester with my daughter recently.

We spent a whole day shopping for wedding outfits and returned empty handed. All that our bags contained was a placating bag of mixed chocs for daughter's husband Mike and a crusty cob, which I had optimistically bought for tea, if we hadn't missed the train back home, that is. 'This must be the dearest ruddy loaf in the country,' was my husband's only comment.

282

He naturally included the £1.70 train fare. 'What were you doing all that time?'

Looking back over the interminable dash from one 'Sale' placard to another, it hardly seemed an hour since we walked so chirpily past the snack bar outside Victoria Station.

My head so filled with visions of endless size 14's waiting to be tried on, I smiled benevolently at a bespectacled elderly gent sipping coffee in a window seat. He smiled back pleasantly, until we were at eye level, then to my surprise he rolled his eyes wickedly, opened his mouth and wobbled his tongue at me, grinning so offensively, I forgot all about fashion euphoria.

First stop was the communal changing room at a store. When trying on, midst some of the slender teenage stock, I sometimes feel like a stump in a forest. One major store thankfully, still retains single cubicles. I tried a beautiful silk two-piece, which looked most elegant on the hanger. Yet I walked out in it to confront daughter looking like Widow Twanky on washday.

The one thing I enjoy on Manchester trips is lunch. Two of us usually visit a food centre or sometimes a restaurant. But time was running out, so we decided to snatch a serve-yourself. When it was my turn the coffee machine unfortunately dried up and by the time I eventually joined my daughter she was ready to resume the hunt.

Monday is normally a good day for a browse. Elderly assistants are mostly fully occupied, muttering and ruminating among their stock, while younger ones are eagerly confessing their weekend sins to each other. The cosmetics are always fully manned with telescopic-sighted staff, ever alert for secret perfume squirters like me.

Selling clothes is not easy, but I wish some assistants would not stoop to insincerity in their efforts. If they must comment, I prefer the plain insulting truth, there is no way of escaping the mirror's verdict anyway.

While daughter and I were indulging in a leg-crossing laugh at me in a black diaphanous cocktail dress, which made me look like one of those fat legless reflections in Blackpool's Hall of Mirrors, a beautiful young assistant walked in and said quite seriously 'Oh, doesn't that suit you.' Meanwhile, back in Piccadilly, a 20-minute gallop away, the first outfits we tried were waiting to be claimed, and only half-an-hour to train time. Could we?

When we eventually arrived at the store we discovered that our suits had been sold and the 20-minute gallop had taken 30 minutes – we had missed the train, the one that would have taken me and my loaf back in time for tea and perhaps a warmer reception!

The following day we bought lovely outfits in Huddersfield – almost as delightful as the first ones we tried on in Manchester!

*

ONLY a few days to go before my hols and I still haven't managed to buy a new swimsuit. I've wandered through chain stores, run my fingers through countless tiny see-through packets with Riviera tanned beauties pictured on the front, but found nothing.

Compared with my contours, they appear to be in the last stages of malnu-trition. With coat hanger shaped hip joints protruding from almost non-existent bikini bottoms.

I feel I have hidden beneath my sensible black lycra long enough and have decided it's time for a change – before it's too late.

My family goes into hysterics when they see the pre-formed plastic cups I once found so glamorously uplifting. How could I ever have imagined this pair of plastic scoops, which were always stand offish anyway, could look natural?

But there is a multi-choice of beachwear in the shops just now. I saw a frail two-piece that looked as if a strong wave could make it even more revealing priced at £12.50.

For big girls there are the fortress-like ensembles, with built-up shoulders and pleated skirts plus a firm control lining guaranteed to cure even the most obstinate hangover. But where does all this flesh go when one sits down or bends over?

The new shiny silk halter-neck one-pieces are tempting and slightly more reasonably priced if you can wear one. C cups would have to remember to sit up straight while wearing this outfit.

I think whoever designed the old Jodhpur breeches had my legs in mind and I wish they'd come up with a swimsuit. Neither cycling, yoga nor dieting will correct their bulge. Apart from a bacon slicer there seems to be no solution. I have learned only to risk being photographed in a swimsuit when there is either a deck chair or a large towel handy.

The carefree childhood days when my sister and I used to giggle hysterically at lumpy middle-aged ladies enjoying a paddle haunt me more and more, now I've become one myself.

There are consolations. We mis-shapes become seaworthy so much faster than our slimmer sisters can. I can run from bathrobe to waist high water in seconds and reverse just as quickly when no one's looking.

Although I hate strangers breathing down my cleavage it is a mistake to buy a swimsuit without a pre-fitting. Sizes can vary dramatically. I bought one once without first trying it on, it fitted perfectly about the bosom, but

284

the body was definitely designed for someone with a longer drop. I could pull the legs down to my kneecaps without disturbing the waistline creases.

A girdle I bought without trying on never did hit it off with my trousers. Every time I wore them together I was pulled two different ways. The front zip would swing round to my left side raising my right trouser leg about six inches, giving me a k-legged appearance my husband found most irritating.

Just before a holiday I always become neurotic concerning family health, praying everyone will be fit enough to enjoy themselves. We have had holidays where one or another has either been recovering from or receiving some anti-social bug.

Some years ago an irate van driver chased our car through Manchester. Apparently, my husband, in between handing out holiday buckets for two of our virus-stricken children to be sick into, had forgotten to signal that he was turning right. After a chase my husband decided to give himself up. But when the van driver saw the pathetic picture in our car – my mother's impromptu paroxysm of acute bronchitis adding just the right touch – his contrition was a joy to behold. He even led us out of Manchester and waved us off!

So fingers crossed, this weekend I hope to be living up to my typical tourist image the natives abhor and – see you soon!
*

DOES one ever become weary of being waited upon? I wish I could afford to answer this question. After one wonderful week of sitting across from the beach at table number 12, I find I am definitely allergic to my kitchen sink, it brings me out in sighs.

To think that some people are lucky enough to spend a large proportion of their lives ordering 'a la carte' and disordering hotel beds, and grudgingly describe it as living in a suitcase – I love it. I found it so easy to slip into the holiday routine.

Take meal times for instance. At home, except Sundays, I normally push down two slices of toast and two beakers of coffee. The only words I can manage are 'come straight back or else' to the dog as I throw him out.

On holiday I am actually smiling 'Good morning' to strangers, before breakfast. I ate porridge, egg, bacon, sausage and still said 'yes please' to another round of toast and marmalade. We gobbled three more courses at lunchtime, three more at the evening meal, shamelessly nodding 'yes please' again to the afters of ripe stilton, even asking for more biscuits to finish off the over-generous lump of cheese.

No wonder my introduction to daughter's trampoline act was such a flop. Young tots were popping up and down like champagne corks at a wedding, yet when I attempted to lift my feet in the air – nothing happened. I bounced up and down alright, it was like being afloat on a stormy ridden raft, but however hard I struggled to lift my feet up, they stuck to the canvas. The only time they lifted was when I tried to get off and fell flat on my face.

I never mastered the dressing for dinner habit. Whatever I wore, the other guests and I quite never matched up. For our first evening I took special care, selecting my poshest suit and discarding, reluctantly, my trousers. The rest had retained their denim. Next evening I shivered in a thin cotton dress, while everyone else looked cosy in their double knits.

Had I known that on the final evening I was to become part of the cabaret act, I would have chosen my bright pink instead of my old black. Until the young virile guitarist pushed a microphone into my hand inviting me to help him sing I was just prepared to sit and watch. While our two swinging teenagers fled to the toilets he gave me my instructions. All I had to do was keep repeating 'ba-ba, ba-ba, ba-ran' while he sang his song.

When I faltered a feeble 'ba-ba' he made everyone laugh as he answered – 'Black sheep have you any wool.'

I was just beginning to get the rhythm when he changed key. He did warn me first, but I thought it was going to be higher, not lower, which added a little confusing harmony for a bar or two. Nevertheless, I kept belting out the 'ba-ba-ba-ran' to the bitter end.

In the second part of his act, when he called me again, I confidently grabbed the mike. But this time I was promoted to music stand. This entailed me holding his words in front of him while he looked into my eyes singing, 'I did it my way.' Had I joined the early toilet trip I could probably have coped better with this static performance. As it was, my feverish foot tapping was somewhat ahead of the music before we reached the end.

Praise for our duet was not quite what I anticipated – but lavish. 'I've never laughed so much in my life,' said one gent. 'I'm still crying,' said another.

But that's the trouble with me, on holiday or at home, I enjoy making a fool of myself. I never worry what people think – until the day after, and then it's usually too late.

Other people's laughter is like potent wine, it goes straight to my head. This can often prove embarrassing to close family. I do try to keep my talents under control when they are 9around. When they aren't – I don't half show myself up!

286

'WHERE can we go?' is a persistent teenage wail at our house. When they were younger it used to be 'What can I do?' I have so many energetic answers to this, now they only want to escape.

Where did I go at their age they often want to know? In my youth there was always a dance also coffee bars had just been imported from America. I remember the Curzon snack bar particularly, where the film-struck like myself felt real starlet material, chewing on doughnuts and sipping 'cawfee.'

When we could afford we went to the pictures on Saturday night. Sundays meant the tennis club or the 'Happy Gang' club, both run by the chapel.

Today's teenagers are short of places to go, but not money. There is a wide explosive wave of boredom that threatens to engulf most youth these days. It often erupts with sickening results.

A band of vandals whistled the night away in St George's churchyard, Cumbria recently. The appalled vicar described the £1,000 damage next day. 'They pushed over heavy headstones, the smashed them with crowbars. The place is littered with wrecked family memorials.'

Recently a gang of older girls attacked our ten-year-old and her friend, on a busy main road. I have already dealt with one member and the others had better watch out. I believe in an 'eye for an eye.' Bullies deserve a taste of their own medicine, in my opinion - it's the only language they understand.

Headmaster John Price won his case recently against a local council who thought he was being too harsh. He believes in punishing misdemeanours like tardiness, smoking, disobedience and bullying. Do it once, you're punished, do it twice, you're punished harder.

It works and he's right. Kids need something to kick against, if they don't find it at home or in school they'll search for it on the streets.

Paradoxically, discipline only succeeds when it is bonded with care. Love and discipline should ideally go hand in hand. With mothers hopping from maternity beds back to jobs, some children have neither. No wonder they grow up feeling rebellious with a desperate craving for attention. No wonder jobs are scarce.

While we were on holiday two motorcyclists screamed down on to the sands, scattering tiny sandcastle builders, they encircled the beach. Meanwhile, to the left, a corpulent figure, wearing only his moustache, tiptoed daintily through the seaweed to the sound of his mate's guffaws.

Up in the town young figures were gathering and chanting like Hitchcock's birds on a store window-ledge. Police cars were hovering nearby, ready for trouble – nothing happened. It was just harmless aggro.

Nevertheless, there was a nag of uneasiness in the pit of my stomach as we drove off towards our peaceful little bay, two miles away.

Ask the older generation what they did in their spare time and the answer is 'Parade.' My mother paraded Grimscar and Waterloo woods. When dad wasn't playing football or eating flapjacks in Lockwood Picture Palace, watching Elmo Lincoln rescuing Pearl White for a penny, he was parading Westgate. On Sunday after church this was a favourite haunt.

My 80-year-old neighbour, also a former Lockwood picture fan, sometimes danced in Honley schoolrooms. Everyone, she said, had two outfits in those days – weekday and best. Best was kept for church on Sunday. Some of her friends took a jug to the local to collect parents' beer. 'A certain class of folk did frequent pubs, but they were looked down on by decent people.'

It is 65 years since my friend Ethel strutted the 'monkey run' or 'bandstand' - a name given to a stretch of Manchester Road. What was the object of all this parading? 'Looking for lads, I suppose,' says my neighbour, with a coy smile.

Sound healthy enough to me. Now the parade ground has been transferred – they are all under cover, seeped in smoke and hiding behind their pints!

*

I NOTICE old photographs are commanding unbelievable prices on the market these days. But how do owners find the courage to part with them?

Mine have a value 'beyond rubies.' Birthdays and anniversaries would never be the same without a chin-wobbling browse through the black and whites.

This week our son celebrates his 21st birthday and I couldn't resist a wallow through the albums. It's lovely to look back to the short time when he could actually be persuaded to hold my hand.

Here's one taken on his first birthday. All you can see is a chubby lower lip hanging beneath a sun hat. That year we discovered he hated Bridlington, sun, sand, going to bed, getting up and waiting for food. He also spoke his first sentence, 'Carry me, mum,' which I quickly translated to 'Carry me, dad!'

We also learned he was a lad of few words. 'I wouldn't talk, would I, mum' became his favourite expression, as friend after friend struggled through exhausting sessions of trying to communicate with him.

Here he is again walking with grandad at Filey. Lower lip trailing because we had sold his pushchair – he was four at the time. He managed to prolong his non-walking lifestyle by squatting in big sister's doll's pram – until the day she ran in, white faced and incoherent. I dashed out in time to see small brother's happy wave, just before he and doll's pram hurtled backwards down our eight front steps. 'Does not like to exert himself,' his first school report confirmed.

On the next school snapshot he and mate are disguised as 'Steptoe and Son' wearing first-prize rosettes. Unfortunately while they were posing someone ran off with their junk filled pram.

The following year he went to his first disco. He came in one teatime in wild excitement demanding a 'crarvut,' his pronunciation for a cravat a strange request since all he ever wore were jeans and T-shirts. But that Saturday afternoon he and his mate set off in their first long trousers, Paisley 'crarvuts' tucked smartly beneath their bulging Adam's apples. Two hours later he trailed in foot weary and uncommunicative, with necktie crushed carelessly in back pocket.

When he eventually found his tongue we learned he was somewhat disappointed with the disco scene. Not even a silk necktie could alter the fact he had two left feet. After ten minutes he left his happily cavorting mate, collected his coat only to find his bus fare had disappeared. Too embarrassed to face his mate he walked home.

He always believed the walk from hearth to coal cellar was destroying his health, so the five-mile trek home must have been crucifying.

Here he is in High School uniform. Don't ask me how he managed to get away with wearing a gold lame shirt under his school tie. It was about this time he first sampled the grape. He staggered in from school at 5pm with the frog-eyed deadpan expression I have grown to recognise, threw his satchel at the dog, made a derogatory remark about mothers in general and collapsed. When he felt well enough to talk about it, a week later, he said it was school dinners and had nothing to do with his girl friend's father's home-brewing activities.

Here he is cruising down the Broads two summers ago with five mates. That's him behind the 'Playboy' magazine.

On leaving school to become an engineer his apprentice report sums up his talent. This unique gift he has for organising others – 'fetch me this, pass me that, come on you lazy beggars,' has turned out to be 'Management Material.'

Now (sniff) he is a man of 21. We still haven't been introduced to a girl friend. 'No, better not ma, it would only upset you,' he brushes me off, or 'She's not your type.'

Yes, here he comes now bless him, tall and straight, with tonight's party invitations, the ones I gave him to post last week, protruding from his pocket. His greeting echoes through the back porch. 'Hey come and look everybody – my spiders have hatched out!'

Congratulations, son.

*

IT DID not occur to me at the age of 22, as I stood poised on the brink of motherhood, that one day my daughters and I would be sharing similar ageing symptoms. As it is, their teenage wails of 'You don't understand' are entirely misdirected because I do – I do.

Am I not struggling with a difficult transition myself? They may be floundering from girl to womanhood but I am in the middle, reluctantly slipping from motherhood to what I fervently hope will be prolonged 'just-being-a-wife-hood.' What are their adolescent pimples compared with my indelible fans of creases? Once you start laughing you are forced to continue, to cover up the scars it leaves.

The young can pour over a whole exciting range of romantically designed fashion, while I am condemned to gaze despondently at the heartless belted pleats, or dated cape collars, destined to droop pathetically over prolapsed bosoms.

My teenagers plead for outfits exactly like their friends, while I lust after something totally different. Still I suppose there are not many 45-year-olds wearing faded grey cords with black Biro stains on back pocket. I achieved these delicate white stripes on my dark velvet shirt by inadvertently scooping it in with the whites. But I rebel against becoming a member of the twin-set and pearls society, I want to come to terms with middle-age – but not yet.

One point I have gathered from 45 years of observation is that style, the ability to look good in anything, is a gift. But these head-turners have one common denominator that it pains me to admit – they are all slim.

At a bowling match last week I heard a daddy chide 'Don't shout at granny when she's bowling.' Granny was a handsome bronzed Athena in late fifties, with a striking bikini-type figure, which put us all off our meat teacakes. This was almost as challenging to a lapsed size 14 as the latest bloated photo of Liz Taylor. Why do some stay ageless while others shrivel up?

The immortal Margot Fonteyn is about to face the ballet stage again at 50. Mind you, I imagine leaping around with Rudolph could be quite rejuvenat-ing. Max Bygraves, looking forty in his late fifties and reputedly earning half a million a year is an example to us all of what an excellent wrinkle remover a high income can be.

A certain freedom of spirit does descend as one passes forty. If I want to escape for an hour or two in the evening with husband, our teenagers cope at home. I use the term with husband loosely, of course. He takes me out and I usually find him when it's time to come home.

Advancing years also bring a feeling of urgency – one has still so much to accomplish before the curtain falls. I'd love to do something really startling, like turn up for a bowling match wearing false eyelashes, or walk into the 'Examiner' readers department with dyed vermilion hair.

When Times columnist Molly Parkin was 40 and grey she decided on green hair. She was in 'an emerald field along the Cornish coast' to quote her book Good Golly Miss Molly, but it was only fully appreciated by babies she said.

I did once return from the hairdressers with unplanned bleached tips. She had some lotion left and I was early. But my striped hair – family name for it - turned a ghastly khaki, which took months to wear out.

I have goals I hanker after: to be able to say one Friday, 'I've done,' meaning the housework, including windows and baking is actually completed, to write a book, to take an American Greyhound tourist bus around the movie stars homes. I'd like to be able to furnish our home with furniture we like, not what we can afford. One day I want to visit my children and their families and be told 'Sit down, mum, I'll wash up,' and many more unfulfilled desires that would only scorch the paper.

In the meantime I'm looking forward to the day when this corselet, which fits like a tourniquet, will hang in folds around my middle or I'll settle for a shout of 'Well bowled,' from my team mates instead of 'Rubbish!'

*

TO enable lucky volunteer helpers to get down to some serious commando training, we usually receive our first school trip warning straight after Christmas.

Last Wednesday, mid enthusiastic cheers from the stay-at-homes, our trusty driver, Jean, swung our tropically-heated coach on to the main road. We each folded our two packed meals into the luggage rack and settled down for our first stop – Little Moreton Hall in Cheshire.

On normal school mornings I often see children drifting towards school with an ice lolly trickling down one paw and a packet of crisps in the other. To counteract travel sickness, eating on the bus is strictly forbidden.

Within half an hour withdrawal symptoms are rife. It's amazing how quickly happily flushed expressions can evaporate, leaving that deathly glow no pill can remove. The pale green were assembled nearest the bucket, while the rest continued trying out various hand signals on surprising tolerant lorry drivers.

A small brain behind was bursting with statistics. 'There are 71 lightning conductors between here and Manchester. It's bad luck to breathe under a bridge,' and in the middle of the M62, 'Please miss, Andrew wants a toilet.'

We arrived at the extremely well preserved Elizabethan mansion and the sick were quickly persuaded back to life. Built about 1460 it started out as a smaller house, but in 1559 the Moreton's decided to extend - I know the feeling. A well-maintained and unusually glamorous female showed us around this intriguing piece of history.

The children had been previously crammed with facts by teacher and con-tinuously buzzed about the 'long gallery,' a feature also added later and used as an exercise chamber for the ladies and a sort of play pen for the children. These galleries were show-off symbols only affordable by the multi-wealthy.

Our friendly guide asked a question and the genned-up were immediately struck to idiocy. Their stares were so vacant you would have thought she had lapsed into Latin. In the private chapel she told us lovely little details regard-ing tapestry kneelers embroidered by a local Women's Institute. 'You've all heard about Women's Institutes,' she encouraged. She might have been referring to an alien planet – reception was so mute. Carved initials in an upstairs chamber caused speculation until our guide explained they were 20ᵗʰ century workmen's not Tudor.

Our charges looked exceptionally intelligent when someone said 'Shop,' and they were soon cashing pound notes like they were going out of fashion.

I indulged in some quiet meditation in the pebbled courtyard. Elizabethan ladies certainly led a workless life. Walking in the long room on wet days, sewing tapestry in the withdrawing room after dinner. The house was so spacious one could imagine ghostly voices from the past.

'Where's your mother – again?' 'Does anyone know what a guardrobe is?' Our cheery speaker pointed to an outside wall. 'There were 16 along here, once.' This ignorance was embarrassing. I could almost visualise the guards hanging their armour on coat hangers in the little allotted guardrobes. 'This was the word for Tudor toilets,' we ignorant were informed.

In the grounds are elevated mounds where the Moretons could stand and survey all the surrounding countryside. A particular hazard for the recalcitrant swag-bellied when dynamic teacher was forming her after lunch rounders' team. Happily some of us were excused games, even without a note.

My favourite quote of the day – from a sweet little blonde who stroked my greying locks and said quite seriously: 'You're growing some dark hair aren't you?' Magic!

*

THE school midsummer break is almost upon us. While teachers prepare to convalesce, parents are praying for the three S's–Sun, Safety and Self-control.

July always makes me feel nostalgic. It is usually the time I take my own children back for another sight at the pretty hamlet where I spent my school holidays. Once more I show them the tumbledown cottage where we lived, now expensively renovated and expertly disfigured by the ever-popular pseudo-Georgian craze.

Thankfully no one had tried to modernise the overhanging laburnums or the sprawling wood opposite.

It never rained during my school holidays – or if it did I never noticed, because all my memories are sun-filled. Although it was in reality a time when most lives were under threat – when the slightest buzz overhead struck one to a speechless halt, to listen for the ominous intermittent drone which meant 'It was one of theirs,' an enemy plane.

This fear did once become absolute when a bomb just missed a nearby RAF camp. As soon as the 'all-clear' sounded we villagers were eagerly scavenging for shrapnel souvenirs; many mantelpieces were proudly adorned with evidence of our participation in the war.

In desperate situations it is human nature to stick together. Our back doors were so tightly packed, we had no choice. One knock opened many doors.

There were often periods of embarrassing poverty when service pensions did not cover luxuries like shoes and insurance payments. One night I was sticking pins in an effigy of our insurance agent, hoping he would be struck down with paralysis until next pension day so I could have my new shoes, when his bombastic knock shook the back door. We kept quiet hoping he would go away. Then our neighbour's voice, 'Knock again lad – I know they're in,' spurred us to action.

Trying not to giggle, we – my mother, sister and me – crept out of the front door, down the path along the road, up the hill, not daring to lift our heads until we reached the freedom of the open fields half a mile beyond. Some time later we retraced our steps, finishing up at our back door to confront an astonished neighbour who was still on guard. We greeted her felicitously – after all she was expecting an air raid shelter any day, which we hoped to share.

Boredom was alien to me. There were endless pursuits stretching before us. Ball games against another neighbour's wash kitchen door, with the promise of an exciting chase if it was occupied - most of our games ended this way. When we were fed up with ball games we could climb the 'Big House' tree, a pastime tolerated since I was matey with the evacuees who were billeted there.

From this lookout we could await the crunch of the ARP warden's best boots, marching their way to his little wooden headquarters. Once he was installed with helmet on nail and boots on table, we entertained him with our impersonations. Enemy aircraft and fire alarms were two of our specialities. As he was also our rent man I had to wax exceptionally nifty on the escape route.

Sometimes we played hide and seek with the milkman's wife, in her hus-band's best mowing field: 'I know you little brats are in there, I can see you,' she would scream into the distance, as we all slipped through the gate behind her.

Ah yes, playing with adults was great sport – unless you were caught. Then it was trouble in triplicate. A hiding on the spot, another when you reached home and most efficacious of all punishments, 'Wait till I write to your father!'

*

MOST Sunday afternoons when sensible wives are snoozing under a news-paper I can be seen pointing my bowling bag in the direction of yet another competition. With husband's advice, 'Don't be short,' meaning aim far enough, ringing through my hairspray – I throw my first wood. It screams off the green and into the gutter and the fight for supremacy has begun. End after end I trail – jaws exhausted with gum chewing – voice croaky with cursing. All too soon I'm smashing my woods back into their nest ready to proceed to the 'if only' stage.

If only she hadn't done this, if only I had thought, if only the sky would fall – if only I could bowl.

Naturally husband has to take his share. If only he hadn't been so insulting. If only he didn't prophesy exactly how far away from winning each bowl would be – before it leaves my hand. If only he could be wrong for once. If only he would shut up. Then there was that match when he kept his mouth shut and I lost 21-2.

I am convinced that there is some vital ingredient hitherto undiscovered by me, which produces winners. We see it every year at Wimbledon, but what is it? Tracey Austin believes in talking to herself. 'I had to keep talking to myself,' she confessed, after beating Billy-Jean, 'Telling myself to stay under control and forget BJ had won almost everything there was to win.'

Jimmy Connors had mom accompanied by his coach who was reprimanded for coaching from the sidelines. His advice? 'Take your time, don't get careless.' American College football coach Woody Hayes always insists his players keep straight faces. 'You just don't laugh your way to victory,' he warns. Words we should have carved on our bowling bags.

'You chat around in groups instead of shouting each other to victory,' nags my husband. 'But that's all they go for, dad, a natter and a laugh, winning is just a bonus,' grins son.

When one sees the bitchiness that overzealousness can produce – happiness seems the lesser evil. I once saw a Monty Python sketch where John Cleese and mate walked into a strange house and proceeded to insult the hostess. When she protested, he threw her into a chair saying 'Sit down, it's only a bit of fun.'

This remark bubbles on my lips whenever I am confronted by autocratic females. Petty officialdom pollutes many English sports. Martina Navratilova was reunited with her mum who came all those miles only to be refused entry to Wimbledon because she hadn't a ticket.

When bowling ladies don't turn up for matches or if they are late they are 'scratched.' 'Does it hurt, mum?' our small daughter once asked. It certainly does, and nearly happened to a friend and me last week.

Our smiles were not returned as we 'signed in' and we were heavily told off for not anticipating six bowlers would not turn up, making our games earlier. Several pairs of eyes shot venom–we ought to be scratched. In case there was still a glimmer of joy left in us, we were told, 'This is no laughing matter.'

A sun-tanned lady wearing dark glasses whined on about having to sit in the sun with nothing to do but wait. I felt my claws begin to bristle, then we were finally forgiven and allowed to play. But no doubt about it – we were in the 'sin bin' for a while and lost the game as well.

Last week at the Isle of Man bowling festival a player made his way back to his room one night to see a young woman knocking on his door. When questioned, she said she was giving the occupant an early call as requested. 'But that is me and I haven't come in yet,' he cried!
*

EVERY week I watch Clive James and Anna Raeburn struggle to unravel 'A Question of Sex.'

The former made his name tearing programmes like this to pieces. Ms Raeburn used to answer sexy questions on the back page of a women's magazine. Apart from stuffing us with meaningless statistics and showing us that both sexes look as comfy as kangaroos on a flag pole the Clive and Anna show is boring chemistry. We did learn, however, that James has the larger lung capacity, this must be the reason he looks more cuddly.

Anna is at her happiest when putting men in their place – which in her opinion ought to be under her big toe.

With the aid of complicated figures and charts she informs us that there are not as many women as men in the medical and dentistry professions. While I worship my lady doctor, I thank heaven for any obstacle that deters lady dentists. The only one I encountered injected what felt like a pint of crushed ice into my top lip and then proceeded to drill a cavity in my front gum. When I managed to manipulate my tyre lip enough to protest she said, 'Never mind, I'm nearly through.' She was! In future I will probably be able to whistle 'In a monastery garden' through the hole in my gum.

No one has yet mentioned on the programme the indisputable fact that basically men are nicer than women. In the emotive area of temperament, men surely have the edge. With their natural sense of fairness they make better bosses - some of them even make better mothers.

For a start their uncomplicated body chemistry does not plunge them into monthly moods, which females are prone to blame their mistakes on.

I can stand some female company longer than others, but I confess to a blatant misogynistic strain in my make-up. No, I have not an overbearing mother, in fact I was the dominant feature at our house, especially when dad was away during the war.

I did have a predatory dancing teacher – who still makes me tremble when-ever we meet. Recently I had a re-union with another ex-pupil in a large store. We had both seen teacher enter and had chosen the same row of nighties to hide behind.

'I have to drag the talent from her,' she used to tell my mother, who was also afraid of her. Growth was the only part of me beyond her control – she never forgave me for being smaller than the rest of our troupe, that and my sallow neck, which she tried unsuccessfully to scrub as white as the other girls' on several occasions. She still gives me nightmares, but I'll say this for her - she taught me to dance, and to wear a smile, however much it hurt – if you knew what was good for you.

Last weekend I attended another bowling competition, not one run by the female bowling Mafia but handled by the men of Brighouse – what a difference as smoothly in tune as their terrific brass band. The women's committee had admirably confined their talents to preparing an excellent tea.

*

WHERE would we be without the conscientious efforts of our eminent scientists? One has just completed a survey on the rate of 'touching' as it varies from country to country, ie how often human beings touch each other in one day.

This highly specialised work has taken him to several café corners, and I suspect several long grass areas–all over the world. He discovered that Puerto-Ricans touched each other 180 times, French 110 times, Americans twice and Londoners never.

I notice he didn't mention Greece, where last week a couple was jailed for making love in public. They were arrested in a seaside village in Northern Crete – surrounded by a crowd of interested onlookers – who were naturally disgusted.

Other scientific experiments indicate that if you touch people they like you more, on the other hand (no pun intended) it is the more powerful person who tends to touch the weaker. Now we know why footballers and politicians rush at each other with outstretched arms and puckered lips.

If a scientist had to study the touching scenes on Blackpool sands during the next fortnight I'll bet his notebook would be a best-seller.

Northerners can be as untouchable as the Southerners until they reach the briney, but there's something about the salty air that loosens the inhibitions, and Blackpool has the loosest in the North.

When our relatives congregate for birthday and Christmas celebrations I genuinely enjoy doling out bear hugs and kisses. Sometimes I can even manage it with the women. I am always first in the queue for greetings or farewells when our neighbour's French relatives visit. I find their double cheek brushing particularly endearing.

It was a sad day for me when our son became a man – on the day he substituted a handshake for his mother's goodnight kiss. No more sissy cuddles for him – now he was nine years old.

According to this latest survey hot countries have the highest body contact rate. Sunshine is always a great unwinder for me. Balmy air fills me full of bon homie but I have to be careful how I use it. Many summers ago my fiance and I were sunbathing with others on the grass in Greenhead Park after our picnic, when a very senior citizen prodded me about the naval with her umbrella and ordered me to 'Get up you naughty girl!'

It was a sultry evening when a shy lad who often caught the same bus as me accompanied me to our gate. As we walked, me chatting animatedly as usual, he suddenly threw his arm around my neck. Feeling slightly ridiculous, he was a foot taller and almost missed, I tried to carry on walking and ignore the added weight on my shoulders. All I had to do was to tell him I was already courting – sounds simple enough – but if I had known this lads name it would have helped.

My mother once arranged a blind date for me with a lad she said she felt sorry for. She said he had no girl friends because he was so bashful, but he wasn't very pretty either, besides being built like Oliver Hardy. I only went out with him because it seemed a shame him having all that money and no one to spend it on.

We went to the Tudor Cinema; the only words he spoke were 'Excuse me, please,' before he ran to hide in the gents when the lights went up.

But are we now becoming more publicly affectionate. If you are about to set off on your holiday why not conduct your own survey and find out? And don't forget – keep in touch!

*

'THEY had a right job with me last time, took four of 'em to get me in the chair.' These words drifted towards me as I persuaded my ice-filled shoes into the dentist's waiting room. Every visit my heart beats so fast it's like having a frog in my top pocket. Suppose you were Anne Boleyn, I try to kid myself, things could be worse. But even head removing has the edge – it's quicker.

All right then, suppose you were about to face a serious operation – but it's good, what could be more serious than having a tooth filled? Pregnancy is a good tranquilliser, if someone had removed all my teeth at the same time I probably wouldn't even have noticed.

On five occasions I have cuddled a new baby and promised myself no more dentist fright, but it never works. Once I get my strength back, I weaken. Still, dentists have changed. Apart from looking younger, their surgery equipment has shrunk. You don't feel as if you are on a building site with overhanging cranes and pneumatic road drills. Everything is so sophisticated nowadays; a diminutive high-speed drill that also squirts water up your nose.

Instead of sitting with neck clamped upright, you can take it lying down and contemplate your eye-level shoes.

A long way from the ghastly wooden steps which children used to have to climb with someone else's mother at Huddersfield's old school dental clinic. They probably had a theory that being accompanied by preceding patient's mum cut out tantrums. In my case it just meant crying louder so my mum could hear downstairs.

I remember once opening the surgery door, sniffing the fumes, and introducing myself with a piercing scream. The two nurses and dentist carried on conversing. 'We hope to try there one summer,' a nurse said as she dragged my forlorn shoulder heaving figure to what looked like the electric chair – a signal for higher pitched yelling. 'Peggy's going up to Scotland, next month.'

The dentist prised my mouth open and jacked-up my jaw. This did not quieten my voice, but took his mind off Peggy's holiday long enough to mutter 'Stop that nonsense.' Peggy smiled charmingly before she blotted out the universe with what looked like a dustbin lid.

My new dentist sometimes masks his lovely smile. On my last visit I caught him spraying his throat like a prima donna, and when he bent over me, his breath was sweet and cool. Wish I could have returned the favour; my daughter reminded me too late as we stepped off the bus, 'Ugh, mum, garlic.' Secret garlic eaters should always carry mints.

Dental visits are so undignified. No make-up, my front tooth staring at me from his tray; rinse and spit, the slobbery battle with stubborn salivary strands that won't let go. The suction tube that makes gluttonous soup-sucking noises you'd rather not be associated with. Try to remove it and you feel like Humphrey Bogart taking of the leeches in 'African Queen.'

Dentists have this tormenting habit of talking to you with your mouth full. They tuck two plugs of cotton wool up each cheek, screw a clamp on to your tooth, fix the vacuum under your tongue, and when your nostrils are beginning to flare like Dizzy Gillespie's, he'll ask politely 'Where did you get to this year, then?'

I suppose it's a gift!

*

IT WAS with mixed feelings of pride and palpitations that I fastened my seat belt last Tuesday and allowed our son to drive the gang and me over to Leeds Market. He only stopped being a learner a week ago, but I was eager to offer the benefit of my many years' experience as navigator.

I hope to take a driving test myself one day. All I need is a brave, tolerant, jolly character with a few years to spare and an abundant supply of duel-controlled cars.

My husband has been trying to teach me – in spasms – for ten years, without success.

The only time he ever swore at me was when I let our car run backwards. Well I didn't let it, it just refused to go forward. I did my best to follow teacher's frantic instructions, 'You should be able to hold it, for Pete's sake, what are you trying to do, you'll ruin these gears . . . you. . . .' But we still slipped faster and faster down the road.

Usually so tolerant, his sense of humour turns off the moment I turn on the ignition. He would go through the starting routine in hushed tones with a face like a bankrupt counting his assets. Tiny giggle bubbles would rise in my throat and I never managed to find a way to stop them exploding. 'Yes, I do really want to drive and I honestly don't know what I'm laughing at,' I had to recite before we set off for every lesson.

He did congratulate me once when I was practising how to reverse on a large empty area of waste ground. At least I thought it was empty until I pulled up two inches in front of a fairground lorry's headlamps. My husband was so impressed I never told him that the first time I noticed the parked vehicle was when he praised me for not hitting it!

Before that, the only place I was allowed to take the wheel was a deserted stretch at Blackmoorfoot. I was not used to seeing anything besides birds and even they started avoiding our patch of road after a time.

I will never forget the day I was granted a drive into our village. I don't know how word got around, but the streets were empty.

At the first corner son remembered an urgent fishing engagement, one by one our daughters decided to take up walking, then when the car started to defy me and run the opposite way, I accepted defeat. I think it saved our marriage.

To show their gratitude my husband and son bought me a brand new bike on my birthday.

Cycling is fine, but I often suffer withdrawal pangs, especially when greedy motorists blast me out of their way. Not possessing the equipment to honk back, I have developed my own sign language. It's remarkable how explicit one can be, using only one hand.

Leaving Leeds City centre is a teeth-grinding experience for a newly fledged driver, not to mention his mother. Luckily my navigational intuition was well to the fore. I was able to shout valuable instructions at all the traffic lights 'Right here, now bear left, straight on,' and couldn't resist a rosy glow of satisfaction as we sped towards Morley – the Huddersfield turn-off would turn up, I calmly assured the pale faces in the back seat.

Of course sons never appreciate one's efforts, 'I wish you'd stop telling me where to turn when you can see I'm in the middle lane, mother,' was all the thanks I received.

IT DEPRESSES me to note the progress made in maternity procedure over the past twenty years. When I first became pregnant Dr Dick Grantly-Read was advocating the art of natural childbirth.

Every Monday afternoon we lay hands clasped on our foetus at our weekly ante-natal classes listening to teacher's promises. If we breathe deeply through our forthcoming contractions, panted eagerly when baby arrived, motherhood would prove to be just another vigorous exercise.

All those tales of terror, the scourge of smockland could now be buried and forgotten. No more pulling on towels or biting straight through lower lips as one relative relates so realistically, you can almost see her sitting there with her three lips.

It was a big bluff, naturally, because as we mothers soon discovered, pain-less childbirth is a medical myth. Nevertheless with adequate care and concern it can certainly be less painful. Dr Grantly-Read definitely took maternity a step forward, away from the idea that suffering was a woman's lot. Trilene – the soporific mixture of gas and air was also introduced.

I remember turning away from it in disgust at an ante-natal rehearsal. What did I want with artificial aids when I could breathe in and out to four counts and pant like next door's bitch at the drop of a scalpel?

I am only thankful none of the other mothers witnessed me screaming for 'more' at my actual delivery, when the nurse tried to separate me from the mask.

Today, according to many young mothers I know, the popular method of childbirth is by induction. This is the unnatural acceleration of baby's arrival, usually by drugs. Normally applied where mother or infant's health is at risk if pregnancy is allowed full term. The proportion of these induced births rose from 15 per cent in 1965 to an alarming 40 per cent in 1974.

Recently, in a hairdressers' I heard two ladies in full-womb discussing their forthcoming events. The question 'When?' cropped up. One was due 'Some-time next month.' 'I'm going in to have mine next Wednesday at ten,' was the other's surprising forecast.

On her last clinic visit she was told she was about to be induced. The decision had nothing to do with her or baby's health; she said it was simply to ease overcrowded hospital conditions during the holiday period.

The sad thing for me was the look of unconcern when it was pointed out by another expectant mum that this operation was merely for convenience of staff.

Mums I have spoken to who have undergone this treatment, experience more painful and stronger contractions compared to their natural births.

Home confinements are no longer encouraged. My first two children were born at home, where the ratio is one patient to one midwife. Nurse and I had time for long conversations concerning baby's welfare. Due to her perseverance I nursed all my five babies.

In my three hospital confinements I never once saw a mother taught the art of breast-feeding. On one ward I was the only one not feeding by bottle.

The policy of aiming for 100 per cent hospital births must be crippling an already debilitated National Health Service. Yet with improved ante-natal services I firmly believe all mothers-to-be would eventually agree with me, health permitting, there is definitely no place like home.
*

IN SPITE of the ghastly weather, home-grown garden produce is miracu-lously flourishing. We are enjoying a glut of vegetables - or another way of looking at it, while other spud-bashers progress to the quick peel method we gardener's wives can look forward to another rigorous month or two of prolonged spud scraping.

Cooked gently and over-dressed in delicious parsley butter, freshly dug potatoes are a feast for kings.

I am still searching for the herbs I so lovingly boasted about planting earlier – only the parsley arrived. Yet in the next plot where our junior carelessly threw a packet of mixed flower seeds, behold a magic garden!

Of course, this is a busy time in the gardener's world. What with all the harvest gathering and basket filling, the beetroot boiling and shallot pickling. Unfortunately, school holidays are also in full blight. The shouting that exudes from our household, my frequent journeys to dustbin, with the pickle tears wet on my cheeks and fingers dripping with beetroot blood, must be quite frightening to our neighbour.

It's all the little extras that make term time seem so far away. The additional boyfriends and girlfriends, an intrinsic fact of family life motherhood bibles neglects to mention.

We also have a nervous cat and gerbil holidaying with us. Every morning cat flees to the darkest, quietest spot, under one daughter's bed. Every three hours I prise it out, trap it against my chest and carry it to be fed and watered in the kitchen. This journey includes a trip past our dog basket where deadly enemy number one is waiting with tail a-wag, setting pussy's claws on edge, or more precisely into my neck. I was on the phone the other day when something whizzed past my ear and thudded at my feet. Cat had either decided to end it all, or accidentally fallen from upstairs banister. Meanwhile, in the back porch a bedraggled little gerbil is wading through an inch of water, struggling to rescue its woolly bed from the deluge. My fault, when the phone rang I had just filled his water bottle and, unable to fathom where it should hang, had placed it on the cage floor, where it had steadily emptied itself.

Then there are the ubiquitous bantam eggs christened 'too pretty to eat.' Every ornament has one. This is the harvest of daughter's school livestock duties. Each morning when I am about to enjoy that particularly relaxing extra half hour in bed, a mighty banging on the back door heralds the arrival of the livestock gang.

'We've come for Amanda' they chorus when I blearily open the door. With rain bouncing of their waterproofs and wellies they looked more like a lifeboat crew.

On the way to our vegetable plot we pass what must be the finest allotment in the north of England which does diminish the quality of one's own harvest somewhat.

The other day I caught a lad pinching gooseberries there. 'Hey! What are you doing?' I shouted. Whereupon he jumped quickly off the wall and ran to join his mates. I gave them my dignified self-righteous stare as I passed – until that nasty terrier sprang from nowhere and egged on by their gleeful shouts of 'Kill!' chased me up the street.

Last night a frightened stray hound left all alone in the empty police station yard kept my husband and I awake – in spite of stuffing our ears with cotton wool and burrowing under our pillows.

As if life isn't difficult enough, we still have no 'Coronation Street.'

*

LOOKING back, it seems as if I spent most of the war years being frightened into nightmares by a gang of ruthless Gestapo, who terrorised me twice weekly, by courtesy of our local cinema.

There I sat, my legs embedded in the hairy plush, while members of the 'underground' had their nails torn out and their fingers broken by Conrad Veight in the name of freedom.

Going home on the bus I was convinced that I was surrounded by German agents, and willing to confess everything at all costs.

1940 was the year my auntie arrived on our doorstep with one large suitcase and two cousins declaring 'We've come to stay until the war is over,' A week later when it showed no sign of halting – she left.

I was six years old when war was declared and until my dad was called up two years later I ignored it. When he left I started paying attention to the daily bulletins concerning 'our troops' who had usually either 'landed in' or 'retreated from' places I had never heard of. But RAF general duties men were never mentioned in dispatches, I discovered.

At first it all seemed an exciting game – with cosy evenings in the air raid shelter – with grown ups in dressing gowns and us all sat around drinking cocoa, waiting for the all-clear to sound.

Then I came of picture-going age and saw the Pathe Gazette newsreels showing column after column of dusty British soldiers. The wounded and the weary being cheered on by the ecstatic liberated. Some wore smiles under their helmets, but although I was only eight – I recognised the fear. One newsreel, still painful to recall, showed Japanese soldiers catching babies on their bayonets – while hysterical mothers were forced to watch.

Every Monday and Friday we ogled this torment. Yet paradoxically our games were far removed from war. We always played Tarzan. The lads took it in turn being Johnny Weismuller while we girls went native. With rhododendrons clipped to our hair we made camps in the treetops for our chiefs.

Every Sunday night we listened to Harry Korris and Enoch 'let me tell you' in a radio favourite 'Hippodrome.' Then while Albert Sandler depressed us with his violin from 'Palm Court' we wrote our letters to dad.

Two other spirit-lowering features were sweet rationing and gas mask drill. I will never forget the day my friend and I, realising it was the first of the month, dashed in for our coupons. We planned to buy two ounce of sweets each, but unfortunately she returned empty handed. It appeared her mother had sold the entire family sweet ration to support the habit that finally killed her.

Most of us were compulsive queuers. A person would only have to lean against a wall for a second, immediately five others would join him. Often, such luxuries as oranges or bananas were suspected.

Everyone did something towards the 'War effort.' I impersonated Carmen Miranda. After all the spy films, my accent was more German than Brazilian, but it made other people laugh.

When victory was finally announced I went to Greenhead Park to watch the celebrations. I was surprised to see one of our neighbours in a sailor hat with her arms draped around its owner. Tears were running down her cheeks, yet I knew her husband was on his way home.

DURING this recent surprise spell of sunshine I have been allowing my thoughts to dwell on the prospect of the forthcoming topless bathing at Brighton.

Not long ago newspapers were full of reports concerning the health dangers to which sun wallowers were exposing themselves. An alarmist view, really, when you consider the sunless English weather we are becoming accustomed to. I have never had an all-over tan in my life. Usually I return from holiday wearing a brown triangle at my throat, two short white skin sleeves and brown legs that finish at the kneecaps.

If Brighton is going bare, I thought to myself this morning; what could be the harm in exposing my thighs to this blistering heat in my own backyard. I should explain that my thighs are not the sort you unveil in public. As a keep fit crony succinctly put it, after she had spent most of the session studying them, 'Your body's not so bad,' she decided 'it's them,' as she prodded my overstuffed uppers.

When I wasn't gnashing my teeth during the latest Miss United Kingdom competition, I couldn't help noticing how unscarred contestant's limbs always appear, as if they have all led a charmed, wartless, non-pimpled existence.

Necks are a noted age give-away, but I feel ten years younger when my thighs are covered. Age and exuberance have left their scars.

That bulge on the left for instance, is the result of a joke that misfired. A friend left me at the bus stop while she dashed home for some forgotten article. Hoping to make her believe the bus and I had departed, I stepped into the entrance to the wood at the back of us, meaning to crouch behind the wall. Only it was pitch black and I forgot about the stone steps. When she returned and eventually discovered where the moaning was coming from, the joke took a lot of explaining.

Then, splattered here and there between the broken blood vessels are the boil craters that have grown up with me. If I have a ballpoint pen handy – and I usually have – I can amuse myself for hours turning them into eyeballs.

So it was this morning, with my dress hem tucked indecently into my drawers, my collar pushed unseemly into my bra and my scars fluttering their countless inked-in eyes provocatively, the dog and I fell asleep on a rug in our back yard.

Now when film stars do this a remarkable metamorphosis occurs. Their skin becomes all golden and glistens like satin, when ordinary mortals sunbathe it's a different story. First the eyelids shrink, and the overheated eyeballs start to bulge, then the lips fold into tiny pleats. Blobs of

305

perspiration boil over into ugly red blotches. You want to swat the fly that is heading for your brains, via your left nostril, but your arms and legs have turned to stone.

The dog and I had just about reached this state of inertia today when a strange man came to read the meter. Covered in confusion, and ink eyes, I tried to spring to my feet, I managed it at the third attempt. With difficulty I unsealed my starched mouth. Something had also happened to my sight. After he had finished I showed him to the back gate and walked into the drainpipe. He ran off without a backward glance.

It is always the same, if ever I decide to uncover my inhibitions – a man appears from nowhere. The last time I crept stealthily out in a pair of shorts, a neighbourly gardener decided to confide his war experiences. I spent all afternoon behind a sheet I had just hung out, with just my head visible above the clothes line. It wasn't only modesty – the poor chap had a dicky heart and I daren't risk letting him see me in those shorts. The shock might have killed him.

*

AS autumn approaches, we look forward to cosy evenings in our favourite armchair, perhaps reading the book we've been postponing all summer, or maybe relaxing our varicose veins to the sound of some long-gone composer.

We look forward to this but . . . we had reckoned without the attack of the Adult Education leaflets. Suddenly we feel we ought to be out there arranging flowers, icing cakes or something.

September has become a popular 'Coming out' season. Throwing comfort to the winds, long queues of enthusiasts can be seen this week signing away their winter evenings.

Of course Christmas usually sorts out the truly dedicated. School events, festive parties, the return of ITV or just the pull of the hearth, will soon sift away the dilettantes.

I know from experience the stamina required seeing an evening course through to the end product. I completed some of my chosen sessions, but unfortunately my trophies never reached exhibition standard.

Two children's overcoats I made were worthy, but display day was so bitingly cold they had to wear them. A piece of pottery I made adorns my tea trolley. I wish I knew what to call it. None of our class had the courage to ask what the lumps of clay we were all rolling out so enthusiastically would eventually become.

My father-in-laws description seems pretty accurate. 'What is it?' he asked when he first saw it. 'Looks like a kipper that's been left out in the sun.' So, it's a curly kipper-shaped thing, which holds three apples when you get the balance right.

My husband and I joined up for a course on modern dance once. We had decided to start going out together now the children didn't want us. As a result of my blatant showing-off, I was immediately promoted to playing Ginger Rogers to our teacher's Fred Astaire, while my husband spent the evening confined to a hopalong column of cha-cha-ing non-starters at the other end of the ballroom.

I have permeated many buses with smells of aired food, as I travelled homeward from Tech. Carrier bags brimming with various casseroles, which the family were waiting to polish off the minute I arrived home.

Although yoga has proved my most endurable vocation, this year I have decided on a change. I reached this decision at our last class while we were meditating. 'Think of some tranquil place you long to be,' said our teacher. My fireside kept looming into focus and I was hard put to suppress my homing instinct.

*

LAST week BBC television took us inside the walls of Westminster Public School, where, for £3,000 per year, boys – and recently girls – can be educated.

Some severely self-assured lads expressed articulate opinions on school life. It was a refreshing change to hear them talking about their school with pride and without that worked-to-death phrase 'Yer know.'

Parents' evenings at the exclusive Westminster looked similar to our com-prehensive affairs, except coffee was served in china cups with saucers.

When asked did she not think that public school atmosphere could give a child a rather narrow outlook; all that mixing with only middle and upper classes, one mother voiced an opinion with which I wholeheartedly agree.

'There is a danger,' she admitted, 'but on the other hand, they are not subject to influence from under-achievers at this school - a threat at comprehensives.'

Being a comprehensive teacher she speaks from experience. Being a parent of four comprehensive-trained pupils, so do I.

I believe this percentage of under-achievers, the couldn't care less element, is a festering affliction of the comprehensive system. Left to smoulder un-checked this bane is often carried forward into a non-career when they leave.

In my schooldays teachers were to be feared – you went to school to learn. Multiplication's were forced repetitiously down our throats each morning. Only when one table could be recited without mistakes were you allowed to tackle the next. Spelling mistakes had to be corrected three times. Laziness was punished by more work repetition. I can recite much of Tennyson's 'Lady of Shalott,' I'm ashamed to say, because I was consistently late for school. It took me a week of dinner time stay-ins to learn it and it cured my tardiness.

We did our homework because if we got bad reports, it meant Saturday morning detention. I hated my first year at Grammar school, I hated the stern, unfriendly teachers, and at the end of term I took home one of my best ever reports.

Since our recent Educational Renaissance teachers now have less power, the deterrents are dwindling. In some schools religious and moralistic instruction are being phased out. We had to earn the respect of our teachers, now the role is reversed.

Given the ability, ambition and a grant, there is no limit to what students can achieve. Nowadays teachers give an almost round-the-clock service, being merely an appointment or a phone call away.

Problems should be non-existent. But without the necessary parental backing all the other advantages are wasted. On parent/teacher interview evenings, there is always an element of parents who are either 'too busy' or too unconcerned to take advantage of this opportunity to discuss their offspring.

Kids who have never known loyalty at home, naturally enough have no use for it at school. If parents don't respect school why should they? Discouraged adolescents are quick to note the breach in liaison – and rebellion takes root.

In Huddersfield our textile heritage is, sadly, on the wane and with it the old working-class standards are dying too. During the worsted boom when mills were thriving, if a man wanted more wages, he had to work more hours, produce more output.

The aim nowadays is simply – more money. No one seems prepared to make sacrifices any more. This selfish attitude is reflected in the present non-marital situation.

Couples are no longer prepared to make promises or accept responsibility. The trend is to live together until the excitement wears off – or someone new comes along. Loyalty is becoming an old-fashioned outmoded emotion.

A friend recently told me that when his full quota of work is completed for the day, he then sits and reads for the rest of the time. Why? His answer was 'Because it is against union rules to do more work.'

It's called progress!

CAN you ride tandem? Whether you can or not the double-bike is coming back on the market, sales have doubled this year, according to George Clark, of the Tandem Centre in London.

We have had quite a few in our household. My parents kept our neighbours entertained for years with theirs. Every Sunday, weather permitting, my mother enclosed in my father's corduroys would fill the saddlebags with sandwiches, while my dad filled the tyres. This was always the signal for much tablecloth and rug shaking in the area as news of the forthcoming take-off got around.

Our tandem was a three-seater. Discarding his former idea of turning our old pram into a sidecar so that we could all ride together, my dad had proudly speculated on a new chair which he fixed on their back wheel to accommodate my sister. When our dog who, whenever we forgot to lock him up was also a keen cyclist, came along it became a four-seater. I rode behind on an old ex-RAF model.

The chance to become a tandem slave came when I was courting. Another cycling duo enthusiastically converted us, and every weekend I took up my position behind my future husband. However much you love your partner, a perpetual view of his back pocket can wax monotonous.

For born leaders like me the suspense is also frustrating. Not knowing when the next gear is likely to change pace, having no control on direction – or as my driver puts it, having no choice but to do as I was told. To relieve this I was put on signal duty, but in the middle of heavy traffic, 'Put your left arm out,' can often be distorted. Then you have the demoralising task of either admitting you were concentrating on your 'Madame Butterfly' aria, or you simply guess and extend your right arm.

I developed a handy 'rubbing out' gesture to cope with wrong hand signals. By polishing the air with an imaginary duster, hopefully I cancelled the preceding signal. In particular smouldering circumstances I would turn and mouth an exaggerated 'Sorry!' to the bewildered faces behind.

We had a small motor fixed to help with hill work, but we soon discovered that although it sounded as if Barry Sheene was about to zoom over the horizon, if we stopped pedalling there was the embarrassing hazard of being overtaken by pedestrians.

Cyclists may believe that in their shorts they are God's gift to the open road, but they have also to realise that once they enter a café, they begin to feel like something which has just crept out of the woodwork.

Wherever you go be prepared to bump into people you know. Like the time we cycled to York and met two snobby acquaintances who looked as if they had just dined with Norman Hartnell, whereas my dusty shorts did nothing to conceal my oil-tattooed legs. As fate determines on such days, we hadn't tainted their path for years, yet an hour later we were under their noses again. This time I was dripping like a used tea-bag. While my hands pulled our rowing boat ashore, my feet had somehow pushed it out again, leaving my rear end in the river. Have you ever tried to follow you irate captain's instructions while you and the rest of the crew are paralysed with laughter? It's a slow body-soaking process.

Aside from the scars, cycling gave me an awareness for which I shall be eternally grateful. That magnificent sight of a no-pedal downhill stretch when your lungs are on the verge of collapse - the wind whistling through your shampoo and set as you speed downhill with your feet up. The bliss of being able to pause mid-pedal and watch a hunting kestrel as I did recently, and being able to get off and walk while cars are throbbing, with traffic light aggro. These are just a scattering of the rewards that come – free of charge – with your first bike or tandem!

*

MY DOG'S days are definitely numbered. Coming up to fifteen years next birthday, he and our sixteen-year-old have grown up together.

They gambolled alongside each other as babies, now they have both reached the same growling stage, snapping their jaws angrily when anyone disturbs them, but sadly he will not grow out of it. No doubt about it – one day soon he will have to go.

He cannot hold his liquor anymore; his incontinence is driving me mad. When a tree is not available he'll make do with one by any other name, such as a chair, table leg, etc. He once disgraced himself by performing a leg-up on my husband's trousers, while he was still inside them. The times I've pleaded with him to let me wash his mouldy old gardening pants!

When the dog mistook him for a clump of rubbish, I could not have put it better myself. Sometimes he limps and wobbles his stiff joints so much as he tries to stand up, he looks a hundred years old. Yet when the wind is in the right direction, he can detect the waft from any seasonal bitch within a mile, with miraculously rejuvenating effects.

I never wanted a black mongrel with non-matching ears and tail and two sandy paws, which he likes to cross over and place in the hearth on cold evenings. I fancied something posh, like a Pekinese. But he looked so cute and cuddly as a pup and the price was exactly right, 'Free to good home.'

In return for free bed and board the last fifteen years, the perpetual ear-caressing from 7pm onwards, I don't kid myself he feels any loyalty towards me. Of course when I'm eating a juicy steak he adores me. He would follow me anywhere – until it was finished. Unlike the majority of pet-pamperers I do not cherish the illusion that he loves me in return.

My dog is acutely intelligent. When husband and me attempted an experiment; my husband pretended to attack me to test dog's reaction, our mongrel rolled over and laughed.

Our canine's coat, glossy as a seal, has only ever been bathed, apart from canal dips, three times. The last because he was lousy and would insist in crouching in uncouth positions of exposure in front of Reggie Bosanquet; feverishly raking the back of his neck with his hind leg, or he would aggressively attempt to nibble his unreachables when visitors were present.

These embarrassing posturings would be accompanied by a syncopated stomping from his non-scratching foot, a stimulating source of amusement when we all joined in one night.

With the aid of some smelly carbolic-like substance from a pet shop I eventually put a stop to this entertainment. Most of his 'cures' came from pet shops or my pill bottles. He hasn't cost us much in vet bills. I hope my teeth are as strong as his are when I reach the same stage. I put his healthy condition down to regularly gnawing on marrow bones.

About the time we were all being urged to travel on an egg, he went a step further and acquired the taste for chicken – alive preferably. He wasn't greedy, one a day would do. Around the seventh day we followed the advice of a farmer friend and tied two chicken corpses around his neck then fastened him up outside. 'You'll see,' our friend promised, 'Leave him there till they rot – he'll never touch another.'

Early next day we visited the doghouse. He had already breakfasted, there was a pile of feathers and four feet left hanging round his neck. But we cured him – we sold the rest of the hens.

The day will surely dawn when someone will have to shh! You know what. But who will nuzzle his silky brow under my hand, whose hot, rough tongue will lick away the midnight movie tears, whose late night stomach gurgles will brighten up Match of the Day, when he's . . . gone? If only he was suffer-ing, passing sentence would be easy. Wouldn't it?
*

PRINCESS Margaret's faux pas at a recent dinner party confirms my own opinion. I refer to the misconception that planned formal dinner parties are fun. Unless you are lucky enough to be among chosen friends, they can be overrated, lonely affairs. Conversation has to be clipped and tailored according to which rung of the ladder you hope to step on next.

Some years ago I had to attend such a gathering. The lush carpeted country inn was teeming with inflated executives. I was introduced to poker-faced strangers and left to chat animatedly with people I would normally avoid like sliced bread.

As wives usually do at these get-togethers, while husbands talk business, I spent most of the evening alone, wondering what had possessed me to accept a cigar, on which I kept puffing merely as an excuse to do something with my hands.

Enveloped in smoke, with a suitably partyish expression on my rapidly greying face, I stood a long as I could. As the need for support increased I made for the nearest object – the piano. The pianist's hands were tripping busily along the ivories. In my fuddled state he looked to be playing a duet.

Gratefully I lunged against the open piano top. I was about to strike up a lightning friendship with the pianist when my cigar inadvertently dropped into the piano works and disappeared.

Mortified, I whispered my dilemma into his ear. Still playing, he nodded sympathetically and said 'Yes please, a gin and tonic.' I hung around waiting for flames to leap out. Nothing happened. My husband returned now and then to replace my empty glass. If he wondered about my sudden obsession with the piano's innards, he never remarked on it. When a trio of stray wives burst into song, not daring to leave the scene of the crime, I made it a quartet. The mystery was never solved and the place is still standing.

On these daunting occasions there is also the problem of being dressed 'properly,' meaning, in the case of females, being clad from head to toe in newly bought. Husband's old party line, 'You always look nice in your blue, love,' doesn't stand a chance.

As a tender teenager I discovered that the danger of being 'run over' was not the only reason why girls should change underwear frequently. This was painfully revealed to me during a naughty party game that we called 'inches.' The boys asked us questions that would have baffled Einstein, and for every question we could not answer we had to raise our skirts an inch - a sort of X-certificate Mastermind.

When my lack of knowledge reached as far as my old fleecy brown school bloomers, I decided my habits would have to change.

American psychologist Dr F Caprio believes that underwear can reveal a person's true character. Efficient businesswomen wear plain white undies. The sexy self-confidents prefer black lace. Women who wear frills want to be dominated.

Men who wear bikini-style underpants are show-off types, out for attention. A man who doesn't take life seriously goes for the gimmicky underwear printed with those laughable suggestions.

Jockey short wearers are open-minded and fair – so says Dr Caprio. Being an old-fashioned girl underneath I'll plump for the down-to-earth type, the family lover – but you'll have to guess what he wears!
*

THE shops have been filled with Christmas stock ever since we returned from summer holidays, but I usually manage to ignore this until after bonfire night.

Once the planning starts, I am swamped by all the other events that sneak alongside. We also have four birthdays and our silver wedding anniversary to be worried through before Christmas dinner.

It is an especially expensive time for students. I scoured the shops with one of our teenagers, trying to find her a Saturday job – no luck. 'How old are you?' one boutique owner asked our 15-year-old. 'Sorry, love, we are looking for Christmas staff, but we need a 16-year-old.' I explained she would be 16 next month, but she was adamant.

We lied about her age at the next shop. 'Sixteen,' we answered. It didn't work. 'Sorry, love, there is a law which states Saturday workers must be seventeen.'

The assistant at the next store apologised for the delay, as she had to climb over huge boxes of Christmas stock waiting to be unpacked. She obligingly rang her superior about our request, while my daughter practised looking eighteen. 'No, and no waiting list either,' was the answer.

At the next stop we were told quite enthusiastically that names were now being taken for next year's list. Finally we gave up trying to be Esther Rantzen and drowned our sorrows in a cup of coffee – after quizzing the staff about Saturday vacancies, first, of course.

On our way home it was depressing to see all the shops decked out with everything money can buy. The magazines offer crafty inexpensive ideas for gifts. Home made luxuries like egg-cosies, toilet-roll covers, even tissue pack covers. One gains endless pleasure from making these, which only recedes when you have to decide who to palm them off on to.

The season's fashionable slit-skirts certainly take the seam sewing out of home dressmaking. There are hardly any about. I don't know whether I am happy about all this leg showing or not. If I were two stones lighter, I'd probably be slashing seams with the rest of them.

I suffer these wild urges occasionally, a sort of last fling at wearing the ridiculous before I am stuck with the sublime. I'd love to turn up at a party wearing a scarlet see-through strapless, slashed to the thigh, with the hip-length hair I never achieved, tumbling over my shoulder. Women in my age group have these fantasies – I understand!

While I was alone with Radio 1 and the washing up last Sunday, I couldn't resist trying out my latest disco routine. Like all experts, I do all my best performances in front of the kitchen mirror. 'Very good, Mrs B,' said the amused voice of daughter's boyfriend, who just happened to be peeping through the banister rails at the time.

*

THIS year will be my twenty-fifth attempt at baking successful Christmas loaves. Last year's efforts were ruined by crunchy currants, euphemistically described as 'seedless' – eating them was like chewing chopped coal. It was embarrassing to hear the crack of tooth on seed as our guests went bravely into the attack.

Being a Christmas bride, coping with festive fare was my first hurdle. Before we married, my mother-in-law had many anxious moments over her son's sensitive stomach; had she seen the punishment it withstood, nay survived during our first year – its strength would have surprised her.

Full husbands are in the habit of enjoying a post-luncheon lie down, mine soon discovered that this was the only way to maintain the concoctions I cooked.

One of my problems was that I always cooked too much. My stews started life in a medium size way, by the time I had added all the ingredients, three pans were bubbling on the stove.

My first Christmas loaf session ended with more mixture than bowl, excluding the sticky blobs hanging from every drawer and cupboard I had contacted in my search for an even larger container. In the end we decided instead of boasting the best fed dustbin in the street, it would be more economical to provide more mouths.

Our first mouth heralded another trial-and-error period. 'Don't waste money on tins of strained baby foods,' was the advice. 'Get a veal knuckle bone and make your own nutritious broth.'

When baby reached the mixed feeding stage, I obediently ordered a veal knuckle bone. My butcher looked quizzical, but promised he would have one ready for my husband to collect at teatime.

At five o'clock a tired daddy staggered in with what appeared to be a dinosaur's jaw bone under his arm. 'What sort of veals had knuckles as big as this' I asked.

None of our pans were large enough to hold it, but with the help of a rolling pin I managed to shatter it and finally hammered it into our pressure cooker. While it spurted like Vesuvius on the oven, I eagerly referred to the chapter on mixed feeding in my baby manual. Let other modern mums hog the homo-genised, my baby deserved the best.

I found the 'on to solids' page and read the words 'one or two teaspoons for the first week.' After extracting this amount, I calculated this would leave us with about four pints of see-through broth.

The first teaspoon was angrily squirted back at me, the second two, formed baby's first bubbles. Around the time of the third boil-up my husband decided this was as good a time as any to declare the aversion to home-made broths and stews and what was wrong with tinned stuff, anyway? Our baby couldn't talk but her eyes carried the same message.

I was fed up with sharing the cooker with this warped knee-joint too, but our bin was already bursting with past specialities de la maison. It was too big to push into our pot-bellied stove, but I set about it with a hammer and eventually succeeded in ramming it through the top. I heard the splutter as gristle met heat, and immediately life took on a new meaning.

Minutes later I was fighting off enormous swirls of acrid, grey smoke. Donning my best leather gloves I struggled to pull the smoking joint through the stove top, but it proved bigger than both of us. My husband had to dismantle the stove later, to retrieve the charred bone. We put the remains to rest in the garden and I bought a tin opener.

*

OCCASIONALLY I allow myself a full-length wallow in front of our bathroom mirror. Believe me, my November image is not a pretty sight. Our recent central heating installation has definitely taken its toll. No heavy shovels to carry, no fire grates to empty, no arguments as to who saw the coal cellar last – in fact no exercise at all.

A simple flexing of finger on button and in every part of our home it is un-believable summer. It's like being permanently swathed in lamb's wool. No need to 'shut that door' or move until supper. Fantastic, especially when the other side of the windows is so miserably rain-splashed. As you will probably have guessed – we haven't had our first bill yet!

My reflection reminds me of the poem, 'O fat white woman whom nobody loves.' What I need is exercise. Cycling is out because (keep it to yourself) I am waiting for someone to mend a puncture. Walking would be all right if you could do it sitting down. The seat on my bike is its most attractive asset, I find.

Still, it worries me to observe how superfluous children's legs are becoming. Every day I see misguided mums chauffeuring their children to and from school. Even babies are denied their pram outings in the fresh air because they spend most of their time strapped to a car seat.

Every Sunday morning my husband used to push our pram around until Yorkshire pud time. Our children knew the route from house to bowling club before they could walk.

Today's riding habit is becoming a serious health threat. I only realised the other day – when I had to stop myself strangling our driver because he parked the car two doors away from the shop I wanted – exactly what a petrol zombie I have become. Yet I often deride friends who shop by car when they only live a ten-minute walk away from our village centre.

Because of today's crime rate we dare not even allow children the after-school freedom to roam that we enjoyed. When I was a child the tea time air was heavy with mothers' voices calling in their young from the surrounding woods and streams. My mother borrowed her sound-off from Tarzan and when she was on the warpath her breath control was magnificent.

My father is a compulsive walker. On the day I was born, it must have been a great disappointment for him to learn it would be another 12 months before I could walk. My sister and I once visualised the way he chose the house we grew up in. He probably stepped off the bus, walked until he dropped, then choked out the words 'This will do Emma, find an empty house, we'll live here.' Everything was always a hike away. We walked two miles to school, and when we arrived home the dreaded note and basket awaited us, meaning another mile long trek to the shop.

Weekends meant a walk from Quarmby to Golcar and tea at my aunt's. A favourite treat was a bus ride to Edgerton Cemetery. After a saunter around the gravestones, with a pause here and a sigh there, the grown-ups would sit on a seat and swap violent deathbed scenes, while my sister and I shared out all the flowers.

One reason I like writing is that you don't use your legs. Since my father retired he is so busy that I have to see him by appointment. I take stock of his 70-year-old sparkling brown eyes, his ruddy ever-smiling face – I wince at his 6am to 10pm energy, and realise he has never taken a sleeping pill in his life. His only panaceas were a spoonful of honey mixed with Old Jamaican and I recall that his mother was still running around at ninety. I then pray it is not too late for me to follow in his footsteps.
*

'ARE you boasting or complaining?' my hairdresser wanted to know when I mentioned my forthcoming silver wedding. I am boasting naturally. In this age when almost everything bears the 'disposable' label, I consider twenty-five years a good innings.

'Have you ever regretted it, dad?' one daughter daringly probed recently. 'Of course he has,' I interfered. His whispered comment in daughter's ear and her responding snigger were not altogether reassuring, so I sought him out later.

I found him up a ladder in our front room. Trying to look coy and dodging the emulsion drips at the same time, I popped the question, 'Wonder what we were doing twenty-five years ago, love?' His answer came in short, sharp brushes. 'I can remember exactly what I was doing.' His paint-splashed face looked grim. 'I was up a ladder painting the ceiling.' Not the ideal moment, perhaps, to introduce a 'This is Your Life' flavour.

I can't recall what I was up to while he was painting the parlour of our first home – probably some vital issue like planning my hen party. I remember our first meeting, as I made my way thirty years ago, towards the printing firm where I started my apprenticeship, thrilled to the 3in hem of my blue overall at the chance to earn thirty bob a week. Eager to learn, I soon became the best tea-maker, pot-washer, fish and chip carrier and joke repeater in the trade.

But fate was waiting to take a hand, for draped over a frame in the composing room was the lad destined to take me away from all this.

It started with our running errands together. King Street will always have sentimental associations for me. Twenty warm pork pies at 3d from the Farm Stores, two dozen iced Swiss-buns from Whiteley's, graduating to shepherd's pie and chips for two at the Kingsway Café and finally the ultimate, back seats at the Tudor Cinema. The last radio programme on Saturday night was Jack Jackson's record show. His signature tune 'Dancing in the Dark' also heralded my parent's bedtime – naturally it soon became our favourite tune.

After a whirlwind courtship, which lasted six years, he finally surrendered and we were married. Over the next fifteen years we welcomed five additions. One consolation of being an overworked, inadequate mother, it leaves less time to be a rotten wife. I have browsed through countless 'successful marriage' manuals written by super couples who pretend they know all the answers. It beats me how anyone dare have the gall when they are in the middle of a marriage themselves.

But I'm hoping its not too late, now the family are almost independent, to concentrate on Old Faithful again, when he comes down from the ladder. It surprises the young to think that the spark is still there after twenty-five years. 'At your age the heyday in the blood is tame' – so spoke Hamlet dis-approvingly to his mother. But I like the remark made by a middle-aged couple on TV: 'It may take longer to climb the mountain but when you reach the summit the view is just the same!' Eat your heart out, Hamlet!

*

SINCE our youngest is now aged 11, it was Father Christmas's last stand at our house last year. This does take some of the pleasure out of the preparations, I admit that, but non-believers still hang up the pillowcases, so there is still the element of surprise to cater for.

Still the five piles to sort out on Christmas Eve, wracking semi-conscious after-party brains at two o'clock in the morning, as to where we hid everything while Santa snores helpfully in his armchair. Then when the sacks have been distributed and we finally hit the sheets, that pleasant nostalgic wallow.

Of Christmases past, when carting prams and bikes up the staircase we wore both ourselves and the decor out, not helped with an unstable Santa often tripping over a sleeping child's slipper. One particular occasion we had to deliver a bike three times. Every time we entered small son's domain with his first two-wheeler, son's eyelids went on the blink – we had to retract quickly. Not easy turning a corner, silently with a non-bendable frame between you, and Father Christmas's vest caught in the pedals.

Time marches on, sleeping son is so well anaesthetised nowadays, the Navy could deliver a battleship without disturbing him.

The doll and pram tradition has altered somewhat. Manufacturers have milked this market to the last detail. Don't put your purse away when you have purchased dolly – this is only the beginning. Next it's all the outfits she needs for her wildly exciting social whirl. Naturally she then needs a wardrobe and furniture, her hair needs regular shampooing with special hair kit, plus a super priced make-up outfit. Latest extravaganza is a car-drawn fully equipped caravan, no less.

We all have our own feelings about this 'peace to all' season. Some refuse to be influenced by it.

To one of our teenagers it means 'no school' and 'I like it – it's just that I never have enough money.' 'All I can think about are my A-level exams after Christmas,' moans another. 'I love all the visitors and food,' beams our youngest, a renowned washer-up skiver.

No need to ask son who celebrates every weekend, regardless, and I know husband hasn't recovered from the phone bill - but I can't help it. I love all the sparkle and glitter, stuffing myself and sleeping it off in front of a TV spectacular, sending cards to all and sundry and trimming the tallest tree I can afford.

I used to love the school Nativity play – now inadequately replaced by a communal church service. It was comforting to watch young Joseph and Mary wave proudly to their mums, the Three Wise nine-year-olds, grinning wickedly beneath their bath towels. I miss hearing the carol singers outside my door, although I made them earn their reward.

My Christmas starts with our candlelit chapel service. I like to grip the true spirit first and go on from there, savouring every merry, matey moment. Meeting up with relatives, making a fool of myself at parties, cooking rich food, opening presents – all washed down with a glass or three of my favourite wine.

Of course I blame being hooked on Christmas on my father. He started it by giving us all those unforgettable fun Christmases year after year. Now I find I just can't give it up!

1980

AS WE step over the threshold of a brand new unopened New Year, one cannot resist just a tiny glance over the old.

Looking back to the summer that never really arrived, our ladies had a happy bowling season, adding a legacy of laughs to our sporting repertoire. This did not win us any cups of course, but it means we do climb down into a lower division, with a smile on our lips.

On the home front my husband had to break the news 'Howard has had an accident – don't panic' three time last year. Our son is so accident prone, he says when he enters 'casualty' the staff all smile in welcome, 'Hi, Howard, how many this time, lad?'

During the Christmas shopping bustle a ranting granny attacked me. I was just browsing along wondering what I could buy, when this pensioner ambles up to me. Putting on my help the aged expression I wished her the seasonal compliments, whereupon she swings back her arm and deals me a swipe across the neck, which made my eyeballs flutter.

'Didn't you retaliate?' my family wanted to know afterwards. I described the dirty look I gave her as I ran away.

'That'll teach her,' said son, 'She won't do it again.' 'Poor old thing,' commented my mother when I showed her my bruises, 'She must have been off her rocker.'

To anyone wavering in the marriage stakes, keep going for the silver, it is worth it. Through this column I would like to thank everyone for the delightful cards, the flowers and the presents. I hope I may be forgiven for saying that the moment that brought the biggest lump to my throat was when our son and four daughters made father and me sit down while they paraded their gifts – a king size quilt, complete with matching cover, sheet and pillowcases. We are so wrapped up in it – time simply has no meaning. And I love husband's daily announcement, 'I've made the bed, love!'

Yes, it's lovely, thanks, and so is eating from unchipped crockery, with matching cutlery, drinking coffee served from a silver pot, cooking with straight-bottomed pans and reading the tear-jerking sentiments over and over again.

The biggest surprise came as husband and I were leaving home to join our guests at the party hotel. I was about to lock up when he said 'Oh you had better take a nightie.' His way of telling me he had also booked the bridal suite for us. Bet there aren't many brides who enter the honeymoon portals with their night attire tucked in a plastic supermarket carrier bag!!
*

THE family were discussing the recent Pools winner, 'Poor chap,' was my husband's retort, 'Whatever will he do with £800,000?' I kept my mouth shut. Our exchequer has not received our festive grand total yet, so he can afford to be naïve.

Although half of me retains an intrinsic working class attitude – that money which has not been earned cannot be enjoyed – the other half would certainly have a high old time with a few thousand before conscience set in.

I could pay off all our debts, keep the central heating on all night, and burn my husband's paintbrushes. Refurnish from attic to cellar with priceless antiquities, and fit our dining room with a shag-pile carpet deep enough to conceal our dog, so my husband wouldn't need to kick him out.

We could dutifully install the grandparents in a heated coastal bungalow, surrounded by arable acres, and buy my dad a lumber yard so he could knock up hen huts to his heart's content. Philip Rickman's book 'A Selection of Bird Paintings and Sketches' would sit on my bookshelf, not because I am a frustrated ornithologist, but I'd simply love to own a book that costs £450.

There is no end to the luxury in which we could wallow. Our students would be rigged out with a complete school uniform – in triplicate – no more blouses steaming on radiators, plus full sporting kit, something we never managed to attain.

Our 11-year-old would be educated privately. Believe me, this would take priority. We could set up a trust fund for all our offspring with . . . certain con-ditions of course. One would be that they never regard pa and me as being unlovable.

Oh boy, it would be extravagance all the way. The horizons are almost unimaginable, our cavernous freezer stocked to the brim at last, and a general dogsbody to take over my duties so my 'I'm off,' threat could eventually become reality. I could actually visit my sister in Australia, and can you visualise the supreme ecstasy of looking at price tickets – after you got the article home?

I would make sure my beloved had his heart's desires, a market garden and a country pub, before I set off for Paris, New York or India. Robert Robinson would not be the only one to slide off an elephant into a maharajah's palace, if I were a rich man.

Should all this richness give me indigestion, spending on others may ease the strain. I could provide an elderly friend with a private nurse and chauffeured Rolls. The nurse would perform the injections, which are a daily dread for her own gnarled arthritic fingers. The Rolls would take her to all the places she wants to go but hasn't the strength.

Perhaps I had better not dwell on the aged or handicapped, because £800,000 could soon be frittered away on putting new heart into them. Such frivolities would soon wipe out a fortune. I did once win £100, three-quarters of which I used to re-cover our suite. The rest went on a family dine-out. Feeling like Paul Getty I swaggered to the bar with my order, 'a champagne cocktail.' If I had demanded a glass of milk the barman couldn't have looked more stunned. I returned red-faced with my usual lager and lime. How was I to know barmen were not enthusiastic about opening bottles of champagne for one cocktail? This never happened in the books I read.

Ah well, back to reality. Cornwall's not so bad early season – is it?
*

A TEACHER of mine, who had the esteemed honour of holding my attention for whole minutes at a time, once informed us that the small paragraphs in newspapers always contain the most interesting news.

Every morning we queued at his desk with torn off flaps of black and white. Consequently, these vital snips catch my eye first whenever I pick up a newspaper.

Today I learn for instance that Dr Arthur Klatsky, of the Oakland California Medical Centre says, after intensive research naturally, there is strong evidence that drinking moderately may reduce heart attacks.

What decent doctors some patients have. Imagine being handed a prescription for a drop of what you fancy three times a day. I believe some do have super understanding GPs.

321

An acquaintance of mine was recently ordered to bed for complete rest. 'No cooking, no cleaning – let your family look after you for a change,' was her doctor's prescription.

Now that is what I call expert medical advice, difficult to acquire these days. I mean, how ill does one have to be to qualify for such treatment?

Many's the time I've hinted that a week in bed would do the trick, usually to my doctor's lowered lids as he scrawls out some scientific cure.

The clue to my condition must lie in the way I say 'hello,' because one astute GP sitting in for my regular doctor once, handed over a completed prescription before I was half-way through my symptoms.

Once I was so desperately incapacitated with what felt like a fractured throat, I expected nothing less than a fortnight's bed rest. Mind you I didn't realise how fast I was sinking until I looked up my symptoms in a lethal Home Medical tome, which I am surprised does not carry a government health warning.

On my way to the throat section, I happened to thumb through the lung disorders, discovering there was a possibility I had also contacted 'Black Lung.' In the heart section I realised my heartbeat was in danger of reaching mortuary pitch, deteriorating with every word I read in fact. By the time I reached 'throats' I was almost too weak to lift the phone, I didn't know who to ring first, the doctor or the undertaker.

'Just carry on with the tablets,' smiled my doctor. No mention of moderate alcohol or feet-up therapy. Of course they don't put us to bed anymore, not like they did in the old days.

Waiting room conversations have advanced drastically, too. Once we swapped coughs and sniffs, now with the wonder drugs there's no end of im-portant diseases you can walk around with.

You cannot even lie in after an operation. Before you know it you are in your slippers and propped in a chair. Have you ever walked into a surgical ward at bed-making time? Not a pretty sight. It looks like a dressing gown sale. These garments appear to be draped everywhere. On closer inspection though you can see they contain tiny, shrunken post-operative faces, all peering longingly in one direction – towards their beds.

But it's better for the blood you see. I am frightened that one day sick beds may become obsolete. The 'How to look after your doctor' notices in surgeries may be replaced by 'Operations while you wait.' Or we could all be sitting outside a garage somewhere under a different sign. 'Have you had your ten year test?' Bionic parts re-serviced here!!

THE skies are grey, the gardens look washed out, Rita has deserted husband, Len Fairclough, yet I find this a hopefully exhilarating time of year.

There's a lot of work to be done in that favourite armchair. Gardeners can fill their pipes and browse through the growing manuals. Scholars can pause before the shock of their mock-exam results. Lady bowlers can contemplate intriguing new ways of camouflaging their bulges, and our holiday deposit is on its way to the Isle of Wight.

Before long I shall be able to start all my days with a copy of the holiday promises propped up against the coffee pot. I am a sucker for the brochure prophecies. 'Wonderful unrivalled views,' 'heated throughout,' 'nestling under a cliff,' are all guaranteed to set me reaching for a stamp. Somehow I never work up the same interest in the foreign brochures, the photos all look alike to me. Open any page whether it is Ibiza, Malta or Portugal, you see the same tall white blocks set against turquoise sky with a swimming pool or two featured in the foreground. Even the swimmers look identical.

After all the bad publicity last year, air strikes, hotels that disappear once you've paid your money, the only thing guaranteed is sunshine, and then not always. Freak weather was a torment everywhere last season.

When I was young we never pored over brochures. Until we saw the tip of Blackpool Tower sail into the top corner of our train window, we lived on our memories from the previous year. We did not have to wonder what sort of bed and board awaited us, every year we visited the same digs, a homely board residence tucked between a row of look-alike doors and windows on a narrow back street.

Every morning we had a long bout of spade trailing before we reached the prom end of Lytham Road, and our daily ride through 'Fairyland,' a child's delight of illuminated clockwork elves and fairies at two old pennies a time. By the time we had crossed the tramlines and queued for deck chairs – it was usually dinnertime.

Since I had my family, we have often holidayed in sea-front cottages. You, the children, beach gear and food can be on the sands for 8.30. Dinner can seem a painfully long way off – sometimes. When we do discover the idyllic we are reluctant to part. When all the family went along, we couldn't stop going to the Pembrokeshire coast. In the same way we never face the disastrous twice. At the moment Rhyl, Bridlington and Devon are off our list.

Rhyl – because we discovered our 'superb luxury flat' was as desirable as our rabbit hutch. Brid made our son bawl for a week. We blamed it on Bridlington anyway, that and our landlady's face. She could do frown and disgust, but she had never mastered smiling.

Devon was a great disappointment after Wales. Our 'sea view' also included a railway line, go-kart circuit and caravan site.

Being able to holiday early and late season is an advantage we often share with pensioners. One such lady kept me on my toes for a week when we stayed in adjacent caravans at Lydstep Haven. Every morning I watched her brush out her hair rollers and powder her nose before the early toilet trip. Me, the original 'Woman in a dressing gown,' was still trying to gather enough co-ordination to plug the kettle in.

By the time I looked fit to face my public she was already pegging out her smalls. When her husband emerged at mid-day, shopping was completed, and a delicious smelling lunch was on the table. A picnic tea, which they liked to eat on the headland above the bay, was packed in the boot followed by a stroll to the pub, then a coastal breather hand in hand, and so to bed. This is one vital ingredient holiday brochures leave out – a good mate.

*

ONE of the advantages of having children is the relief you enjoy when they are temporarily not there. A whole day uncontaminated by one's offspring can seem truly delightful.

In order to gain full benefit you need to be pretty well bogged down by these dominating little darlings first, of course. Like banging your head con-tinuously on that open cupboard door, it's lovely when you shut it.

This is why I look upon my husband's periodic days off – when we plan all manner of childless pursuits together – as brief lifesavers.

On one of his mystery tours we finished up eating chicken from a basket in an ancient country pub somewhere near Halifax. If I wondered about my husband and publican being on first name terms, I kept my mouth shut. Later I learned it was a watering hole for his bowling team when in the vicinity.

This week we took our picnic to an auction. An esoteric sale of pottery, porcelain, silver, jewellery and old furniture. Naturally I completed the necessary first, I popped a casserole in the oven, only the chips to fry when we returned. This is the next best thing to having tea made for you, a fall-out from baby days. On our busy shopping days I used to leave jacket potatoes baking on the top shelf, sausages sizzling underneath and a rice pudding simmering in the oven bottom. When you stagger back home the welcoming smell which rushes to greet you is worth the few minutes' preparation.

We arrived at the draughty saleroom ten minutes before eyes down, to find most of the furniture occupied. Under clouds of pipe smoke and pork-pie hats, stern faced dealers sat a-brooding. I managed to find myself a chair about two inches from the floor that no one else had managed to fold their frame into. With my knees so near my nostrils, I felt a bit like a grasshopper.

This was a sale with a difference for us, because we had someone else's money to play with. Our son-in-law had given us permission to bid up to £100 for a piece of Japanese bric-a-brac he fancied. Just in front of my eyeballs the glass and silver sparkled expensively, but if my bank balance looked healthier the dignified old furniture, which looked as if it had been polished lovingly for decades, would have my vote.

A damsel nearby was soon buying silver as if it was gold. Her fingers were all bound to the tip in huge Victorian rings, a handicap at coffee times I noted, but she never imbibed.

It's easy to feel one 'knows nowt about owt' with all the nodding and winking that goes on for items you wouldn't give house room. Two pewter plates, looking like the old junk our children made their mud pies on, fetched £50. Just as surprising, a beautiful mahogany sideboard sold for only a fiver.

Selling the 330 lots was serious business; I was bound to giggle at the auctioneer and his clerk turning their heads from left to right in complete harmony, rather like a vaudeville duo, as they followed the bids. He didn't waste time, his advances leapt upwards in tens, four nods and you were often into a hundred. 'This is very trying, sir,' a chap was admonished when he kept offering bids only £1 higher.

One item was described in the catalogue as 'important pair of Worcester vases.' We discovered why when they were sold for £1,300.

At this climax in the proceedings, I also discovered my chair had wheels. As I bent forward to oggle, it ran out of control. I shot forth at high speed knocking a table over, shocking two old gents, nearly chopping a woman's finger off and raising the auctioneer's left eyebrow.

Ah, but what an honour it must be when his highness the auctioneer knows one's name without having to ask first. It makes one feel so humble to note the recognition, as he scribbles down a dealer's name automatically following a sale. None of the 'What name did you say?' and 'Spell it, please,' we ordinary mortals have to suffer, which makes you feel as if you stepped off another planet.

Eventually 'our' objet d'art was held up for all to view. 'Right,' smiled the auctioneer, 'Shall we start the bidding at – say £100 for this item?' He didn't stop until he reached £310, leaving us speechless – and art-less!

READING about dear old Sandy Powell celebrating his 80th birthday reminded me of when the old Palace Theatre was still alive and well, echoing with top variety acts like Sandy, Jimmy James, Max Miller, the pianist Semprini, singers, dancers and even dramatic actors reciting lines from Shakespeare.

Every Saturday mum, dad, sister and I enjoyed our shillings worth in the front row of the balcony. Entertainment was rife in Huddersfield at that time. We seemed to have cinemas on every corner and a first-class repertory company at the Theatre Royal.

I was an avid cinema-goer from the age of six – but there is an indefinable magic in seeing live performances, which I am sorry my own children miss. No wonder some of us were stage struck. 'What did you really want to be when you left school?' my boss once asked me when it was evident I was in the wrong job.

'A film star,' I answered straight away. She eventually stopped laughing and tried again. But I was serious, I had only sniffed the greasepaint in a small way but, had I not met my husband to be, I would probably still be on the front row of the chorus, waiting for my big break.

Ah yes, I can hear the sniggers. But I have rubbed shoulders with the famous. Hughie Green stood in front of me once when he was looking for talent in our theatre dressing room. I provoked Albert Modley into changing his script when we were both appearing at the Leeds Empire; and I was a Carroll Levis discovery! Only when he discovered me he didn't know what to do with me. But that's another story.

The Saturday nights at the Palace triggered it all off when my sister and I would curl our naked knees into scarlet plush, playing guess the adverts from the front cloth until the supreme moment when the white-gloved MD raised his baton and the splendour began.

We didn't need a programme to tell us the dancers came first and the star always followed our tubs of ice cream. We chuckled over acts like the armless man we once saw who lit a cigarette with a match held between his toes. Whenever jugglers, balancing acts or singers appeared, my sister and I excused ourselves and went and explored the theatre.

Most popular on our list was the strong man/frightened female act. A huge bemuscled ox-like man in satin trousers, usually bald, would crack his bull-whip repeatedly while his dainty mate would cringe all over the stage. Cymbals crashed and purple lights flashed. We loved it, I couldn't wait to get home to my whip and top and try it on my sister.

Later on, when I was in panto at the Theatre, our show included a similar act. Night after night we peeped from the wings as he swung his delicate damsel gracefully above his head, then threw her like an empty pop can into a corner, where she spun in ever-decreasing revolutions on her navel until he picked her up and threw her somewhere else.

Curious as to their off-stage relationship, we wondered if he was really so cruel. We chorus girls used to hang around their dressing room listening for clues. Silence. His autograph in my book was even more puzzling. He scrawled 'May God keep you in the palm of His Almighty hand.' Was he a Bishop – resting we pondered.

Ah well, that's show biz.!

*

HAVE you been watching the effervescent Barbara barking out canine commands on BBC television's Training Dogs the Woodhouse Way? Doggy-love oozes from her tongue as she bounds around laughing and panting at her learner puppies to 'Come – sit – stay.'

It's the owners who come in for some reprimanding. 'Oh do move your dog away from that nasty puddle, dear,' one handler was admonished. She couldn't have looked guiltier if she had left the watery message herself.

The healthy looking 70-year-old Mrs Woodhouse was quoted recently as saying she is in fact never ill. She believes in freezing germs to death. If you want to cure flu her advice is to get out in the cold, which viruses detest, and they will immediately depart to pounce on the cosseted and cosy, in their sick beds.

One can imagine her on a bitingly frosty morn, ensconced on a breezy hill top bringing her germs gloriously to heel: 'Go – now – at once! There's a good virus.'

Although I applaud her efforts, personally I believe training animals is easy. I am living in hope that one day some terrifically overpowering personality will give us a weekly session or two on how to train and control adolescents. Just simple commands for a start, like 'Sit, stay, turn it down.'

I would love to see mine react as docilely as our dog to my suggestions; indeed I am prone to contemplating more and more of late what quality my life may hold if, say, I had chosen to have five dogs instead of five children?

No more brain-rotting breakfast quizzes: 'Where's my biology book, skirt, comb, games kit and bus fare?' 'Why don't we get Swiss cereal anymore?' 'Because this week you had new socks and luxuries like new bras, pants and socks have to come from somewhere.' And of course dogs never interrupt your pep talk on economy cuts with irrelevant questions like 'How much did your hair cut cost then?' Or spend hours on the phone oohing and ahing over friends' new outfits, and then sit gazing despondently

327

at 'old' shoes that cost twenty quid last Saturday, before demanding pathetically 'Mum, why are we so poor?'

At least dogs would not cry heart-brokenly on teacher's shoulder, like my youngest did recently, sobbing unmercifully because 'My mum's just made me a new suit and – sniff – sob – I don't like it.'

I have this cruel streak you see. I sit up all night sewing expensive velvet into a trouser-suit, in order to enjoy the look of complete loathing on daughter's face when she tries it on the morning after.

I am just as heartless in the kitchen. Instead of giving them their favourite meat and two veg, day after day, I go to sadistic lengths preparing Italian pasta with rich nutritious sauce, all for the pleasure of seeing the suicidal expressions when I explain that, no, Lasagne is not garnished with Yorkshire pud.

There is no limit to my meanness. How can I suggest my teenagers wear the same disco outfit twice! I mean, who wants to dance opposite someone in the blinding semi-darkness wearing the same trousers one wore last Saturday? 'Why can't a woman be more like a man?' asks Henry Higgins. But why can't children be like dogs, say I?

Happy footnote: My 15-year-old pet dog was on his last legs seven days ago. Thankfully next door's bitch saved his life. She came into season at the weekend – he looks ten years younger already!
*

'WHEN people ask what is it like to be over 50, I can't tell them,' said Katie Boyle in a Sunday newspaper interview recently.

Aged 53 and newly married to her third husband, the wealthy impresario Peter Saunders, she can't tell us what being over 50 feels like because, she confesses, she doesn't feel her age.

Katie has the sort of natural beauty one wants to fire cream pastries at. Famed for her advice to magazine readers, the Marchese Caterine Imperiali de Francavilla, to give her the title she was born to, offers words of wisdom on how to cope with the menopause. She tells us she ignored it.

'If I get hot flushes, I just fan myself, I have several which I keep close at hand.' She certainly has my admiration; and if I had the sort of friends who wouldn't bat an eyelid if I selected a fan and wafted myself every half-hour, I should certainly try this.

I realise, too late, I have been treating this menopause all wrong. Instead of ignoring my glowing facial transformations – the colourful transition from pale porridge to pink, pink to puce, then when you reach scalp lift-off back to pale cod again – my friends and I fall about laughing, which usually triggers a repeat.

328

My family is becoming quite experienced at ignoring the 'bursting into tears' syndrome. This is the part I confess I like least. When you are trying to command a ship, tears do nothing for one's superiority. Although I'm working on it, the unexpected variety is even harder to bear.

For instance, I have been producing technicolour washing quite accidentally for years, and I still don't know why husband's white vest suddenly turned powder-puff pink, while daughter's pink lingerie finished up sludge grey.

Withering comments are just something I have learned to live with, yet in the middle of a well-rehearsed defence the other day, concerning a pair of burgundy-tinged blue jeans, all of a sudden I am crying like a baby.

Still, tears are recommended as a beautifier, and are purported to leave the eyeballs sparkling clear. If they could squirt to the ground without touching my skin, I might indulge more often.

Experimenting with make-up can be rejuvenating, but it's a pity one cannot be allowed to walk around in daylight for a few hours to test before buying.

I admired the peachy silk tones of my new moisturiser in the kitchen mirror last week. Then, as is my wont, I sneaked another peep at my refection in a pan lid in the hardware shop window. What a transformation! Was that radiant orange sun really me? Every time I spoke to anyone I had to either blow my nose a lot or stand in the shade. So it was particularly surprising to be told by an old school chum, 'You never look any older.'

By only using half a squelch of make-up I have managed to regulate my New Guinea fever look to a modest Bridlington beige.

Naturally, I intend to continue wearing it!

*

ONE hundred and twenty million Americans are a total of 1.444m lbs over-weight, which sounds like a lot of hamburgers.

If you are struggling to eat thin for spring, statements like that don't help, because you can't resist the feeling that surely all those people can't be wrong. How do the successfully slim manage it? How do they maintain their whispy waistline? They have to start somewhere, and I guess it is in front of the mirror after a bath before they have pulled themselves together.

Very often behind a sylph-like wife towers a tough but proud husband. 'Hey Fatty,' some helpfully encourage. Mrs A Turton, of Wombwell, weighed a solid 17stone until her husband offered to pay her a pound cash for every pound weight she lost. Today, she is a jubilant 10stone and husband says it was worth every penny.

My friend, Mrs P, whom I will describe as 'cuddly' because I value her friendship decided to take her weight problem to a hypnotist. I did a Mike Parkinson on her recently, a sort of probe between the layers, over a couple of slim-line lagers. What prompted you to take this vast step Mrs P? Well I'm just fat and I don't want to be.

But was there a moment you can remember vividly, when you said to yourself, I can't go on, I must be slim? No, I just felt bloated and blown up. How much did you weigh? A lot. Come on Mrs P, how much. No, I'm not telling you.

Well I didn't break any sound barriers there, so let's face it, Mike Parkinson can breathe easy - his job is safe.

Anyway, Mrs P's excess was enough to drive her to the eyes of a hypnotist who, for a fee, puts her into a relaxed position every Saturday, and then tells her she must only eat three small meals per day, definitely no nibbling in between.

He has been telling her this every week since Christmas, and she feels it is working. She obediently shed half a stone quite painlessly during the first few sessions, but now admits it's dragging a bit. Back to Mrs P, and another couple of slim-lines please, luv.

Has the rest of the family made any comments on your efforts? If I wrote it in large letters on a 6ft placard and hung it on the wall, they wouldn't notice. When we were going up the path the other night my husband did say 'If you are losing any weight, I haven't noticed it yet.'

At first the talk-ins were on a weekly basis, now she has a three week rest in between. Her Zvengali probably feels she has digested the basic message by now and just needs 'topping up' every three weeks.

I know Mrs P has tried various methods and still remains her cuddly jocular self. One year she attempted to lose a little extra for charity, but her husband begged her to fatten-up – her over-developed temper was reducing him to tears. I wish her the best of luck in her efforts, and if she does eventually reach her target I promise to publish her photo as my slimmer of the year. How's that for an incentive, Mrs P?

If all else fails, remember that an efficient worker is more likely to become overweight than his less productive co-worker is. The former spends less energy at his job while the latter burns up calories working around his task. A California University came up with that little gem – sounds like a load of hamburgers to me!

IT'S only 4ins long and hasn't been a member of our family for a week, yet already my husband is making a fool of himself over Houdini, our baby hamster.

After our last pet catastrophe, when one of our guinea pigs decided to add his mate's head to his diet, I vowed never again. Thank goodness I discovered his voracious appetite in time. How often had I snuggled his warm little nose under my chin, innocently unaware of his carnivorous thoughts that were probably festering between his perky little ears.

I resisted our youngest daughter's lies I've heard before, 'I'll feed him, clean him, trail the sawdust home, etc.' But a hamster seemed the only answer when she accused me of providing all our other children, except her, with a baby sister or brother.

I put my foot down concerning his living quarters. In spite of the tears, Houdini will have to be satisfied with his bungalow. I refuse to be bullied into buying one of the plastic two-tier hyper-expensive, upstairs, downstairs residences, one mortgage is enough.

Then of course it needs an exercise wheel. I rush with everyone else when it wakes up, to watch it pedal frantically, but it seems so undignified. Like circus elephants being forced to sit on chairs. 'Look how happy he looks,' daughter reassures.

Admittedly it has an open-mouthed glazed-eyed expression, but who wouldn't after all that treadling. Occasionally he misses a step and gets catapulted to the side of the cage. Mind you when the wheel has been creaking continuously for an hour, I have to suppress an urge to nudge him off, when no one's looking, hoping for a non serious coma.

'He needs a hamster fun boot,' daughter suggested. This item is an orange plastic 'Mother Shoe' boot with a hole marked 'in' at the toe and one marked 'out' at the heel. Beware! Unless hamster can read this brings no joy.

The other night my husband, whose only concession to pet pampering is to put his slippers on when he kicks the dog out, surprised us all when he sauntered into the dining room carrying Houdini carry-cot style in his plastic boot. Two minutes later hamster is lying shamelessly on his back giggling like Esther Rantzen while dad tickles his tum.

Alas – then Houdini made his first mistake, he crawled out of the hole marked 'in.' Well he tried to, but it was like squeezing a tube of toothpaste. All the contents slipped to the back, no matter how he squirmed and squeaked, he was well and truly stuck. Our daughter hasn't screamed so much since I refused to let her wear her new split skirt for school. 'Oh daddy – get it out,' she pleaded, as poor Houdini, sadly not living up to his name, swung head first from the boot pawing the air like a trapezist whose partner is late.

Then it happened. Suddenly pet-loving dad is dancing around with boot and hamster dangling from his finger. 'Yaroooo . . . !' and other inspired fractures of language scorched the air, but hammy's teeth were firmly sunk in flesh. He let go of bloodied finger after a bounce on the floor and crawled quickly away, as quickly as he could that is with a boot attached to his rear.

We tried everything to rescue him. Dad sawed with a bread knife while I covered animal's eyes with a pot towel. No luck – and scissors made no impact either. Eventually my husband snapped it in two with the pliers – the boot I mean.

We were all extremely happy. But what happens now – will he get blood poisoning? Should we have given him something for the pain?

And perhaps my husband ought to have an injection too!

*

'YOU are like me – as long as it is all right at the front you're not bothered about the back.' This remark was intended to complement my new hairstyle and the bearer and I, believe it or not, are still friends.

Do you ever have difficulty in expressing yourself? Do the words you intend to say often undergo a strange metamorphosis on the journey from brain to mouth – so that you finish up saying one thing but mean another? Well, join the club, it happens to us all, young or old.

I was a teenager when I amused a bus load by asking for 'two to tango' thereby repeating the lyric of a current pop-song instead of ordering two tickets to town. At the scruffy age of twelve I left a fish shop clientele with suspicious looks on their faces when I absentmindedly chanted our family night cap 'Goodnight and God bless,' as I left with my chips.

Even perfectionist Robin Day has his muddled moments. Not long ago I saw him make a right muck-up while introducing his panel for a television question programme. 'Well I have a very mixed bag with me tonight,' he growled, turning immediately to the charming lady guest on his left, 'Miss Margaret Macdonald, of Scotland.' While the audience heartily applauded, Miss Macdonald quickly recovered to waste a forgiving smile on the abrasive Robin, who was already grunting at his next guest.

He hadn't noticed his innuendo but Margaret and I had. I'd like to bet she did an efficient job of reminding him afterwards.

Newspaper bereavement announcements are always sad, but I saw one recently which read doubly tragic. It concerned an elderly lady who 'died suddenly after much suffering at her daughter's residence.' One can only imagine the trials she underwent under daughter's eagle eye.

Some mistakes are better left alone. My husband and I were undergoing much suffering at our son's school once, during a parent's evening. Being informed by his tutor what an accomplished comedian he was and how every-body loved him even though he had no future was beginning to take its toll. So it was quite a pleasant surprise to be told by one teacher that his work showed great promise; indeed his report was so glowing, we dared to stop counting the floorboards for once and actually met teacher's eye. I only just controlled an impulse to press my lips to his Doc Marten's as we left. 'Yes – I wish there were more hardworking lads like your Richard,' he beamed.

Actually our lad's name is Howard – but it seemed a shame to spoil a beautiful friendship.

But we all make mistakes like the New York prostitute who sidled up to corpulent actor and wit Robert Morley and cooed 'Hey big boy, where are you going?' 'Actually I'm going to Australia – to play Alec Guinness's role in the Old Country' was his answer.

The recent report concerning the doctor, who decided to swap his trousers for a skirt, sounds a desperately tragic confusion. Certainly this should not alter his/her medical status. Yet understandably some patients felt the need to make a transfer. My sympathy is for the doctor, but I confess that if my doctor turned up in a frock my worst problem would be keeping my face straight.

*

PEOPLE who complain live longer – the passive are more likely to die first. Doctors have discovered that among the elderly, it's the complainers who outlive the submissive.

So stop taking things in your stride, start living now – go out and nag at somebody today. At least we needn't worry about the young being short-lived if my mutinous brood are any indication, they could prove immortal. The problem is my generation were not brought up to complain. At home and at school we were taught to endure – or else. Every Sunday it was taken for granted my sister and I would stand for tea, if we had company. Not just out of respect - we hadn't enough chairs.

When the ice cream man rang his bell it was always penny cornets for us kids and twopenny wafers for the adults. I only argued once – that afternoon I didn't get my cornet.

Complaining was classed as being cheeky. Great store was set by having good manners, being courteous, being seen and not heard. It was important to create a good impression on our elders. Virtues that are apparently on the decline today, freedom and noise seem to take priority. Authorities bend over backward protecting our youth from any sort of distress. Yet overcoming adversity is one of the greatest character builders I know.

Working mothers are blamed for their children's misdemeanours. It has become fashionable to excuse young 'latch key' rebels, because they are bored. What is to stop them getting on with some housework or shopping or perhaps cooking mum's tea for a change?

My mum had to work to support us during the war. It was the blight of my life having to clean out the grate and light the fire and lay the table before she came home at 5 o'clock while my mates were out getting into all sorts of trouble. In my opinion it's the hardworking mum who needs pampering.

So I must admit I have had to learn the subtle art of complaining. One of my relatives is an expert at putting down the ignorant. When she was tired of waiting for an insolent young draper to finish chatting up his girlfriend once, she eventually leaned across the counter and politely said, 'Awfully sorry to interrupt, I know having to serve customers must make conversations so frustrating – DO YOU MIND!'

This attitude works better than a frayed temper approach. When one of my daughters came home in her new shoes, leaning like the Tower of Pisa, I tried it on a shoe shop manager. 'The heels are pointing the wrong way and she has only worn them at weekends' I complained. 'Just for discos?' he grinned sar-castically. That remark put an end to my courteous cover-up. To cut a long battle short, my final spluttering was 'Are you calling me a liar?'

The blood was galloping round my eyeballs now, he had the sort of 'I'm in charge' composure which made you want to run your fingers through his rows of tidy shoes, then throw them at him one by one. I was really at my complaining peak when he suddenly disappeared through a gap in the shoe boxes. Surprisingly he did not return with a copper, but presented me with a new pair of shoes.

'And tell them you want your money back,' my family advised me from their armchairs as I obediently toddled back with our hamster's fun boot; which had almost put our pet in a wheelchair for life when he got stuck in it. The pet shop manageress was so humble I needn't have splashed out on a packet of chewing gum, normally a valuable confidence booster.

Funny how things turn out. There she is pleading with me to take the money, there am I saying – no – it's not that – and of course it is not you fault. I know, I know, my passivity is killing me!

334

WILL someone tell me why our television dancers have stopped dancing? And why anyone should imagine the libidinous rubbish which has gradually replaced it, should be regarded as family entertainment.

Watching Kenny Everett with our family, including our 11-year-old, is always an embarrassment for me because I find him as funny as Monday morning; but when the steamy 'Hot Gossip' make their entrance, that's when I really start squirming. Instead of the bright and snappy routines we used to expect from a dance group, now all they do is writhe around the stage wet-lipped, open-mouthed and performing pelvic contortions.

Gone are the healthy smiles, all now wear similar pained expressions. Still, having to gambol around in underwear four sizes too small, which threatens to be swallowed up entirely by some of the cheeky antics, must take its toll.

Soggy bottom lips are popular in these routines and helps if you can look hungry enough to eat the camera all the time. Uncontrolled cleavage is another feature of these exhibitions, I swear some of those titillating tops are surely glued on. But any performer who can gyrate the head continuously and not walk into the next girl, or tip the pelvis in all directions without doing themselves a mischief, deserves something I suppose, even if it's only a pair of crutches.

Dancing, as we knew it seems to be going out of style. When I was a chorus girl, success meant being an accomplished ballet, tap or musical comedy performer. We didn't have to body-throb to the beat, but we managed to be quite entertaining in our tap shoes and sailor suites. Our teacher once confided that when she was in competitions, the adjudicator used to sit under the stage where all the tap beats could be clearly heard. Today when 'Foxy Feeling' and 'Hot Gossip' throb their way on to our screen during 'family' shows, I feel like creeping under the stage myself.

One can only imagine what qualities television dancers require nowadays. 'Right dear, how many provocative ways can you perch on a stool?' Say what you like, I loved the Tiller Girls with their high kicks and normal expressions.

I wonder what will happen to the large wardrobe baskets that used to hold the costumes backstage, outfits will probably be tucked neatly into a handbag now.

Our beloved Saddler's Wells has also been infiltrated by the modernistic scourge according to a recent television programme, which showed ballet dancers crawling all over each other liked depraved snakes, with weird voices chanting instead of music.

A wild-eyed choreographer talked a lot about 'emotive feelings' and 'images,' he must have known what he was talking about, I certainly didn't.

When a be-tighted Prince tripped across the stage behind an arm-waving ballerina, we knew where we were. If we didn't, the movements were so beautiful and the music so stirring it didn't matter, we were entertained.

Isn't that what we pay for?

*

'IT WON'T be long now,' a strange face whispered at me as I sat in our car a fortnight ago in town. At least I thought she was a stranger until she explained: 'The bowling season, you dope!'

Then I remembered straight away, she was a 'round-pegger' from Almond-bury or was it Golcar? That's the way we lady bowlers remember each other from season to season, by our shape and form.

We become 'that big corner-bowler' or 'her with the voice and teeth,' or even 'that flat-footed, big-chested, thin-faced woman who can't bowl.'

And so with the frost nibbling hungrily on our double-wrapped dimensions, we ladies are treading the turf once again. It's goodbye to the mid-day snoring trio in my kitchen, where dog, hamster and me usually put our feet up for half an hour after lunch. Now the games have started every spare minute will be spent on the bowling green.

How did I first enter this cunning craft, I often ask myself. It was flattery that bowled me over, really.

'I bet you'd make a bowler if you practised,' smiled an opponent once after she'd wiped the green with me during an open-for-all club competition. Not realising winners often waffle on like this when flushed with success, I believed her, and felt my first stirrings of green fever.

Sometimes I believe her words even now, several unsuccessful seasons later. Bowling victories rush to the brain like champagne; no one in their right senses takes any notice of the bluffing that accompanies a win.

'Ooh, I've bowled terrible, I don't know how I did it,' victors lie through their teeth to the defeated.

Losers have then to make 'well bowled' sound convincing, whereas some of us simply take pleasure in ordering our drink, a compensation for which the victor has to pay. Not compulsory, but in my numerous defeats, I have only been left low and dry twice.

In early season when the east wind is gnawing at our vitals, the liquor bill is pretty high; whisky and rum are excellent blood and spirit levellers.

Beneath the wool caps and chapped lips we are a matey little band, which appears to aggravate our male counterparts. 'Gerron wi' yer bowling,'

336

they shout when females wander across the green together, jaws ticking over furiously as we discuss current affairs.

'Have you heard about Jack and Elsie?' Men are silent on the turf, all their shouting is done when they are out of reach, with a pint in their hands. What they fail to realise is there is an art in drifting across a green in serious discussion with a mate, when woods are bombing in from all directions, and one day we hope to master it.

Husbands do not make good bowling supporters – they do their best. They stand around the green pointing out our mistakes before we make them. 'Nowt for this anyway, rubbish, run away bowl, I said put some in' all this advice before the wood is halfway across the green.

A friend of mine once asked an elderly character's advice on bringing up children 'Lad, if tha' wants to know t' best way, ask them that's niver 'ad any, they know all abaht it'

In the same way all the perfect bowlers are the ones standing around watching you lose. But you learn to smile and repeat useless platitudes like 'It's only a game,' while inside you're doing your 'Please God act.' Just give me one at this end God and I promise I'll behave. And when you've sweated and struggled to a victory and you can't wipe the smile off your face, you then wax philosophical 'No honestly – it was just luck,' you lie!

*

ONE of the most satisfying sentences I read last week, concerned famous gourmet Egon Ronay and his being turned away from an Ullswater hotel!   It was nothing personal – there just wasn't any room for him, they were full up! But I'd love to have been the one to tell him. 'Sorry, we can't do with you today dear, too busy.'

One day in the future when I open my exclusive tea-rooms, somewhere in Lakeland or maybe the Dales, I look forward to the honour of giving some food critic the full up sign. Food is such an individualistic institution I abhor the idea of one man's taste being able to influence a nation's eating habits.

I haven't started looking yet for my tumbledown cottage, with an acre or two of land to keep hubby happy, while I am busy in the kitchen – he will provide the veg for our summer tables. We shan't serve anything too fancy, ours will be a sort of homely 'Mrs B's Pantry' with home-baked bread and home-made jam and fresh cream oozing from oven-warm scones. Perhaps in my old age, I could learn to love a cow, or at least learn to watch my husband milk one, then we could be almost independent.

My herbal teas, lime and mint, would be another speciality, and I would take a few bookings for dinners on certain evenings when I wasn't gourmeting around the hotel restaurants myself, picking up ideas that is. I shall have a sign saying 'Dogs, hikers and children most welcome,' with little doggy hitch-up posts attached to all my tables in the garden. In my dreams of course, it is perpetual dine-in-the-garden weather, all animals would be fed on fresh scraps, no canned food in my pantry.

I may take non-pet owners if I like the look of them, but the management reserves the right to refuse admission to anyone I don't like the look of. While you wait for your meal, why not take a stroll around my husband's chrysanths or pick your own fruit? In winter when we are tired of cruising the oceans, then we will retire to our little cottage, where I can get on with my latest book on 'How we opened our first tea garden.' Well, that's my dream.

You remember what Bloody Mary sang in South Pacific – 'You gotta have a dream, if you don't have a dream, how you gonna have a dream come true?'

I know many couples are fearful about the future, 'what if one of us dies?' and all that. Well, at least you will have had the pleasure of a mutual dream, whether it materialises or not. No one can take that away, is the way I look at it. Like looking forward to a holiday, often the anticipation is more exciting than the actuality.

Of course my husband makes protest noises from time to time. He seems to think I don't take the financial side seriously enough. But as I keep telling my father when he isn't tripping off on holiday, or buying new radios – I can't wait to get on that pension.

Cooking is one of my favourite pastimes and talking to strangers another. Combine these with a winter full of writing – who could ask for more? But he probably got the idea of becoming rich overnight, from a Leeds hotel where we were wedding guests once. The reception food was so fabulous we couldn't wait for breakfast, the following morning.

Unfortunately, he read the small print first and immediately avoided the hyper-expensive three-course breky. We made do with the continental at £2.75 which consisted of tenpence worth of cereal, a pot of coffee, and as many croissants as you could eat!

But if – say in another ten years time you are strolling in the Dales, worn and weary, looking for a good cup of tea and a wholesome wedge of home cooked meat and potato pie - why not look us up? Just follow your nose and the sound of yapping dogs!

WHAT an amazing society we live in! At a recent christening a baby nestling in his proud mother's arms – had six Godfathers. 'Anyone of the six might have been the father,' explained a guest. 'The family came to this really aristocratic solution.' Each Godfather provided a Christian name and mummy, daughter of a Peer, gave her maiden name as surname.

I feel sure baby will find it spiffing fun receiving his six presents every year and writing 'with love to daddy,' six times in return – right until he is old enough to understand what it means – in fact.

Meanwhile at the Tate Gallery three security guards sit in solemn well-paid silence – watching over three piles of coal. These coal heaps reminiscent of the mess my coal man used to leave in my back yard if I didn't watch him, are the creation of the late Marcel Broodhaer, an artist, not a coal merchant, I hasten to inform. His work is the subject of the Tate's latest exhibition. One can only contemplate the cost of this security exercise and pray it is justified.

Of course I am merely an ignorant tax payer who has yet to discover any artistic significance in a pile of coal, and can't visualise anyone – anyone with a gas fire anyway – running off with a sack of it, much less getting away with it. Wouldn't a hundred weight of coal be difficult to disguise?

Even if one is a coal freak, where does one display these objets d'art? Too big for the sideboard and who but a short-sighted coal man would dump them on the front lawn?

Now here's one for the cricket lovers. Fancy a day out with a difference? Over to Trent Bridge for the opening day of the forthcoming Test Match against the West Indies. 'Why not give your favourite customers their most memorable day out' is the invitation from a sports firm. Take them to Trent Bridge, give them a sherry reception, a champagne buffet luncheon, afternoon tea, all while watching play from the exclusive licensed restaurant, everything taken care of by the firm.

All you have to do is find £50 a head per day. Plus VAT naturally.

Then back at the supermarket we have shoppers protesting over the latest price increases. Wholesale prices are their highest level since 1977. Mean-while cheap butter is being shipped to Russia and French farmers have burned an effigy of Margaret Thatcher in protest of her blocking an EEC agricultural subsidy – Confusing isn't it?

As if this is not enough to contend with I have just discovered what the world in general thinks about we 'smallies.' According to Ralph Keyes author of 'The Height of Your Life,' tall is all and bigger is better. By the age of 30 we have all shrunk an inch, so when I am 60 I should make an eligible mate for the little guy in 'Fantasy Island.'

Mr Keyes also points out that there are no short Miss Worlds. Why not, I would like to know. Why should this height discrimination exist?

Tall girls may be elegant, willowy and graceful. But we shorties are cute, cuddly and easier to carry.

Anyway, if as he says, Ingrid Bergman had to shuffle along a specially dug trench when filming with the shorter Humphrey Bogart and Sophia Loren had to stand Alan Ladd on a crate before she could kiss him – being tall is not much fun either! Now you can chat among yourselves for a week while I dash off to the Isle of Wight.

*

YES, thanks, we had a most enjoyable Sunday to Sunday at Ventnor on the pretty blossom-covered Isle of Wight.

Before the sun curled the skin on my arms and nose like new potatoes – I wallowed in it all day. Husband and I were even scorched enough to wet our toes in the briney. But one dip was enough to anaesthetise a whole leg in a matter of seconds, and we only just managed to limp back to our deck chairs on white bloodless feet.

Being a Cancerian I am supposed to be happiest near water - this is true. I loved the sound of the waves cleaning up the shore as I lie in bed, and am fascinated watching it trickle ever nearer my deck chair as the tide comes in. But ask me to sail on it and I am petrified, which does rather detract from the pleasure of visiting islands.

A Bridlington sea captain once told me that poor sailors should always stay on deck. As I sat alone on the deck of his ship listening to him describe the sickly coastline through a loudspeaker, it did pass through my mind that perhaps the captain was just a lonely man.

But I was not seasick. Drenched, miserable and sorry I'd ever said 'Hello Sailor,' maybe. But my stomach remained intact.

A ferry from Southampton to Cowes took one hour – or 3,600 seconds – whichever way you look at it. And I looked at it with both hands clinging to the nearest lifeboat. With a gale-force wind trying to blow my ears inside out I wrestled with thoughts of the Titanic and the old question when shipwrecked – whom do you save first, your husband or your children? There is only one answer to that, I panic then drown.

The return ferry seemed easier. Whether this was due to a blissfully calm sea or just before we boarded I fell down a hole and ripped my knee I don't know. An old schoolmate once told me that whenever she had toothache she used to grip the other cheek so hard the toothache didn't seem so bad.

I can now inform her that if you fall just before you board a car ferry and blood is oozing from your knee, and you think you may never bowl again, you are home and dry before you know it.

One unspoiled area of the island that will always evoke happy memories is the petite village of Godshill. The main street is lined with exquisitely maintained, plump little white cottages with thatched roofs, and abounds with tea-gardens and an exclusive tavern where one can eat snails.

We tiptoed around the dignified old church that stands on a hill overlooking the village. The atmosphere was so ethereal and timeless that it deemed somewhat incongruous when the minister leaned over my shoulder as I browsed through the visitors' book and whispered, 'I have to catch a bus in two minutes.'

I love pondering over past visitors' remarks. Adjectives like 'lovely' and 'peaceful' seemed to be most popular. Then I came across an intriguing sentence written by a couple from New York. 'Huggy and I enjoyed the long grass best.' I had a giggle at the thought of Huggy living up to his name in the graveyard, until my sober-minded spouse explained they would probably appreciate meandering through any sort of grass after the dust of New York.

Holidays take on a slightly different slant when half the family remain at home. I spent the week before composing memos to the effect of: Feed hamster and dog, water plants, turn iron off, check lights, lock doors, etc.

The first thing I saw as I came home and passed my kitchen window looked like a pile of decaying spaghetti dangling from my window basket.

The prostrate forms of dog and hamster were only sleeping, I was relieved to discover on investigation, and not extinct as I first suspected.

'I did all the washing,' greeted one daughter, proudly indicating the four mountains of washing curled up waiting to be ironed.

*

WHENEVER we ride on a motorway I feel thankful I never found anyone capable of teaching me to drive. Keeping sane and in the correct lane takes more initiative than I'll ever have. We motorwayed down to Birmingham last week and even before we started I was a-quiver with indecision. Firstly, should I belt up or not?

Since a relative's accident, I feel particularly uneasy about this. She was thrown from the car, to escape with concussion, a couple of cracked ribs and her life! Had she been strapped in to the now crushed and practically non-existent front seat, would she have been so lucky?

On the other hand another relative lost the sight of one eye when she was smashed against the windscreen, could it have been worse if she had not been strapped in? Anyway just to be sure I clicked in and controlled an impulse to take along son's crash helmet too! Motorway gazumping is not quite the nightmare since the five gremlins grew up. Yet whenever we ride alone, I am nostalgic. Now there is little relief from the motorway monotony. No tearful protestations, when our car wheels roll over the mangled body of a dead animal.

'I've told you it's a crow.' 'No its not it's a rabbit.' 'Rabbits don't have beaks.' Big wail from youngest. 'I didn't see it dad.' No obsession with toilets when the Services Ahead sign looms up either.

When there was seven of us plus potty, my driver didn't mind me leading a sing-song or doling out points to magpie and oak tree spotters, or if I got fed up, offering 20 points for a blue-haired man wearing a red mac and carrying a black and white poodle under his arm.

The scenery can be unusually breathtaking sometimes, even on a motorway. When we were driving to the Lakes last summer we saw a figure silhouetted against the sky, above us on a bridge. As our car approached he dropped his pants, turned around and proudly presented his naked rear to the oncoming traffic. Cheeky! We had hitherto been in a nodding stupor but his performance certainly opened our eyes. It had a similar effect on the heavens, for there followed a crack of thunder and a flood was unleashed.

On tedious journeys one finds oneself occupied with strange thoughts. What prompted this young man to publicly unveil his potentials, I asked myself. Was it a compulsive habit he could not control? Or was he simply indulging in a momentary urge, like the one I struggle with when I want to pull my tongue out at passing strangers.

Did his mother make him wear too-tight trousers in his youth? Psychiatrists can usually trace quirks back to mother. When I think of the innumerable occasions that I said to my children, 'I'll be glad to see the back of you,' I feel somewhat uneasy myself. At least it's a harmless occupation.

We now know why football idiots bash each other's faces in. 'I like doing it,' one offender explained recently.

Then there was the time a balloon burst when we were speeding up the M1. My apoplectic husband thought a tyre had blown and braked immediately. I thought we were being assassinated and when we discovered the tatters of coloured rubber on our children's laps, they very nearly were.

Last week, as we approached Tamworth, we discovered something worth noting; a snack bar of taste, real taste. On the outside it looked like a tatty caravan, inside delicious individually brewed coffees in earthenware mugs were served to us for 15p by a charming lady who called me 'sunshine' and my husband 'sweetheart.'

On the way back we risked a Services establishment. The last time I visited such a place the chef looked as 'high' as the grease marks on his walls. It took him five minutes to translate my order and another five to navigate the soup ladle.

What a difference last week! They were clearly expecting Egon Ronay. Waitresses were waitressing, cleaners cleaning, servers serving, and everything on the menu was displayed. One of the Lowry prints on the immaculate walls was slightly awry, but we enjoyed our coffee nevertheless – and yes, 'oill give it foive!'

*

AS my grey hairs increase I find I am becoming more and more interested in survival – mine. I have always been addicted to the 'How to' manuals. 'How to Eat, 'How to Stop Eating,' 'How to Relax' and 'How to Jog' all find their way to my shelves.

Some are a little beyond my scope like Mr and Mrs Vidal Sassoon's beauty book. When I copied her hairstyle, I found I looked more like him, but these epics have seen me through many a bad patch. Shepherd Mead's 'How to Stay Medium-Young Practically Forever' was particularly stimulating as it gave me the courage to send off my first article.

One book I intend to read is 'Change and Choice – Women in Middle Age,' which is all about women over 50 having more zing than ever. It sounds just up my street.

It contains interviews from women who insist that the menopause is merely the gateway to a more exciting life ahead, a life in which we should feel fitter, more energetic, take up new careers and interests, and travel to different places.

In other words ladies, our liberation has hardly begun. One day, the reasons why young men marry older women shall all be revealed. I have only read the reviews, but I feel better already and will certainly buy it.

It is 20 years since I read Betty Macdonald's 'Anybody Can Do Anything,' but I still believe it. Providing there's a book about it I'll tackle it.

Dr Magnus Pike, still energetically clawing the air in his 71st year, tells us in his latest book, 'Long Life – Expectation for Old Age' that one of the blessings of growing old is that you can enjoy eating rhubarb or mutton fat because the taste buds diminish. Sounds fun, hic! He also adds that couples can continue to be sexually fulfilled as long as they wish. Apparently whether you favour rhubarb, dripping or an early night, there

343

will be something to satisfy all appetites – providing we can keep going long enough.

Although brain cells decrease with age some scientists made discoveries when they were 100 years old reports Magnus. According to scientist Virginia Satir, what the world needs to survive is four hugs per day - eight are good for maintenance and twelve for growth. The question is, are you getting your healthy share of hugs?

I must confess the idea of being on hugging terms with everyone sounds great, in theory. But when our yoga class was asked to massage each other once, I was ready to roll up my mat in embarrassment. My partner that evening was my daughter's mother-in-law.

Now Eileen and I have an excellent relationship and other couples were soon enthusiastically kneading each other like Friday night bakers. Even my daughter started poking half-heartedly at my mother's varicose veins, but my partner and I were blushing body-pinchers. In the end I swallowed my reluctance and performed some hefty biceps massage I learned when my husband was a crippled footballer. It put Eileen out of action for a week but she didn't hold it against me!

Now I can't say I have experienced this non-touch inhibition with the opposite sex – on the contrary – but that's another story.

One tonic you can't afford to miss is your share of sunshine, as good as a bottle from the doc and much cheaper. Get out and notice the effect the pleasant weather has on everyone.

Have a laugh at the odd outfits the first waft of spring brings forth. Walk to your nearest bowling green and admire the blooming rows of bent backs as husbands' creep out of hibernation and - Good Health!

*

'MUM, what are veins made of?' a typical breakfast question fired by my 11-year-old daughter. 'Oh, chewing gum,' the first answer to surface, is not suitably lucid. What are they made of anyway? Perhaps a handful pulled from my nearest limb would satisfy her curiosity. I pour forth an imaginative description using aids like 'spaghetti' or 'tubes of muscle.' She smiles 'Don't you know?'

Knowing all the answers is an art I never mastered. The other day my hairdresser told me I had a nice chin. Like Mark Twain I can live for two months on a good compliment. 'Have I really?' What an observant chap! 'No you haven't – I'm only joking,' was his reply. Lesson one, never question flattery, merely be thankful.

I like the answer produced by Lord Snowdon when he appeared on Mike Parkinson's show. Mike was dithering around the question of finance.

'Er – Lawd Snudden, I believe you were offered quite a considerable sum . . .' he ventured. Lord Snowdon quickly blocked this particular channel with his smouldering reply, 'Yes, I bet you do!'

Oh, to be mistress of the withering retort or to develop the degree of abstruseness which enables politicians to bury all questions under a cloud of last year's statistics. 'How can we end unemployment? Well let's take a look at last year's statistics.'

It surprises me how many patients leave their doctor's surgery without an answer to the pertinent question: 'What's wrong with me, doc?' I always feel better if my illness has a name, especially if I cannot pronounce it. I learned not to enlighten the medical profession with my own diagnosis when my first born was three. 'She's got measles,' I greeted our physician with when he came to visit (this was when they did). I don't think he ever forgave me.

I can never find the right words to release the clutches of the zealous sales assistants who guard the changing cubicles in dress shops. How does one exit gracefully without buying? The trials I undergo in the curtained cube – rehearsing my get away. 'Too big, madam?' and like Tommy Cooper she'll produce a smaller size from behind her back. Perhaps if I act deaf or could have been suddenly struck with facial paralysis that makes speech impossible?

I have already performed my struck deaf act on two occasions. It takes the nerve of J R Ewing. The first was when my dog did a whoopsie on an elderly lady's clean path she was sweeping it at the time. Looking straight ahead I continued pulling the other end of the lead and tried to look deaf. Barbara Woodhouse would have been proud.

The other occasion was one Christmas when I sat pretending to read a newspaper while to my left an angry refuse man stood tapping his collecting tin on the window. He could see me quite plainly, but playing deaf seemed less painful than confessing I was broke.

The paper was a mistake actually. Had I not been reading it I could have pretended I was blind, too. Who knows, he might have left me a tip!
*

'NO holes in your ears until you leave school,' I said when one daughter first brought up the subject of ear-piercing.

Mind you, she chose an unfortunate time to ask. I had just been watching a David Attenborough subject grinning beside his native hut – or was it his wife? A commendable feat, nonetheless, because besides having an ugly whalebone wedged between his nostrils he had two boulders swinging from each ear lobe, which were stretched to somewhere around where his loincloth would have been.

His mates had presumably left their ear-rings at home, they just had long holes flapping around their shoulders. My daughter played her ace: 'Everyone else has – why can't I?'

'Barbaric,' 'primitive,' 'expensive' were words I used to defend my decision. So the following day her gran took her to town and paid for the ear-studding. Not only have I disobedient daughters, but a dissident mother also.

Naturally the 'me too' epidemic immediately struck her younger sisters, but gran had spent up. 'When you are older' was too long for our next daughter, then 15. Next evening she performed a home darning-needle operation on her left ear. She liked it so much – she punctured it again, higher up, two holes in one and the other ear as yet, untouched.

One Saturday afternoon, son was smouldering near the fire and I was about roll his snoring body away from the heat, when I noticed something glittering in his ear. My shouts and wail eventually penetrated his stupor and I must say he was almost as shocked as me when he felt the ring in his left ear. He muttered something about 'a bet' and after checking his wallet next opening time he sold it to his sister.

So it was with a somewhat sheepish expression that I crept into our kitchen last weekend with two gold studs embedded in my bright purple lobes. The protest was unanimous. Why? After all the denunciations! I keep asking myself the same question as I dab with spirit and turn the screws daily.

It all started when this hairdresser was combing through where my hair had once been. I've seen similar 'What about a wig?' expressions when other hair-dressers have given up the struggle to find suitable words to compliment their handiwork. So I was surprised when he said 'Have you tried ear-rings?'

Some time later eldest daughter and I paid a kind lady (with her ears well hidden, I noticed) to fire the gold studs. Before you could say 'Let me out,' our ears were shot and we hadn't bolted. We are thrilled to bits with our new ears and can't wait to swap our studs for some of the dainty butterfly or lovers' knots we keep staring at in jewellers' windows.

'Course you get the 'earie' conversations all the time about surgeons having to amputate etc. 'Thought your ears were pierced Elsie,' 'They were, but every time I tried to push my ear-rings in I fainted.'

I have given strict orders – if I faint will someone keep pushing till they are through, OK!

WHEN the weather is fit and I have no pressing bowling engagements, or if it is too early for television, I like to take a stroll around my husband's allotment. I know this will never replace wielding a hoe for him, but he likes me to smile approvingly at his potato shoots occasionally or sympathise with him over that patch full of stones, which he has frayed the edge of his spade on night after night.

I admire his broad beans as he explains to me while he has given them a change of scenery this year. I gaze dutifully into what looks like an elongated polythene play-pen for rows of bamboo canes – which he explains is his chrysanth nursery: a cosy wind-screened haven where hopefully his cherished debutantes will burst forth in obedient profusion later on in their coming-out season.

Then I stare knowingly at his brasica and nod understandingly over his spring onion in the salad section. I kneel painfully on a gritty path and watch him lovingly and with special tenderness separate his baby seedlings and tuck them comfortably into a cold frame, giving them a long cool drink before he shuts them up for the night.

Good gracious is that the time already? Coronation Street must be almost over, and we still haven't wandered through our greenhouse. When entering this esoteric area of his kingdom, the plants look so privileged and snooty I always feel as if I ought to be wearing a hat.

Here we have box after box of delicate greens all snuggled in moist black earth, neatly rolled bundles of string, a tickling stick for his tomato plants, bottles of root tonic and fertiliser. It makes me feel such a heel for all the times we sit down and enjoy all the produce he trails home without so much as a thought for all the hard work and tender care that all gardeners everywhere put into their vegetable growing.

One chap we knew used to save all the liquid left after cooking veg and carry it to his garden, faithfully feeding it back to his growing plants.

Perhaps we can show our gratitude by doing full justice to their produce in our cooking.

If you want a tasty recipe, quiz any of the old gardeners and you'd be surprised how much they know about cooking. I was boasting about the size of my husband's leeks at a bowling match recently – I tend to salve my con-science this way when I have just undergone a serious bout of non-gardening. Apparently (it was pointed out to me) some of us cut off too much of the dark green tip. We had a fine leek harvest last year and although I tarted them up with cheese when I was in the mood, before the end of the season we were all a shade leek-bound.

Well, it seems there are several ways to cook them. My new friend told me he liked leek fritters, and there was nothing tastier in his canny old opinion than leek pudding.

For the fritters, simply slice into one-inch rings, dip in batter and deep fry.

This is the pudding recipe as related to me: 'I cuts a bit of toppin of me leeks, then I roll 'em up in suet paste, wraps the lot in a large white handkech', fasten each end wi' a safety pin.' 'What no seasoning?' I felt bound to ask. 'No you gets enough flavour from the ham.' 'Ham?'

'Meanwhile I have a shank simmering in some lentil broth an' I drops the puddin' in this for half hour or so.'

It sounds finger-lickin' good and I only wish I could remember the old chaps' name to thank him.

When our leeks mature enough I certainly intend to try it.

*

WHAT do you think of the weather so far then? As I write I wallow in glorious heat provided by my kitchen radiator. Outside its all grey skies and long faces. Still, by the time you read this it could be cotton dress and sun lotion in full swing.

The signs are all there, surely an abundance of dandelion heads cannot be wrong – summer must start soon.

Contrary to what most parents' fear, rain does not always mean miserable holidays for children. Youngsters love getting soaked.

Dress them in wellies and sou'wester; let them frolic in grimy puddles, wash their hands in filthy sludge – they wax content. Let the sun shine down blistering and they become sons of want. 'I want some ice cream,' 'I want some pop.' They are cranky, you're prickly and dad's pockets are soon empty.

Teenagers seem blissfully ignorant of the elements. 'Put your coat on,' I ordered mine as she was about to go forth in a torrential downpour dressed in jeans and sweater. She looked baffled. 'Why? It'll only get wet.'

When I was a child on annual holidays at Blackpool, my sister and I prayed every night for rain. Whenever we wanted to go in: The Tower, circus, Madame Tussauds or the Fun House, the stock answer was 'When it rains.' We were innocently unaware of how much rainy days cost.

During my own children's inclement holidays, we found jigsaws, penny arrows and crayoning books a Godsend. Allowing an angry sea to throw her waves at us once provided us with an evening of vigorously cheap family entertainment. We sat holding hands on a ledge just above the beach and screamed with delight every time the spray hit us.

Now that there are only three of us, wet days conjure up a loaf around second-hand bookshops, or if small daughter gets compulsively involved in the amusement arcades, we can nip in the snack bars opposite for a quick coffee. Recently we heard an elderly lady talking to the waitress. The pensioner was talking about breaking in a new landlady. 'She doesn't allow smoking. I used to look forward to a cig and a chat in the lounge being on my own all day, but she's removed all the ashtrays. I sneaked into my room for a crafty smoke last night, but this morning she opened all the windows and kept talking about the foul smell tobacco leaves – so I go for walks on my own now.' Landladies have a lot to answer for.

I was a long time discovering that people actually bought clothes to wear in wet weather. In my junior days wet weather meant going to school in my mother's mac which only just missed the puddles. I usually had an assortment of inherited family scarves wrapped around my body and head. My wellies were still too big although I wore two pairs of army socks. But it was wartime and we were all in the same impecunious state.

Boys boasted patched britches, girls were proud of their much-darned woollies. Everything was bought two sized too big. Hems were let down year after year. Females were not afraid to wear mended stockings. One friend made a good living from 'invisibly' mending them.

Frayed collars and cuffs were 'turned' for extra wear. Lads could be heard clomping to school a mile away, irons nailed to their clogs prolonged active life. I can remember cringing as they slid across the school yard, sparks flying in all directions as iron met stone. In those days the unpatched were the most noticeable.

Today's ephemeral lifestyles, where nothing is intended to last, so sadly reflected in non-marriage relationships, have built a vast gap between generations which can unfortunately never be bridged.
*

ALL this sport on television – the victorious, the cups and the trophies are a persistent reminder to me of all the records that I must have broken over the years with my sporting efforts. I feel sure there must be other dedicated failures like myself who may be harbouring unrecognised talents.

Take tennis for example. I have been a dedicated tennis player ever since I missed our school coaching by dragging my appendicitis on for almost a term. Every summer I can be seen or heard smashing a tennis ball passionately against our coal cellar door, unless the dog is quicker than me and runs off with it and (Barbara Woodhouse forgive me) fails to bring it back. He gets 'sit' confused with 'git'! Nevertheless I recently hit the ball sixteen times without missing – is this a record?

On holiday my super tennis-playing spouse took me on court for an hour. During which I galloped, ran, swooped, dived, strained one arm six inches longer than the other, ground my racket frame to a splinter, spent so much time retrieving balls from the adjoining playground, that my see-sawing daughter asked me why I wasn't playing tennis. Despite all this energetic exercise I never won a point - a record surely?

My dancing days were plagued annually by the dreaded tap and ballet competitions. On stage a pianist would pound out my intro while I stood petrified in the wings awaiting the cue to come tapping forth. Once in front of the adjudicator sat in judgement at her raised table, my mind and feet lost contact. My feet would automatically tap out something, but for the first sixteen bars I was lost.

The sight of teacher's fist waving frantically from off-stage usually kept me going as long as the music. The only award I received for this torture was a card with the message, 'A pleasing sense of eye-line.'

For the past seven years I have been trying to win some recognition for my bowling efforts. My hands are nearer the ground than most, what with pushing five prams around over the years but my muscles are reasonably developed.

My teenagers' have been a considerable help to my game this season. Every time we have a row, I reach for my bowling bag, I've had my hair cut short, and become adept at chewing gum. I have made a profound personality study of all the Wimbledon personnel this week, trying to pick up useful hints.

Bjorn has his concentration, Virginia Wade her crouch and mumble. What does she mutter to herself throughout her matches? I particularly made note of the Borg philosophy, 'Every match I believe I shall win. A man who comes to the court thinking he cannot win, has lost already.' Last week I stepped on to a bowling green with these words burned in my mind. Half an hour later I stepped off having scored five points to my opponent's twenty-one. Now, I have developed my own homily: 'A bowler who comes to a match thinking he cannot lose – is in for a trouncing.'

We also have post-mortems after the event. 'What happened Mrs B?' 'Well her woods were a lot weaker than mine, she's also a left-hander as well you know, and of course she had all the luck.'

My husband naturally sums it up much more succinctly. 'She was outbowled, love.'

Last week as woods bumbled over hailstones, I watched the permanently pleated faces, as bowlers wandered across the green dressed like deep-sea divers. 'We're all here to enjoy ourselves,' said my companion. But my game has improved. When I lose I can now smile cheerfully at my partner and repeat 'Good game' as if I meant it!

*

THERE come a time in every mum's life when she has to take spotty, stringy-haired offspring on one side and attempt to explain the complications of being an eleven-year-old.

After already shuffling through this issue with three other daughters and a son I find it does not get any easier. 'What are you trying to say, ma?' my son grinned at my initial efforts to advise, 'Cos you're saying it all wrong, and I'm gonna miss my bus.' I found our first daughter's biology notes a useful aid when her turn came. Anything I didn't understand she obligingly translated.

The next two daughters were remarkably attentive when I talked about their approaching teenhood. We were walking home from a school concert and the darkness was a useful ally. They were so unusually silent, perhaps they wanted to ask a question? 'Yes, can we have some chips please?' was the unanimous demand.

This year enlightening Amanda was helped by the fact that she and friend Samantha have two mateable hamsters. Together we enthusiastically digested the breeding facts of hamster life. Their mating season, not unlike ours, is between April and October. Sam's female has all the right statistics, broad in the beam, well furred and not too fat; she helpfully comes into season every five days, and should start getting hot feet about this time, according to the book.

All they had to do was put the couple together, watch and wait. I missed their first date, but apparently had I been present and blinked I would have missed it anyway. Sam's female took one look at our handsome loveable Houdini and dealt him a swift bat to the nose, whereupon a mortified Amanda immediately snatched him back.

Here endeth the first session. The second meeting was arranged at Sam's house, every movement being cautiously watched by the timorous owners. Whenever the two animals looked like getting close, one or other was promptly snatched back to corner.

According to Sam's mum who rang later to ask how Houdini was, this dragging back to corner happened several times and was all that was allowed. 'Do you think we ought to do something? Our hamster has been furiously gnawing at her door all night.' I looked at Houdini swinging from the top of his cage by his teeth, was that smoke rising from his little suspended feet?

351

I tried to explain to daughter, hamsters, like humans, don't immediately fall in love. They need time to get to know each other; they have to be left alone.

Sam's ham may have won second prize in the school pet show, but Houdini is not necessarily impressed. After all he was unplaced in the same show.

And although we love his interminable Esther Rantzen smile, perhaps he would prove more appealing to lady hamsters were he not such a bright khaki.

Saturday night we arrived home to find an empty hamster cage and an exceedingly uncommunicative dog, who at my command 'Find' unco-operatively remained in his basket and ran his tongue over his nose. While fish and chips congeal, daughter bawls and I imagine Houdini already dispelling all frustrations on his first mouse, husband discovers small bundle of fur cowering in the hall. Amanda now concludes there's a lot to be said for the celibate life.

All we have to do is convince Houdini!

*

WHENEVER there are one or two blowing together, be it pipes, horns or trombones, I always find fetes, carnivals or garden parties more endearing.

There is something about the blast of a band that brings out the best in all of us, no matter how rotten you feel, despite the devastating weather, even sodden soles cannot resist tapping to the beat.

Brass bands represent a working class culture which may fade a little now and then, but one which is never allowed to die. Every so often they burst into popularity again.

Brighouse and Rastrick started our clogs dancing again with their exuberant rendering of the 'Floral Dance.' Brian Glover is reviving interest at present on ITV's 'Sounding Brass.' What a pity that chapel and church have made no effort to reinstate the traditional Whitsuntide march which has happy memories for most Yorkshire folk.

At the recent 'Racial Harmony' entertainment in Greenhead Park a major effort was made by all races and creeds to exhibit their differing art and culture. Black, brown or white, there was something for everyone.

Hot dogs, home made cakes, samples of Indian food, samosas and spiced nuts were temptingly displayed on tables in the arena. All selling so briskly, the Italian café proprietor looked quite white as he surveyed his empty chairs.

We were sustained from start to finish by all modes of music. I swung my handbag gaily in time with the bag pipers' sporrans, which I always find stomach-stirring.

You could see by the length of their necks that some of the drummers had been carrying their instruments for a long time.

One had his drum on such a tight rein his neck appeared to be at right angles to his body, which enabled him to watch his feet as he drummed.

Then I found myself in the middle of a writhing throng, all throbbing furiously to the reggae beat of 'North Star,' a West Indian steel band. I just copied the antics of a brown-faced gent in front, who also managed to balance an outsized fish on his head.

Their dancing, like their wide smiles, is so infectious you can't resist. 'I can't stop, man,' confessed one drummer in a flat cap when their leader, noticing the beer tent, tried to end it all.

The majorettes, obedient, betighted angels of all shapes and sizes – with their eyes so hypnotically fixed straight ahead, you feel they could carry on walking over roundabouts, horses and trees, without once blinking – always make me weep, even when they play in tune.

I missed the Asian contribution, sadly, because I find their weird strains too good for the soul. Drifting towards the source of a savoury odour I did indulge in a samosa, a sort of fried Cornish pasty. One bite and the taste buds explode in a myriad of tongue-rupturing electric shocks. My ensuing breath could have ignited a cigarette at 20 paces. Delicious! Never felt cold again all afternoon.

The Plexus folk trio rounded off the afternoon so beautiful on the ear – as long as they played I wanted to sit and listen, even on wet grass. 'Matchbox Men' composed by Bernie Parry, was an additional luxury.

The highlight for some of us, of course, was Birkby Junior steel band with their talented fingers clenched on drumsticks and a mixture of flaxen and woolly heads buried in their pans – definitely a group to watch out for.

Taught by two North Star members and directed by two teachers, the calypso rhythm of these under eleven's transported us above the rising damp to a land of sunshine and Boney M. And please don't think that I am prejudiced – but one of the good-looking tambourine shakers is my daughter.

*

HAS this depressingly wet nasty soggy awful weather affected the British holiday takings?

Last Wednesday with the sun burning through our anoraks we decided to take a trip to Blackpool and find out.

It kept fine until we reached the South Shore, where everyone seemed to be enclosed in plastic. Damp dads were barking at whimpering children, mums were growling at everything, small babies tucked away under pram hoods were the lucky ones.

Across the prom a seagull was guarding the empty paddling pool. Vacancy signs were in most hotel windows. Our daughter, Amanda and friend were thrilled to bits – bad weather meant no delaying their visit to the Pleasure Beach. Pleasure? Flailing arms and bloodcurdling screams surrounded us and this was only mums threatening dissident toddlers.

Then there was something called 'Loop the Loop,' where a train shoots backwards then swings full circle, my stomach heaved horribly at the thought; which is why I probably stuff myself every visit.

My husband gets his kicks watching the various ways that frightened ladies express their suffering – while I nip off for a hot dog, with onions served by a student reading physics – from a book propped against the ketchup.

Then while husband waits for another trainful of masochists to descend, I tackle 35p worth of mussels. There were several empty seats in the Pancake House where I had coffee while the children topped up the slot machines. I could have enjoyed a pancake, there was one almost untouched by my husband's elbow, but he would have seen me.

Holidaymakers who had braved the rain were doing their best to make up the day's takings. Children were queuing to be daubed with clown make-up, a photographic gimmick was to pose in Victorian gear, gent seated, lady resting delicate palm on his shoulder, costumes provided.

The rain tippled steadily on the empty saddles of the hoses, while the merry monarch rolled about in raucous laughter outside the fun house. This year his mirth did not seem quite as infectious.

Later, a stroll down the prom revealed multi-scurrilous messages to man-kind scrawled everywhere – on walls, T-shirts and hats. It used to be 'Kiss me Quick,' now anything connected with JR is a best seller. One large pile of T-shirts no-one seemed to be buying carried the inscription: 'O Lord help me to keep my mouth shut until I know what I am talking about.' Badges carried obscene invitations. 'I am a virgin,' one boasted, with small print underneath which read 'This is a very old badge.'

Buxom belles of all ages in disco garb, stiletto heels, blouses cut low, skirts slashed high, paraded the prom – pausing under the awnings now and then to protect their mascara.

354

After tea the clouds miraculously rolled away and we enjoyed an hour or two of sunshine. Things perked up on the sands. Donkey bells were jingling again, a couple of pensioners soaked their bunions in salt water, and some broad shouldered hairy chests were soon bouncing in the briny. But, for once, I was more interested in tracking down that fish and chip aroma – and we didn't have to queue. When you don't have to queue at Blackpool, believe me business is bad!

*

WHY do television quizmasters have to be comedians? Or more importantly why do comedians have to turn quizzical?

One can understand a stand-up comic board with the same nightly patter deciding on a change. What could be more obvious with this incessant gift of chat than to chair a quiz show? Commendable. Until they start duplicating their original performance at the expense of defenceless contestants.

Interminable quizzer Bob Monkhouse is cursed with a particular retentive memory that unfortunately never recorded a full stop. Once his eyes connect camera, the quips trigger forth unmercifully.

Charlie Williams did convey to us during his excruciating painful initiation into 'Golden Shot' exactly how naked an artist can be without his material. Separate a comic from his jokes and he's truly gagged.

I'd like to thank Nicholas Parsons for his Sunday 'Sale of the Century,' one of the funniest shows on television, although Nicholas is not a comedian. He learned his trade playing straight man to the late Arthur Haines and delivers all his lines as if was looking into a mirror. Whether admonishing a hasty button-pusher, 'No, Daphne, you must let me finish . . . .' or condescendingly chiding a wrong answer, before smugly reading the correct one from his card, he's a delight. While he proudly shows off the prizes, he loves to push contestants into place. 'This is what you could have won – no, stand behind me Eric, please' - and so hilariously patronising. 'I'm sorry Daphne but you did not answer within the 15 seconds – I'm afraid I must give it to Eric.'

I like Terry Wogan best on photographs. The masterful Magnus Magnusson with all the cloak and dagger effects, perspiring victim clutching black chair, face spotlighted mercilessly in Magnusson Viking glare – it's as entertaining as a horror movie.

Robert Robinson who talks as if his top and bottom set are wired together, deserves something for controlling the 'Call My Bluffers' and not pervading the show.

'Face the Music's' Joseph Cooper seemed more like a benevolent uncle who had just popped in for a cuppa and a chat. It was so moving watching him bash his finger ends on that dummy keyboard miming a piano solo every week. I never laughed once.

Ted Rogers always gives me the impression of being worked from behind. In 3-2-1, his speciality is firing alliterative twaddle at the audience for several minutes without taking a breath – an exercise that makes everyone clap heartily when it's all over.

Watching Larry Grayson giggle at Isla is like having to eat something you don't like – twice over. Before he had his teeth and hair tailored I enjoyed his fey chatter.

But let's face it, who can possibly follow Bruce Forsyth, the perfect Master of all Ceremonies. Until she stopped twirling and started talking Anthea was more of an asset too.

Deal me out of his latest card game – my heart is not in it. But his talent is too good to waste. I hope he still has one or two more tricks up his sleeve!!

*

'WISH I could relax,' is becoming a universal plea. Surprising how many never learned this habit. To be able to relax comes naturally, I find if you have a heavy workload.

Sounds paradoxical, it's true, but the more I have to do, the easier relaxing becomes. I just split the load in two and organise a sofa-rific lounge in between – an idea I pinched from the sagacious Winston Churchill. Then, hopefully, I return to duty – er – refreshed.

My heart goes out to the non-workers of the world, because they miss one of the greatest institutions of the working day – the morning 'break,' that tantalising pause between discipline and treadmill, the essential ingredient necessary for successful productivity. Of course it depends on your occupa-tion and scale as to how you are allowed to spend it.

For textile workers on 'What you earn,' it's a hasty brew-up, drunk while you work, followed by a quick 'drag' in the toilets.

At one printing firm I was expected to join a card school in the toilets. If I played my cards right, I didn't have to wash up. I washed up for two weeks then left.

During my two days standing at a conveyor belt counting biscuits, I could have coffee, if someone remembered to relieve me.

In a chain store where I once worked staff were allowed the luxury of two 15 minute breaks in the excellent canteen.

When I was a teenage apprentice with a bookbinding firm, I spent some of the happiest breaks of my life listening to my ex-army mate's stories concerning his victories in war-ridden Cairo; until our forewoman put a stop to it, that is. According to him Cairo women are the most desirable in the world. Mind you he went straight there from Lockwood!

For housewives with children, organising a break in routine is difficult. During school holidays it's almost impossible. Today I have cleaned three bedrooms and with one still to do, surely this qualifies me for an interval.

Lunch tray complete, I decide to dine outdoors where the sun is actually casting shadows. Hang on – where's my chair? Right, here we go under window facing sun – lovely. A short delay while I belt dog that thinks the tray is for him, and knocks my tea over.

Back again, tea replaced start lunch. Sun burning gloriously on my perspiring flesh – blast that wasp. Ah, this is my Utopia. Just shows how unused to heat I have become. My scorched face is beginning to feel like Dr Jekyll's after he took the potion. Layer after layer feels to be melting away. Must find the sun lotion. Son used it last in 1976, I discover it still in his case.

This is a good opportunity for an illicit bask in daughter's sexy sun top. Now let's see how should I describe myself in this three-sizes-too-small strapless statistic squasher. Stunning? Electrifying? Repulsive? The postman's not ready yet for this transformation, better not. Back to chair, sandals off, feet on flower tub, what a life, just let the old eyelids droop.

'Shriek,' I'm being attacked by a wild elephant! Turns out to be our dog taking a short cut across my knees to savage whoever dared walk past our back gate. Still the best guard dog in the world, bless him.

My heart settles into gear again. The strain of daughter's piano playing drift through the window. If she plays that piece just once more I swear I'll . . 'Amanda, out here in this sunshine, now.'

Daughter emerges in her summer gear: Polo neck, padded jacket, cords and wool knee socks.

Why is my daft, dozy, senile mongrel still barking hysterically at an empty road? He misunderstands my 'Sitah! – Comah,' and gallops hell for leather in opposite direction. Shouts emanate from bathroom, 'Mum, come and find my bikini.' I'd forgotten what sunny days were like.

*

WHAT is so unique about falling for the first ambitious young starlet who sets her cap at you – when you are a top name in showbiz circles?

The 'Sundays' are filled with the soggy confessions of those whose minds have been passionately turned by the attentions of their young lovers.

In some cases not only their mind but their speech has been affected.

Sixty-one-year-old Dick Emery, who has just made wife number five redundant, had a gym built into his last home so he could have a daily work-out. 'Something inside me makes me determined to keep trim.' That guy is certainly all heart.

'I am still amazed that women find me attractive,' he sighs, sounding exactly like one of his comical caricatures. 'I won't give up showbiz until the day I die and I'll probably carry on in Heaven.'

Here, I think the old sinner may be setting his immortal sights optimistically high and in the wrong direction.

Telling newspapers 'quite frankly' about one's peccadilloes certainly brings in the cash and publicity, even if it does read like a load of old tripe.

Comedian Eddie Large has also walked out on his 35-year-old wife and two children after she supported him through 15 years of building up his name and waistline.

In retrospect do these clowns have any regrets? Are they tortured with guilt and remorse? Eddie has one: 'I should have come out in the open instead of letting the news leak,' he concludes. 'My children are my number one concern – I would swim through shark-infested waters to protect them,' a solution which must sound most appealing to them just now, I imagine.

A pity really that this sort of puerile overstatements sell newspapers and lines pockets. Just to balance the books I believe the monogamus deserve a line or two.

Writer Roald Dahl nursed his wife, film star Patricia Neal, through a serious stroke. He spent years nursing her back to speech and mobility. Today she is tackling cameo roles again, thanks to her own courage and the love and loyalty of her husband.

DJ Sam Costa has been wed 42 years to wife, Esther. Fifteen years ago comedian Eric Barker was maimed by a stroke. 'Despite all his problems Eric is still my biggest strength,' says his wife, actress Pearl Hackney, currently playing the late Renee Bradshaws's mother in 'Coronation Street.'

Eventually we all reap what we sow and I could not resist a snigger when the omnivorous Bernard Manning, unable to take the heckling at a Manchester club recently, left the stage. According to club owner, Joe Pullen, when a coloured lad threw a few verbals back, Bernard blew up and walked off. Some of his comedy is quite superfluous to the rest of his act, which when he is in form, is brilliantly funny.

WHEN I was a juvenile 'Babe in the Wood,' one certain seat in the orchestra stalls at the Theatre Royal was occupied every Friday by the same worshipping face.

Was the attraction our flying ballet we fairies asked ourselves? After all, we never gave the same performance twice. The scene-shifters, who also piloted our high wires, appeared to be both blind and deaf that year. Our producer, dressed in his King Rat costume could be seen clawing the curtains twice nightly in hopeless exasperation as we flew across the stage missing ill-placed scenery by inches.

Some of our ancient manipulators were also chronic worriers; frightened to death they may miss a pint between scenes. We would be hanging in the air in our final pose – me in the centre, a fairy on either side holding my hands, and two below holding a foot each.

In their anxiety to be first to the bar, the stagehands would start pulling the fairies in from each side of me – while they were still clinging to my limbs. It was fascinating to watch, but terrifying to experience – if you could stop laughing. I almost became a split personality.

The bleary-eyed dipso who worked my wire was also a compulsive con-versationalist. Consequently, instead of making the rehearsed there-and-back flight, I often had to float around indefinitely waiting for a merciful lull in conversation.

At one point his view of my descent was blocked by part of the woodland glade and I was not fully grounded which meant having to balance gracefully on my toenails until it was time to rise again.

He frequently counteracted this by zooming me so high up into the flies that only my ballet shoes were visible. My mother's pretentious reports to relatives of how high I flew 'right up to the roof' were not always an exaggeration.

But despite our famous aerial contortions, it later transpired, when our favourite fan became a perpetual pest, forever hanging around the principal boy's dressing room that her interest alas was not in us.

'She's here again,' we sneered every Friday, ignoring the fact that our own autograph books were piled on the same artists dressing table awaiting the signatures, that we spent hours examining afterwards for evidence which revealed that Big Star actually knew us.

We were shameless showbiz worshippers, and I have never outgrown this trait.

The year I suffered cartilage trouble and had to wear a horrid knee support was my happiest. All my autographs contained a 'little miss legs' message.

When Harry Worth walked into me once at Yarmouth I almost fainted with gratitude. 'But you can't stand his act,' was my husband's ignorant remark.

This is the amazing thing; love or hate, the thrill of meeting a famous face is still the same.

Last week we were enjoying a drink in a Leeds hotel when my husband casually announced he had just seen Eddie Waring in the foyer. Before you could say 'early bath' I was on a pretend toilet visit. Yet his television appearances drive me mad.

Unknown to me until it was too late Dickie Henderson was also sitting chatting – merely an ashtray away. 'Hey isn't that Annie Walker serving on?' Son likes his little joke.

In Blackpool's Manchester Hotel I once smiled seductively at the late ace trumpeter Eddie Calvert. And whatever husband says – I know it was Eddie Calvert.

Should I ever be lucky enough to be introduced to a showbiz personality I don't know what I would say.

When my sister-in-law and I saw commentator Peter Dimmock leaving a racecourse we sadly said the wrong thing. 'Ooh, look,' we exclaimed, pointing ecstatically, 'It's Richard Dimbleby!'

*

WHEN I popped into the chippy last Friday for my favourite dinner of the week the proprietress was overwhelmingly sociable.

'Have you some better work in this week, luv?' she beamed. I gave her my plastic smile and asked her what she meant. She tried again.

'Have you finished that load of bobbins you were on about?' I was baffled. Then, after a close look, she grinned an apology and it dawned on both of us she had mistaken me for someone else who apparently worked in a nearby mill. 'She's your living image, luv,' was enough to set my curiosity on fire.

So that's why people are always asking me if I have just finished work. Here I am thinking it's my clothes. To see ourselves as others see us is dangerously tempting. So, not immediately recognising the unfamiliar name of my double, I dashed home to quiz my daughters.

When I repeated the name, oh yes, they all knew her, a small woman, yes, a small woman. Not much satisfaction yet. Dark hair perhaps. No, they didn't think so, but it was difficult to say as she always wore a woolly cap pulled over her ears. 'She has funny little eyes and a grey moustache,' one daughter added helpfully. 'You know her surely.' No I'm sure I would remember.

Anyway, my eyes could not be described as little, and I certainly do not have a grey moustache – it's black.

Still, I suppose it's inevitable with all the faces in the world that one or two must look similar. Every time I see Annie Walker pull a pint in the Rover's Return I always confuse her with her look alike Barbara Cartland. The resemblance between these two doyens is incredible.

When Kate Bush was performing the other night I kept getting her face mixed up with the image of young Egyptian King Tutankhamen – or was it his mummy Nephatites?

Barry Manilow always reminds me of a chap who comes to our bowling club. Barry Manilow is younger, his hair is blonde (not the colour of soiled string like this bloke, and my friends arms are six inches longer) probably something to do with his stooping gait. But his face is Barry's. We also have a Charlie Drake, minus the curls, but with a wig he could fool anybody.

Often it's the voice that hits a memory chord. Margaret Thatcher's phonetics are exactly like an infant's teacher I know who always addresses parents in a hushed monotone, as if they are geriatrics with only a month to live.

In my youth, when Liz Taylor was wasting her charms on 'Lassie,' I tried to look like her. Getting ready for dances took hours.

With little to start on, but armed hopefully with my Woolworth's make-up, two ounces of mascara on each eyebrow, vivid tangee lips, plus the tightest waistband my heartbeat could stand – I joined the happy band of other Liz Taylors at the Town Hall.

Now when I see my own daughters leaving for dates, with grotesque purple eyelids and greasy lips, I marvel how my mother kept silent. But she just kept on knitting silently even when she caught my full frontal, and probably spent the rest of the night picking up dropped stitches.

A midwife told me once she never noticed faces. 'Bums and faces look alike to me, dear,' she laughed, only she didn't use the word 'bum!'

*

WHATEVER it is about cricket that hypnotises our males, certainly has the reverse effect on me. Mind you, I must admit, I am the sort of sports viewer who can fall asleep during a boxing match. I have been known to read one and a half library books during 'Match of the Day.' But cricket! There is this strange hush of inactivity that defies any hobby I try to tackle.

The hollow, irritating drib-drabs of applause – Richie Benaud's adenoidal pontificatings; I always feel he ought to be running around inside a Dalek with a voice like his. Have you noticed how he talks without moving anything but his bottom lip? This is known as the fatal cricket-watchers paralysis – all cricket lovers are struck down with it during the season.

It is the sort of game where nothing ever happens unless you go to the toilet or look the other way, consequently addicts develop this stiff-necked immo-bile glazed eye attitude. Conversations with them are unbelievable.

'Sheila's had a wonderful holiday in Torquay,' I still attempt to converse. Husband's head turns about three degrees towards my chair while his eyeballs stay where they are, facing Geoff Boycott. Sometimes he adapts a Clint East-wood expression and talks out of the side of his mouth, this saves him the aggravation of moving his head, thereby easing the strain on his eyeballs.

Questions have often to be repeated or rephrased: 'Sheila is gorgeously tanned, they've just got back from Torquay.'

With eyes still at silly mid-off he swings2 his lips in my direction, 'Has she! That's 87 runs they need now Ian,' Ian is daughter's boyfriend. When the game is almost over, 'Er let's see now – where has she been, Bournemouth wasn't it?' 'He's caught! Hee hee hee! Fetch Howard quick!' A hair-dripping Howard gallops in and performs a victory dance. Dog shakes his ears in disbelief.

I wish I could have this rejuvenating effect, by simply catching a cricket ball. Their eyes are all sparkling with a 'pint of mixed' expression. When I think of all the side-splitting sagas that I have related which received nothing but polite forced apologies for a smile, I could spit at that chap who caught the ball.

At least we can turn it off now. Turn off? By courtesy of the other channel, we now have the added luxury on continuing on the 'other side' until 6.30 when former players will discuss it until the cameras fade.

I've also seen this cricket phenomenon reduce strong-minded lions to manipulative lambs.

All one has to do is seen to be involved in some television programme other than the cricket he has just rushed home to watch, which is now showing on the 'other side' and which he would give blood to see.

First he flashes you a brilliant top-teeth smile – guaranteed to melt the heart of a witch – in any other circumstances. He then walks over to the window feigning interest in the garden, until he sees the long grass. He draws the curtains; you can almost hear his mind searching for the right approach. Perching uncomfortably on your chair arm, he tentatively slips a paw around your neck. You can feel the giggles bubbling around under your pinny – but nothing will betray your steely concentration.

He looks at his watch for the twentieth time. Then at last breaks: 'Er, um, are you watching this, petal?'

Oddly enough – and this is what is so diabolically infuriating about cricket – you begin to feel it is your patriotic duty to give in to this mania and while he kneels in front of the telly, eyes fixed, finger poised on button, awaiting your signal – like a fool you nod your head and owz zat! You've been caught again!

*

HUMPHREY Littelton does it for a magazine and Egon Ronay does it for a living. This week we followed their example; searching for the best value in pub food. With one irrevocable difference – we paid our own bill.

My husband, acting as chief scout, has been seeking a suitable haven where he and his lads, namely the rest of the bowling team, can feast and confidently stagnate, after a gruelling day at York races.

Their annual dawn to dawn airing, 'Don't wait up petal,' starts with full English breakfast at the nearest pub, then its back to the bus lads and forward to York. After their hot and tiring journey, the passengers retire parched and weary to – another pub. The race to be first to the bar begins.

Men certainly have the knack of doing these trips in style. Mention a day trip with the family and they'll start decorating a bedroom. For a club jaunt they start saving in January, obediently coughing up the weekly contribution to be stashed away secretly in the care of a trusted mate.

'How much now?' merely brings an enigmatically glint to their eyes. Wives can only guess, but some treasurers, hitherto of scrupulous character, who wouldn't take the hair from your comb, have been known to find the lure of it irresistible and have vanished with the swag never to return.

Meanwhile after an hour or two discussing their favourite topic – 'want another?' – our racing heroes surface for a while, some may even see a horse.

I have never been able to fathom when they eat lunch, or if they do, but by six o'clock most of them are ready for solids, and steak is a strong favourite.

Collecting menus from pub restaurants has proved an education and I have become an avid bar-snacker in the process.

Not so long ago the term conjured up what looked like 'cork' pies and curly teacakes under a glass cover at the end of the bar. Today's buffets are a mouth-watering technicolour experience, with a sophisticated blend of colour-ful salads, every cold cut you can mention tastefully sliced and garnished, and beautifully arranged on immaculate linen.

There is also a variety of 'hots,' One choice included lasagne and home-made steak and kidney pie. Chicken in the basket and scampi are now definitely non-starters.

The standard of culinary art was superb at the place we finally chose for the outing's evening meal. Once again we by-passed the restaurant and lunched in the bar-buffet. The onion soup accompanied by chunky French bread and butter looked a meal in itself until we perceived the bar layout. Exquisite salads were all arranged in small dishes and were constantly being re-filled to retain freshness. Everything looked delicious.

The cheery Madame-in-charge had clearly been brought up with a family of discus throwers, to her 'small' meant not scraping out the bottom of each dish. She shovelled huge slices of ham and beef topped up with spoonfuls of prawns, coleslaw, pickles and dressed green salad. There were also trays of turkey and pork plus an empty dish with a golden border of crumbly piecrust – the remains of 'chef's special' chicken pie.

For dessert – yes once you start there's no stopping - you are compelled to continue with desirable concoctions twinkling seductively at you from the bar top.

Three of us chose mousse, which proved quite difficult – how does one order three? I couldn't decide whether mousses or mices was correct, but madame was Scottish and 'mousses' quite tickled her tartan. Made with fresh raspberries, cream and wine – divine and husband's apple pie was 'lovely.'

We concluded with a bottomless cup of Cona with lashings of cream. 'There's another jug of coffee if you want dearies.'

That's four mixed meat salads, three raspberry mousse, one apple pie and about twenty cups of coffee – total damage £12.80 (inc VAT)!

This lunch 'snack' was so satisfying it sustained me until my bedtime cuppa and with a little encouragement, could become my favourite sport!
*
HOW did you feel when you struggled to pull back the curtains this morning? Exhausted after the haul from bed to window? Weary from wincing at the same old view, which in my case is either a workman's quiff peeping from a 6ft gash in the road, or his drill-happy mate struggling to gain control of his teeth and eyeballs as he clings with both hands to the dithering machine.

What we need is a packet of roast peanuts. Grandpa McKenzie, a 95-year-old Canadian eats 1lb of roasted peanuts every night. He never retires before midnight, smokes like a chimney and drinks a bottle of whisky a week. When he retired 30 years ago he became a part-time accountant; in his spare time he fiddles with the local band. Exercise has never been his strong point he admits. Yet he is reported as having twice the energy of youngsters aged sixty.

More good news to come. Chinese take-aways could be helping to avoid the risk of a heart attack. An American doctor discovered this revelation recently.

When studying the blood taken from a man during an experiment, he found it did not clot normally. When questioned it was revealed that he had just feasted on a plate of hot bean-curd, a common ingredient in Chinese cooking.

Intrigued the doctor had the same Chinese chef whip up a similar meal for other students to try – and as he expected their blood was equally slow to clot.

A fiendishly cunning race the Chinese, they have also been eating a fungus called moyee for centuries, fully aware that it not only contributes to longevity but potency too.

Who can blame them? If it's efficacious I'll try anything – well almost. I have never yet been able to look an oyster in the eye and swallow it. Even their legendary aphrodisiac properties cannot alter the unattractiveness of them.

Among my collection of ancient cookery books, I have a recipe for stewed oysters that should prove a stimulating starter for any meal. Printed in 1893 it suggests 'about three score of oysters' concluding with a cautionary footnote regarding price. 'Oysters are so very expensive, try those sent to this country from the United States and Canada in tin cans; which contain about 50 oysters and are sold from 6d to 1s per can.'

In the 19th century appetites must have been extraordinary. In the same book is a recipe for pot-au-feu (stew to you and I) which starts of with 'Take 4lb of beef . . . .'

One delicacy considered good for the constitution and which contains few calories has become a popular feature on our bowling night. I can personally vouch for its energy giving qualities. Battling for the league cup is nearly as exciting as fighting for possession of the communal plate of mixed tripe, provided by our club steward.

Before I was initiated it always reminded me of the crepe soles on shoes. But eating this quivering delicacy at home is not the same as struggling for a vinegary morsel from the communal plate on Thursday nights. It was the same when one of our players turned up with a gruesome looking bag of tricks called black pudding. We all grimaced and shuddered, yet finished up fighting harder for a slice of this than we had during the match! Washed down with half of lager, most commodities taste unbeatably succulent I find.

I consider myself particularly lucky to have all these health-giving foods, peanuts, pork scratchings, tripe, brewer's yeast, all at my own local bowling club. When I've finished who knows, I may just pop along for a blood-flushing parcel from the oriental establishment on the corner. Good health!
*

ON Sunday afternoons, when the Monday pain starts, I like to turn to 'A life in the day of' featured in one of the supplements. It's interesting to learn how others organise their days.

'I have a perfect life,' admits Luciano Pavaroti, the opera singer, who is rich, handsome, famous, talented and who loses 4lb in weight during each performance and is still only 42 years old.

The older the writer the more inspiring their days seem to become. Each dawn is regarded as infinitely precious. 'Time has slowly speeded up,' is a way a retired editor puts it.

It's early morning cuppas in bed for wives of artist John Bratby and Malcolm Muggeridge; prepared by their husbands, of course. Like bus riding, breakfast appears to take on a new meaning during retirement. So much so that when I am fortifying myself with a second cup of coffee before the 7am bathroom scramble, I console myself with the hope that I may live long enough to enjoy breakfast again. At present each awakening is more harrowing than its predecessor.

Before I shake each body and give the call I know I am going to regret, I allow myself the luxury of a straightforward glare into each sleeping face. This is the only time I can without getting stung since they reached independence. Once their fallen arches touch the carpet, loving glances are taboo.

Michael Miles used to run a TV quiz where contestants were gonged if they said 'yes' or 'no' before the allotted minute was up.

If he took a place at our breakfast table we should, without doubt, be rich, idle quiz winners. With all this abrasiveness to off-load on someone before we don our 'face the world' images, 'yes' and 'no' are non-starters.

Each request has to be measured carefully against the insult it could provoke. 'Pass the sugar, please,' is a blatant invitation for typical breakfast homilies: 'What did your last slave die of, hard work,' or 'Lie down and I'll fan you.'

The early males look as horrible as the females but they are quieter. It takes fifteen minutes to get son Howard from dreamland to gatepost. First, he has to be shouted at repeatedly until his eyes open and his mouth closes.

This usually takes ten minutes. Five minutes later, after hearing him fall down the front steps, we know he's heading in the right direction. Beg him to eat and he says it will upset his routine too much.

Scholars are at their most boring during breakfast. Either demanding money you haven't got for some trip you thought you'd already paid for twice over, or altering tea arrangements.

The sausage fiends expected tomorrow are coming today, which means no chop for me again and 2lb of sausage for me and dog when everyone is other-wise engaged tomorrow.

But Tuesday is crisis day. It has something to do with the preceding wash day and my never being able to stand at the ironing board for longer than three hours at a time.

I try and iron something for everyone, but if I press the pink it's their day for black; the jeans I struggled to tame are inevitably the ones with the broken zip.

On Wednesday teenage Louise manages to smile, 'Oh yes, I need a fiver, please,' just before we hear her bus driver across the road put his foot on the brake, and she needs it before his foot moves again.

While we sleep all the combs and brushes disappear. I once had to comb my hair with a fork before an urgent dental appointment.

Do families actually sit around the breakfast table sipping orange juice through a smile anymore? Or is this pleasure limited exclusively to the 'Southfork' clan?

*

LIKE me you have probably guffawed and grimaced at the stupidity shown by some television quiz contestants. And like me, you must have wallowed in exasperation as the glaze-eyed and gormless fail to answer questions a five-year-old could. Last weekend I played the part of a gormless bird-brain myself!

To appease my spouse's manic 'see how it works' curiosity, the family and I were persuaded, some time ago, to audition for ATV's 'Family Fortunes.'

First of all let me explain that I have trouble putting the correct name to faces of our own children, but this did not deter my husband. 'No one can be so dumb,' he's fond of saying when others fail. So I went along uneasily to the auditions held in Leeds. My first nervous collapse occurred when researcher Miss Claudia Hovarth rang about two weeks later to announce we had been chosen. We were about to be televised! The thrill was overwhelming, and didn't fade until I put down the phone.

By the time the rest of the family came home my health and well-being had deteriorated so much I could hardly get the news out. My husband said later that he thought there had been a death in the family.

For one hour after the news of our success, egos soared. Then one by one all except father backed out. But his lengthy address on £1,000 divided by six soon had us chomping at the bit once more.

A letter followed informing us that weekend accommodation for six had been booked and paid for at a posh hotel near Elstree Studios.

Looking back I can see small, but ominous indications of what the weekend was about to unfold for me: Holding my hand under the wrong orifice when using a soap dispenser in a motorway toilet, thereby filling my jumper sleeve with pink slime. Being given the wrong room key, fetching hotel manager to open door, dropping cases, plugging in kettle and switching on TV and then running next door to daughter's room only to realise too late I had locked myself out. What does maitre d'hotel think when he opens our door for second time in five minutes to find kettle boiling mad, television playing full blast and cases not even unpacked?

At noon the following day a mini-bus drives us to the studio where we meet five more families and after placing our gear in the dressing rooms we then troop into canteen for lunch.

To calm my nerves I nonchalantly order a medicinal brandy and squirt soda siphon so severely that it transfers everything from my glass on to the bar top. Sympathetic barmaid who has already watched me miss the ashtray and flick ash in son's beer several times refills glass and shows me how to use siphon without drowning her customers.

Canteen food good and cheap, but my appetite fled the minute we were introduced to our intelligent looking opponents. From now until 5.30pm con-testants are confined to the 'Fortunes' studio for rehearsals.

Camera technicians, engineers, researchers, various earphoned youths, a producer, director and of course, our host, Bob Monkhouse all concentrate on moulding six dithering white-cheeked families into vital contestants.

Whatever preordained image we may have had, Bob Monkhouse in the flesh is a kind, hardworking, 100 per cent professional, and that goes for the rest of his team, including the canteen staff who all do their best to keep us on our feet.

If you want to know the rest of the saga, don't miss next week's thrilling episode entitled 'Montgomery and his part in my downfall!'

ABOUT a third of what actually takes place during a show eventually arrives on your television screen.

Blank pauses seemed to play a large part when my family and I appeared on 'Family Fortunes.' The computer needs time to fill in the answers, and of course empty, adverts have to be slotted in; mistakes occur – Bob may leave out vital clues for technicians that could involve a replay. It is all highly con-fusing for weak-kneed amateurs.

Three shows were recorded consecutively the night we performed. Just enough time in between for producer to assemble the next families and Bob Monkhouse to change into another immaculate outfit. No need to mention the part played by the live audience – could hardly be a dead one – but you could be forgiven for thinking this, what with all the instruction to 'Applaud.' 'Laugh,' 'Silence,' etc.

All afternoon is spent rehearsing. Before we took our positions on the set for a mock trial, we were each given a name badge and genned up on how to be perfect contestants by director Bill.

Smart Alecs are not encouraged. 'Leave the jokes to Bob, dears. The idea is to just be yourselves.' Sounds good advice, but difficult when your face won't stop melting and your legs feel like five penn'orth of boiled tripe. After the salutary bit, 'Any Questions?' son surprisingly raises a hand and quivers, 'Any toilets?'

An ever-quipping Bob Monkhouse nurses the first two families through their ordeal. Once he has been introduced to us he disappears, and director Bill takes over our game. We cannot quite master the art of smiling at our opponents. An ear-phoned technician pulls faces behind his camera, but it's no good, my lips are twitching so violently all I manage is a Humphrey Bogart leer.

Meanwhile the rest of the family win a thousand make-believe pounds. This is only pretend but my confidence is such that I heartily attack half-an-inch of roast beef from the superb free cold buffet at teatime. We take our director's advice: 'The camera is very revealing,' and limit ourselves to one glass of the free wine. A girl staggering under a large bag visits every table and doles out travel expenses to husbands, who visibly relax. I break all records for toilet visits until 7.15 – time to dress.

The dressing rooms have reached monsoon heat in our absence. While others change into see-through lightweights, I don my winter sports that seemed a good idea 10,000 years ago. Time drags cruelly at this point. Mirrors everywhere, nothing to do but study our defects. While daughter works on her sixth hairstyle, son and me compare spots, his are larger and closer together, mine are all by my nose, nurtured beautifully by the dehydrating temperatures.

Son-in-law nonchalantly unaware of price tag still on back pocket plays shove halfpenny.

I am just beginning to have second thoughts about my Fleetwood market earrings when Duncan arrives and trots us down to make-up.

Husband's nose and ears come in for a lot of powdering. Monitor above mirror busily recording our pre-contestants, who have already started on their ordeal. Son emerges spotless but looking as if his face has been whitewashed. Any other time I would have laughed.

Suddenly it's all happening – the lights, the applause, the mole on Bob Monkhouses' upper lip – the strained faces waiting for me to think of a World War II leader and, B-L-E-E-P, it's all over. Naturally I knew the answer was 'Monty.' I just wanted to see my husband's nervous tic every time he hears this name, and make a fool of myself in front of millions!!

That's showbiz!

NB: Enid was not permitted to divulge the outcome of the show having had to sign a form to that effect. However, it was a nail-biting finish. After the five rounds of questions both teams were level and a tie-break round was played. They were asked to name three famous World War II leaders. I pressed the buzzer first and named Winston Churchill, which was the top answer and won our team the right to name the other two. Enid was stuck, didn't give an answer and was bleeped. Son, Howard said Hitler, which was also bleeped, that left one more chance. Son-in-law, Michael said Roosevelt, which was correct. I was convinced the final name was Montgomery but dare not whisper, because if you are caught cheating you are thrown out of the game. Final contestant, daughter Heather, said Stalin that earned her a bleep. It was then thrown open to the other team to discuss among themselves. Lo and behold they said 'Montgomery' and the game was lost - William

*

I HEARD him crawl into the back porch at dawn. Naturally all the doors were locked and bolted, but he had been warned.

Of course, I've known something was up for some time now – women sense these things. Nothing you can put your finger on, but he's been so distant lately, walking over to the window in the middle of my conversations or pretending sleep when I kick him from my half of the bed.

When I think of all the evenings I rubbed his legs until my glowing palm would have pressed trousers, because his joints had this habit of seizing up when he sat in one position too long.

I didn't notice any joint stiffness this morning when he galloped the back steps two at a time. Once he was ever pestering me to go out with him, he seemed happy, nay boyish, in my company.

Nowadays he's out of the house, off on his own every occasion possible without so much as a glance in my direction.

The other night I felt so perturbed by his behaviour I even contemplated following him, but he was down the path out of sight. His stiff joints accelerating like an old Chaplin movie; unfortunately I chose the night follow-ing my keep-fit class and my displacements were still inflamed – I couldn't catch him.

I suppose it's partly my own fault he is seeking solace elsewhere. I know I have slipped into the habit of pleading a headache or telling him to get lost when he starts acting playful.

Hopefully this phase will burn itself out, but it's the children I feel sorry for, they are so ashamed when the other kids gloat about his nocturnal carryings on.

The company he keeps leaves a lot to be desired. They're a shaggy-haired ungroomed lot, used to living rough and eating out of tins. He used to prefer my home cooking, mention dinner now and he rushes to the door. It's - excuse me while I grab a tissue – it's heartbreaking. I could stand him sneaking off without warning the minute he opens his eyes, if he didn't stay out so late. At his age, I mean, it's so worrying.

Then when he eventually does drag is wasted form to bed, he's moaning and groaning in his sleep all night long. Let's face it, all the evidence points to that fat bloated bitch up the road, but it doesn't matter how I plead with him, one whiff of her exclusive scent and he becomes her slave.

This morning when I saw his once young and active body, now as ravaged as an ex-president's, the draught from the kitchen door was gently wafting the pendulous flap that used to be his chin. I noticed the sunken eyes and sagging lips, once full and moist, but now a dry and fraying wreath for his bad teeth. Like it or not, I decided it had to stop.

I turned the key in the lock, tied him to the chair and told him the facts of life and how if he wished to remain, he had better alter his ways. Believe it or not, he collapsed in a slobbering heap at my feet, it was disgusting.

Dragging oneself out of bed to let in late night teenagers is hard enough to bear, but when our teenage dog is wailing to be let in each dawn, then howling to be let out the minute you re-kindle the sheets – believe me it is definitely no joke!

THE party season is galloping ferociously towards us once again. Who knows what exciting invitations may flood the letterbox one of these chilly mornings?

Will it be a curt summons to appear before auntie for the annual relative round-up; a nostalgic noggin in someone else's armchair, or are you the type who commands those exotic 'Come in disguise' invitations, 'dressed up hysterically' is the way my mother describes it.

For one party I heard of the suggested gear was leather and lace, only no one knew which sex was supposed to wear what. Confusing but fun.

Whatever you feel about parties at least there is no danger of being invited to Margaret Thatcher's latest. This year she has come up with a novel gimmick which could catch on. Last night the annual 'do' for members of the Cabinet took place at number 10. Invitations were duly sent. After they had been accepted each Minister was informed the price for this privilege would be £21.25 per head. No mention of VAT or service charge.

Small dinner parties, I mean the free non-gratis kinds are my favourites. Over-crowded house parties are sadly overrated.

Standing alone with an empty glass trying to appear glad your husband gets on so well with the opposite sex can be an ageing experience.

Many Christmases ago I unwittingly shaped my image for all parties to follow. I was in scintillating party mood, rib-tickling gems flowed through my teeth – I was everybody's favourite wise-crack.

Whether this was due to the hock or perhaps the moon moving out of Uranus, who knows but I set a sparkling precedent that night which, unfortunately, I am not only expected to live up to, but improve on each year!

'Here she is folks!' Hosts threw me to the hounds the minute they tore of my overcoat. The strain of being an amusement is killing me. There's this serious character trapped inside me screaming to get out. But there is no escape, the minute I stop to catch breath someone says 'What's wrong?'

I find strange characters come up to me and start grinning expectantly, and I'm only reaching for a sausage roll.

One year I did manage a short escape, but it meant listening to the clinical details of a garrulous gourmet's womb disorders, all through the lasagne.

Then there are the athletic get-togethers. One drink and you are expected to indulge in death-defying leaps for spinning dinner plates, or retrieve an orange from inside some guy's beard, if the garlic fumes don't get you first.

Other Christmas displeasures that leave an ugly taste are artificial Christmas trees, shop made mince pies, gift vouchers, modern carols, packet stuffing and Bing Crosby's 'White Christmas.' Santas showing their pin stripes and anyone who moans that it's all a waste of money and cards that ignore the Christmas message ie: the birth of Christ.

I once saw a strip cartoon that showed two snooty dames choosing cards. One had a picture depicting the virgin birth. The caption said: 'Look at this Fiona they're even trying to bring religion into Christmas now!'
*

IN her beautifully British classic country tweeds Penelope Keith definitely looks to the manor born. Wearing those exquisitely cut silk blouses and the smooth fitting wool skirts she might have slipped straight from the glossy pages of 'Country Life.'

I bought a similar outfit recently – a pure wool wrap-over skirt and a tie-front silk shirt, the best of British. I wanted to look tall, slim and smart – a sophisticated pastiche of the elegant Miss Keith.

Granted my shorter legs are a different shape, there is a gap in our ages and I may be a heavier model, but why do I still look like Whistler's mother? Why can't I slip meekly into middle age? Though not like writer Doris Lessing, who describes it like this, 'And then not expecting it, you become middle-aged and anonymous. No one notices you, you achieve a wonderful freedom, it is a positive thing you can move about unnoticed and invisible.'

Could anything sound more depressing? When I start feeling unnoticed and invisible I usually go out and buy a new outfit. The wrap-over skirt certainly provided a new image and a wonderful – if draughty – sense of freedom.

When I tried it on in the shop, it was quite well behaved. The giant beanstalk assistant stopped trying to sell me the lettuce leaf Indian cotton, which looked as if it needed watering anyway, when she saw me in the skirt. She smiled down approvingly from the skylight and clinched the sale when she confessed I looked taller.

That night I wore it and felt my first burst of freedom when I bent to fasten my shoes and my knees slipped out to greet me.

I practised a few more disgusting poses in front of the wardrobe mirror, by simply pushing one knee forward the two skirt fronts fell majestically apart. Another step and my elastic was showing – a brand new image was unfolding before me. When I dashed down the stairs, my two skirt fronts billowing behind, my husband raised his eyebrows, but he was looking at his watch. When I climbed into the car beside him with only my tights

373

visible, he did become slightly neurotic, but luckily there were no coppers about to arrest me.

During the evening at least half a dozen respectables tactfully pointed out the gap in my front. 'Be careful when you dance, it looks shocking.' One masculine remark for which I shall be eternally grateful, went something like 'co-oar!!' Much later when confidence was in full flow and we were all dancing like candidates for a 'Hot Gossip' contest, I suddenly realised my partner, a young husband kindly on loan, was not trying out a new finger pointing, nervous twitching routine, he was trying to attract my attention and seemed anxious about my blouse front. I checked but it looked OK.

'Quick!' he whispered frantically 'fasten your top buttons.' I think I would have been less offended had he asked me to undo them! Decidedly, middle-age is stabbing me in the chest. But I intend to fight it – noticeably!!
*

MOST Saturday I can be seen loitering with intent over the cookery magazines in the town centre bookshops. You've probably fallen over my bags many a time.

One certainly needs a strong stomach for this because some offer the most odious suggestions. Do housewives really insult their lamb roast with items like 'minty yoghurt sauce'? Or stuff their birds with chestnuts and watercress? Are guests actually supposed to enjoy eating a 'cheesy onion custard' between two slices of French bread? And I can't believe anyone could be cruel enough to conclude a meal with 'potted' Stilton.

Some of the soupy suggestions are totally unnerving. In our household, soup was always served with a fork and very often as the main meal. But what a heady brew! The smell was so tantalising we couldn't hang our coats up quick enough.

No one ever questioned mother's ingredients too closely, but we recognised the remains of the Sunday joint, and cabbage played a vital part – the rest was a secret between ma and the stew pot. It tasted so good we were past caring anyway; even if she never did partake of it herself.

My own, which I make with fresh sewing beef plus an assortment of vegetables will never live up to the old fashioned 'stick to the ribs' broth my mother dished up on washday.

Today's lewd apologies, delicacies like cucumber soup and lettuce soup offered in the colour mags, seem diabolically tame by comparison.

Every household develops its own culinary secrets; trying to pin some of the crafty oldies down to what they actually put in to their delectable dishes is like asking Prince Charles to name his future bride. Naturally tastes differ—one man's cheesecake is another man's indigestion.

Going over my Christmas recipes I realise what a metamorphosis they undergo each year. I find I am always trying to improve on last year's dinner, leaving out this and adding a little more of that, ever in search of perfection.

We all have favourites: mine are sauces. When they taste delicious enough to be eaten alone, they are a complement for any bird. All my energies go into perfecting them. I have a collection of ancient recipes and most of my sauces are a pot pourri from these antiquities.

My turkey stuffing started life as a sloppy, bitter mush, screaming for adjustment. Today it is almost right and nothing like it was. We favour a crispier, savoury sort, achieved by dividing a mixture of breadcrumbs, onion, suet, parsley and mixed herbs, all moistened with an egg. Roll them into small dumplings and place them around the sizzling turkey for the last half-hour. Turn them after fifteen minutes and they pick up the juices, which helps to brown and flavour them.

Bread sauce seems so bland without the onion so I developed what I think is a tastier version by cooking chopped onion gently in butter, then add bread-crumbs and top of the milk until the mixture looks really sloppy, season and stick with cloves. Keep it going in the oven until needed.

This year I intend to enrich my trifle the Delia Smith way. That is by smearing an egg custard, using double cream, on top of the sherry-soaked sponges before the whipped cream topping. Sounds scrumptuously fattening and supremely irresistible!

*

OUR average spending increased last year by 17 per cent, despite the squeeze. So says the government's new family expenditure survey. Apparently we are gradually increasing the number of electric gadgets and installing more heat.

The biggest item of spending was an average of £21.83 (or 23.2 per cent of weekly earnings) on food. More families are running second cars, but the lowest household expenditure was recorded in Yorkshire and Humberside.

Another survey indicates, however, that husbands are spending less on clothes than their wives are. Official figures reveal that last year men spent an average of £1.35 per week on outer clothes compared with £2.16 by women. And it shows – doesn't it girls?

If fashion was once ruled by class with the proletariat wearing the overalls and middle-class trying to look like the classically courtured upper class, nowadays it's all a question of age.

At the top of my 'scruffy' list come the teenage lads who imagine that lashings of aftershave and a comb will take them anywhere. Long hair, a pair of jeans, a graffiti covered jacket and battered training shoes; or a skull-cut, baggy clown pants and big boots, are the eternal uniform of some of our youth.

When I was at school, clipped heads and ugly black boots were the trademarks of boys from a nearby orphanage – they hated it.

Next come the over-forties, the Desperate Dans of pub land. Life for these tubby trendies is a trying business; trying to squeeze their excess into tailored shirts or trying to zip the underflow into those crippling tight pants. Trying to cover the mushroom-top Previn hairstyle brushed well down into the eyebrows.

This obsession for hair manifests itself in horrifying ways. Wild sideburns and untamed beards are allowed to grow rampant. Oddly enough this group are liberally soaked in aftershave, too.

Although joggers who live and breathe in track suits all look middle-aged, once they stop and allow their circulation to settle down, some are quite young.   Next in line are the turgid young executives. I would guess that this group spends the most on working gear. Being exquisitely tailored all day they like to wear as little as possible socially. Light slacks, flimsy slim-fit shirt and a bunch of car keys. If they have time they'll throw a couple of gold medallions round their neck to complete the picture. They like to relax and let their hair breathe at parties, hence the burst of brush from his recklessly plunging neckline.

For style with distinction and good taste, look to the over-fifties. Whether it's a fine wool sweater or chunky suede trimmed tweeds, these are the smarty pants that would feel naked without a tie. Denims will ever represent working gear, greasy overalls to this lot.

For weekday jaunts it's sports jacket and Terylenes, and for weekends a three-piece suite, well brushed and pressed. The only perfume emanating from this model is shaving soap.

It's a long time since the days when boys wore skirts until they were three years old and went into their first long trousers the day they started work.

The first suite I ever saw my dad wear was a navy blue with white pin stripe. With it he wore a dark orange overcoat, a grey trilby hat and copper-coloured shoes. It was an incongruous get-up known as a demob suite, but he looked like a film star to me.

If you want to learn a thing or two about grooming, look around at some of our pensioners. Note the mirror-like toecaps and the clean cut hairlines. Some of the suits may be well worn, but you can't beat the pleat of solid worsted.

*

ONE of the pleasanter aspects of my life used to be eating. All my treats were edible. Fresh cream delights to jolly along my shopping sprees, long vigils in a certain chocolate cabin queue for my indulgence of assorted panaceas.

Luscious carbohydrate suppers, with vinegar soaked chip butties or savoury fry-ups to quell my non-maternal instincts after another teenage attack. Then there were the periods of rest, which round off this delightful occupation.

Ah yes – halcyon days, and it wasn't the fear of heart disease that set me on the miserable road to thin-landia. I have always been prepared to take the consequence of my excesses and have no fancy for prolonged decrepitude. The biblical promise of three score years and ten sounds about right to me.

It was my crowning glory – vanity - which helped me to start this calorie cutting life sentence. I decided to have my perm removed and go straight.

My magazine clipping promised a wet-lipped wildly attractive short-cut, the result in the hairdresser's mirror looked like my father's RAF cut.

One can always depend on daughters for unbiased, honest, suicide-inducing opinions. My eleven-year-old ran down the garden path to give me hers. 'Ooer, your head's shrunk,' was her first observation. Did she approve of shrunken heads? 'It looks daft,' was her second. 'Your head looks too little,' seemed to be the majority vote. My own feeling was, buy a big hat, or reduce my body to fit my head.

By refusing all things soothing; in-between snacks, second helpings, cakes and suppers for the last twelve months, I am now only one stone overweight for my height. I wear high heels and pretend I'm large boned and my clothes, usually at full stretch, fit comfortably now.

But why has society conditioned us to believe that thin is beautiful, I ask myself every time I see a meringue?

Once, fat meant affluence. Corpulent Lady Dowagers were the envy of the starving peasants. Reuben's beauties were a heavy-thighed, full-bellied lot. Look around at the starch filled faces of the cuddlies, they all appear flawless and bonny, bubbling over with warmth and vitality. Dangerous observations for we 'lifers' on a permanent diet!

Even more harmful is a Radio 4 programme broadcast on Monday nights, 'Fat guy on a bike.' BBC producer Tom Vernon, 19 stones of cheerfully proud flesh is cycling and consuming his way around Italy in search of anecdotes, atmosphere, pasta and wine. This loveable dumpling believes thin is miserable and after one broadcast almost has me believing it too. Help!

A lot of my success is due to the demon nicotine. Being an after eight smoker, this has replaced the snack I usually take with my drinks.

And after 8pm eating is the scourge of the fuller figure. One theory blames the brown fat we keep at the back of our necks. If you don't burn it quickly enough it blows you up. Weighing it all up – when you are fat you feel ugly – when you are thin you feel hungry!

*

EVER since my first child was born Santa and I have carried the sacks on Christmas Eve. The minute four pairs of eyelids have stopped twitching and the fractured nutshells and empty wineglasses have been cleared away, Santa and I have tackled the sobering business of filling the sacks.

But first, the inevitable Christmas hunt.

'Where did you put Howard's stuff?'

'Me? You were in charge of his. I don't know what you did with them.'

'Who did we buy this for?'

Over the years we have stuffed parcels in some unlikely spots, inside the piano, next door's top cupboard, and one year we locked them in our front vestibule, hid the key in a different place every time we used it.

It was a perfect hideaway if I could only have remembered where I hid the key. The most successful spot proved to be son's wardrobe. Finding it more convenient to leave his clothes wherever he stepped out of them, he never did discover the treasure tucked away at the back of his clothes cupboard.

When all the Christmas harvest is finally gathered in and divided into four clusters - another panic. The planned gifts you so proudly preened over when first bought now appear to have shrunk pathetically.

Amid Santa's mutterings about wasted money you privately wonder if the piles are evenly balanced. Year's back we wondered if son would understand that his train set cost more than all his sisters' presents combined. Would the two middle girls recognise their old school desks under the shiny red paint?

378

Incidentally, they have told me since that the name of their school stamped underneath was the first thing they looked for.

It seems odd now watching 22-year-old son eagerly probing the parcels under the tree trying to guess the contents, that one year he refused to unpack his pillowcase.

It was father who had to ride around on his wooden train and spin his top. Three-year-old son screamed every time we tried to coax him.

It happened at the beginning of our Santa act, the early years when we were actually waiting for them to awake, just before we progressed to the 'Don't you dare open your eyes before daylight' stage. The minute we heard their light click on we were outside their bedroom door, listening intently for the first gasp of satisfaction – silence. No splinter of plastic, no crunch of tooth on toffee, not a sound. The suspense was choking. This was no joke, surely we deserved a delightful yelp or two. We decided to barge in and find ways of making them glad.

A strange sight met our eyes. Although son was sitting up with both eyes open, he was not screaming as normal for his shredded wheat, but simply staring marble-eyed at the full sack below his toes. His sister was also sitting, white-faced, hypnotised by hers. They both looked as if they expected something horrible to creep out of the sacks any minute. It was unnerving, especially in the mouse season. Excitement appeared to have paralysed them.

Dad sat on daughter's bed and pulled her sack nearer. 'Come on, let's see what Santa's left,' he coaxed pulling a mini vacuum cleaner out of the top. Before it was half way out, son's chubby claws were clamped around the handle. Within seconds he had removed the dust bag and was pursuing the dog. When we tried to prise him away from it he went purple. When we dragged him back to his own sack he ran the vac over it. He vacuumed the garden, the flowers, the dog's breakfast, and our guest's feet. The dog moved in next door.

The vac ate with him and slept with him – but I refused to take it to town with us. Finally we had to pretend Santa actually meant it for him and had inadvertently placed it in the wrong sack.

Redundant Santa and I are now reduced to placing our surprises beneath the tree, since they became teenagers. But it's still my favourite sport. I love it: the gifts, the feasting, the awful television shows and the lovely warm tipsy feeling of thankfulness I feel at Christmas with my family around me.

Be happy, be thankful and, if you can't manage gratitude for what you have, try being thankful for what you don't have. Merry Christmas to you all.

*

I ALWAYS feel that looking back is slightly unhealthy and should not be encouraged. Having put one's hand to the plough, what's the point of raking up the muck you've just trampled through? Yet standing here at the portals wondering if you dare risk a resolution or two, passing judgement on the old year is like most wholesome habits, too fascinating to resist.

This 1980 was not a successful year for the film industry and J R Ewing must take some of the blame. Those exquisitely furnished Southfork breakfasts around the pool which no one ever ate – the beautifully coiffeured ciphers and their unflagging services to the lip-gloss industry, JR's indelible constitution, his superb dental care, his daddy's denim blue eyes and momma's homely cardigans – all added a hypnotic dimension to Saturday night viewing.

On the home front, redundancy and short-time, Metro buses cut down on staff and raised the fares so high even those lucky enough to be in work can't afford them. Meanwhile, British Rail lower their fares and regular passengers complain at the standing room only effect this has.

Writer Tom Sharpe has a lot to answer for regarding my neglected house-work and high spirits. His books were the funniest I read during the year. One hilarious paragraph can lighten the load for a fortnight. Almost as efficacious was Douglas Adams' 'A Hitchhiker's Guide to the Galaxy,' originally on radio and also on record. Saw one film last year 'Airplane' – a send-up of airways everywhere, a belly-laugh from the first take-off.

I was pleased to receive a letter from famous television personality, Katie Boyle, who kindly pointed out a spelling error in my column. 'Be a darling and if you write about me again please spell my name correctly,' and even more delighted to correct the mistakes in her letter.

My sympathies go to Princess Grace, whose daughter, Caroline, obtained a divorce – daughters just won't be told. Was proud to see Mary Martin show her son Larry Hagman on the Palladium stage what professionalism really means.

My favourite sonnet of the year came from gardener Geoff Smith, who compared one of his flowers with 'a mug of bedtime cocoa.'

Thanks to Bjorn Borg for showing us that it pays to keep your mouth shut and to Alex Higgins for taking the starch out of snooker viewing.

Other notable events – son's engagement, he and fiancee are now happy co-supporters of a mortgage, wall-to-wall Scalextric and a sandwich toaster.

There seemed to be more deaths than I ever remember. One day you read some famous figure is dead, next day everyone has been in love with him at a profit!

Elton John had a transplant and grew a flat cap. Meanwhile, Elvis still lives.

If I could have one moment of 1980 again I would choose the three seconds of our television debut on Bob Monkhouse's Family Fortunes. That tortuous void when all the war leaders ever recorded in my memory decided to go AWOL. I would shout the name 'Montgomery,' our winnings be doubled, but most of all, I wouldn't look such an idiot at the beginning of March when we go on view!

A Happy New Year to all!

*

THE father who objects to his son being taught 'cissy' subjects like cookery and needlework sounds as if he could do with a lesson or two on the facts of life himself. He says his son will be ill equipped to find a job.

If our job situation continues its downward plunge, dear Merseyside Father, the only occupation your son is likely to follow, is standing in the dole queue where the well and ill-equipped stand side by side. Where cooking, sewing and anything that diverts young minds from the frustrations of being one of the country's unemployed millions will definitely be considered a primary art.

Even before he leaves school, knowledge of cookery can add a new dimension to his life. One boy from a comprehensive school was quoted in the Press as saying: 'I especially like cookery because I can make things to eat for myself before my mother gets in at night.'

And I would like to point out to Mr Merseyside that if your son were lucky enough to find a wife to support him, his cooking and sewing would be a definite asset.

During my schooldays my mother's hacking cough often confined her to bed. My stomach still quivers when I remember the concoctions my dad served under the name of tea. He made up his own recipes – they all tasted the same – poisonous.

He once made scones with salt instead of sugar and we nearly drank the tap dry. But the next morning my mother had stopped coughing and we were all on syrup of figs.

Besides joining the girls for cookery, I believe boys ought to be taught to wash and iron and change nappies.

Also there ought to be compulsory courses on 'How to cope on the dole.' What sort of info you are required to give once you reach the girl at the desk. How to fill in forms correctly, how to release frustration without harming others. How to manage on the handout when it costs £1 bus fare whenever you sign on and £1 for medical prescriptions.

When my daughter, who has been on the dole for three weeks, went to collect her antibiotics, I put my pride in my pocket and asked if there was any reduction for redundant teenagers. 'Only if she is on social security' was the answer. Which to my mind is a ludicrous way of saying: only if she is receiving extra benefits.

Pupils should also be taught the art of directing their money past the pub doors. What alternatives have they? In bleak weather, pubs offer superior comfort, reality-blunting refreshment and good cheer.

Leisure centres do offer cheap amenities for those who haven't become too despondent – and can afford the bus fares.

But for most healthy energetic adolescents eager to earn their first wage, the dole buys a bleak and sickening non-existence.

Girls should also be encouraged to what were hitherto considered masculine pursuits. Home maintenance, particularly decorating says my hus-band. While jobless daughter is out 'despairing' each evening with her jobless mates, he is condemned to the back kitchen with a paintbrush.

I am not an ardent women's libber, quite the reverse. For instance I violently disagree with maternity leave for expectant mothers. I believe a child is entitled to mother's complete attention until it is five, at least. And I think that our school-leavers are entitled to a better prospect than a few weeks temporary work while dilettante mothers give birth.

THE END

In support of

Macmillan cancer relief

During the last few weeks of Enid's life both her and her family received comfort, counselling and wonderful care from the team of Macmillan nurses

In appreciation of their help William and his family have decided to donate all profits received from the sale of this book to Macmillan Cancer Relief

We ask that you give as generously as you can with the minimum cost of the book being £10

Macmillan Cancer Relief provides the expert care and emotional support that makes a real difference to people living with cancer

Macmillan offers a range of innovative cancer services and are at the heart of improving cancer care throughout the UK

Macmillan Cancerline 0808 800 2020   www.macmillan.org.ukd